DEFEATING DISINFORMATION

Global platforms present novel challenges. They are powerful conduits of commerce and global community, and their potential to influence behavior is enormous. *Defeating Disinformation* explores how to balance free speech and dangerous online content to reduce societal risks of digital platforms. The volume offers an interdisciplinary approach, drawing upon insights from different geographies and parallel challenges of managing global phenomena with national policies and regulations. Chapters also examine the responsibility of platforms for their content, which is limited by national laws such as Section 230 of the Communications Decency Act in the United States. This balance between national rules and the need for appropriate content moderation threatens to splinter platforms and reduce their utility across the globe. Timely and expansive, *Defeating Disinformation* develops a global approach to address these tensions while maintaining, and even enhancing, the social contribution of platforms. This title is also available as open access on Cambridge Core.

Bhaskar Chakravorti is the Dean of Global Business at The Fletcher School of Law and Diplomacy at Tufts University, the founding executive director of Fletcher's Institute for Business in the Global Context, and chair of Digital Planet. He is chairman of the Advisory Board of Mastercard's Policy Center for the Digital Economy and is a frequent commentator, author and speaker on the digital economy, AI and the impact on global inclusive growth.

Joel P. Trachtman is Professor of International Law and Henry Braker Professor of Commercial Law at The Fletcher School of Law and Diplomacy at Tufts University. He is the author of ten books and over 100 scholarly articles and chapters on international economic law. He is also a frequent media commentator on trade law issues.

Defeating Disinformation

DIGITAL PLATFORM RESPONSIBILITY, REGULATION AND CONTENT MODERATION ON THE GLOBAL TECHNOLOGICAL COMMONS

Edited by

BHASKAR CHAKRAVORTI
The Fletcher School at Tufts University

JOEL P. TRACHTMAN
The Fletcher School at Tufts University

CAMBRIDGE
UNIVERSITY PRESS

CAMBRIDGE
UNIVERSITY PRESS

Shaftesbury Road, Cambridge CB2 8EA, United Kingdom

One Liberty Plaza, 20th Floor, New York, NY 10006, USA

477 Williamstown Road, Port Melbourne, VIC 3207, Australia

314–321, 3rd Floor, Plot 3, Splendor Forum, Jasola District Centre, New Delhi – 110025, India

103 Penang Road, #05-06/07, Visioncrest Commercial, Singapore 238467

Cambridge University Press is part of Cambridge University Press & Assessment, a department of the University of Cambridge.

We share the University's mission to contribute to society through the pursuit of education, learning and research at the highest international levels of excellence.

www.cambridge.org
Information on this title: www.cambridge.org/9781009438629

DOI: 10.1017/9781009438636

First published 2025

A catalogue record for this publication is available from the British Library

Library of Congress Cataloging-in-Publication Data
NAMES: Chakravorti, Bhaskar, editor. | Trachtman, Joel P., editor.
TITLE: Defeating disinformation : digital platform responsibility, regulation, and content moderation on the global technological commons / edited by Bhaskar Chakravorti, The Fletcher School at Tufts University; Joel P. Trachtman, The Fletcher School at Tufts University.
DESCRIPTION: Cambridge, United Kingdom ; New York, NY : Cambridge University Press, 2024. | Includes bibliographical references and index.
IDENTIFIERS: LCCN 2024030767 (print) | LCCN 2024030768 (ebook) | ISBN 9781009438629 (hardback) | ISBN 9781009438643 (paperback) | ISBN 9781009438636 (epub)
SUBJECTS: LCSH: Disinformation. | Online social networks–Law and legislation. | Social media–Law and legislation. | Digital media–Law and legislation. | Internet–Law and legislation. | Electronic commerce–Law and legislation. | Freedom of speech. | European Parliament. Digital Services Act (2022)
CLASSIFICATION: LCC K564.C6 D44 2024 (print) | LCC K564.C6 (ebook) | DDC 343.09/944–dc23/eng/20240712
LC record available at https://lccn.loc.gov/2024030767
LC ebook record available at https://lccn.loc.gov/2024030768

ISBN 978-1-009-43862-9 Hardback
ISBN 978-1-009-43864-3 Paperback

Joel would like to dedicate this book to his late sister, Gail. Bhaskar would like to dedicate this book to his late brother, Subhankar, who passed away while we were putting the finishing touches on the book, and to his wife, Gita, his son, Tarit, and his daughter, Sahana, who kept nagging him to be done with the finishing touches.

Contents

Contributors

Christoph Busch is Professor of Law and Director of the European Legal Studies Institute at the University of Osnabrück, Germany. Additionally, he is an affiliate fellow at the Yale Information Society Project, at Yale Law School, New Haven. His areas of research include the regulation of digital platforms, consumer law, digital services, personalized law and algorithmic regulation. He is also a member of the European Commission's Expert Group for the EU Observatory on the Online Platform Economy, which provides expert advice on EU platform regulation. For the Expert Group, he coauthored the report "Uncovering Blindspots in the Policy Debate on Platform Power" published in March 2021. In addition, in 2021, the European Commission appointed him as a member of the EU Consumer Policy Advisory Group, which is the Commission's main forum to consult with stakeholders on EU consumer policy.

Bhaskar Chakravorti is the Dean of Global Business at The Fletcher School of Law and Diplomacy at Tufts University, the founding executive director of Fletcher's Institute for Business in the Global Context and chair of Digital Planet, one of Fletcher's leading research and convening initiatives. Chakravorti serves on the Fletcher faculty as Professor of the Practice of International Business. He also served on the Global Future Council on Innovation for the World Economic Forum and was nonresident senior fellow at the Brookings Institution, is chair of the Advisory Board for the Mastercard Policy Center for the Digital Economy, senior advisor for Digital Inclusion at the Mastercard Center for Inclusive Growth, a senior fellow at the Centre for Social and Economic Progress and on the Advisory Board of the UNDP's Center for Private Sector in Development and consultant to the World Bank. A former partner of McKinsey and the Monitor Group, faculty member of Harvard Business School and a distinguished scholar at MIT's Legatum Center, Chakravorti is the author of the book *The Slow Pace of Fast Change: Bringing*

Innovations to Market in a Connected World (Harvard Business Press, 2003) and hundreds of articles, and is the creator of the widely used Digital Evolution Index.

Vasudev Devadasan is a project officer at the Centre for Communication Governance, National Law University Delhi, as well as a research consultant at the Supreme Court of India. His research has covered the impact of technology on constitutional law and democracy, in particular the regulation of free speech and press and election law.

Daniel W. Drezner is Professor of International Politics, a nonresident senior fellow at the Chicago Council on Global Affairs, and the codirector of The Fletcher School at Tufts University's Russia and Eurasia Program. Previously, he taught at the University of Chicago and the University of Colorado at Boulder. He has also held positions with Civic Education Project, the RAND Corporation and the US Department of the Treasury and received fellowships from the German Marshall Fund of the United States, Council on Foreign Relations and Harvard University. Drezner has written seven books, including *All Politics Is Global* (Princeton University Press, 2008) and *Theories of International Politics and Zombies* (Princeton University Press, 2011), and edited three others, including *The Uses and Abuses of Weaponized Interdependence* (Brookings Institution Press, 2021).

Carlo Garbarino is Associate Professor of Tax Law at SDA Bocconi, where he is the director of the Tax and Accounting Observatory of SDA Bocconi and teaches in the Executive Master of Finance. Garbarino is the author of several monographs in Italian and English, dealing with various dimensions of international taxation and international tax treaties. His thorough knowledge of domestic law is matched by that of international matters, with particular attention to the emerging issues of global governance. He developed a comparative approach in the tax field connected to the circulation of policy models, resonant with the latest developments in institutional law and economics. Part of the top 5 percent SSRN, he is one of the most well-known scholars of comparative and international taxation.

Eric Goldman is Professor of Law at Santa Clara University School of Law in the Silicon Valley. He also codirects the High Tech Law Institute and supervises the Privacy Law Certificate. His research and teaching focuses on Internet, IP and advertising law topics, and he blogs on these topics at the Technology & Marketing Law Blog (http://blog.ericgoldman.org). *Managing IP* magazine has twice named him to a shortlist of North American "IP Thought Leaders," and he has been named an "IP Vanguard" by the California State Bar's IP Section. Before joining the Santa Clara Law faculty, he was an assistant professor at Marquette University Law School in Milwaukee and practiced law in the Silicon Valley.

Dominik K. Hofstetter is a Swiss-trained jurist with an LLM. in International Law from The Fletcher School at Tufts University (2022). During his LLM, Hofstetter pursued thesis research on the principle of international comity and the comity abstention doctrine in US jurisprudence under the Alien Tort Statute as an independent researcher at Harvard Law School. Hofstetter served as a research assistant to Professor Joel P. Trachtman and Professor Thomas Burri, researching matters in the fields of international economic law, artificial intelligence and public international law. He is assistant editor of *The International Court of Justice and Decolonisation: New Directions from the Chagos Advisory Opinion* (Cambridge University Press, 2021).

Mark Jit is Professor of Vaccine Epidemiology and head of the Department of Infectious Disease Epidemiology at the London School of Hygiene & Tropical Medicine (LSHTM). He also holds visiting professorial appointments at the NUS Saw Swee Hock School of Public Health and the School of Public Health, University of Hong Kong. His research group focuses on epidemiological and economic modeling of vaccines to support evidence-based public health decision-making. Jit has published over 250 papers covering a range of vaccine-preventable or potentially vaccine-preventable diseases including COVID-19, measles, HPV, pneumococcus, rotavirus, influenza, Group B Streptococcus, dengue, EV71 and RSV as well as methodological papers advancing the ways vaccines are evaluated.

Jhalak Mrignayani Kakkar is both executive director at the Centre for Communication Governance (CCG) as well as Visiting Professor at the National Law University Delhi. Kakkar is an expert member of the Global Partnership on AI (GPAI) Multistakeholder Experts Group Plenary and member of the Working Group on Data Governance. She is an expert member of the United Nations Broadband Commission Working Group on AI Capacity Building and also serves on the board of the Global Network Initiative. Kakkar also serves on the steering committee for the Action Coalition on Meaningful Transparency.

Simone Lipkind is the Research Associate for Middle Eastern Studies at the Council on Foreign Relations. She graduated summa cum laude and Phi Beta Kappa from Tufts University, where she received her BA in Arabic and International Relations with a focus on the Middle East and South Asia.

Federico Lupo-Pasini is Associate Professor in Commercial and Corporate Law at Durham Law School. Lupo-Pasini joined the Law School in 2018 as Associate Professor in Corporate and Commercial Law. His research focuses on international financial law and financial regulation. Previously, Lupo-Pasini also worked as a consultant for various international organizations and governments around the world on financial policy and international trade policy. Since 2017, he is an advisor to the government of Northern Ireland on the trade implications of Brexit.

Shashank Mohan is a program manager at the Centre for Communication Governance, National Law University Delhi. As a lawyer and public policy researcher, his focus lies in technology policy. His research has covered areas of digital privacy, online speech, intellectual property, intermediary liability, artificial intelligence, net neutrality and open access to knowledge and the Internet. He also previously served as Counsel to the Software Freedom Law Centre, India (SFLC.in).

Artur Pericles L. Monteiro is the Wikimedia Fellow at the Information Society Project and Associate Research Scholar at Yale Law School. He is an editor of the Digital Future Whitepaper Series. His work focuses on platform governance, anonymity, freedom of speech, privacy and data protection. He has spoken at conferences at Yale Law School, the Knight First Amendment Institute at Columbia University and George Washington University. Previously, Artur was head of research at InternetLab, an independent research center on law and technology in Brazil. He holds a doctorate in law, an MSc, and an LLB from the University of São Paulo (Brazil), where he led the clinic on free speech and the Internet.

Farah Pandith is an adjunct senior fellow at the Council on Foreign Relations, foreign policy strategist and former diplomat. Farah is a pioneer in the field of countering violent extremism (CVE), has been a political appointee in the George H. W. Bush, George W. Bush and Barack Obama administrations. She served on the Secretary of Homeland Security's Homeland Security Advisory Council (HSAC) from 2015 to 2017, where she also chaired the HSAC subcommittee on countering violent extremism. Her book, *How We Win: How Cutting-Edge Entrepreneurs, Political Visionaries, Enlightened Business Leaders, and Social Media Mavens Can Defeat the Extremist Threat* (Custom House), was published in 2019. She was a senior advisor and commissioner on the Center for Strategic and International Studies' CVE Commission Report, is a senior advisor at the Anti-Defamation League and maintains an affiliation with Harvard University's Kennedy School of Government.

Joel P. Trachtman is the Henry J. Braker Professor of Commercial Law at The Fletcher School of Law and Diplomacy and director of the Center for International Law and Governance at Fletcher. Joel has served as a member of the boards of the *American Journal of International Law*, the *European Journal of International Law*, the *Journal of International Economic Law*, the *Cambridge Review of International Affairs*, and the *Singapore Yearbook of International Law*. He has consulted for a number of governments and international organizations, including the United Nations, the World Bank and the OECD. From 1998 to 2001, he was academic dean of The Fletcher School, and during 2000 and 2001, he served as dean ad interim.

Jufang Wang is the deputy director of the UK-based Oxford Global Society and the coordinator of its Digital Cluster. Previously, she was the deputy director of the Platforms, Governance, and Global Society (PGG) program based at Wolfson

College, Oxford University and had been a senior news editor and manager for many years in China.

Josephine Wolff is Associate Professor of Cybersecurity Policy and has been at The Fletcher School at Tufts University since 2019. Her research foci include liability for cybersecurity incidents, international internet governance, cyber-insurance, cybersecurity workforce development and the economics of information security. Her first book, *You'll See This Message When It Is Too Late: The Legal and Economic Aftermath of Cybersecurity Breaches*, was published by MIT Press in 2018. Her second book, *Cyberinsurance Policy: Rethinking Risk in an Age of Ransomware, Computer Fraud, Data Breaches, and Cyberattacks*, was published by MIT Press in 2022.

Acknowledgments

In carrying out the research project that produced this volume, we relied on advice and support from many colleagues. The project could not have been completed without support from a generous gift from the Omidyar Network, which provided financial support, but even more importantly, expert advice on the problems addressed here. At the Omidyar Network, we worked with Anamitra Deb, Ellen Jacobs, and Gus Rossi. The project also could not have been completed without the assiduous and scholarly research, organization, diligence, patience, and sheer hard work of Dominik Hofstetter. Similarly excellent research assistance, with only slightly less intense involvement, was also provided by Arpitha Desai, Eshita Eshita, and Mitakshi Lakhani. Ravi Shankar Chaturvedi's support in project management was invaluable. We are also grateful to our colleagues at The Fletcher School – Abidemi Adisa, Christina Filipovic, Anuradha Herur, Dorothy Orszulak, and Maria Pereira – for their support through the project and help in organizing the conference associated with this initiative. It was a pleasure to work with the authors of this volume who each added extraordinary depth and perspective to the final product.

Abbreviations

AEED	Assessoria Especial de Enfrentamento à Desinformação
AI	artificial intelligence
ARSP	algorithmic recommendation service providers
BCBS	Basel Committee on Banking Supervision
BRICS	Brazil, Russia, India, China and South Africa
CAC	Cyberspace Administration of China
CCAC	Central Cyberspace Affairs Commission
CCP	Chinese Communist Party
CD	compact disk
CDC	Código de Defesa do Consumido
CFR	Charter of Fundamental Rights
CFTC	Commodity Futures Trading Commission
CGI	computer-generated imagery
CJEU	Court of Justice of the European Union
CSAM	child sexual abuse material
CVE	countering violent extremism
DMA	Digital Markets Act
DMCA	Digital Millennium Copyright Act
DPDP	Digital Personal Data Protection Bill
DSA	Digital Services Act
DSC	digital services coordinator
ECD	e-commerce directive
ECPA	Electronic Communications Privacy Act
EMIR	European Market Infrastructure Regulation
ESMA	European Securities and Markets Authority
EU	European Union
FATF	Financial Action Task Force
FCTC	Framework Convention on Tobacco Control

FOSTA	Fight Online Sex Trafficking Act
FSB	Financial Stability Board
GAC	Grievance Appellate Committee
GATT	General Agreement on Tariffs and Trade
GCIG	Global Commission on Internet Governance
GDP	gross domestic product
GDPR	General Data Protection Regulation
GIFCT	Global Internet Forum to Counter Terrorism
IAP	internet access provider
ICANN	Internet Corporation for Assigned Names and Numbers
IGO	international governmental organization
IHR	International Health Regulations
IISP	internet information service provider
IMF	International Monetary Fund
INIS	Internet News Information Service
IOSCO	International Organization of Securities Commissions
IP	internet protocol
IPC	Indian Penal Code
IPPPR	Independent Panel on Pandemic Preparedness and Response
ISC	International Sanitary Conference
ISIS	Islamic State of Iraq and Syria
ISP	internet service provider
IT	information technology
ITU	International Telecommunications Union
MEITY	Ministry of Electronics and Information Technology
MIIT	Ministry of Industry and Information Technology
MPS	Ministry of Public Security
MRA	Mutual Recognition Agreement
NAFTA	North American Free Trade Agreement
NetzDG	German Network Enforcement Act
NGO	nongovernmental organization
NPPA	National Press and Publication Administration
NRTA	National Radio and Television Administration
OECD	The Organization for Economic Cooperation and Development
OHCHR	Office of the High Commissioner for Human Rights
OTC	over-the-counter
P2P	peer-to-peer
PD	publicity department
PEPFAR	President's Emergency Plan For AIDS Relief
PHEIC	public health emergency of international concern

PIP	pandemic influenza preparedness
PIPL	personal information protection law
RARIIS	Regulation on Algorithmic Recommendation of Internet Information Services
RGOIE	Regulation on Governance of Online Information Ecology
RIIS	Regulation on Internet Information Services
RINIS	Regulation on Internet News Information Services
SARS	Severe Acute Respiratory Syndrome
SESTA	Stop Enabling Sex Traffickers Act
SPS	sanitary and phytosanitary measures
SSMI	significant social media intermediaries
TBT	technical barriers to trade
TCO	terrorist content online
TFEU	Treaty on the Functioning of the European Union
ToS	terms of service
TRIPS	trade related intellectual property rights
TRN	Transnational Regulatory Network
UDAP	unfair or deceptive acts or practices
UGC	user-generated content
UN	United Nations
UNESCO	United Nations Educational, Scientific and Cultural Organization
URL	uniform resource locator
USC	United States Code
USMCA	United States–Mexico–Canada Agreement
VLOP	very large online platform
VLOSE	very large online search engines
VPN	virtual private network
WHO	World Health Organization
WTO	World Trade Organization

1

Introduction

Comparative, Generative, and Synthetic Analysis of International Dimensions of Platform Responsibility

Bhaskar Chakravorti and Joel P. Trachtman

From the giants – Facebook, YouTube, TikTok, and WhatsApp – to the corners occupied by Discord, Caffeine, and NextDoor, there is no scarcity of digital platforms to browse and in which to lose onself.[1] Social media has come a long way since its early days of Six Degrees or Friendster. More than half the world's population is on one or more such platforms and they spend 15 percent of their waking hours on them. Collectively, they watch a billion hours of YouTube videos a day and between sharing personal updates, pictures of the last meal, breaking news, and outright falsehoods, half a billion stories are posted on Facebook every day.[2] It is no wonder, therefore, that social media platforms have enormous power to shape narratives and influence behavior.

This raises the question of who bears responsibility for what appears on the platforms, how the content is shared, and who gets to see it. Users cannot be expected to – reliably and consistently – self-regulate their posts. It is natural to expect that in the absence of a set of rules and editorial intervention, the communicative power and global nature of the platform space will be severely compromised. The responsibility of the platforms for the use of their power to control and disseminate content is statutorily limited by national laws, such as Section 230 of the Communications Decency Act in the US or the Digital Services Act in the EU. Legislative efforts to demand and guide appropriate content moderation and to avoid private abuse of this power offer essential safeguards, but they are in tension with several competing concerns. Any restraints on content must be balanced against the commitment in liberal states to avoid excessive government regulation, especially of speech. Less liberal states will have different policies, and even liberal states differ with respect to their priorities. The US focuses on free speech,[3] while the EU more frequently compromises free speech for other values. Second, users must

[1] The idea of a "platform" itself merits some discussion. We shall defer it to a later chapter by Eric Goldman (Chapter 2).

[2] *Top social media fun facts in 2023*, Amra & Elma (2023), https://www.amraandelma.com/social-media-fun-facts/, (last visited Mar. 2, 2024).

[3] *See* Michael Glennon, Free Speech and Turbulent Freedom (2024).

have the opportunity to exercise their creative urges and possibly develop businesses based on the content they post. The tools to exercise such creative urges have been given an added boost by the wide availability of applications enabled by generative artificial intelligence (AI). Third, social media offers a powerful way to tap into the "wisdom of the crowd" for information and bottom-up insights on a wide range of issues from breaking news stories to reviews of products and any restraints ought not to skew the outcomes.

Yet another complication is that digital platforms are borderless (except in countries where they are blocked), while state-imposed rules and regulations that govern content on platforms are country-specific. Diverse – and sometimes contradictory – national rules can splinter platforms and potentially undermine their utility. Intermingled among all of these issues are the very different sets of political, commercial, and personal interests of the principal actors – users, platforms, and regulators. As we look ahead, a fourth actor is poised to become a principal as well: AI that may not have "interests" that drive the decisions made by underlying algorithms but is an autonomous player that can evolve beyond the control of its human creators and their intentions.

With these issues as context, can a global approach be developed to address them while elevating the quality of content and limiting material that could lead to harm? This is the question that motivated the book.

As we consider setting boundaries around harmful content, there are four challenges to be addressed:

- *Volume*. First, platforms host primarily user-generated content; the number of users and the amount of content are enormous, as is the frequency of posting – billions each day. Platforms make it costless for many people to share content among varying and potentially very large groups. Where user-generated content may violate national substantive laws, such as those applying to defamation, pornography, intellectual property protection, consumer protection, trafficking, pornography, election protection, etc., it is difficult for national regulators to keep up. While it is easy to say that what is illegal in the real world is also illegal in the virtual world, the virtual world raises novel problems of enforcement. Some states respond by delegating some aspects of enforcement to platforms themselves, sometimes leaving it to the platforms to establish private regulation that may exceed the powers of government regulation, especially in free speech areas.
- *Diversity*. Second, regulators and lawmakers in every country are guided by their own legislative, bureaucratic, and political agendas. Each might operate at a different pace, and each might want to push forward regulations to suit local conditions and political and economic interests. As a result, while reform of Section 230, the internet platforms' current

intermediary liability regime in the US, is being debated, other jurisdictions, notably, India, Brazil, Australia, Kenya, the UK, and the EU, have taken or are considering taking their own actions to hold platforms responsible for content. This could result in a chaotic patchwork of rules worldwide. The patchwork of rules could splinter the platforms in ways that are costly not just to the platforms, but to society at large.

- *Indivisibility.* Third, to a significant extent, platforms are valuable precisely because they are global, establishing a global common communications space and providing generous economies of scale and scope. This very global nature makes platforms vulnerable to divergent national regulation. States set rules focused on their own territory, but these rules inevitably have effects beyond their territories. On the other side, states that wish to have different rules – to assert digital sovereignty" – may be unable to effect their policies, especially if they are not the home state of the platform. While technological devices can be used to reestablish "borders" for platforms, these may be incompletely effective.
- *Scarcity.* Finally, there could be unintended consequences of well-intentioned actions by regulators and lawmakers of any one country; such unilateral action might skew the incentives for the social media companies in ways that could, ironically, make matters worse globally. The platforms could respond to regulations imposed by one country, say the US, by over-allocating resources to ensure protections for users in the US and not run afoul of the laws; but given limited resources, this could come at the cost of resources under-allocated elsewhere. As an example, consider the 2021 Facebook papers revelations that the company had allocated 87 percent of its content moderation resources to monitoring US content, even though less than a tenth of all Facebook users are in the US. Moreover, the greatest risks of dangerous content are in societies with weaker political and legal systems and with more vulnerable populations. Aggressive action by US regulators could result in outcomes that make conditions worse for these societies unless the new regulations proactively create mechanisms to guard against such risks. The worst-case scenario is that societies with the least resources and low global "share of voice" suffer the most as the companies must respond to other demands.

If the overarching goal is to "defeat" disinformation – a term we use to cover a broad range of harmful content – the failure to address these discontinuities will result in potentially insufficient and inefficient restrictions.

In response, The Fletcher School carried out a timely and novel collaboration between two key centers, its Institute for Business in the Global Context and its Center for International Law and Governance, to coordinate expert analysis and research designed to examine the dynamics of these challenges and their possible resolutions. We began with the specific question of reforming rules that make platforms responsible or immunize them from responsibility for content they host, ranging from modification of Section 230 to more focused rules requiring moderation and takedown, defining hate speech, restricting non-consensual image-sharing, defining cyber bullying, prohibiting misinformation to consumers, and outlawing threats to elections and civil discourse, etc.

As we investigated the question of platform responsibility, we examined whether there is useful guidance or precedent offered by other regulations and widely agreed-upon international standards in other fields, such as international finance, international taxation, international public health, and initiatives aimed at countering violent extremism, that govern companies and have cross-border implications.

We assembled a set of experts to contribute chapters aimed at a broad audience of policymakers, lawmakers, and industry decision-makers. The chapters are organized in three categories: comparative, generative, and disciplinary analyses.

Comparative Chapters. The comparative chapters examine specific countries' policies, and the bases for those policies, in this area, seeking to understand how different national social goals and structures demand different types of rules. These chapters include leading technologically advanced jurisdictions like the US, the EU, China, India, and Brazil. These chapters were prepared by experts in the relevant area and contain in-depth analyses responding to specified questions and based on experience, study, and interviews with leading thinkers and policymakers. Eric Goldman (Chapter 2) summarizes the legal framework governing social media platforms in the US by highlighting three pillars: the constitutional protections for free speech and press, Section 230, and the limits on state regulation of digital platforms. Christoph Busch (Chapter 3) provides an overview of the EU regulatory framework and its nuanced "due diligence" approach to content moderation, along with the potential international effects of EU rules on platform responsibility. Jufang Wang (Chapter 4) considers the general principles that govern China's online content governance and how it exercises governmental control of its information space, along with a brief case study on TikTok. Artur Pericles (Chapter 6) characterizes Brazil as a "battleground" where proposals for platform responsibility have been advanced and disputed; he provides an overview of existing and proposed frameworks, and of recent developments there and the lessons they offer. Finally, Jhalak Kakkar, Shashank Mohan, and Vasudev Devadasan (Chapter 5) provide an overview of the regulatory frameworks that govern content on social media platforms in India and their evolution as well as the challenges and petitions that have been filed as the rules have evolved.

The overall picture is one of considerable diversity across countries and steady evolution. The latter is often in response to a consideration of rules in place in other regions or to external events where social media content has played a role or petitions and challenges to existing rules. This initial set of chapters help with setting the stage for many of the key issues that must be addressed.

Generative Chapters. The generative chapters examine other partially analogous global regulatory issues to generate proposals for addressing the issues at both the rule-making stage and the rule-application stage. Federico Lupo-Pasini (Chapter 8) focuses on the Basel Committee on Bank Regulation capital requirements on banks and the potential lessons from financial regulation. Carlo Garbarino (Chapter 9) considers the OECD Base Erosion and Profit Shifting International Taxation Project. Mark Jit and Dominik Hofstetter (Chapter 7) offer a comparison based on the global response to infectious disease, examining how the international community might respond to "misinformation pandemics." Farah Pandith and Simone Lipkind (Chapter 10) explore the experience of countries looking to counter violent extremism. These examples have a crucial factor in common: they deal with issues that are subject to national regulation and enforcement but have significant implications beyond national boundaries. The generative chapters explain the global scope of the problem, detail the process and institutional structures by which rules have been promulgated and applied, and briefly compare these contexts to and suggest lessons learned for content moderation and platform responsibility rules.

Disciplinary Analyses. The issues at the heart of defeating disinformation on social media platforms are complex and defy straightforward solutions. Clearly, even the insights drawn from a breadth of comparative and generative analyses can fall short of delivering answers. The reason for this is that the underlying factors have disciplinary characteristics that draw upon a combination of microeconomics, international law, international politics, and technology policy. Each disciplinary lens offers insights into the drivers behind possible solutions and the barriers that might get in the way. This set of chapters considers these drivers and barriers and offers potential paths forward in addressing the complexities using the lens of these individual disciplines. Josephine Wolff, adopting a technology policy perspective, considers different policy goals related to social media platforms along three different types of obligations: responsibilities to target particular categories of unwanted content, responsibilities for platforms that wield particularly significant influence, and responsibilities to be transparent about platform decision-making. Wolff (Chapter 11) explores which of the policy goals present the greatest opportunities for international coordination and agreement and the lessons learned from the comparative and generative chapters. Daniel Drezner (Chapter 12) argues, from the perspective of an international political scientist, that we are destined for what he describes as a hypocritical system of "sham governance," with token agreements negotiated at the global level but with inadequate enforcement mechanisms. He concludes that regulation is likely to remain national – and fragmented. Bhaskar Chakravorti (Chapter 13) adopts a microeconomist's perspective and examines the incentives structure that are at the heart of social media platforms run as businesses and discovers that they lead to a "disinformation paradox." The attempts to moderate content by regulators acting independently across nations leads to an increase in harmful content worldwide. Joel Trachtman (Chapter 14) observes that the approach of international law is to address issues vertically relating to specific regulatory areas, such as human rights, election integrity, consumer protection, privacy, defamation, human trafficking, competition, tax, etc., rather than to examine horizontally how these issues manifest themselves on social media platforms. However, as Trachtman observes, digital platforms present special challenges given the enhanced frequency and velocity of interaction that create novel law enforcement difficulties; and, thus, special structural and procedural rules are required to meet these challenges.

We convened the authors alongside several additional experts representing a wide cross-section of viewpoints – from Meta as well as its Oversight Board, Meedan, the National Conference on Citizenship, the *New York Times*, and the Government of Denmark – at The Fletcher School for a symposium that included a public discussion and debate of their ideas, key issues, and potential solutions. In the conclusion of this book (Chapter 15), we summarize the overarching ideas, and prescriptions for public and private policy, that have been derived from this project. With the year 2024 as the biggest election year worldwide in human history and growing fears of AI-aided disinformation, the explorations and findings covered here could not have been more timely; 2024 will, surely, alert us to the many ways in which the moderation of content – or lack thereof – on digital platforms is of enormous social and political relevance. It is our sincere hope that the chapters to follow help us gain perspectives on the depth of the challenges and pathways to possible solutions.

2

The United States' Approach to "Platform" Regulation

Eric Goldman[*]

2.1 INTRODUCTION

This chapter summarizes the United States' legal framework governing internet "platforms" that publish third-party content. It highlights three key features of US law: the constitutional protections for free speech and press, the statutory immunity provided by 47 U.S.C. § 230 ("Section 230"), and the limits on state regulation of the internet. It also discusses US efforts to impose mandatory transparency obligations on internet "platforms."

2.2 WHAT IS A "PLATFORM"?

The term "platform" has emerged as a standard descriptor for internet services and has been incorporated into US legislation. Nevertheless, this term is problematic.

First, the term "platform" often refers to internet services that facilitate user-to-user communications – with Facebook viewed as the archetypical platform and the primary target for regulatory intervention. Yet user-to-user online communications take place in a wide range of services, including consumer review services, wikis, message boards, private messaging services (such as email services and private chat tools), online marketplaces, online dating services, livestreaming video services, video hosting services, "social media," and much more. There is no consensus about which services constitute platforms. Sometimes platforms refer to all of these services and others;[1] sometimes the term narrowly describes only "social media"

[*] This chapter addresses developments through December 1, 2022.

[1] For example, a proposed bill in Minnesota defined "social media platforms" as any "electronic medium … that allows users to create, share, and view user-generated content, " UNLAWFUL SOCIAL MEDIA ACTIVITIES (May 4, 2022) 325F.6945, https://www.house.leg.state.mn.us/cco/journals/202122/J0504102.htm?fbclid=IwARoogeZn77rqZ2VX7NiuaX8iOnY8U-sWwV2zToKe7dN2E6ODpZoaNqepfEo#12992.

(another term without a precise definition); and sometimes it is used in other ways. Furthermore, numerous synonyms to the platform term are used in legislation and common parlance. The lack of standardized terminology creates scope problems for a chapter like this.

Second, the term "platform" can obscure or trivialize a service's editorial and publication functions. The nomenclature implies that the entities do not qualify for stringent constitutional protections applicable to "publishers." For example, platforms are sometimes analogized to common carriers or utilities because those entities get diminished constitutional protections. Alternatively, sometimes platforms are analogized to "public squares" or other government-provided functions that must comply with the constitution – a different way of curtailing services' editorial discretion, but no less censorial in intent. Because the term "platform" subverts internet services' editorial, curatorial, and publishing functions, it has significant political valence and consequences.

To sidestep the semantic and substantive problems created by the "platform" term, this chapter instead uses the term "internet services"[2] to cover all online services that publish third-party content.

2.3 CONSTITUTIONAL PROTECTION FOR FREE SPEECH

The First Amendment of the United States Constitution says, "Congress shall make no law . . . abridging the freedom of speech, or of the press."[3] This provision provides strong and wide-ranging protections against government censorship of speech.

2.3.1 *Content Protected by the First Amendment*

The First Amendment generally requires heightened scrutiny of speech restrictions, though the level of scrutiny varies. For example, government restrictions based on the speaker's viewpoint generally get the most demanding level of scrutiny (called "strict" scrutiny); government restrictions on commercial speech get a less rigorous, but still meaningful, level of scrutiny (called "intermediate" scrutiny). Government regulations rarely survive strict scrutiny, and they usually survive the lowest level of scrutiny (called "rational basis" scrutiny). The outcomes are less predictable when intermediate scrutiny applies.

Some types of content are characterized as receiving no First Amendment protection at all, including child sexual abuse material (CSAM), obscenity, incitements to violence, and defamation. However, each of those exclusions is defined

[2] Sometimes these services are called "user-generated content services" or "UGC services." The term "internet service provider" typically refers only to internet access providers.

[3] Elsewhere, the Constitution makes clear that these obligations apply to all government actors, not just Congress.

narrowly. For example, incitements to violence may be punished only when the speech is likely to lead to imminent unlawful violence.

As a result, many categories of speech that are regulated internationally may be constitutionally protected in the United States and thus subject to little or no government restriction. Some examples are as follows:

- "Hate speech": Unless the speech fits into one of the content categories that do not get First Amendment protection, it is not constitutionally permitted to restrict odious views about other people. As just one example, the First Amendment protects distribution of Nazi images and paraphernalia and public support for the Nazi party and its ideals (including declarations of Nazi affiliation).
- "Cyberbullying": Cyberbullying activities are often protected by the First Amendment, including typical online bullying behavior like name-calling, dehumanizing references, brigading, doxing, and uncivil behavior. Cyberbullying behavior becomes actionable only in extreme cases, such as when it constitutes criminal stalking, criminal harassment, or imminent threats of violence.
- "Terroristic" content: In general, the First Amendment protects content published by or about terrorist organizations that does not fit into one of its exclusions.
- "Pornography": With limited exceptions, the First Amendment protects nonobscene and non-CSAM depictions of sexual activity, no matter how "hardcore."
- "Misinformation": The First Amendment protects many categories of "false" information.[4] False political statements are routinely permitted unless they are defamatory, and the First Amendment imposes heightened standards for defamation claims in those circumstances.[5] The First Amendment also protects health misinformation provided by nonexperts, such as scientifically unsupported statements against vaccines or downplaying concerns about the COVID pandemic.

The First Amendment limits speech restrictions in any government-operated online speech venue. In other words, government-operated social media accounts may be unable to moderate constituents' comments that contain hate speech, misinformation, or pornography without violating the First Amendment.[6]

4 For example, false public claims of military honors are protected. United States v. Alvarez, 567 U.S. 709 (2012).

5 Usually, plaintiffs must show that the defendant made the statement with "actual malice" of the falsity, a very difficult standard for plaintiffs to satisfy. *See* New York Times Co. v. Sullivan, 376 U.S. 254 (1964).

6 Knight First Amendment Inst. v. Trump, 928 F.3d 226 (2d Cir. 2019), *vacated as moot*, Biden v. Knight First Amendment Inst., 141 S.Ct. 1220 (2021).

In practice, this means the government largely cannot manage users' antisocial behavior in any online speech venue it operates.

2.3.2 *Protection for Internet Services as "Publishers"*

The First Amendment protects the freedoms of speech and press, though the "press" freedom rarely gets invoked. For disseminators of third-party content, their editorial decisions are usually treated as their "speech" and are subject to the highest level of First Amendment protection. As a concurring justice explained in *Miami Herald v. Tornillo*, the "government may not force a newspaper to print copy which, in its journalistic discretion, it chooses to leave on the newsroom floor."[7]

Nevertheless, because of their unique structural dynamics, several types of communication providers get reduced First Amendment protection, including telephony/telegraphy providers and broadcasters. These diminished First Amendment principles do not extend to internet services, however. In 1997, the Supreme Court said that its prior telephony and broadcasting rulings "provide no basis for qualifying the level of First Amendment scrutiny that should be applied to the Internet."[8]

Instead, when internet services perform editorial or curatorial functions, the First Amendment protects those functions to the same degree it would protect offline content publishers. As one court explained, "Like a newspaper or a news network, Twitter makes decisions about what content to include, exclude, moderate, filter, label, restrict, or promote, and those decisions are protected by the First Amendment."[9]

The First Amendment should negate all attempts to impose strict liability for disseminating third-party content.[10] However, it permits the imposition of liability based on higher levels of scienter, such as intent, knowledge, and recklessness, and perhaps a "should have known"/negligence standard as well. As a practical matter, Section 230 (discussed momentarily) typically moots the need for courts to explore the interplay between the First Amendment and internet service scienter. Thus, it is not clear what level of internet service scienter regarding third-party tortious or criminal content is required to impose online publisher liability under the First Amendment.

2.4 STATUTORY PROTECTION FOR FREE SPEECH (SECTION 230)

2.4.1 *Overview*

In 1996, Congress enacted 47 U.S.C. § 230 as part of the Communications Decency Act, which says the following:

7 Miami Herald Publishing Co. v. Tornillo, 418 U.S. 241 (1974) (concurrence of Justice White).
8 Reno v. ACLU, 521 U.S. 844 (1997).
9 O'Handley v. Padilla, 2022 WL 93625 (N.D. Cal. Jan. 10, 2022).
10 Smith v. Cal., 361 U.S. 147 (1959).

(1) Treatment of publisher or speaker: No provider or user of an interactive computer service shall be treated as the publisher or speaker of any information provided by another information content provider.
(2) Civil liability: No provider or user of an interactive computer service shall be held liable on account of – (A) any action voluntarily taken in good faith to restrict access to or availability of material that the provider or user considers to be obscene, lewd, lascivious, filthy, excessively violent, harassing, or otherwise objectionable, whether or not such material is constitutionally protected or (B) any action taken to enable or make available to information content providers or others the technical means to restrict access to material described in paragraph (1).

Translating these provisions into simpler language:[11]

- Section 230(c)(1) says that websites and other online services are not liable for third-party content.
- Section 230(c)(2)(A) says that websites and other online services are not liable for the content filtering decisions they make, even if they are partially responsible for the content.
- Section 230(c)(2)(B) says that vendors of anti-threat software filters, such as anti-spam, anti-spyware, anti-virus, and parental choice vendors, are not liable for their blocking decisions.

These provisions are subject to statutory exceptions discussed below.

Defendants need Section 230(c)(1)'s immunity only when the law would otherwise impose liability. This immunization is not a technical loophole or a "get-out-of-jail-free" card. It is a critical policy choice that Congress made to get the benefits provided by internet services that otherwise would be foreclosed by liability concerns.

Section 230(c)(1) is a globally unique policy. No other country has adopted a legal rule like it. The United States has entered into trade agreements with Mexico and Canada,[12] as well as Japan,[13] that nominally require those countries to adopt Section 230–like protection, but those countries have not taken steps to honor those commitments.[14]

[11] For a more comprehensive description of Section 230, *see* Eric Goldman, *An Overview of the United States' Section 230 Internet Immunity*, The Oxford Handbook of Online Intermediary Liability 155 (Giancarlo Frosio, ed. 2020).

[12] United States-Mexico-Canada Agreement (USMCA) Article 19.17.

[13] Agreement Between the United States of America and Japan Concerning Digital Trade (US-Japan Digital Trade Agreement) Article 18.

[14] US-Japan Digital Trade Agreement: Side Letter on Interactive Computer Services, October 7, 2019, https://ustr.gov/sites/default/files/files/agreements/japan/Letter_Exchange_on_Interactive_Computer_Services.pdf (saying that "Japan need not change its existing legal system").

2.4.2 *Elements of a Section 230(c)(1) Defense*

A defendant qualifies for a Section 230(c)(1) defense[15] when it satisfies the following three elements:

1. *Interactive Computer Service Provider/User.* The definition of "interactive computer service" includes internet access providers (IAP). By definition, anyone online necessarily uses an IAP to connect to the internet, so Section 230(c)(1) protects all services, and users of those services, from liability for third-party content. Sometimes Section 230 (c)(1) is mistakenly characterized as a "gift" or privilege to "Big Tech," but it equally benefits "Small Tech" and individual internet users.
2. *Publisher or Speaker Claims.* Section 230(c)(1) says that defendants "shall not be treated as the publisher or speaker" of third-party content, but this phrase is not limited to causes of action that expressly reference "publisher" or "speaker" in the claim elements. Instead, this phrase applies to any cause of action where the imposition of liability would treat the defendant as the publisher or speaker of third-party content.

However, Congress has enumerated four statutory exceptions to Section 230:

- Federal criminal prosecutions: If the US government brings a criminal prosecution of federal law, Section 230 does not apply.[16] However, Section 230(c)(1) does apply to civil claims based on federal crimes[17] and to state criminal prosecutions (with the exception of FOSTA discussed below), when based on third-party content. To reinforce the point: with respect to third-party content, internet services only need to comply with the single national standard of federal criminal law, not the cacophony of state criminal laws with diverse standards.
- Intellectual property claims: Federal intellectual property claims (except for claims under the Defend Trade Secrets Act) are excluded from Section 230(c)(1). For example, federal copyright claims are not covered by Section 230(c)(1), though Congress has enacted a separate safe harbor, 17 U.S.C. §512 (the DMCA Online Safe Harbor), for claims over third-party copyright infringement. State IP claims are also excluded from

[15] This part will focus on Section 230(c)(1). *See A Review of Section 230's Meaning & Application Based on More Than 500 Cases*, INTERNET ASSOC., July 27, 2020, https://archiveia.org/publications/a-review-of-section-230s-meaning-application-based-on-more-than-500-cases/ (discussing the relative infrequency of Section 230(c)(2) litigation).

[16] Sometimes critics of Section 230, including judges, claim that Section 230 creates a lawless zone for third-party content. This is plainly erroneous because federal criminal law always governs internet services (plus, content originators are always liable for their own content).

[17] Jane Doe No. 1 v. Backpage.com, LLC, 817 F.3d 12 (1st Cir. 2016); Gonzalez v. Google LLC, 2 F.4th 871 (9th Cir. 2021).

Section 230 in most of the country, but the Ninth Circuit Court of Appeals (covering the western United States) has applied Section 230 (c)(1) to state IP claims (such as trade secrets, publicity rights, and state trademark claims) based on third-party content.[18]

- The Electronic Communications Privacy Act (ECPA) and state law equivalents. This exception is largely irrelevant in practice.
- FOSTA. In 2018, Congress enacted FOSTA, a complex bill that targeted online promotions of sex trafficking victims and commercial sex more generally.[19] Among other consequences, FOSTA amended Section 230 (c)(1) to exclude state criminal prosecutions related to the promotion of sex trafficking and commercial sex, as well as private claims related to the promotion of sex trafficking.

3. *Information Provided by Another Information Content Provider.* Conceptually, this provision says Section 230(c)(1) only applies to third-party content, not first-party content. Thus, content originators remain liable for their content, but no one else online is liable alongside them. Of course, works are often prepared jointly or collaboratively, and internet services could potentially contribute to the development of users' content. However, courts applying Section 230(c)(1) typically reject plaintiffs' arguments to characterize user content as first-party content based on standard editing practices by services, such as reformatting content or engaging in content moderation.

To get around this first/third-party distinction, plaintiffs can claim that they are enforcing the services' contract or marketing promises made by the service. However, perhaps surprisingly, some courts have used Section 230(c)(1) to reject private lawsuits alleging services breached their public promises when courts think those lawsuits seek to hold the services liable for third-party content.[20]

In addition to Section 230(c)(1)'s statutory exclusions, courts have developed common-law exceptions for the following claims: promissory estoppel,[21] civil conspiracy,[22] failure to warn,[23] and defective software design (so long as the defect does not result in the publication of third-party content).[24] Additional common-law exceptions may apply when defendants allegedly moderated content with anti-competitive animus,[25] consummates an online marketplace

[18] Perfect 10, Inc. v. Ccbill LLC, 488 F.3d 1102 (9th Cir. 2007).

[19] For a fuller explanation of FOSTA, *see* Eric Goldman, *The Complicated Story of FOSTA and Section 230*, 17 First Amendment L. Rev. 279 (2019).

[20] *See, e.g.*, Murphy v. Twitter, Inc., 60 Cal. App. 5th 12 (Cal. App. Ct. 2021).

[21] Barnes v. Yahoo!, Inc., 570 F.3d 1096 (9th Cir. 2009).

[22] Tanisha Systems, Inc. v. Chandra, 2015 WL 10550967 (N.D. Ga. 2015).

[23] Doe v. Internet Brands, Inc., 824 F.3d 846 (9th Cir. 2016).

[24] Lemmon v. Snap, Inc., 995 F.3d 1085 (9th Cir. 2021).

[25] Enigma Software Group USA, LLC v. Malwarebytes, Inc., 946 F.3d 1040 (9th Cir. 2019).

transaction,[26] or encourages illegal content or designs its service to require users to input illegal content.[27]

2.4.3 *Implications of Section 230*

Some things that are not relevant to a Section 230(c)(1) defense:

First, Section 230(c)(1) has no prerequisites or formalities to qualify for the defense. A provider or user of an interactive computer service automatically gets Section 230(c)(1)'s immunity from liability for third-party content. In contrast, the DMCA Online Safe Harbor requires internet services to undertake numerous preparatory steps before they can qualify for the safe harbor – and any skipped step automatically disqualifies the service from the safe harbor's coverage.

Second, defendant scienter is irrelevant to a Section 230(c)(1) defense. An internet service may "know" about problematic third-party content or actions and still benefit from Section 230(c)(1)'s immunity. Thus, "takedown notices" or other legal demands for content removal do not affect an internet service's eligibility for Section 230(c)(1).[28] If the service otherwise qualifies for Section 230(c)(1), the service can ignore the takedown notice with no legal consequence. (In contrast, failure to remove allegedly infringing content in response to a takedown notice disqualifies the service from claiming the DMCA Online Safe Harbor).

Due to the irrelevance of scienter to Section 230(c)(1), the jurisprudence lacks the normal kinds of inquiries into the defendants' conduct or state of mind that one typically finds in US tort law cases. It does not matter to Section 230(c)(1) if plaintiffs allege that the service's employees reviewed the material at issue, or that the service had demonstrable evidence that it knew it had other instances of harmful content, or that the service had previously removed the same or similar content.

Third, Section 230(c)(1) does not depend on the internet service's lack of financial interest in the third-party content. Section 230(c)(1) applies to third-party content that the service pays to obtain.[29] Section 230(c)(1) also applies when the internet service shares revenue with the content supplier and when the internet service is paid to disseminate third-party

[26] HomeAway.com, Inc. v. City of Santa Monica, 918 F.3d 676 (9th Cir. 2019).

[27] Fair Hous. Council v. Roommates.com, LLC, 521 F.3d 1157 (9th Cir. 2008).

[28] E.g., Marshall's Locksmith Service Inc. v. Google LLC, 925 F.3d 1263 (D.C. Cir. 2019) ("it is 'well established that notice of the unlawful nature of the information provided is not enough to make it the service provider's own speech'").

[29] E.g., Blumenthal v. Drudge, 992 F. Supp. 44 (D.D.C. 1998).

content, such as advertisements,[30] in either case even though the internet service derives financial benefit from the illegal content.

Fourth, Section 230(c)(1)'s immunity applies regardless of how vigorously the service moderates content. It protects services that do zero content moderation at all (an unsustainable model given the exceptions to Section 230), services that have humans fully pre-screen all third-party content and select only some of that content for publication, and every option or configuration between those two extremes. As a result, internet services do not have an obligation to pre-screen third-party content either manually or using automated filters, though they are free to deploy such techniques without risking their eligibility for Section 230(c)(1) immunity.

Fifth, if a US court has jurisdiction over the matter and is applying US law, Section 230 will apply to foreign plaintiffs[31] and claims over foreign activities, such as a Canadian deindexing court order[32] and foreign terrorist attacks.[33]

2.4.4 *The Interplay Between Section 230(c)(1) and the First Amendment*

Internet services can always assert a First Amendment defense, but Section 230 supplements the First Amendment defense in important ways. If Section 230 and the First Amendment would both lead to the same substantive outcomes with respect to the publication of third-party content online,[34] Section 230(c)(1) acts like a "procedural fast lane" to resolve litigation more quickly and cheaply than would be possible

[30] *E.g.*, Ramey v. Darkside Productions, Inc., 2004 WL 5550485 (D.D.C. 2004); Goddard v. Google, Inc., 640 F. Supp. 2d 1193 (N.D. Cal. 2009); Calise v. Meta Platforms, Inc., 2022 WL 1240860 (N.D. Cal. 2022).

[31] *E.g.*, Force v. Facebook, Inc., 934 F.3d 53 (2d Cir. 2019); Igbonwa v. Facebook, Inc., 786 F. App'x 104 (9th Cir. 2019). For more on this topic, see Anupam Chander, *Section 230 and the International Law of Facebook*, 24 YALE J.L. & TECH. 393 (2022) ("in all of the cases that I have been able to discover involving foreign parties or events, with one exception, defendants successfully invoked Section 230, except in cases where the courts did not reach that issue because the defendant won on other grounds"). Prof. Chander says he "could not locate cases where Section 230 was asserted by a foreign defendant." *Id.*

[32] Google LLC v. Equustek Solutions Inc., 2017 WL 11573727 (N.D. Cal. 2017).

[33] Force v. Facebook, Inc., 934 F.3d 53 (2d Cir. 2019); Gonzalez v. Google LLC, 2 F.4th 871 (9th Cir. 2021) ("because § 230(c)(1) focuses on limiting liability, the relevant conduct occurs where immunity is imposed, which is where Congress intended the limitation of liability to have an effect, rather than the place where the claims principally arose. As such, the conduct relevant to § 230's focus is entirely within the United States – i.e., at the situs of this litigation"). Also, the SPEECH Act prevents the enforcement of defamation-related foreign court orders by US courts if the order would violate Section 230. 28 U.S.C. §§4101–4104.

[34] This is not the case. For example, the First Amendment provides less protection to commercial speech than non-commercial speech, but Section 230 treats both equally and thus provides greater protection for commercial speech than the First Amendment requires.

with a constitutional defense.[35] Among other reasons, Section 230(c)(1) empowers courts to dismiss claims at the earliest litigation stages (e.g., a motion to dismiss) when courts may be otherwise reluctant to make constitutional determinations, saving the internet services from incurring high litigation costs and getting dragged into discovery. These procedural benefits have substantive effects by encouraging internet services to moderate content without fearing the price tag of each decision.

When "lawful-but-awful" content is protected by the First Amendment, internet services never can be liable for that content – with or without Section 230(c)(1)'s immunity. In those circumstances, many regulatory and public complaints about the content's availability online are more appropriately directed to the First Amendment, not Section 230. In other words, Section 230(c)(1) revisions will not create any new legal incentives for the services to redress lawful-but-awful content. Instead, Section 230's immunity provides extra-legal comfort to internet services to do the socially valuable work of cleaning up harmful speech – work that the First Amendment would not permit the government to do itself.

2.4.5 *Liability for Account Terminations and Content Removals*

Internet services usually have the unrestricted editorial discretion to terminate or suspend user accounts or remove or downgrade user content without incurring liability. Users have lost dozens of cases over these decisions, and no plaintiff has gotten a courtroom victory over terminations/removals.[36] Those defense wins are based on a variety of theories (depending on the plaintiff's precise claims), including:

- Private internet services aren't state actors or sufficiently linked to the government to be obligated to comply with constitutional requirements.
- Internet services typically defeat contract claims because their terms of service expressly reserve their right to terminate accounts and remove content as they see fit.
- Section 230 protects the services' decisions. In particular, courts often treat the plaintiffs' content as third-party content,[37] thus evaluating the case using Section 230(c)(1) rather than Section 230(c)(2)(A) (which would require the service to show good faith decision-making). Though Section 230 plays an important part in this jurisprudence, it has been in play in less than half of the termination/removal cases.[38]
- The plaintiffs cannot satisfy the prima facie elements of the claim.

[35] *See* Eric Goldman, *Why Section 230 Is Better Than the First Amendment*, 95 Notre Dame L. Rev. Reflection 34 (2019).

[36] Eric Goldman & Jess Miers, *Online Account Terminations/Content Removals and the Benefits of Internet Services Enforcing Their House Rules*, 1 J. Free Speech L. 191 (2021).

[37] *E.g.*, Federal Agency of News LLC v. Facebook, Inc., 432 F. Supp. 3d 1107 (N.D. Cal. 2020).

[38] Goldman & Miers, *supra* note 36.

2.4.6 *What Happens When Section 230 Does Not Apply to Claims over Third-Party Content?*

Section 230(c)(1) applies to an essentially infinite number of state law claims predicated on third-party content. However, when a case fits into Section 230's statutory and common law exclusions, what rules apply then?

Every plaintiff must establish the prima facie elements of their claim. Sometimes, those elements do not apply to internet services for third-party content. For example, there have been numerous lawsuits against social media services for allegedly providing illegal "material support to terrorists." Many of those lawsuits have failed because the applicable statute simply does not reach the provision of content publishing tools. (Those lawsuits have also failed on Section 230, First Amendment, and other grounds).

As another example, some plaintiffs overcome a Section 230 defense by alleging that the defendant service failed to warn them that other users could harm them. Nevertheless, those lawsuits cannot establish the prima facie elements of negligence.[39]

If a plaintiff establishes a prima facie case, the defendant can assert a First Amendment defense. As discussed above, the First Amendment should negate strict liability for third-party content, plus services can interpose any defenses available to the content originator (such as the First Amendment limits on defamation liability).

The IP exception to Section 230 includes federal copyright, federal trademark, and (in some parts of the country) state IP claims. First Amendment defenses are not usually tenable for federal copyright or trademark claims, though they apply to some state IP claims.

With respect to federal copyright claims based on third-party content, internet services routinely qualify for the DMCA Online Safe Harbor.[40] Upon receipt of a takedown notice, the service makes a choice: it can expeditiously remove the targeted item or waive the DMCA Online Safe Harbor and accept whatever default liability may apply. If a service does not qualify for the DMCA Online Safe Harbor, a successful plaintiff must show that either (a) the service knew of the infringing content and materially contributed to the infringement or (b) the service had the right and ability to control the infringing conduct and directly profited from it.

With respect to federal trademark claims, no federal statute parallels the DMCA Online Safe Harbor.[41] Nevertheless, the courts have generally followed the same legal principles: a service is not liable if it expeditiously stopped third-party trademark infringements after receiving takedown notices.[42]

39 Beckman v. Match.com, LLC, 743 Fed. Appx. 142 (9th Cir. 2018); Doe No. 14 v. Internet Brands, Inc., 2016 U.S. Dist. LEXIS 192144 (C.D. Cal. 2016).

40 17 U.S.C. §512.

41 15 U.S.C. §1114(2)(A) provides a safe harbor for "innocent" printing of third-party materials, but this provision is rarely litigated because the "innocent" requirement is tautological.

42 Tiffany Inc. v. eBay, Inc., 600 F.3d 93 (2d Cir. 2010).

With respect to state IP claims based on third-party content that are not preempted by Section 230, the laws are too diverse, and the cases are too infrequent, to summarize.

2.5 STATE REGULATION OF THE INTERNET (THE DORMANT COMMERCE CLAUSE)

The United States vests regulatory power both in the federal government and in subnational regulators, such as state legislatures. In practice, however, state legislatures have numerous limits on their authority over internet services, including the First Amendment, Section 230 (which expressly preempts most conflicting state laws regarding third-party content),[43] federal preemption, and constitutional limits on personal jurisdiction.

In addition, the US Constitution restricts the ability of states to regulate the internet through a doctrine called the "Dormant Commerce Clause." The Constitution gives Congress the authority to regulate interstate commerce, and by negative implication, that power is allocated exclusively to Congress and not to the state legislatures. State regulation of internet services often has Dormant Commerce Clause implications because of the services' global and national reach. Some reasons why a state law might violate the Dormant Commerce Clause:

- Two or more states enact conflicting laws that make it impossible for an internet service to simultaneously comply with each law.
- A state's law regulates activity wholly outside of the state, such as a law purporting to govern how a service outside the state facilitates an interaction between two residents of other states.
- A state's law erects barriers to an out-of-state service providing services in-state.

However, Dormant Commerce Clause challenges against state internet laws are infrequently advanced, and those challenges succeed only occasionally. More often, overreaching state internet laws are struck down on First Amendment grounds.

2.6 TRANSPARENCY AS REGULATION[44]

In addition to, or instead of, dictating content moderation decisions outright, legislatures are requiring internet services to provide greater "transparency" about their editorial practices and operations. These regulations can take many forms,

[43] 47 U.S.C. §230(e)(3). The non-preempted state laws are the ECPA-equivalents, state IP claims outside the Ninth Circuit, and FOSTA claims.

[44] For a fuller treatment of this subject, *see* Eric Goldman, *The Constitutionality of Mandating Editorial Transparency*, 73 Hastings L.J. 1203 (2022), https://papers.ssrn.com/sol3/papers.cfm?abstract_id=4005647.

including requiring internet services to publish their editorial policies, provide explanations to affected users about content moderation decisions, and publish aggregated statistics about their content moderation practices.

The constitutionality of mandatory editorial transparency requirements is actively being litigated, and the final resolution is uncertain. Much depends on how the courts frame the requirements. If the disclosure requirements are like standard compelled commercial disclosures, the requirements will get relatively relaxed constitutional scrutiny. If the requirements distort editorial decisions by publishers, then they are more likely to get stringent constitutional review.

Whether or not states create new transparency requirements for internet services, government enforcement agencies are demanding disclosures from Internet services by invoking consumer protection laws, such as state "UDAP" (unfair and deceptive acts or practices) laws and other restrictions on "false" advertising. These information demands are more likely to be upheld by a court than broad-based statutory disclosures, but not all of them would survive judicial scrutiny. For example, the government regulators sometimes choose their enforcement target on partisan grounds, which makes the investigation look like impermissible retaliation for constitutionally protected speech.

2.7 CONCLUSION

Online speech freedoms have become inextricably intertwined with partisan politics, which creates irreconcilable conflicts. Oversimplified, Democrats want internet services to remove more content, even if it is constitutionally protected; while Republicans want internet services to publish more content, even content that hurts society or the internet service's audience. Although both sides are unhappy with the current legal framework governing internet services and would favor censorial interventions, their solutions advance two radically different visions of the internet's future.

Given the partisan split on content moderation expectations, internet services are now routinely subject to partisan attacks on all sides. The services cannot satisfactorily navigate these attacks, because (as with any partisan topic) any accommodations to one team automatically anger the other team. As a result, the partisanship creates a dangerous ecosystem for terrible policy ideas, especially when one partisan party controls all of the applicable regulatory apparatus. This means the US legal framework described by this chapter could change dramatically – and almost certainly not for the better – imminently.

3

Platform Responsibility in the European Union

From the E-Commerce Directive to the Digital Services Act

Christoph Busch

On February 17, 2024, the Digital Services Act (DSA) became fully applicable in the European Union (EU). The DSA, which has been portrayed as Europe's new "Digital Constitution," sets out a cross-sector regulatory framework for online services and regulates the responsibility of online intermediaries for illegal content. Against this background, this chapter provides a brief overview of recent regulatory developments regarding platform responsibility in the EU. The chapter forms part of the volume's comparative research project focused on inconsistencies among jurisdictions, the international effects of national structures for responsibility, and the possibility of international coordination of reform. In this context, the chapter seeks to add a European perspective to the global debate about platform regulation. Section 3.1 provides an overview of the regulatory framework in the EU and recent legislative developments. Section 3.2 analyzes different approaches regarding the enforcement of rules on platform responsibility. Section 3.3 takes a closer look at the regulation of content moderation by digital platforms in the EU. Finally, Section 3.4 adds some observations on the international effects of EU rules on platform responsibility.

3.1 GENERAL OVERVIEW ON PLATFORM RESPONSIBILITY

Platform responsibility in the EU is based on a combination of horizontal and sector-specific rules. For more than twenty years, the central pillar of the regulatory framework for digital services at EU level has been the E-Commerce Directive[1] (ECD).[2] Over the past few years, it has been complemented by sector-specific regulatory initiatives (Section 2). Furthermore, several Member States have recently

[1] Directive 2000/31/EC of the European Parliament and of the Council of 8 June 2000 on certain legal aspects of information society services, in particular electronic commerce, in the Internal Market (Directive on electronic commerce), http://data.europa.eu/eli/dir/2000/31/oj (hereinafter *ECD*).

[2] *See* Alexandre de Streel and Martin Husovec, The e-commerce Directive as the cornerstone of the Internal Market: Assessment and options for reform, Study for the IMCO committee of the

enacted national laws imposing responsibility on platforms in specific subject areas (Section 3). With the proposal for a Digital Services Act (DSA),[3] published in December 2020, the European legislator has taken an important step toward a comprehensive reform of the regulatory framework for platform responsibility (Section 4). A political agreement[4] on the outline of the DSA was reached in April 2022 and the DSA was formally adopted in October 2022.[5]

3.1.1 *The E-Commerce Directive*

The ECD, which laid the foundations for the EU regulatory framework for digital services, did not provide a positive basis for establishing when a provider of online services can be held liable for illegal content online. Instead, it created a horizontal framework of conditional exemptions from liability for different types of online service providers.[6] For hosting providers, including online platforms, legal immunity was based on a knowledge standard. Unlike Section 230 of the US Communications Decency Act,[7] which gives absolute immunity to publishers (other than immunity from Federal criminal law and certain intellectual property and sex trafficking claims), the ECD shielded platforms from liability only if they did not know that they are hosting illegal content. Under Art. 14 ECD, a platform operator was not liable for information stored at the request of a user, subject to the satisfaction of two alternative conditions. First, if "the provider does not have actual knowledge of illegal activity or illegal content."[8] Second, if "the provider, upon obtaining such knowledge or awareness, acts expeditiously to remove or disable access to the illegal content."[9] According to well-established case law of the European Court of Justice, the applicability of these safe harbor provisions depends on whether the intermediary has played a "neutral role" or an "active role."[10] In the cases *Google France v. Louis Vuitton*[11] and *L'Oreal v. eBay*,[12] the European Court of

European Parliament (May 2020), https://www.europarl.europa.eu/RegData/etudes/STUD/2020/648797/IPOL_STU(2020)648797_EN.pdf.

3 European Commission, Proposal for a Regulation on a Single Market for Digital Services (Digital Services Act) and amending Directive 2000/31/EC, COM (2020) 825 final (hereinafter *DSA Proposal*).

4 DSA, Provisional Agreement (Apr. 23, 2022). The text of the provisional agreement is available here: https://www.europarl.europa.eu/meetdocs/2014_2019/plmrep/COMMITTEES/IMCO/DV/2022/06-15/DSA_2020_0361COD_EN.pdf (hereinafter *DSA Provisional Agreement*).

5 Regulation (EU) 2022/2065 of the European Parliament and of the Council of 19 October 2022 on a Single Market For Digital Services and amending Directive 2000/31/EC, http://data.europa.eu/eli/reg/2022/2065/oj (hereinafter *DSA*).

6 *See* Arno R. Lodder & Andrew D. Murray, EU Regulation of E-Commerce 47–54 (2017).

7 47 U.S.C. § 230.

8 *See* ECD, *supra* note 1, art. 14(1)(a).

9 *See* ECD, *supra* note 1, art. 14(1)(b).

10 *See also* ECD, *supra* note 1, Recital 42.

11 CJEU Case C-236/08, Google France v. Louis Vuitton, ECLI:EU:C:2010:159 (Mar. 23, 2010).

12 CJEU Case C-324/09, L'Oreal v. eBay, ECLI:EU:C:2011:474 (July 12, 2011).

Justice has stated that the liability exemptions do not apply to service providers who play an active role, which would give the provider knowledge or control over the activity or information that is hosted. The safe harbor rule is complemented by Art. 15 ECD, which underlines that platform operators have no general obligation to monitor information on the platform.

3.1.2 *Sector-Specific Legislation and Self-regulation at EU Level*

In the light of the dynamic development of the digital economy over the past two decades, it became evident that the ECD in its present state no longer provides an adequate regulatory framework for the emerging "platform society."[13] In response to the rise of large online platforms, the EU has adopted over the past few years a variety of regulatory initiatives, including sector-specific legislation and measures based on self-regulation. These initiatives, which were meant to complement the ECD, seek to provide a regulatory response to the increasingly complex digital environment and the dissemination of illegal and harmful content.[14] Some of them focus on specific services (e.g., audiovisual media services),[15] others address specific types of illegal content (e.g., illegal hate speech,[16] terrorist content).[17] Others again tackle the dissemination of content that is harmful, but not necessarily illegal (e.g., online disinformation).[18] This piecemeal approach added to the fragmentation of the regulatory landscape and failed to provide a comprehensive update of the ECD, in particular in terms of responsibilities and regulatory oversight.[19] A few examples may illustrate this sector-specific approach.

Hate speech. Regarding illegal hate speech, the EU opted for self-regulation by platforms. Thus, in May 2016, the European Commission published the EU Code

[13] *See* José van Dijck, Thomas Poell & Martijn de Waal, The Platform Society: Public Values in a Connective World (2018).

[14] Ilaria Buri and Joris van Hoboken, *The Digital Services Act (DSA) Proposal: A Critical Overview* 5 (DSA Observatory, Oct. 28, 2021), https://dsa-observatory.eu/wp-content/uploads/2021/11/Buri-Van-Hoboken-DSA-discussion-paper-Version-28_10_21.pdf.

[15] Directive (EU) 2018/1808 of the European Parliament and of the Council of 14 November 2018 amending Directive 2010/13/EU on the coordination of certain provisions laid down by law, regulation or administrative action in Member States concerning the provision of audiovisual media services (Audiovisual Media Services Directive) in view of changing market realities, 2018 O.J. (L 303) 69–92 (hereinafter *AVMS Directive*).

[16] European Commission, *The EU Code of conduct on countering illegal hate speech online* (June 30, 2016), https://commission.europa.eu/strategy-and-policy/policies/justice-and-fundamental-rights/combatting-discrimination/racism-and-xenophobia/eu-code-conduct-countering-illegal-hate-speech-online_en#theeucodeofconduct.

[17] Regulation (EU) 2021/784 of the European Parliament and of the Council of 29 April 2021 on addressing the dissemination of terrorist content online, 2021 O.J. (L 172) 79–109 (hereinafter *TCO Regulation*)

[18] European Commission, *EU Code of Practice on Disinformation* (2018), https://digital-strategy.ec.europa.eu/en/policies/code-practice-disinformation.

[19] Buri and Hoboken, *supra* note 14, at 8.

of Conduct on Countering Illegal Hate Speech Online.[20] Initial signatories of the Code of Conduct included Facebook, Microsoft, Twitter, and YouTube. Today, the list of signatories also includes TikTok, LinkedIn, Twitch, and other platforms.[21] Considering that there is no formal definition of "hate speech" in International Human Rights Law, the Code of Conduct, adherence to which is voluntary, builds on the definition of illegal hate speech adopted by the Council of the European Union.[22] Under the Code of Conduct, the signatories made several voluntary commitments to counter the spread of illegal hate speech. In particular, they committed themselves to put in place mechanisms that allow them to review the majority of notifications on illegal content submitted by users within twenty-four hours and remove or disable access to such content, if necessary. In addition, platforms pledged to intensify cooperation between themselves and other platforms and social media companies to enhance best practice sharing. The implementation of the Code is evaluated through regular monitoring rounds. The performance reports are published by the European Commission.[23]

Disinformation. Another subject area, where the EU has promoted platform self-regulation, is the fight against disinformation. In September 2018, the European Commission released the Code of Practice on Disinformation,[24] under which the signatories (including Facebook, Google, Twitter, TikTok, and several advertising industry associations) voluntarily commit to take measures to minimize the spread of online disinformation. In order to coordinate these efforts, the Code of Practice contains a wide range of commitments: from transparency requirements for political advertising, to the termination of fake accounts, to the demonetization of disinformation campaigns.

Following a revision process launched in 2021, a revised and strengthened Code of Practice was released in June 2022 by the European Commission. It is planned that the new Code of Practice shall become part of a broader regulatory framework in combination with the future DSA. In particular, for very large platforms (VLOPs)[25] and very large search engines (VLOSEs)[26] with at least forty-five million

[20] European Commission, *supra* note 16.

[21] *Id.*

[22] Council Framework Decision 2008/913/JHA of 28 November 2008 on combating certain forms and expressions of racism and xenophobia by means of criminal law, 2008 O.J. (L 328), (defining illegal hate speech as "all conduct publicly inciting to violence or hatred directed against a group of persons or a member of such a group defined by reference to race, color, religion, descent or national or ethnic origin").

[23] European Commission, *supra* note 16.

[24] EU Code of Practice on Disinformation, *supra* note 18. In May 2023, the social media platform X (formerly Twitter) announced its intention to exit the voluntary Code, *see* Luca Bertuzzi, *Twitter Set to Exit EU Code of Practice on Disinformation, Sources Say*, Euractiv (May 26, 2023), https://www.euractiv.com/section/digital/news/twitter-set-to-exit-eu-code-of-practice-on-disinformation-sources-say/.

[25] DSA, *supra* note 5, art. 33.

[26] *Id.* art. 33a.

average monthly active users, adherence to the Code of Practice will constitute a risk mitigation measure required under Art. 27 DSA. In 2023, the EU adopted two series of designation decisions under the DSA designating twenty VLOPs and two VLOSEs.[27] Following their designation, the companies will have to comply with the full set of new obligations under the DSA. The examples above show that the DSA will not entirely replace the existing regulatory instruments but rather incorporate them into a more comprehensive governance framework that combines horizontal and sector-specific rules, as well as binding and non-binding instruments.

Terrorist content. The controversial EU Regulation on addressing the dissemination of terrorist content online (TCO Regulation),[28] which came into force in June 2021, establishes uniform rules to address the misuse of hosting services for the dissemination to the public of terrorist content online, which have direct effect across the EU as of June 7, 2022. Under the TCO Regulation, hosting service providers, including social media platforms, video-sharing services, and cloud services, may be required to remove flagged "terrorist content"[29] across the entire EU within specific time frames.

Notably, national authorities have the power to issue "removal orders" requiring hosting service providers to remove or disable access to terrorist content in all EU Member States "as soon as possible and, in any event, within one hour of receipt of the removal order."[30] In addition, the TCO Regulation includes a number of measures to ensure transparency, accountability, and the protection of legal rights. For example, platforms will have the right to challenge a removal order in court.[31] Furthermore, they must put in place complaint-handling mechanisms that allow users whose content has been removed to request a reinstatement of the content.[32]

When the DSA entered into force, it did not replace the TCO Regulation. Instead, the DSA explicitly mentions the TCO Regulation in the list of sector-specific legislation that will continue to apply as *lex specialis*.[33] The same applies to

[27] The first set of VLOPs, designated in April 2023, includes Alibaba AliExpress, Amazon Store, Apple AppStore, Booking.com, Facebook, Google Play, Google Maps, Google Shopping, Instagram, LinkedIn, Pinterest, Snapchat, TikTok, Twitter, Wikipedia, YouTube, and Zalando. The second set of VLOPs, designated in December 2023, includes three platforms that host sexually explicit content: Pornhub, Stripchat, and XVideos. In addition, in April 2023, the European Commission designated two VLOSEs: Bing and Google Search. *See* Press Release by European Commission (Apr. 25, 2023, Brussels) *Digital Services Act: Commission Designates First Set of Very Large Online Platforms and Search Engines*, https://ec.europa.eu/commission/presscorner/detail/en/ip_23_2413; *see also* Press Release by European Commission (Dec. 20, 2023) *Commission Designates Second Set of Very Large Online Platforms under the Digital Services Act*, https://ec.europa.eu/commission/presscorner/detail/en/ip_23_6763.

[28] TCO Regulation, *supra* note 17.

[29] *See* the extensive definition of "terrorist content" in the TCO Regulation, *supra* note 17, art. 2 (7).

[30] *Id.* art. 3(3).

[31] *Id.* art. 9.

[32] *Id.* art. 10.

[33] DSA, *supra* note 5, art. 2(4)(c).

the Audiovisual Media Services Directive, which was revised in 2018 and contains new rules on how video-sharing platforms (e.g., YouTube) shall deal with illegal content.[34]

3.1.3 *Regulatory Initiatives of the Member States*

It is not only the European legislator who has contributed to making the regulatory landscape in Europe increasingly complex through sector-specific regulation. Member States have also contributed to this by introducing national legislation on digital services and online platforms. For example, as the ECD does not contain any harmonized rules on notice-and-action procedures, several Member States have enacted such rules in their national legislation.[35] In addition, some Members more recently introduced strict requirements for platforms to remove specific types of illegal content (e.g., illegal hate speech) within a short time frame. A prominent and rather controversial example is the German Network Enforcement Act (NetzDG) of 2017, which stipulates due diligence obligations for social media platforms.[36] In particular, the NetzDG specifies that content that is "manifestly unlawful" must be removed or blocked within twenty-four hours of receiving a complaint.[37] Other examples of national platform laws that require the deletion of illegal content within short time limits include the Austrian Communication Platforms Act[38] and the French Loi Avia (although key provisions of the latter were struck down by the French Constitutional Council in June 2020).[39] These national initiatives and the growing risk of regulatory fragmentation was one of the main drivers of the European Commission's effort to update the legislative framework for online

[34] AVMS Directive, *supra* note 15.

[35] *See* Impact Assessment accompanying the Proposal for a Digital Services Act, SWD (2020) 348 final, 28–29, https://digital-strategy.ec.europa.eu/en/library/impact-assessment-digital-services-act.

[36] Gesetz zur Verbesserung der Rechtsdurchsetzung in sozialen Netzwerken [Netzwerkdurchset zungsgesetz] [NetzDG] [Act to Improve Enforcement of the Law in Social Networks] BUNDESGESETZBLATT, Teil I 3352 (Sept. 1, 2017), translation at https://www.bmjv.de/SharedDocs/Gesetzgebungsverfahren/Dokumente/NetzDG-engl.pdf; for a critical evaluation, *see, e.g.*, Rebecca Zipursky, *Nuts about NETZ: The Network Enforcement Act and Freedom of Expression*, 42 FORDHAM INT'L L.J. 1325 (2019); Patrick Zurth, *The German NetzDG as Role Model or Cautionary Tale? Implications for the Debate on Social Media Liability*, 31 FORDHAM INTELL. PROP. MEDIA & ENT. L.J. 1084 (2021).

[37] NetzDG, *supra* note 35, art. 3(2)(ii).

[38] Bundesgesetz über Maßnahmen zum Schutz der Nutzer auf Kommunikationsplattformen [K ommunikationsplattformen-Gesetz] [KoPl-G] [2020] BGBl. I Nr. 151/2020.

[39] Décision 2020-801 DC du 18 juin 2020 visant à lutter contre les contenus haineux sur internet [Law 2020-801 of June 18, 2020 aiming to counter hateful content on the internet], JOURNAL OFFICIEL DE LA RÉPUBLIQUE FRANÇAISE 0156 [J.O.] [OFFICIAL GAZETTE OF FRANCE], June 25, 2020; *see also* Aurelien Breeden, *French Court Strikes Down Most of Online Hate Speech Law*, N.Y. TIMES (June 18, 2020), https://www.nytimes.com/2020/06/18/world/europe/france-internet-hate-speech-regulation.html.

platforms and ensure that platforms are regulated at the EU level.[40] In November 2023, the European Court of Justice decided that national laws may not subject a communication platform provider established in another Member State to general and abstract obligations (e.g., reporting obligations).[41] In its decision, the Court held that such a regulatory approach would be in breach of the ECD's country-of-origin principle. This ruling further limits the regulatory options of Member States vis-à-vis online platforms.

3.1.4 *The Digital Services Act*

In December 2020, the European Commission published the then much-anticipated proposal[42] for a Digital Services Act (DSA) to update the regulatory framework for online platforms.[43] The proposal was part of a more comprehensive legislative package that also includes the Digital Markets Act (DMA).[44] Together, the DSA and the DMA create a new regulatory framework for the governance of digital services in the European Union.[45] The DMA aims at ensuring a contestable and fair market across the digital sector by stipulating *ex ante* rules applicable only to large online platforms that act as "gatekeepers"[46] between business users and end users.[47] In contrast, the DSA has a much broader scope and aims at updating the existing rules on platform responsibility for the provision of digital services.

[40] Buri and van Hoboken, *supra* note 14, at 6

[41] CJEU Case C-376/22, Google Ireland and Others, ECLI:EU:C:2023:835 (Nov. 9, 2023).

[42] DSA Proposal, *supra* note 3; for an overview see Christoph Busch & Vanessa Mak, *Putting the Digital Services Act in Context: Bridging the Gap between EU Consumer Law and Platform Regulation*, 10 Journal of European Consumer and Market Law 109 (2021); *see also* Miriam C. Buiten, *The Digital Services Act: From Intermediary Liability to Platform Regulation*, 12 J. JIPITEC 361 (2021).

[43] This section draws on Christoph Busch, *Regulating the Expanding Content Moderation Universe: A European Perspective on Infrastructure Moderation*, 27 UCLA Journal of Law & Technology 32 (2022).

[44] Regulation (EU) 2022/1925 of the European Parliament and of the Council of 14 September 2022 on contestable and fair markets in the digital sector and amending Directives (EU) 2019/1937 and (EU) 2020/1828 (Digital Markets Act), http://data.europe.eu/eli/reg/2022/1925/oj (hereinafter *DMA*).

[45] *See* Martin Eifert, Axel Metzger, Heike Schweitzer & Gerhard Wagner, *Taming the Giants, The DMA/DSA Package*, 58 Common Market Law Review 987 (2021).

[46] On September 6, 2023, The European Commission has designated Alphabet, Amazon, Apple, ByteDance, Meta, and Microsoft as "gatekeepers" under the Digital Markets Act, requiring them to comply with its regulations within six months for their twenty-two core platform services. *See* Press Release by European Commission (Sept. 6, 2023, Brussels) *Digital Markets Act: Commission Designates Six Gatekeepers*, https://perma.cc/KR8U-JQ8D.

[47] *See* Alexandre de Streel, *The European Proposal for a Digital Markets Act – A First Assessment* (Jan. 19, 2021), https://cerre.eu/publications/the-european-proposal-for-a-digital-markets-act-a-first-assessment.

3.1.4.1 General Framework of Platform Liability

Regarding platform liability, the DSA keeps up the conditional exemptions from liability of providers of online services.[48] One important difference compared to the ECD is that they will be contained in an EU Regulation, which unlike EU Directives requires no implementing legislation within individual Member States and therefore increases the level of harmonization.[49] Generally speaking, the DSA makes three contributions to the regulatory framework for content moderation by (1) setting out general rules of liability for providers of intermediary services; (2) establishing a regime of due diligence obligations, with a special focus on online platforms including social media; and (3) strengthening the cooperation between national authorities in charge of the public enforcement of online regulation.[50]

The liability rules for providers of online intermediary services set out in Chapter II of the DSA form the legal backdrop for content-related decisions taken by platform operators and other providers of digital intermediary services.[51] These rules determine under which circumstances online intermediaries, such as ISPs, hosting providers, or social media platforms, are legally required to remove content. The DSA abstains from the difficult task of drawing a line between legal and illegal content. Instead, it defines a number of liability exemptions by establishing when a provider of online intermediary services *cannot* be held liable in relation to third-party content. The safe harbor regime of the DSA broadly follows the existing model of the ECD.[52]

The DSA defines liability exemptions based on an intermediary's specific functions: mere conduit,[53] caching,[54] and hosting.[55] For the first two categories of providers, the DSA establishes a broad liability exemption as long the providers are "in no way involved with the information transmitted."[56] In contrast, for hosting providers, legal immunity is based on a knowledge standard. In other words, the DSA shields hosting providers from liability only if they do not know that they are hosting illegal content. This general rule is supplemented by two important limitations: First, Member states must not impose a general obligation to monitor content

48 For an overview, *see* Martin Husovec, Principles of the Digital Services Act (forthcoming).

49 *See* art. 288 of the Treaty on the Functioning of the European Union (TFEU).

50 *See, e.g.*, Martin Eifert et al., *supra* note 43.

51 *See* DSA, *supra* note 5, arts. 4–10.

52 *See* ECD, *supra* note 1, arts. 12–13; *see also* Sebastian Felix Schwemer et al., *Liability Exemptions of Non-Hosting Intermediaries: Sideshow in the Digital Services Act?*, 8 Oslo L. Rev. 4, 27 (2021) (discussing the liability exemptions for non-hosting providers under the ECD).

53 DSA, *supra* note 5, art. 4.

54 *Id.* art. 5.

55 *Id.* art. 6.

56 *Id.* recital 21.

on providers.[57] Second, it incorporates a Good Samaritan rule, whereby providers who carry out self-initiated investigations in order to detect and remove illegal content will not lose their liability exemption for this reason alone.[58]

3.1.4.2 Due Diligence Obligations

The above liability rules are complemented by several due diligence obligations for online intermediaries. Because of the broad range of intermediary services covered by the new rules, the DSA does not apply a one-size-fits-all approach. Instead, it follows a "risk-based approach" and formulates a catalog of "asymmetric due diligence obligations."[59] In doing so, the DSA distinguishes four levels of regulation:

Level 1 contains a basic set of rules, which applies to the broadest category, that is, all providers of online intermediary services. This category includes all providers of mere conduit, caching and hosting services.[60]

Level 2 applies to all providers of hosting services, such as cloud storage providers and webhosting services.[61]

Level 3 contains some additional provisions that apply only to online platforms,[62] defined as a provider of hosting services that, at the request of a recipient of the service, stores and disseminates to the public information.[63] This category includes online marketplaces, social networks, and app stores.

Level 4 adds some specific due diligence obligations for "very large online platforms" (VLOPs), and "very large online search engines" (VLOSEs), which have more than forty-five million average monthly EU users (i.e., roughly 10 percent of EU citizens).[64] In contrast, very small platforms are exempt from most due diligence obligations.[65]

This model of asymmetric regulation, under which the rules become more numerous and stricter as we go from Level 1 to Level 4, is an expression of the principle of proportionality. In terms of substance, the DSA introduces, for the first time, a number of due diligence obligations with regard to content moderation. For example, all providers of online intermediary services have to include information about their content moderation policy in their terms and conditions.[66] They also

57 *Id.* art. 8.
58 *Id.* art. 7.
59 DSA Proposal, *supra* note 3, at 6.
60 *See* DSA, *supra* note 5, arts. 11–15.
61 *Id.* arts. 16–18.
62 *Id.* arts. 19–32.
63 *Id.* art. 3(i).
64 *Id.* arts. 33–43.
65 *See, e.g., id.* arts. 19, 29.
66 *Id.* art. 14(1).

have to publish annual reports with meaningful and comprehensive information about their content moderation activities, including details on the use of automated tools for content moderation (*Level 1*).[67] In addition to these general requirements, providers of hosting services must provide harmonized notice-and-action mechanisms and justify removal decisions with a statement of reasons (*Level 2*).[68] Providers of online platforms must also provide users with meaningful possibilities to challenge decisions to remove or label content via an internal complaint system and an external out-of-court dispute resolution mechanism (*Level 3*).[69] Finally, VLOPs and VLOSEs are subject to additional rules to ensure more comprehensive public oversight of their content moderation practices (*Level 4*). In particular, VLOPs and VLOSEs are obliged to develop appropriate tools for assessing and managing systemic risks and take measures to protect the integrity of their services against manipulation, including disinformation campaigns or interference with electoral processes.[70]

Most of the rules regarding content moderation in the DSA have been drafted with user-facing platforms such as Facebook, Twitter, or YouTube in mind. But the DSA also responds to the expansion of content moderation practices by expanding its content moderation rules, both in the horizontal and vertical dimensions.[71] In this sense, some of the content moderation rules stipulated by the DSA apply also to nontraditional platforms (e.g., public groups on messaging services) and to actors deeper down in the content moderation stack (e.g., cloud services, content delivery networks).

3.2 ENFORCEMENT OF PLATFORM RESPONSIBILITY RULES

Enforcement of platform responsibility was a weak spot of the ECD, which mainly relied on self-regulatory initiatives and gave Member States wide discretion regarding the choice of enforcement methods (Section 1).[72] In contrast, the DSA puts a strong emphasis on procedural aspects and enforcement.[73] In doing so, it combines different methods including self-regulation and administrative liability (Section 2).

67 *Id.* art. 16.
68 *Id.* arts. 16–17.
69 *Id.* arts. 20–24.
70 *Id.* arts. 33–43.
71 *See* Busch, *supra* note 40.
72 *See, e.g.*, Melanie Smith, *Enforcement and cooperation between Member States: E-Commerce and the future Digital Services Act, Study for the IMCO committee of the European Parliament* (Apr. 2020), https://www.europarl.europa.eu/RegData/etudes/STUD/2020/648780/IPOL_STU(2020)648780_EN.pdf.
73 *See, e.g.*, Ilaria Buri & Joris van Hoboken, *The DSA Supervision and Enforcement Architecture* (DSA Observatory, June 24, 2022), https://dsa-observatory.eu/2022/06/24/the-dsa-supervision-and-enforcement-architecture/.

3.2.1 *The E-Commerce Directive: Self-regulation and Wide Discretion for Member States*

The ECD did not provide for an effective oversight and enforcement framework at the European level. Instead, it merely suggested that the European Commission and Member States encourage the drawing up of codes of conduct by trade, professional, and consumer organizations.[74] Examples of such codes are the above-mentioned EU Code of Practice on Disinformation,[75] the EU Code of conduct on countering illegal hate speech online,[76] and the EU Product safety pledge.[77] With regard to civil liability and private rights to sue, the ECD only vaguely instructs Member States to "ensure that court actions available under national law allow for the rapid adoption of measures, including interim measures, designed to terminate any alleged infringement and prevent any further impartment of the interests involved."[78] Regarding administrative enforcement, the ECD mainly limits itself to stipulating that "Member States shall have adequate means of supervision and investigation necessary to implement" the ECD.[79] Similarly, the ECD does not prescribe which type of sanctions Member States shall apply to infringements of national provisions implementing the ECD. Instead, the choice of sanctions is left to the discretion of Member States. Using the standard formula of EU Directives, the ECD merely stipulates that those sanctions shall be "effective, proportionate and dissuasive."[80]

3.2.2 *The Digital Services Act: Strong Emphasis on Oversight, Enforcement, and Sanctions*

Unlike the ECD, the DSA puts a strong emphasis on oversight and enforcement and devotes a detailed chapter on "implementation, cooperation, sanctions and enforcement."[81] Generally speaking, the enforcement of the due diligence obligations imposed by the DSA on platforms is shared between Member States and the European Commission. For starters, the Member State where the platform has its

[74] ECD, *supra* note 1, art. 16(1)(a).
[75] *See supra*, note 18.
[76] *See supra*, note 16.
[77] *See* European Commission, Product Safety Pledge: Voluntary commitment of online marketplaces with respect to the safety of non-food consumer products sold online by third party sellers (June 25, 2018), https://ec.europa.eu/info/sites/default/files/voluntary_commitment_document_2021_v5.pdf; *see also* European Commission, 6th Progress Report on the implementation of the Product Safety Pledge (Apr. 22, 2022), https://ec.europa.eu/info/sites/default/files/6th_progress_report_product_safety_pledge.pdf.
[78] ECD, *supra* note 1, art. 18(1)(a).
[79] *Id.* art. 19(1).
[80] *Id.* art. 20.
[81] DSA, *supra* note 5, Chapter IV, arts. 49–88.

main establishment will have exclusive powers for the supervision of the DSA rules, except where such powers are attributed to the exclusive or shared competence of the European Commission.[82] In particular, the European Commission is granted exclusive powers regarding the specific obligations set out in Section 4 Chapter III DSA, which apply only to large online platforms (VLOPs) and very large online search engines (VLOSEs). For fulfilling this role, the Commission is granted far-reaching powers of investigation, enforcement, and monitoring (similar to those in antitrust cases) in respect of VLOPs and VLOSEs.[83] In December 2023, the European Commission has opened formal proceedings against the social media platform X (formerly Twitter) in order to investigate whether X may have breached its obligations under the DSA regarding risk management, content moderation, dark patterns, advertising transparency, and data access for researchers.[84]

For coordinating the enforcement of the DSA, each Member State must appoint a Digital Services Coordinator (DSC).[85] The DSC will be an independent authority responsible for supervising platforms and other intermediary services in their Member State and for coordinating supervision by sectoral authorities. It is envisaged that national DSCs and the Commission cooperate closely and provide each other mutual assistance in the enforcement of the DSA. Cooperation between DSCs shall be facilitated by the setting up of a European Board for Digital Services, which consists of all national DSCs and the European Commission.[86]

The DSA is also more explicit with regard to the type of sanctions that may be imposed in case of infringements. In particular, the DSA states that the competent enforcer – the DSC or the European Commission, as the case may be – can, in the most serious cases, impose a fine of up to 6 percent of the total worldwide annual turnover in the preceding financial year.[87] Moreover, periodic penalty payments of up to 5 percent of the average daily income or worldwide annual turnover in the preceding financial year per day may be imposed.[88]

As this brief overview shows, the DSA focuses on public enforcement and introduces a centralized regulatory model for VLOPs and VLOSEs with the Commission as the primary regulator. The choice of this model seems to be

[82] *Id.* art. 56(1). For platforms which do not have an establishment in the EU, the Member State where the legal representative (as required under art. 13 DSA) is established or the European Commission (in case of VLOPs and VLOSEs) shall have powers for the supervision (arts. 56(2), 56(6) DSA). If a platform fails to appoint a legal representative, all Member States or the European Commission (in case of VLOPs and VLOSEs) have those powers (art. 56(7) DSA).

[83] DSA, *supra* note 5, arts. 64–83 (including, for example, the power to request information, take interviews and conduct inspections).

[84] *See* Press Release by European Commission, Commission opens formal proceedings against X under the Digital Services Act (Dec. 18, 2023), https://ec.europa.eu/commission/presscorner/detail/en/IP_23_6709.

[85] *Id.* art. 49.

[86] *Id.* art. 61.

[87] *Id.* arts. 52(3) and 74(1).

[88] *Id.* arts. 52(4) and 76.

influenced by the difficulties that have arisen in enforcing the General Data Protection Regulation[89] (GDPR).[90] In particular, it occurred that some national data protection authorities were rather slow to respond to complaints and requests for cross-border cooperation by authorities from other Member States. Against this background, the DSA also establishes a detailed cooperation mechanism that seeks to ensure that the enforcement of the DSA will not be compromised by an inactive DSC. In particular, in case of disagreement among DSCs, the European Board for Digital Services may refer the matter to the Commission in order to speed up the enforcement procedure.[91]

While the DSA focuses on administrative enforcement, it is important to note that the public enforcement model is complemented also by other methods of enforcement. In this sense, Art. 54 DSA, which was introduced only during the trilogue negotiations between the European Commission, the European Parliament, and the Council of the European Union, underlines that platform users "shall have the right to seek, in accordance with Union and national law, compensation from providers of intermediary services, against any damage or loss suffered due to an infringement by those providers of their obligations" under the DSA. In other words, a violation of the due diligence obligations stipulated by the DSA may also give rise to civil liability. However, the DSA leaves the details of such individual claims to the laws of the Member States. Finally, violations of the DSA may also give rise to class actions (or, more precisely, "representative actions") under Directive (EU) 2020/1828.[92]

3.3 SPECIFIC PLATFORM RESPONSIBILITIES REGARDING CONTENT MODERATION

Content moderation by digital platforms has become a focal point of the policy debate on platform regulation.[93] Some argue that platforms are not doing enough to reduce the dissemination of illegal or harmful content. Others criticize platforms for exercising too much censorship. Against this background, this section will explain how the DSA regulates content moderation by platforms, in particular the scope of

89 Regulation 2016/679, of the European Parliament and of the Council of 27 April 2016 on the Protection of Natural Persons with Regard to the Processing of Personal Data and on the Free Movement of Such Data, and Repealing Directive 95/46/EC (General Data Protection Regulation), 2016 O.J. (L 119) (hereinafter *GDPR*).

90 *See* Buri and van Hoboken, *supra* note 14; *see also* Buiten, *supra* note 39, para. 78.

91 *See* DSA, *supra* note 5, art. 59.

92 *Id.* art. 90.

93 *See generally* James Grimmelmann, *The Virtues of Moderation*, 17 YALE J. L. & TECH 42 (2015); Jack M. Balkin, *Free Speech in the Algorithmic Society: Big Data, Private Governance, and New School Speech Regulation*, 51 U.C. DAVIS L. REV. 1149 (2018); Kate Klonick, *The New Governors: The People, Rules, and Processes Governing Online Speech*, 131 HARV. L. REV. 1598 (2018); Hannah Bloch-Wehba, *Automation in Moderation*, 53 CORNELL INT'L L. J. 41 (2020).

platform responsibility for detection and moderation, and limits on platform discretion to moderate.

3.3.1 *General Framework: No General Monitoring Obligations and Good Samaritan Rule*

The DSA defines content moderation as "activities, automated or not, undertaken by providers of intermediary services that are aimed, in particular, at detecting, identifying and addressing illegal content or information incompatible with their terms and conditions, provided by recipients of the service."[94] As mentioned before, such activities to detect and moderate specific types of content are not only taken by operators at the platform level but also deeper down in the internet stack at the infrastructure level.[95] The definition provided by the DSA is rather broad in two respects: first, it not only covers decisions to remove content and disable user accounts but also other measures that influence the "availability, visibility and accessibility" of content, such as downranking and de-amplification. Second, the definition is not limited to "illegal content" but also includes measures taken with regard to information which is incompatible with the terms and conditions of the online service provider. Therefore, content moderation under the DSA includes also measures taken regarding content that is legal but nevertheless considered objectionable.

As explained in Section 3.1, the DSA establishes a knowledge-based limited liability regime that is built around a notice-and-action mechanism. These rules determine under which circumstances online intermediaries, including social media platforms, are legally required to remove content. In this sense, the liability rules for providers of online intermediary services form the legal backdrop for content-related decisions taken by online platforms.[96] Another key provision that determines the legal framework for content moderation decisions is Art. 8 DSA, which underlines that "no general obligation to monitor the information which providers of intermediary services transmit or store, nor actively to seek facts or circumstances indicating illegal activity shall be imposed on those providers." While any "general obligation" to monitor is prohibited, courts may impose "specific obligations" to monitor activities on the platform in order to tackle repeat infringers or the reappearance of identical or content with "equivalent meaning."[97]

[94] *See* DSA, *supra* note 5, art. 3(t). According to this definition moderation activities may include "measures taken that affect the availability, visibility, and accessibility of that illegal content or that information, such as demotion, demonetization, disabling of access to, or removal thereof, or that affect the ability of the recipients to provide that information, such as the termination or suspension of a recipient's account."

[95] *See* Busch, *supra* note 40.

[96] *See* DSA, *supra* note 5, arts. 4–10.

[97] *See, e.g.*, CJEU Case C-18/18, Glawischnig-Piesczek v. Facebook, ECLI:EU:C:2019:821 (Oct. 3, 2019).

A notable addition to the EU regime of platform liability is Art. 7 DSA, on "voluntary own-initiative investigations." According to Art. 7 DSA, online intermediaries will not automatically lose the conditional exemption from liability "solely because" they carry out voluntary investigations or take other measures for "detecting, identifying and removing, or disabling access to, illegal content" or "take the necessary measures to comply with" requirements of national law or EU law, including those set out in the DSA. The purpose of Art. 7 DSA is to incentivize online intermediaries to engage in voluntary content moderation of harmful and illegal content by introducing a sort of "Good Samaritan" protection.[98] It is unclear, however, whether this aim will be achieved. In particular, the scope of the protection offered by Art. 7 DSA will need further clarification. During the trialogue negotiations between the European Commission, the European Parliament, and the Council of the European Union, the wording of the provision has been amended to the effect that voluntary own-initiative investigations are only covered by the Good Samaritan protection if they are carried out "in good faith and in a diligent manner". It is unclear, however, which level of diligence is required with regard to content moderation activities by platforms. At least some clarification is provided by Recital 26 of the DSA, which underlines that the condition of acting in good faith and in a diligent manner should include "acting in an objective, non-discriminatory and proportionate manner and with due regard to the rights and legitimate interests of all parties involved." While the DSA does not formulate an explicit requirement of platform neutrality, the reference to the principle of non-discrimination makes it clear that an arbitrary unequal treatment of content within the framework of content moderation would be a violation of the due diligence requirements.

3.3.2 *Asymmetric Due Diligence Obligations: Risk-Based Approach to Content Moderation*

In addition to the general rules set out in Arts. 7–8 DSA, there are a number of more specific rules on content moderation that are scattered throughout the DSA. These rules stipulate graduated due diligence obligations regarding content moderation depending on the type and size of intermediary. In this sense, they follow the asymmetric model ("risk-based approach") of the DSA.

3.3.2.1 Transparency and Reporting

According to Art. 14(1) DSA all providers of intermediary services, including social media platforms, must provide in their terms and conditions "information on any restrictions that they impose in relation to the use of their service." This information

[98] *See* Buri and van Hoboken, *supra* note 14, at 17.

shall include details on "any policies, procedures, measures and tools used for the purpose of content moderation, including algorithmic decision-making, and human review as well as rules of procedure of their internal complaint handling system."

These general transparency requirements are supplemented by Art. 15 DSA, which stipulates detailed reporting obligations.[99] In particular, it requires providers of intermediary services to publish a yearly report on any content management they engaged in during the relevant time period.[100] This report shall provide "meaningful and comprehensible information about the content moderation engaged in at the providers' own initiative."[101] Furthermore, detailed information about the use of "automated means for the purpose of content moderation" must be included in the report.[102]

On September 26, 2023, the European Commission launched the DSA Transparency Database, a first-of-its-kind platform that collects data in accordance with Art 25(5) of DSA and provides public access to content moderation decisions made by online platform providers in the EU. This initiative aims to enhance online transparency and accountability.[103]

3.3.2.2 Fundamental Rights and Proportionality

The DSA not only stipulates transparency and reporting requirements regarding content moderation policies but also regulates how providers of intermediary services shall implement their content moderation procedures. Pursuant to Art. 14(4) DSA, they "shall act in a diligent, objective and proportionate manner in applying and enforcing the restrictions" referred to Art. 14(1), "with due regard to the rights and legitimate interests of all parties involved, including the fundamental rights of the recipients of the service, such as the freedom of expression, freedom and pluralism of the media, and other fundamental rights and freedoms as enshrined in the Charter."[104] In other words, Article 14(4) DSA sets a benchmark for content moderation decisions by providers at all levels of the content moderation stack. All providers of intermediary services are obliged to take due consideration of

[99] Providers of intermediary services that qualify as "micro or small enterprises" within the meaning of Recommendation 2003/361/EC are exempt from the reporting obligations. DSA, *supra* note 5, art. 13(2).

[100] DSA, *supra* note 5, art. 13(1).

[101] *Id.* art. 15(1)(c). This information shall include details about the "use of automated tools, the measures taken to provide training and assistance to persons in charge of content moderation."

[102] *Id.* art. 15(1)(e). In this regard, the reports shall include "qualitative description, a specification of the precise purposes, indicators of the accuracy and the possible rate of error of the automated means used in fulfilling those purposes, and any safeguards applied."

[103] Press Release by European Commission (Sept. 26, 2023) *Digital Services Act: Commission launches Transparency Database*, https://digital-strategy.ec.europa.eu/en/news/digital-services-act-commission-launches-transparency-database.

[104] *Id.* art. 14(4).

fundamental rights enshrined in the EU Charter of Fundamental Rights (CFR),[105] particularly the freedom of expression and information, the freedom to conduct a business, and the right to nondiscrimination.[106]

Similarly, Recital 47 of the DSA underlines that the design, application, and enforcement of content-related restrictions should be "non-arbitrary and non-discriminatory." It remains to be seen whether these references to the principle of nondiscrimination will be interpreted by the European Court of Justice as the legal foundation of a requirement of neutrality with regard to content moderation. In this context, it might also be of interest that during the legislative process, a possible prohibition of content moderation for media content was discussed.[107] On the one hand, it was argued that such a prohibition could strengthen the independence of the media, but, on the other hand ,it could undermine the goal of tackling disinformation. Finally, the proposed ban was not included in the text of the provisional agreement on the DSA.

3.3.2.3 Notice-and-Action Mechanism and Complaint Handling

The DSA requires providers of hosting services, including providers of online platforms, to set up a user-friendly electronic *notice-and-action mechanism* that allows "any individual or entity to notify them of the presence on their service of specific items of information that the individual or entity considers to be illegal content."[108] This mechanism shall enable users to notify hosting service providers of allegedly illegal content. If such a notice is sufficiently substantiated and fulfills the requirements set out in Art. 16(2) DSA, the provider is considered to have actual knowledge of the illegal activity. This triggers application of the liability rule under Art. 6 DSA. In other words, the hosting service provider will be liable for the illegal content unless the provider "acts expeditiously to remove or to disable access to the illegal content."[109] However, providers are only deemed to have actual knowledge of the illegal content where the notices "allow a diligent provider of hosting services to identify the illegality of the relevant activity or information without detailed legal examination."[110] If a hosting provider decides to remove or disable access to the illegal content or otherwise restricts the visibility of specific items of information,

[105] *See* Charter of Fundamental Rights of the European Union, 2000 O.J. (C 364) [hereinafter CFR].

[106] DSA, *supra* note 5, art. 14(4). *See also*, *id.*, recital 3; CFR, arts. 11, 16, 21.

[107] *See* Julian Jaursch, *No Content Moderation for Media Publishers? Proposed Amendment for Digital Services Act Is a Lesson in Unintended Consequences*, Tech Policy Press (Nov. 10, 2021), https://techpolicy.press/no-content-moderation-for-media-publishers-proposed-amendment-for-digital-services-act-is-a-lesson-in-unintended-consequences/.

[108] DSA, *supra* note 5, art. 16(1).

[109] *Id.* art. 6(1)(b).

[110] *Id.* art. 16(3).

Art. 17 DSA obligates the host to provide the uploader of that content with a detailed statement of reasons for removal.[111]

For online platforms, the DSA adds a further element to increase the effectiveness of the notice-and-action mechanism. Pursuant to Art. 22(1) DSA, providers of online platforms shall take the necessary technical and organizational steps to cooperate with specialized "trusted flaggers" (e.g., consumer organizations or other NGOs) and to ensure that notices provided by them are decided upon with priority.[112] Providers of online platforms are also obliged to set up an internal *complaint-handling system*, which enables users to lodge a complaint against decisions to remove content or terminate the service.[113] Furthermore, users who are affected by the provider's decision must be given the opportunity to appeal the decision to an impartial dispute resolution body whose decision is binding on the platform provider.[114]

3.3.2.4 Systemic Risk Management

For very large online platforms (VLOPs) and very large online search engines (VLOSEs), the DSA provides even more extensive regulations.[115] They will be required to undergo annual risk assessments to identify any significant systemic risks stemming from the services.[116] The scope of this risk assessment includes the "dissemination of illegal content," "any actual or foreseeable negative effects for the exercise of fundamental rights," and "any actual or foreseeable negative effects on civic discourse and electoral processes, and public security."[117] When assessing such systemic risks, several factors shall be taken into account, including the design of recommender systems and "other relevant algorithmic systems"[118] as well as the functioning of the content moderation systems.[119]

In order to counter the above-mentioned systemic risks, VLOPs and VLOSEs must put in place reasonable, proportionate, and effective mitigation measures. Such measures may include adapting their content moderation systems (e.g., by adjusting the speed and quality of processing notices related to specific types of illegal content) or by adjusting their terms and conditions.[120] The effectiveness of

[111] *Id.* art. 17(1).

[112] The status of "trusted flaggers" is awarded by the national Digital Services Coordinators. DSA, *supra* note 5, art. 22(2).

[113] *Id.* art. 20.

[114] *Id.* art. 21.

[115] *Id.* arts. 33–43.

[116] *Id.* art. 34.

[117] *Id.*

[118] *Id.* art. 34(2)(a).

[119] *Id.* art. 34(2)(b).

[120] DSA, *supra* note 5, art. 35.

these measures will be assessed at least annually by an independent audit.[121] Furthermore, VLOPs and VLOSEs are required to publish transparency reports every six months, as opposed to once a year.[122]

Influenced by the conflict in Ukraine, a new "crisis response mechanism" was introduced into the final version of the DSA during the trialogue negotiations,[123] which sparked a controversial debate.[124] Under this provision, the European Commission may require VLOPs to react to a public security or public health crisis by initiating an urgent crisis response. For example, VLOPs could be required to intensify their fight against the dissemination of disinformation. Such measures may include, for example, "adapting content moderation processes and increasing the resources dedicated to content moderation."[125] Similarly, VLOPs may be obliged to take "awareness-raising measures" and promote "trusted information."[126]

3.4 INTERNATIONAL ASPECTS OF PLATFORM RESPONSIBILITY

This final section will briefly address three aspects that may be of particular relevance for US readers: the application of EU platform responsibility rules to platform operators based outside the EU (Section 1), the obligation to designate a legal representative in the EU (Section 2), and the global reach of court orders to remove certain content (Section 3).

3.4.1 *Application to Foreign-Based Platforms*

The DSA will have extraterritorial reach beyond the EU. More precisely, the rules set out in the DSA will apply to all intermediary service providers, irrespective of their place of establishment, to the extent that they provide services to users in the EU.[127] Whether the intermediary services are provided in the EU is determined by a "substantial connection" test. A substantial connection is deemed to exist where the provider either has an establishment in the European Union or, its absence, on the basis of the existence of a significant number of users in the EU or the targeting of activities toward one or more EU Member States.[128] This regulatory approach

[121] *Id.* art. 37.

[122] *Id.* art. 42. In particular, the report must provide details about the results of the risk assessment (art. 34), the risk mitigation measures (art. 35), and the independent audit (art. 37).

[123] DSA, *supra* note 5, art. 36.

[124] *See* Morgan Meaker, *Ukraine War Prompts Europe's New Emergency Rules for the Internet*, WIRED (Apr. 25, 2022), https://www.wired.com/story/europe-digital-services-act/.

[125] DSA, *supra* note 5, Recital 91.

[126] *Id.*

[127] *Id.* art. 2(1).

[128] *Id.* Recital 8 ("The targeting of activities towards a Member State could also be derived from the availability of an application in the relevant national application store, from the provision of local advertising or advertising in the language used in that Member State, or from the

follows the model of other EU instruments such as the GDPR[129] and the Regulation on addressing the dissemination of terrorist content.[130]

3.4.2 *Requirement to Designate a Legal Representative in the EU*

The extraterritorial application of the DSA would fail in practice if the competent authorities were unable to enforce the rules against a platform operator that does not have an establishment in the EU. Therefore, the DSA requires service providers based outside the EU to designate a legal representative in one of the EU Member States.[131] The representatives shall not merely be a "mailbox" for communications by Member States' authorities, but they can be held liable for noncompliance with the obligations under the DSA.[132] Similar obligations to designate a "representative" or a "responsible person" have been stipulated in other EU laws with an extraterritorial reach, such as the General Data Protection Regulation,[133] the Market Surveillance Regulation,[134] and the recent proposal for a General Product Safety Regulation.[135] Also the Regulation on addressing the dissemination of terrorist content online requires platforms that do not have their main establishment in the EU are required to designate a legal representative in the EU "for the purpose of the receipt of, compliance with and the enforcement of removal orders and decisions issued by the competent authorities."[136]

3.4.3 *Global Reach of Court Orders to Remove Content*

Another issue that may be of interest from a US perspective is the territorial scope of court orders to remove content. In this context, the recent decision of Court of Justice of the European Union (CJEU) in *Glawischnig-Pieczik v. Facebook* gave rise

handling of customer relations such as by providing customer service in the language generally used in that Member State.").

[129] *See* GDPR, *supra* note 85, art. 3.

[130] *See* TCO Regulation, *supra* note 17, art. 1(2).

[131] DSA, *supra* note 5, art. 13(1).

[132] *Id.* art. 13(3).

[133] Regulation 2016/679, of the European Parliament and of the Council of 27 April 2016 on the Protection of Natural Persons with Regard to the Processing of Personal Data and on the Free Movement of Such Data, and Repealing Directive 95/46/EC (General Data Protection Regulation), 2016 O.J. (L 119), 48–49.

[134] Regulation 2019/1020, of the European Parliament and of the Council of 20 June 2019 on Market Surveillance and Compliance of Products and Amending Directive 2004/42/EC and Regulations (EC) No 765/2008 and (EU) No 305/2011, 2016 O.J. (L 169), 14.

[135] European Commission, Proposal for a Regulation of the European Parliament and of the Council on General Product Safety, Amending Regulation (EU) No 1025/2012 of the European Parliament and of the Council, and Repealing Council Directive 87/357/EEC and Directive 2001/95/EC of the European Parliament and of the Council, at 42, COM (2021) 346 final (June 30, 2021).

[136] *See* TCO Regulation, *supra* note 17, art. 17(1).

to concern.[137] In the case, which concerned a defamatory post on Facebook, the Austrian Supreme Court issued a preliminary ruling request to the CJEU. Among other things, the CJEU was asked whether a national court could extend an injunction against Facebook so that it had effect worldwide. The CJEU dealt with this question rather briefly and underlined that the ECD does not impose any territorial limitation on the scope of the measures that Member States are entitled to adopt. Therefore, the CJEU argued that the ECD "does not preclude those injunction measures from producing effects worldwide."[138] However, as the Court underlined, it is necessary to take due account of the relevant international law.[139] Unfortunately, the CJEU did not further elaborate on how a worldwide effect could be reconciled with public and private international law. This was a missed opportunity considering that only a few days earlier, in *Google France v. CNIL*, the CJEU had decided that a de-referencing request based on the "right to be forgotten" under Art. 17 GDPR does not oblige a search engine to carry out a worldwide de-referencing.[140]

[137] Glawischnig-Piesczek v. Facebook, *supra* note 93.
[138] *Id.* para. 50
[139] *Id.* para. 51, 53.
[140] CJEU Case C-507/17, Google France v. CNIL, ECLI:EU:C:2019:772 (Sept. 24, 2019).

4

Platform Responsibility with Chinese Characteristics

Jufang Wang

4.1 INTRODUCTION

While the US-based platforms like Facebook, YouTube, and Twitter dominate the social media markets in most countries, China, as the world's second largest digital economy,[1] has its own platform ecosystem, where indigenous platforms like WeChat, Weibo, and Douyin are the major players.[2] China's authoritarian political system, together with this unique platform ecosystem, has shaped how it approaches platform responsibility for content moderation.

In liberal democracies, debates around platform responsibility have focused on whether to and increasingly how to regulate platforms and mainly revolve around balancing the two oftentimes incompatible objectives: making platforms accountable for illegal or harmful content and protecting freedom of expression. In contrast, Chinese platforms, despite holding dominant market power over online information distribution and consumption,[3] fall under the heavy regulation of the government and are required to take the "primary responsibility" (主体责任) for content governance (to be discussed later).[4]

[1] According to a Chinese government source, the scale of China's digital economy reached around $7.25 trillion in 2022, ranking second in the world for many years, *China's Digital Economy a New Growth Engine to Drive Modernization*, CHINA VOICES (Apr. 28, 2023), http://english.scio.gov.cn/m/chinavoices/2023-04/28/content_85259744.htm (last visited June 6, 2023).

[2] WeChat is China's multifunctional platform with functions including social media, instant messaging, and mobile payment; Weibo is a Twitter-like micro-blogging platform; Douyin is China's domestic version of TikTok.

[3] *The Report on the Development of China's New Media*, MEDIARESEARCH.CN. (July 27, 2020), http://xinwen.cssn.cn/sy_50320/zdtj/zxxsgd/202007/t20200727_5160945.shtml (last visited June 6, 2023).

[4] The "primary responsibility" requirement is a basic principle of China's platform governance and has been included in many Chinese regulations concerning platform responsibilities. *See, e.g.*, Regulation on Governance of Online Information Ecology (promulgated by the Cyberspace Administration, Dec. 15, 2019), art. 8.

This chapter examines how China approaches platform responsibility for content moderation, bearing in mind its relevance to the global debates around this issue. First, it discusses the general principles for China's online content governance. This is followed by a more detailed analysis of how China defines illegal and harmful content, sets platform obligations, and enforces regulations. As part of a wider project that compares the platform responsibility in different jurisdictions, this chapter then conducts a brief case study on TikTok, the China-originated video-sharing platform that has gained global popularity, to illustrate the following interactions: how China's laws and regulations influence TikTok's content moderation policies and practices in overseas markets and how TikTok's content moderation is influenced by other nations' laws and regulations.

4.2 GENERAL PRINCIPLES OF CHINA'S ONLINE CONTENT GOVERNANCE

Before analyzing China's approach toward platform responsibility, it is necessary and useful to understand the general principles of China's online content governance. Such principles mainly include differentiating the regulation of traditional media and online media, requiring websites and online platforms to take "primary responsibility" for content governance, exerting stricter control over "news" content, and centering on public opinion management (or control).

4.2.1 *Differentiating Traditional and Online Media*

Compared to the regulation of traditional media, which are mostly state-owned or state-controlled (in terms of ownership), China exerted a looser control over digital media services, at least until a decade ago when online content platforms emerged as the main gateways for online news and information. Chinese traditional media outlets (such as newspaper, radio, television, and magazine) are required to have a *sponsor unit* (主管主办单位) recognized by relevant media regulators, apart from meeting other preconditions.[5] Such sponsor units can be a department of the party or the government, a state-owned enterprise, a public institution, or an official media organization.[6] They retain "ultimate responsibility" over the content published by their affiliated media outlets and thus have a strong "incentive" to ensure

[5] *See, e.g.*, Jonathan Hassid, *Controlling the Chinese Media: An Uncertain Business*, 48(3) Asian Survey 414 (2008); Yuezhi Zhao, Understanding China's Media System in A World Historical Context, in Comparing Media Systems Beyond the Western World 143–73 (Daniel C. Hallin & Paolo Mancini eds., 2012); Regulation on the publication of newspapers (promulgated by the National Press and Publication Administration, 2005), https://www.gov.cn/zhengce/2021-12/09/content_5724647.htm.

[6] *E.g.*, Guoguang Wu, One Head, Many Mouths: Diversifying Press Structures in Reform China, in Power, Money, and Media: Communication Patterns and Bureaucratic Control in Cultural China 45–67 (Chin-Chuan Lee ed., 2000).

they comply with government requirements.[7] In contrast, digital media services do not necessarily need such a sponsor unit, making it possible for private companies to enter the digital media market. Currently, all of China's major social media platforms are owned by private internet companies.[8] As these platforms do not have a sponsor unit, they maintain more discretion on content moderation than traditional media.

Both traditional and online media are required to obtain a license from relevant media regulators in China. Unlike regulatory agencies in liberal democracies, which "typically operate at arm's length from the government," China's media regulators are government departments subject to the directives of the Chinese Communist Party (CCP)'s Publicity Department (PD).[9] China has different regulators for traditional and online media. The National Radio and Television Administration (NRTA) and the National Press and Publication Administration (NPPA) are the regulator for radio/television sector and the print media respectively. The Cyberspace Administration of China (CAC), which is also the office of the Central Cyberspace Affairs Commission (CCAC) led by President Xi Jinping, is China's central and primary online content regulator, overseeing all online content (including online content produced by traditional media organizations).[10] While the regulatory responsibilities of the NRTA and NPPA mainly lie in license reviewing and issuing for traditional media outlets, they (as well as other government ministries such as the Ministry of Culture and Tourism) occasionally issue content guidelines that may also apply to online content and impose punishment on platforms.[11]

4.2.2 *IISPs: "Primary Responsibility" for Content Governance*

Just like traditional media, Chinese internet information service providers (IISPs, including social media platforms) are required by government regulators to moderate content they host. This requirement can be traced back to the *Regulation on Internet Information Services* (RIIS) in 2000 (China's first of its kind), which requires all IISPs to monitor illegal content and stop immediately the distribution of such content when detected.[12] In recent years (since around 2014), as platforms increasingly become the

[7] Hassid, *supra* note 5, at 419.

[8] For example, WeChat is owned by Tencent, Weibo by Sina, and Douyin by ByteDance.

[9] Zhao, *supra* note 5, at 154.

[10] State Council's Notice on Authorizing the CAC to be the Regulator of Internet Information Content Governance (promulgated by the State Council, 2014), http://www.cac.gov.cn/2014-08/28/c_1112264158.html.

[11] For example, in 2018, the NRTA (once referred to as SAPPRFT) ordered ByteDance to permanently close a popular joke app for hosting vulgar content. *See* Frank Hersey, *China's Media Regulator Orders Permanent Removal of Toutiao's Jokes App*, TECHNODE NEWS (Apr. 10, 2018), https://technode.com/2018/04/10/toutiao-joke-app-removed/ (last visited Aug. 6, 2023).

[12] Art. 16, Regulation on Internet Information Services Management (promulgated by the State Council, Sept. 25, 2000), http://www.cac.gov.cn/2000-09/30/c_126193701.htm.

dominant gateways and gatekeepers for online information, Chinese authorities have repeatedly emphasized that websites and platforms must take "primary responsibility" for content governance. For example, during a symposium on Cyber Security and Informatization in 2016, President Xi noted, regarding the governance of online information, "Internet companies should take the *primary responsibility* and government regulators should strengthen their supervision, and they should establish a relationship of close cooperation and coordination."[13] This "primary responsibility" requirement has been included in all relevant regulations concerning platform responsibility since 2017, illustrating that it has become a basic principle for China's online content governance. Here, Chinese platforms' "primary responsibility" mainly concerns user-generated content, as platforms generally don't moderate content from media organizations and government-run accounts (although such content is still subject to platforms' keyword filtering systems and user complains and reporting systems).[14]

China's approach regarding platform content responsibility has been classified by MacKinnon et al. as "*strict liability*," compared to the models of "broad immunity" (e.g., in the US, where platforms enjoy the "safe harbor" protection respect to third-party content with a few exceptions like sex-trafficking information) and "conditional liability" (e.g., in the EU and many countries, where platforms enjoy immunity if they take down illegal content upon actual knowledge of its existence).[15] It is worth noting that, just like in the EU and many other countries, Chinese platforms also enjoy "conditional liability" regarding tort damages. According to the *Civil Code of the People's Republic of China* (which replaced China's *Tort Liability Law* and several other civil laws in 2021), if online service providers take necessary measures in a timely manner upon receiving notices from the infringed users, they are not held liable for the damages.[16] Therefore, classifying China's approach of platform responsibility as "strict liability" can be misleading. In other words, Chinese platforms may be "strictly liable" to government regulators for hosting some types of banned content (as defined later, such as politically sensitive content), but they only have "conditional liability" for infringements of users' rights and interests caused by content they host.

4.2.3 *Stricter Control over "News" Content*

Chinese media and internet regulators set out stricter rules over media services that produce or host news information. According to the *Regulation on Internet News*

13 Xi Jinping, *Speech at the Symposium on Cybersecurity and Informatization*, Gov.cn (Apr. 25, 2016), http://www.gov.cn/xinwen/2016-04/25/content_5067705.htm (last visited Aug. 6, 2023).

14 This was confirmed by my primary interviews with executives from several major Chinese platforms and official news websites (interviews were conducted during 2017–2022).

15 Rebecca MacKinnon, Elonnai Hickok, Allon Bar & Hi-in Lim, *Fostering Freedom Online: The Role of Internet Intermediaries*, UNESCO (Jan. 2015).

16 Articles 1195–1997, Civil Code of the People's Republic of China (promulgated by the National People's Congress on May 28, 2020), http://www.npc.gov.cn/npc/c30834/202006/75ba6483b8344591abd07917e1d25cc8.shtml.

Information Services (RINIS), IISPs that produce, host, or reprint news content are required to obtain an Internet News Information Service (INIS) license from the CAC or its local offices.[17] Here, "news" content is defined in a narrow sense, referring to news reports and commentaries about public affairs (including politics, economy, military, and foreign affairs) and breaking social incidents.[18] Thus, sports or entertainment news is generally not subject to this limitation in China.

An INIS license specifies which type(s) of news services the license-holder can provide: news gathering and production, news reprinting, and communication platforms. Only news organizations and their controlled subsidiaries can apply for a license for news gathering and production, which means privately owned online platforms can only apply for a license to host news (as a communication platform) and/or "reprint" news from allowed news sources. At the time of writing, the most recent list of allowed internet news providers, released by the CAC in 2021, contains a total of 1,358 allowed news sources at both the national and local levels, including traditional media outlets, news and government websites, and Weibo and WeChat public accounts run by media organizations and government departments (or party and public institutions).[19] While the list greatly expanded the scope of allowed news sources for reprinting from its 2016 version, *Caixin*, one of China's best-known investigative journalism outlets, was removed from the list, which was seen as a new signal of China's increasingly tight media controls by some overseas media organizations.[20]

The limitation on news gathering, production, and reprinting is an important rule that allows Chinese government regulators to control the sources of news. However, it can be difficult to define what is or is not "news" content in practice. For example, many individuals publish commentaries on social issues of public concern through their social media public accounts, a considerable percentage of which could be classified as news commentaries. As a response, the CAC promulgated in 2021 the *Regulation on Public Accounts Information Services of Internet Users*, which stipulates that both public account operators and online platforms must obtain an INIS license to publish or host news content.[21] While this regulation demonstrates Chinese regulators' concerns over social media being used by individuals to bypass

[17] Provisions on Management of Internet News Services (promulgated by the Cyberspace Administration, May 2, 2017), http://www.cac.gov.cn/2017-05/02/c_1120902760.htm.

[18] *Id.* art. 2.

[19] Internet User Public Account Information Services Management Provisions (promulgated by the Cybersecurity Administration, Jan. 24, 2021), http://www.cac.gov.cn/2021-01/22/c_1612887880656609.htm.

[20] *See, e.g.*, Josh Horwitz & Brenda Goh, *China Updates Official News Sources List, Excludes High-profile Caixin*, REUTERS (Oct. 21, 2021), https://www.reuters.com/world/china/china-updates-official-news-sources-list-tightening-information-oversight-2021-10-20/.

[21] Art. 5.2, Policy Notice on Defining the Scope of Necessary Personal Information for Common Types of Mobile Apps (promulgated by the Cybersecurity Administration, Mar. 12, 2021), http://www.cac.gov.cn/2021-03/22/c_1617990997054277.htm.

government controls over news sources and exerts more pressure on both platforms and individual authors, the difficulty for online platforms to judge what constitutes "news" is still there and no individuals have so far been granted an INIS license. In practice, major platforms like WeChat and Weibo often (intentionally or unintentionally) allow or temporarily allow some content from individual authors that may challenge official narratives.[22]

China's control over news content is closely linked to its policy toward foreign social media platforms. This is because social media platforms usually host a huge amount of news content and thus must apply for an INIS license, at least in principle.[23] To apply for an INIS license, an entity must register in China and its main executives and editor-in-chief must be Chinese citizens.[24] In addition, foreign capital is not allowed to establish an INIS, even in the form of partnership with Chinese capital.[25] These limitations mean foreign social media platforms are de facto blocked in China. In October 2021, LinkedIn announced that it would shut down its social networking business (but would launch a jobs-only site) in China, due to facing a "challenging operating environment and greater compliance requirements."[26] The closure of LinkedIn's social networking business means that all major foreign platforms are now either blocked, or have retreated, from China. As for why LinkedIn had been allowed to operate in China, one possible explanation is that the platform is generally viewed as a career-networking site, rather than a typical social media platform that hosts news content. In addition to strict control over news-related platforms, China's requirements for platforms regarding content moderation (discussed later) also make it very difficult, if not impossible, for foreign social media platforms to operate in the country.

4.2.4 *Content Governance Rationale: Public Opinion Management*

The rationale behind China's stricter control over news content lies in Chinese authorities' concerns over public opinion management since news content is deemed as having the power or potential to influence public opinion (as illustrated in the common Chinese phrase "news and public opinion work"). This is exactly why China imposes extra obligations on platforms "with characteristics of public opinion or capable of social mobilization," which are required to conduct security assessments

[22] Chenchen Zhang, *Contested Disaster Nationalism in the Digital Age: Emotional Registers and Geopolitical Imaginaries in COVID-19 Narratives on Chinese Social Media*, 48(2) Review of International Studies 219 (2022).

[23] In practice, some major Chinese platforms like Toutiao (among China's most popular news-aggregating platforms) operated for years without an INIS license. Toutiao, launched in 2012 by ByteDance, successfully obtained an INIS license in 2021.

[24] Art. 6, Provisions on Management of Internet News Services, *supra* note 17.

[25] *Id.* art. 7.

[26] *See, e.g.*, *Microsoft Shutting down LinkedIn in China*, BBC (Oct. 14, 2021), https://www.bbc.com/news/technology-58911297 (last visited Aug. 26, 2023).

when launching new applications or new technologies.[27] China blocks foreign social media platforms for the same reason, given that global platforms like Twitter and Facebook have proven to be important tools facilitating communications during political turmoil or uprisings, especially seen in the so-called Arab Spring.[28]

As the fundamental rationale for China's online content governance, public opinion management, which comprises both public opinion guidance and public opinion supervision,[29] is embodied in all Chinese regulations concerning platform responsibility. For example, the above-mentioned RINIS states that INIS providers must "stick to correct guidance of public opinion, play the role of public opinion supervision, and facilitate a positive and healthy Internet culture."[30] However, in these regulations, the purpose of public opinion management is often framed as promoting public interest, ensuring online safety, and maintaining social order in China.[31]

4.3 THE CHINESE APPROACH TOWARD PLATFORM RESPONSIBILITY

China adopts a patchy framework and an iterative approach in setting out platform responsibility for content moderation. During the last decade, China has promulgated around two dozen separate regulations in this area. Some of these regulations concern all types of platforms; and others target a specific type of online platform (such as instant messaging, microblogging, and livestreaming platforms), a specific technology used by platforms (e.g., blockchain, algorithmic recommendation, and deepfake), a specific service provided by platforms (e.g., online comments, public accounts, and online groups), or a specific issue brought about by platforms (e.g., personal data protection and consumer/user protection).[32] Despite its patchy nature, China's platform regulation has demonstrated considerable consistency in defining illegal and harmful content, platform obligations, and enforcement methods.

[27] Regulation on Security Assessment of New Technologies and New Applications of Internet News Information Services (promulgated by the Cybersecurity Administration, Oct. 30, 2017), http://www.cac.gov.cn/2017-10/30/c_1121878049.htm.

[28] *See, e.g.*, Simon Cottle, *Media and the Arab uprisings of 2011: Research Notes*, 12(5) JOURNALISM 647 (July 2011); Gilad Lotan, Erhardt Graeff, Mike Ananny, Devin Gaffney, Ian Pearce & Danah Boyd, *The Arab Spring: The Revolutions Were Tweeted: Information Flows during the 2011 Tunisian and Egyptian Revolutions*, 5 INTERNATIONAL JOURNAL OF COMMUNICATION 31 (2011).

[29] Jufang Wang, *China's Public Opinion Control in the Platform Era: News, Media Power, and State-Platform Collaborative Governance* (Sept. 2019) (PhD dissertation, University of Warwick), https://wrap.warwick.ac.uk/151733/.

[30] Art. 3, Provisions on Management of Internet News Services, *supra* note 17.

[31] *Id.*

[32] All relevant laws and regulations are listed on the CAC website and can be accessed under http://www.cac.gov.cn/zcfg/More.htm (last visited Aug. 26, 2023).

4.4.1 *Defining Illegal and Harmful Content*

Building on earlier laws and regulations, China's *Regulation on Governance of Online Information Ecology* (RGOIE), which took effect March 1, 2020, defined three types of online content: banned (or illegal) content, harmful content, and positive content. It requires content producers and online platforms not to produce or distribute "banned" content, to prevent and resist "harmful" content, and actively to produce or distribute "positive" content.[33] Content guidelines of Chinese platforms often combine these requirements with their own rules (such as rules concerning content monetization and user reports and complaints).

The RGOIE specifies a series of "banned" content,[34] which can be classified into three types. The first type is of a "political" nature, including content that is (1) against the basic principles of China's constitution (such as China's socialist system and the leadership of the CCP); (2) jeopardizing national security or national unification, leaking national secrets, subverting state power, and damaging national interests; (3) smearing national heroes and martyrs; (4) propagating or inciting terrorism and extremism; (5) sabotaging China's national unity or religion policies through inciting hatred and discrimination among different ethnicities or propagating cults and feudalistic superstition; or (6) spreading rumors and disturbing economic and social orders. The second type of banned content includes pornography, gambling, and inciting violence, murder, or other crimes. The third type contains defamation, infringing others' legal rights and interests such as reputation and privacy[35] and other illegal content according to the laws and regulations (such as copyright-infringing content and selling illegal items). These types of banned content reflect the characteristics of China's legal system. For example, spreading pornographic content through the internet and gambling (for profits rather than for recreation) are potentially criminal offenses in China mainland (Criminal Law, chapter six). China's defining of banned content, especially content of a "political" nature, concerns public opinion management. For instance, adding "smearing national heroes and martyrs" to the list of banned content has been viewed by some as the CCP's attempt to control the narratives about China's history, as heroes and martyrs often represent values endorsed by the authority and relate to the interpretation of history. In recent years, several Chinese platforms have been censured or punished for hosting content that was deemed as "smearing national heroes."[36]

[33] Arts. 6, 7 and 11, Regulation on Governance of Online Information Ecology, *supra* note 4.

[34] *Id.* art. 6.

[35] In China, cyber bullying is a sub-type banned content under "infringing others' rights and interests."

[36] *See, e.g.*, *China Orders ByteDance's Toutiao to Fix Search, Saying National Hero Smeared*, EURONEWS (Nov. 12, 2019), https://www.euronews.com/2019/11/12/china-orders-bytedances-toutiao-to-fix-search-saying-national-hero-smeared.

In contrast, "harmful" content listed in the regulation is mainly concerned with social stability and morality. The listed types of harmful content include: (1) exaggerating or sensational titles; (2) sensationalizing scandals, gossips, and misdeeds; (3) insensitive comments on natural disasters or severe accidents; (4) sexual content; (5) violent and graphic content; (6) inciting discrimination among different groups and people from different places; (7) propagating vulgar and low-taste content; (8) enticing minors to imitate dangerous acts or developing bad habits; (9) other content harmful to online content ecology.[37] The emphasis on social stability and moral goodness is an important feature of China's online content governance,[38]and the government has legalized its online content governance (sometimes content censorship) through framing it as benevolence and protection.[39]

In addition, the regulation (RGOIE) lists several types of "positive" content that include propagating major policies and strategies of the Party, highlighting China's economic and social development, effectively responding to public concerns and guiding the public to develop consensus, displaying a multi-facet China, etc. It encourages online platforms to display and present positive content prominently.[40] This aligns well with the Chinese party-state's rationale for online content governance: public opinion management. Its goal is to build an online ecology that propagates "positive energy"[41] that may help to distract the public's attention from the negative news and criticisms of the government. As Bandurski observes, the term "positive energy" is "at the very heart of political discourse" in the Xi Jinping era, a tool for internet governance and control.[42]

4.3.2 *Protection of Users and Privacy*

While China's platform governance has centered on public opinion management, government regulators have paid increasing attention to the protection of users (especially minors) and personal data in recent years, showing the adaptability of the party-state regarding regulation in the platform era. For example, the *Regulation on Algorithmic Recommendation of Internet Information Services* (RARIIS), which took effect in March 2022, includes a dedicated section for user protection. The regulation requires algorithmic recommendation service providers (ARSPs) to protect the rights and interests of different types of users, including minors, the elderly,

[37] Art. 7, Regulation on Governance of Online Information Ecology, *supra* note 4.

[38] Di Cui & Fang Wu, *Moral Goodness and Social Orderliness: An Analysis of the Official Media Discourse about Internet Governance in China*, 40(2–3) TELECOMMUNICATIONS POLICY 265.

[39] Min Jiang, *Authoritarian Informationalism: China's Approach to Internet Sovereignty*, 30(2) SAIS REVIEW OF INTERNATIONAL AFFAIRS 71.

[40] Art. 11, Regulation on Governance of Online Information Ecology, *supra* note 4.

[41] *Id.* art. 2.

[42] David Bandurski, *The CCP's "Positive Energy" Obsession*, CHINA MEDIA PROJECT – CHINA NEWSPEAK (Dec. 15, 2015), para. 2 http://chinamediaproject.org/2015/12/15/chinas-obsession-with-positive-energy/ (last visited Aug. 26, 2023).

consumers, and workers (who rely on platforms for orders). The RARIIS stipulates that ARSPs (including social media platforms) should not recommend content that may lead minors to imitate dangerous acts or develop bad habits such as addiction,[43] should strengthen the monitoring and moderation of online fraudulent information to protect the elderly,[44] and their algorithms should ensure fair treatment of consumers and workers.[45]

Another example of user protection is witnessed in the Chinese government's policy document targeting livestreaming platforms, issued in February 2021.[46] A major aim of this guideline document is to protect minors on these platforms. It specifies that platforms should not allow users under sixteen to open a livestreaming host account and should seek the consent of the guardians of minors between sixteen and eighteen before allowing them to open an account.[47] In addition, livestreaming platforms should develop a "minor mode" for minor users and block content that is harmful to them (such as obscene and pornographic content). Another purpose of this policy document is to protect users from excessive and irrational consumption (such as paying high tips to livestreaming stars) – a prominent phenomenon on Chinese livestreaming platforms. The guideline document requires platforms to set a series of limits regarding tips, such as the total amount of tips per day from a single user.[48] It also requires platforms to not allow minors to tip livestreaming hosts; when a tip is verified from a minor who used an adult account, platforms should refund the money.[49]

As for the protection of personal data, China has issued relevant laws, regulations, and policy notices in recent years, including the *Personal Information Protection Law* (PIPL)[50] and the policy notice on *Defining the Scope of Necessary Personal Information for Common Types of Mobile Apps*.[51] Among them, China's PIPL establishes a series of basic principles for personal information collection, including informed consent from users, minimum collection (only collecting necessary information), special care for "sensitive" personal data, and consent from parents or

[43] Art. 18, Regulation on Algorithmic Recommendation of Internet Information Services (promulgated by the Cyberspace Administration, Mar. 1, 2022), http://www.cac.gov.cn/2022-01/04/c_1642894606364259.htm.

[44] *Id.* arts. 19.

[45] *Id.* arts. 20 and 21.

[46] Notice on Guidelines of Strengthening the Governance of Online Livestreaming Norms (promulgated by the Cyberspace Administration, Feb. 9, 2021), http://www.cac.gov.cn/2021-02/09/c_1614442843753738.htm.

[47] *Id.* art. 6.

[48] *Id.* art. 10.

[49] *Id.* art. 6.

[50] Personal Information Protection Law (promulgated by the Standing Comm. Nat'l People's Cong., Aug. 20, 2021).

[51] Policy Notice on Defining the Scope of Necessary Personal Information for Common Types of Mobile Apps, *supra* note 21.

guardians of minors who are under the age of fourteen.[52] The above-mentioned policy notice[53] defined what is the "necessary" personal information that various types of platforms need to collect when providing basic services. For example, for instant messaging platforms, the necessary personal information includes users' telephone numbers and accounts of their contacts;[54] for social networking platforms, such information only includes users' telephone numbers;[55] while for livestreaming platforms and short-video platforms, no personal information is necessary for providing basic functions.[56]

On November 25, 2022, the CAC, in conjunction with the Ministry of Industry and Information Technology (MIIT) and the Ministry of Public Security (MPS), issued a new regulation governing deep synthesis technology and services, commonly known as "deepfake" technology. This regulation, officially titled the Regulation on the Administration of Deep Synthesis of Internet Information Services (the Deep Synthesis Regulation),[57] came into effect on January 10, 2023. Deepfake technology, which involves the use of advanced machine learning and AI to create or alter visual and audio content, can be used to generate synthetic media where a person's likeness in an image or video is replaced with another's. The Regulation is part of China's effort to increase supervision over this technology. It stipulates that providers and deployers of this technology are not allowed to produce and spread illegal content and fake news information;[58] and deepfake service providers should label content produced by this technology in a way not affecting the use of end-users and make some deepfake services such as synthetic face and voice and face swapping immediately recognizable if they may mislead the users.[59] These stipulations reflect the party-state's concerns that this new technology may be used to influence public opinion and social stability, but they also concern the protection of users' rights and interest.

4.3.3 *Major Obligations for Platforms*

China's regulations regarding platform responsibility for content moderation have laid down a series of obligations for platforms, which form the specifics of what the government calls platforms' "primary responsibilities." Major obligations include:

52 Arts. 13, 28 and 31, Personal Information Protection Law, *supra* note 50.

53 Policy Notice on Defining the Scope of Necessary Personal Information for Common Types of Mobile Apps, *supra* note 21.

54 *Id.* art. 3.

55 *Id.* art. 4.

56 *Id.* arts. 27 and 29.

57 The CAC website (Dec. 11, 2022) *Regulation on the Administration of Deep Synthesis Internet Information Services*, http://www.cac.gov.cn/2022-12/11/c_1672221949354811.htm.

58 Art. 6, Regulation on the Administration of Deep Synthesis Internet Information Services.

59 Arts. 16, 17, Regulation on the Administration of Deep Synthesis Internet Information Services

Establishing an editor-in-chief: This requirement is for all INIS providers,[60] including social media platforms. It means social media platforms, just like traditional media, must have an editor-in-chief who takes ultimate responsibility for content on their sites.

Real-name user registration: While internet users can use most services provided by platforms without registration, they must register with their real identities before they can post content (although they can still use nicknames for account names). Platforms are required to verify users' identities through mobile phone numbers (which also require real-name registration in China), ID cards, and other methods.[61]

Real-time content monitoring and moderation: Under the above-mentioned US and EU "broad immunity" and "conditional liability" models, platforms are not subject to "general monitoring or active fact-finding obligations."[62] In contrast, Chinese platforms are required to conduct "real-time" monitoring and moderation of content.[63]

Including links to government-run user reporting website: All Chinese IIS providers are required to include links, in a prominent way, to the website of Illegal and Harmful Information Reporting Center (12377.cn) run by the CAC.[64] Through the link, users can easily report various types of illegal and harmful content, such as political sensitive information, rumors, fraud information, and pornographic content.

Keeping user records: All IISPs are required to keep user records for at least sixty days.[65] For some types of platforms such as microblogging platforms, the required user-record keeping period is 6 months.[66]

Grading-and-classifying (分级分类) management mechanism: Platforms are required to establish this management mechanism regarding user accounts and user content. Here, "grading" means platforms should assess the credit of user accounts and provide services to them accordingly. If certain users are found to have posted illegal or harmful content on a platform, then their credits should be downgraded by the platform and thus the services they can use will be limited accordingly. For users who have seriously breached relevant laws or regulations such as posting

60 Art. 6, Regulation on Management of Internet News Services, *supra* note 17.

61 E.g., art. 7, Regulation on Microblogging Information Services (promulgated by the Cyberspace Administration Feb. 2, 2018), http://www.cac.gov.cn/2018-02/02/c_1122358726.htm.

62 E.g., art. 8, Regulation (EU) 2022/2065 of the European Parliament and of the Council of 19 October 2022 on a Single Market For Digital Services and amending Directive 2000/31/EC (hereinafter *DSA*).

63 E.g., art. 9 Regulation on Governance of Online Information Ecology, *supra* note 4.

64 *Id.* art. 16.

65 Art. 14.2, Regulation on Internet Information Services Management, *supra* note 12.

66 Art. 16, Regulation on Microblogging Information Services, *supra* note 58.

rumors, platforms should add them to a "blacklist" and take corresponding measures (e.g., closing their accounts and preventing them from re-registration under another name).[67] "Classifying" means platforms should classify user accounts and content into different categories according to factors including the number of followers and the content areas (such as political, economic, and entertainment).[68] For user accounts producing content in areas such as politics, platforms are required to exercise stricter monitoring and moderation. According to the CAC, this management mechanism aims to achieve a "precise, focused, and dynamic" management of user accounts,[69] forcing platforms to concentrate their moderation resources on key content areas and influential user accounts.

3.4.4 *Enforcement Methods*

China adopts a mixed method in enforcing regulations regarding platform responsibility. While civil and criminal laws are applicable, administrative measures are China's main method in pressuring platforms to fulfill the "primary responsibilities" for online content governance.

China's *Civil Code* has articles about the liability of internet service providers (ISPs) regarding tort damages. According to the law, if an internet user commits a tort, the injured person shall be entitled to inform the ISP and ask it to take necessary measures (such as content deletion or blocking); the notice to the ISP should include initial evidence and the real identity of the infringed.[70] After receiving the notice, the ISP should send the notice to the concerned internet user and take necessary measures based on the initial evidence in a timely way; otherwise, it is jointly liable for the extended damage of the tort.[71] The infringed is also liable for the damage to the internet user and the ISP for wrong notice.[72] If an ISP is aware or should be aware that an internet user is infringing the civil rights and interests of others and fails to take necessary measures, it shall be jointly liable for the infringement.[73]

Criminal laws are also applicable to platforms for hosting illegal content. So far, it is rare that platform or website executives have been prosecuted according to

[67] E.g., art. 13, Policy Notice on Defining the Scope of Necessary Personal Information for Common Types of Mobile Apps, *supra* note 21.

[68] E.g., art. 9, Regulation on Microblogging Information Services, *supra* note 58.

[69] Guideline on further pressuring websites and platforms to fulfil the primary responsibilities for content governance (promulgated by the Cyberspace Administration Sept. 15, 2021), http://www.cac.gov.cn/2021-09/15/c_1633296790051342.htm.

[70] Art. 1195.1, Personal Information Protection Law, *supra* note 50.

[71] *Id.* art. 1195.2.

[72] *Id.* art. 1195.3.

[73] *Id.* art. 1197.

criminal laws. Kuaibo, once a popular but now-defunct video-streaming platform in China, is a case in point that involves criminal laws. The platform, allowing users to watch pirated videos through P2P technology, was found to host a huge number of pornographic videos. In 2016, Wang Xin, the CEO of Kuaibo, was sentenced to forty-two months in prison and fined 1 million Yuan (around $150,000); and three other senior executives were also given prison terms.[74] This case attracted great public attention in China and signaled the resolve of government regulators to hold platforms liable for hosting illegal content like pornographic videos. According to a judicial interpretation document from China's Supreme Court and Supreme Procuratorate, hosting over 200 illegal videos (in the case of Kuaibo, over 30,000 pornographic videos) is classified as "leading to the spread of a great deal of illegal information" and is against China's Criminal Law.[75]

In addition to civil and criminal laws, China mainly resorts to administrative measures to enforce platform responsibility. Such measures mainly include government-initiated "internet-cleaning" campaigns, summoning platform executives, ordering platforms to suspend content updating or even close a service, ordering app stores to remove the concerned apps (usually temporarily), and issuing fines. For example, during various internet-cleaning campaigns, online platforms are required to self-check their sites thoroughly and deal with problematic user accounts and content. As a result of a campaign targeting the "chaotic situation" around public accounts run by individuals on platforms in November 2018, 9,800 public accounts were suspended or closed across platforms.[76] Platform executives (mostly editors-in-chief) have been frequently summoned by government regulators, especially the CAC and its local offices, in recent years. During these summoning meetings, government regulators often point out the existing problems of the concerned platforms and require them to redress them.[77] Sometimes, platform summoning sessions are accompanied with a fine in more serious breaches. For example, from January to November 2021, Weibo was frequently summoned by government regulators and fined forty-four times, totalling at 14.3 million Yuan (around 2.2 million dollars).[78]

74 Kevin Schoenmakers, *Streaming App CEO Sentenced to 42 Months for Lewd Content*, Sixth Tone (Sept. 13, 2016), https://www.sixthtone.com/news/1329/streaming-app-ceo-sentenced-42-months-lewd-content.

75 Interpretation of the Supreme Court and Supreme Procuratorate on the application of law in cases such as the illegal use of Internet Information Services and facilitating Internet crimes (issued by the Supreme People's Court and Supreme People's Procuratorate Oct. 21, 2019), http://www.cac.gov.cn/2019-10/25/c_1573534999086260.htm.

76 *The CAC Campaign on the Chaotic Situation of Public Accounts: Punishing 9, 800 Accounts and Summoning Weibo and Wechat*, Beijing News (Nov. 12, 2018), https://baijiahao.baidu.com/s?id=1616941232655485724&wfr=spider&for=pc (last visited Aug. 31, 2023).

77 *Id.*

78 Press Release, The Cyberspace Administration of China, The Cyberspace Adminsitration of China Summoned and Punished Sina Weibo (Dec. 14, 2021), http://www.cac.gov.cn/2021-12/14/c_1641080795548173.htm.

It is worth noting that while Chinese regulators do use fines as a punitive measure to ensure platform compliance, the amount is not comparable with some Western regulators. For instance, the EU's DSA imposes fines up to 6 percent of the global revenue of a platform for serious breaches.[79] In contrast, Chinese regulators rarely issue heavy fines on platform companies, with the 18.2 billion Yuan fine on Alibaba for *antitrust reasons* in 2021[80] and the 8.026 billion Yuan fine on Didi for violation of network security and data security laws in 2022 being two exceptions.[81] For violations of content-related regulations in China, the highest amount of a fine is 500,000 Yuan.[82] However, unlike their Western peers, Chinese platforms seldom appeal against the decisions of government regulators, despite having such rights according to China's Administrative Procedure Law (amended in 2017). This demonstrates China's authoritarian nature and the asymmetrical power relations between the Chinese government and online platforms, given that the government can simply revoke the license of a platform under extreme circumstances.

3.4 A BRIEF CASE STUDY ON TIKTOK

This section conducts a brief case study on the video-sharing platform TikTok and its sister platform Douyin (available only in China), owned by the Beijing-based ByteDance, to illustrate how China's relevant laws and regulations influence the content moderation practices of TikTok in overseas markets. Meanwhile, by examining how TikTok adjusts its content moderation policies in overseas markets, this study also sheds light on how other nations' laws and regulations shape the practices of a global platform with a Chinese origin.

TikTok and Douyin are two similar but separate apps. Douyin, launched in 2016, is China's most popular short-video platform with over 600 million daily active users as of August 2020;[83] while TikTok, launched in 2017 in global markets, is the world's leading destination for short videos, boasting over 1 billion monthly active users as of September 2021.[84] The two platforms share the same logo and most user interface features (though Douyin has more advanced e-commerce features at the time of writing). They also have similar recommending algorithms that are mainly based on

79 European Commission. (May 20, 2022). *Questions and Answers: Digital Services Act*, https://ec.europa.eu/commission/presscorner/detail/en/QANDA_20_2348.

80 *China Fines Alibaba Record $2.8 Billion after Monopoly Probe*, Bloomberg News (Apr. 10, 2021), https://www.bloomberg.com/news/articles/2021-04-10/china-fines-alibaba-group-2-8-billion-in-monopoly-probe#xj4y7vzkg.

81 Evelyn Cheng, *China Fines Didi More Than $1 Billion for Breaking Data Security Laws*, CNBC (July 12, 2022), https://www.cnbc.com/2022/07/21/china-fines-didi-more-than-1-billion-for-breaking-data-security-laws.html.

82 Press Release, The Cyberspace Administration of China, *supra* note 75.

83 ByteDance, *About Our Products (Douyin)*, https://www.bytedance.com/zh/products (last visited Aug. 28, 2023).

84 *Thanks a Billion!*, TikTok (Sept. 27, 2021), https://newsroom.tiktok.com/en-us/1-billion-people-on-tiktok (last visited Aug. 28, 2023).

users' interests. However, ByteDance has established a "wall" between these two platforms: Chinese mainland users can only download Douyin and overseas users can only access TikTok. Thus, the two platforms have different users and user content, and their user data are also stored in different locations: Douyin's data is stored in mainland China; TikTok's data is stored in Singapore, the United States, and soon also in Ireland and Norway.[85] While sharing many features, content moderation practices and moderation algorithms of the two platforms are quite different, given that they need to comply with laws and regulations in respective jurisdictions.[86] Douyin must comply with China's content governance requirements, including carrying out real-time content monitoring (through keywords filtering and others) and censorship of certain content; while TikTok is subject to the laws and regulations of countries and regions where it operates.

In overseas markets, content moderation policies and practices of TikTok have been criticized for various reasons. In liberal democracies, TikTok has been accused of censoring content that may displease Beijing. In 2019, *The Guardian* reported that TikTok's leaked internal documents instructed its moderators to censor videos that mention Tiananmen Square (i.e., the 1989 political turmoil in Beijing) and Tibetan independence.[87] The platform has also been criticized for censoring content from black creators and other marginalized groups,[88] and its internal content guidelines were exposed to even require moderators to suppress posts by users deemed too "ugly" or "poor" for the platform.[89] In response, TikTok claimed that the leaked moderation guidelines were either outdated or never put into use,[90] and other alleged censorship incidents were due to mistakes of automatic moderation (in the case of blocking content from some black users). Apart from censorship criticism, the platform has also been temporally banned or threatened to be banned for hosting "immoral" or "obscene" content in more conservative jurisdictions such as Pakistan, Bangladesh, and Indonesia.[91] In some authoritarian countries like Vietnam, the platform has been blamed for spreading anti-government content

[85] Ryan Morrison, *New European Data Centers Won't Stop Calls to Ban TikTok*, TECH MONITOR (Mar. 9, 2023), https://techmonitor.ai/policy/privacy-and-data-protection/new-european-data-centres-wont-stop-calls-to-ban-tiktok.

[86] Interview with a senior manager of ByteDance (May 2023).

[87] Alex Hern, *Revealed: How TikTok Censors Videos That Do Not Please Beijing*, THE GUARDIAN (Sept. 25, 2019), https://www.theguardian.com/technology/2019/sep/25/revealed-how-tiktok-censors-videos-that-do-not-please-beijing.

[88] Abby W. Ohlheiser, *Welcome to TikTok's Endless Cycle of Censorship and Mistakes*, MIT TECHNOLOGY REVIEW (July 13, 2021), https://www.technologyreview.com/2021/07/13/1028401/tiktok-censorship-mistakes-glitches-apologies-endless-cycle/.

[89] Sam Biddle, Paulo Victror & Tatiana Dias, *Invisible Censorship*, THE INTERCEPT (Mar. 16, 2020), https://theintercept.com/2020/03/16/tiktok-app-moderators-users-discrimination/.

[90] *Id.*

[91] *Bangladesh Court Orders Ban on TikTok, PUBG, Free Fire to "Save children,"* NEW STRAITS TIMES (Aug. 17, 2021), https://www.nst.com.my/world/region/2021/08/718633/bangladesh-court-orders-ban-tiktok-pubg-free-fire-save-children.

and for not doing enough (as Douyin does in China) in dealing with addiction and thus posing a threat to the country's youth population.[92]

The above criticism over TikTok's content moderation illustrates how China's laws and regulations may have influenced the platform's overseas practices. Keywords like "Tiananmen Square [turmoil]" and "Tibetan independence" are taboos on the Chinese internet, indicating that TikTok, at least at its initial stage, may have adopted a keyword filtering system that was required by China's regulations. Even TikTok's bizarre rule regarding being "too ugly" can also be traced back to its Chinese origin, as Douyin was once famous in China for its posh content creators – a strategy to attract users when the platform was newly launched. Such explicitly discriminatory content policy wasn't a big issue in China, partly because government regulators' focus has been on content concerning public opinion management (as discussed earlier). As a result, Chinese platforms usually pay much more attention to politically sensitive content (i.e., content that may damage the image of the CCP and government) than to other types of problematic content such as discrimination, obscene and vulgar content.

However, content moderation policies and practices of TikTok have also been shaped by laws, regulations, and norms of overseas markets, to a much greater extent. TikTok's Community Guidelines include sections *Youth Safety and Well-Being*, *Safety and Civility*, *Mental and Behavioral Health*, *Privacy and Security*, *Sensitive and Mature Themes*, etc.[93] While the guidelines address some concerns mostly relevant to TikTok, such as *Mental and Behavioral Health* that focuses on issues like suicide and self-harm, disordered eating and body image, dangerous activities and challenges, they are not that different from the Community Guidelines of other global platforms like YouTube[94] and Facebook. Also, like its Western peers, TikTok publishes quarterly transparency reports since January 2021, including its Community Guidelines enforcement reports.[95] In contrast, the Community Guidelines of TikTok are totally different from those of Douyin. The User Service Agreement of Douyin lists over twenty types of banned or harmful content,[96] most of which are identical or similar to those listed by the government in the above discussed RGOIE. TikTok's Community Guidelines demonstrate its efforts in presenting itself as a *global* rather than a *Chinese* platform, following

[92] Lam Le, *Vietnam Pressures TikTok to Censor More Content or Face a Ban*, Rest of World (May 24, 2023), https://restofworld.org/2023/vietnam-tiktok-ban/.

[93] TikTok, *Community Guidelines* (Mar. 2023), https://www.tiktok.com/community-guidelines?lang=en (last visited Aug. 28, 2023).

[94] *See* YouTube, *Community Guidelines*, https://www.youtube.com/howyoutubeworks/policies/community-guidelines/ (last visited Aug. 28, 2023).

[95] TikTok, *Community Guidelines Enforcement Report* (Oct. 12, 2023), https://www.tiktok.com/transparency/en-us/community-guidelines-enforcement-2023-2/ (last visited Aug. 28, 2023).

[96] Douyin, *User Service Agreement* (Sept. 15, 2023), https://www.douyin.com/draft/douyin_agreement/douyin_agreement_user.html?id=6773906068725565448 (last visited Aug. 28, 2023).

"international legal frameworks" and "industry best practices" (shaped by major Western platforms like YouTube and Facebook).[97]

In addition, when implementing Community Guidelines, TikTok has adopted a "localization" strategy. In March 2020, ByteDance dismantled its entire Beijing team responsible for overseas content moderation and assigned the task to overseas teams.[98] The company stated that its regional and country teams "localize" content moderation in accordance with "local laws and norms."[99] Besides, ByteDance appointed Shouzi Chew from Singapore as TikTok's CEO and Vanessa Pappas (former head of TikTok US) as the platform's COO in 2021 (Pappas stepped down from the role in June 2023).[100] While TikTok's localized moderation strategy may help to alleviate criticism over its content moderation to some extent, it is worth mentioning that it also caused some controversy within China. On China's online Q&A platform Zhihu (China's equivalent of Quora), there are discussions about whether TikTok is still a Chinese company since the platform hosts lots of "anti-China content" and its Chinese owner does not have (or voluntarily gives up) control over its content moderation policies.[101]

3.5 CONCLUSION

This chapter examined China's general principles for content governance and its approach to platform responsibility, both of which have distinct Chinese characteristics. As regards general principles, it is important to understand China's fundamental rationale for online content governance: public opinion management. Following this rationale, China exerts stricter control over all online information services (including social media platforms) that host "news" content, which de facto blocks foreign social media platforms from operating in China. The Chinese characteristics of platform responsibilities are embodied in its defining of illegal and harmful content, its heavy platform obligations, and administrative measures for enforcement, all of which reflect China's authoritarian nature and the asymmetrical power relations between the government and private platforms. China's requirements for platforms to proactively monitor, moderate, and sometimes censor content, especially political sensitive content, make it almost impossible for foreign social media platforms to survive without full compliance. Despite its authoritarian

[97] TikTok, *Community Guidelines*, *supra* note 93.

[98] *TikTok to Stop Using China-Based Moderators to Monitor Overseas Content*, The Wall Street Journal (Mar. 15, 2020), https://www.wsj.com/articles/tiktok-to-stop-using-china-based-moderators-to-monitor-overseas-content-11584300597.

[99] Lavanya Mahendran & Nasser Alsherif, *Adding Clarity to Our Community Guidelines*, TikTok (Jan. 8, 2020), https://newsroom.tiktok.com/en-us/adding-clarity-to-our-community-guidelines.

[100] TikTok, *TikTok Names CEO and COO* (Apr. 30, 2021), https://newsroom.tiktok.com/en-us/tiktok-names-ceo-and-coo.

[101] Zhihu, *Does TikTok Still Belong to China (Question and Discussion)?*, https://www.zhihu.com/question/487405502 (last visited Aug. 28, 2023).

nature, China has also demonstrated adaptability in developing its constantly evolving platform regulation framework. This is especially shown in its many regulations regarding user and privacy protection.

The case study on TikTok (and Douyin) shows that a global platform's content moderation policies are shaped by both its original country and the region and countries where it operates. On the one hand, the laws and regulations of the original country may have impact on users from other jurisdictions through a global platform's content moderation practices. In the case of TikTok, China's laws and regulations may have influenced its content moderation in global markets. This was certainly the case before March 2020, when the company dissolved the Beijing-based moderation team. On the other hand, content moderation of a global platform is also influenced by local laws and norms. This is clearly illustrated in the case of TikTok, which has regional and country-specific teams tasked to carry out content moderation.

5

Safe Harbor and Content Moderation Regulation in India

Jhalak Mrignayani Kakkar, Shashank Mohan, and Vasudev Devadasan

5.1 INTRODUCTION

Social media platforms in India are regulated under the Information Technology Act, 2000 (IT Act). When enacted, the IT Act did not (and possibly could not) envisage the rise of social media platforms and thus, the legislation makes no specific reference to them. However, the IT Act regulates "intermediaries" – defined as entities that receive, store, transmit, or provide any service with respect to third-party content, or user generated content (UGC).[1] As the activities conducted by social media platforms predominantly fall within this definition, with respect to UGC, platforms have been regulated as intermediaries under the IT Act for the last two decades.

In 2021, the Indian government issued the Information Technology (Intermediary Guidelines and Digital Media Ethics Code) Rules 2021 (Intermediary Guidelines).[2] These Guidelines, which constitute delegated legislation under the IT Act expressly defines a "social media intermediary" as an intermediary that primarily enables online interaction between two or more users and allows them to upload, share, and disseminate content using its services.[3] The Intermediary Guidelines further

[1] The Information Technology Act, 2000, § 2(1)(w).

[2] Information Technology (Intermediary Guidelines and Digital Media Ethics Code) Rules (2021), Part III [hereinafter Intermediary Guidelines]. The Intermediary Guidelines (2021) replaced earlier guidelines which had been in effect since 2011. The 2011 guidelines did not specifically define social media intermediaries. The Intermediary Guidelines 2021 introduce numerous conditions in addition to their predecessor, which have been explained in detail in this chapter. *See* discussion *infra* Sections 5.1.3, 5.4.

[3] Intermediary Guidelines, Rule 2(w). Subsequent guidance by the Indian government clarified that entities enabling commercial transactions or providing access to the internet, search engines, email services, and online storage services would not qualify as a social media intermediary. *See* Ministry of Electronics and Information Technology, *Frequently Asked Questions (FAQs) – The Information Technology (Intermediary Guidelines and Digital Media Ethics Code) Rules, 2021*, 10 (2021), https://www.meity.gov.in/writereaddata/files/FAQ_Intermediary_Rules_2021.pdf (last visited Nov. 3, 2021).

differentiate between (i) "intermediaries," (ii) "social media intermediaries," and (iii) "significant social media intermediaries" (SSMIs, i.e., social media intermediaries that have more than 5 million registered Indian users)[4] – imposing additional obligations on SSMIs.[5] The Guidelines also impose certain distinct obligations on SSMIs that provide messaging services.[6] Finally, the Guidelines distinguish between foreign and domestic SSMIs by requiring foreign SSMIs to have local officers who are resident in India – officers who may also be subject to personal liability.[7]

On October 28, 2022, amendments were made to the Intermediary Guidelines introducing additional compliance obligations for intermediaries in an attempt to make the rules and regulations/privacy policies more accessible to the users. These amendments also introduced a mechanism for the establishment of government-appointed grievance redressal committees (GACs). The GACs offer an appellate procedure to aggrieved users who are not satisfied with content-related decisions made by intermediaries.[8] Moreover, on April 6, 2023 amendments were made in the Intermediary Guidelines to include "Online Gaming Intermediaries" as intermediaries to impose due diligence obligations on them and a "Fact Checking Unit" of the central government to identify fake, false, or misleading information about any central government business to help intermediaries take down such content.[9] A number of petitioners, including a stand-up comedian and various news media organizations challenged the amendment introducing the Fact Checking Unit on constitutional grounds in the High Court of Bombay (a state level constitutional appeals court). On January 31, 2024, the High Court delivered a split verdict with one judge agreeing to strike down the provision and the other declaring it as constitutional and legally sound. The case will now proceed to a third judge for final determination.[10]

As social media platforms constitute intermediaries hosting and transmitting UGC under the IT Act, they are distinguishable from entities that publish their own content. Platforms are also regulated distinctly from print and broadcast media, which are governed by the Press Council of India Act (1978) and the Cable Television Networks (Regulation) Act (1995), respectively. Crucially, unlike

4 Ministry of Electronics and Information Technology, S.O. 942(E) (notified on Feb. 25, 2021).

5 Intermediary Guidelines, Rules 2(1)(v), 2(1)(w), 4. *See* discussion *infra* Sections 5.1.3, 5.4.

6 Intermediary Guidelines, Rule 4(2). *See* discussion *infra* Section 5.4.4.

7 Intermediary Guidelines, Rule 4(1)(a). *See* discussion *infra* Section 5.3.3.

8 Ministry of Electronics and Information Technology, The Information Technology (Intermediary Guidelines and Digital Media Ethics Code) Rules (2021), https://www.meity.gov.in/writereaddata/files/IT%20Intermediary%20Rules%2C%202021%20updated%20on%2028.10.2022.pdf/ (last visited Feb. 16, 2024).

9 *Id.*

10 Sharmeen Hakim, *Bombay High Court Delivers Split Verdict on Please Challenging IT Rules Amendment, Govt to Not Notify "Fact Check Unit" for 10 Days*, LiveLaw, https://www.livelaw.in/top-stories/bombay-high-court-judgment-it-amendment-rules-2023-social-media-fake-news-fact-checking-unit-kunal-kamra-vs-union-of-india-248120/ (last visited Feb. 16, 2024).

publishers, broadcasters, and distributors who are typically strictly liable for content they publish, where intermediaries do not have "actual knowledge" of unlawful content on their network and comply with the conditions set out under the IT Act, they are exempt from liability.[11]

Finally, it is also relevant to note that at the time of writing, the legality and constitutionality of the Intermediary Guidelines remains under dispute. Several individuals, organizations, and platforms have filed petitions challenging various provisions of the Intermediary Guidelines in High Courts across the country. The Union government has requested that all these proceedings be clubbed and heard together by the Supreme Court of India.[12] In May 2022, the Supreme Court directed High Courts to stop hearing the challenges to the Intermediary Guidelines,[13] which would suggest the challenges to the Intermediary Guidelines will be heard by the Supreme Court in an omnibus fashion.

5.1.1 *Centrality of Safe Harbor to Platform Regulation*

The Intermediary Guidelines, coupled with the rules on government blocking of content,[14] form the core regulatory structure that governs platform conduct in India. Section 79 of the IT Act offers intermediaries conditional legal immunity (or "safe harbor") for unlawful UGC on their networks. One condition for safe harbor under Section 79 is compliance with the Intermediary Guidelines, which set out various additional obligations that intermediaries must comply with to avail of this safe harbor.[15] As set out in Sections 3 and 4, through the Intermediary Guidelines, the government has imposed wide ranging obligations on platforms as condition precedent for safe harbor. However, the power of the government to prescribe *when* platforms must remove content to retain safe harbor is circumscribed by the Supreme Court decision in *Shreya Singhal v. Union of India*.[16] The Court interpreted "actual knowledge" in Section 79 to mean a court order, effectively ruling that intermediaries could not be compelled to take down content at the behest of private complainants to retain safe harbor and that platforms would only lose safe harbor if they failed to remove content after receiving a government or court order.[17]

[11] Chinmayi Arun, *Gatekeeper Liability and Article 19(1)(A) of the Constitution of India*, 7 NUJS L. Rev. 73 (2015).

[12] Sohini Chowdhury, *IT Rules 2021: Supreme Court to Hear Centre's Plea to Stay Interim Orders Passed by High Courts on July 27*, LiveLaw (2022), https://www.livelaw.in/top-stories/supreme-court-it-rules-cable-tc-amendment-rules-online-media-ott-regulation-204329 (last visited Aug. 1, 2022).

[13] Skand Bajpai v. Union of India WP (Civil) 799 of 2020, order passed on May 9, 2022 (Supreme Court of India).

[14] Information Technology (Procedure and Safeguards for Blocking for Access of Information by Public) Rules, 2009 [hereinafter Blocking Rules].

[15] *See* discussion *infra*, Sections 5.3.1.3, 5.4.

[16] (2015) 5 SCC 1 (Supreme Court of India).

[17] *Id.*, ¶ 122. *See* discussion *infra*, Section 5.3.1.2.

This has limited the government's ability to institute a traditional notice-and-take-down regime for online platforms, where platforms risk losing safe harbor if they fail remove content pursuant to user complaints.

To avail of safe harbor under Section 79, an intermediary must:

1. Either limit its functionality to providing access to a communication system over which UGC is transmitted
   OR
   must not: (i) initiate the transmission; (ii) select the receiver of the transmission; and (iii) select or modify the information contained in the transmission;[18]
2. Comply with the Intermediary Guidelines;[19]
3. Upon receiving "actual knowledge" (interpreted by *Shreya Singhal* to mean a court order), or being notified by the appropriate government or its agency, of unlawful content on its network, remove the concerned material without vitiating any evidence;[20] and
4. Not aid, abet, or induce the commission of an unlawful act on its network.[21]

Additional detail on each of these limbs is provided in Section 3.1 ("Defence to liability"). As noted previously, a key condition to avail of immunity under Section 79 of the IT Act is compliance with the Intermediary Guidelines (i.e., delegated legislation). The Ministry of Electronics and Information Technology (MEITY) has relied on the Intermediary Guidelines to regulate platform behavior, imposing obligations ranging from transparency reporting and cooperation with law enforcement, to requiring users be provided with a hearing prior to their content being taken down, under the Intermediary Guidelines,[22] with platforms in breach of these obligations at risk of losing safe harbor. The obligations imposed on platforms under the Intermediary Guidelines are discussed in Sections 3 and 4.

The corollary of this approach is that the exclusive tool to hold social media platforms accountable is through the threat of losing safe harbor, which can only be enforced through individual actions brought before a court of law for hosting unlawful content. This approach may be contrasted with jurisdictions that employ a regulator to penalize platforms for a variety of problematic behavior. For an intermediary to be penalized in India, an action must be brought against it for hosting unlawful content that proves (i) the illegality of the content hosted by the intermediary, (ii) the secondarily liability of the intermediary in hosting the illegal

[18] The Information Technology Act, 2000, § 79(2)(a)–79(2)(b).
[19] The Information Technology Act, 2000, § 79(2)(c).
[20] The Information Technology Act, 2000, § 79(3)(b).
[21] The Information Technology Act, 2000, § 79(3)(a).
[22] *See* discussion *infra*, Sections 5.3.4, 5.4.

content, and (iii) the intermediary's ineligibility for safe harbor. The efficacy of this approach is analysed in Section 5.3.

The immunity provided by Section 79 is nonetheless vital for platform operations in India because, if platforms are ineligible for such immunity, they risk incurring both civil and criminal liability for content they host. Without such immunity, the regulatory environment around platforms is not suitable for the creation of a dynamic information and communication system that platforms provide today. This is because Indian law includes a wide range of content-related offenses. These content areas are discussed in detail in Section 2. While no platform has finally and definitively been held liable for hosting unlawful UGC, the wide range of criminalized content in India may incentivise platforms to comply with Section 79 and the Intermediary Guidelines to retain safe harbor.

5.1.2 *Content Removal by Government Orders*

The Indian government is also empowered to directly block content on the internet under Section 69A of the IT Act in the interests of "the defence, security, or sovereignty and integrity of India, its friendly relations with other States, public order, or to prevent the incitement of an offence related to these categories." This provision was used between 2020 and 2022 to block over one hundred mobile applications in India, including popular platforms such as TikTok, WeChat, PUBG, and Helo.[23] The Indian government claimed these applications had been transmitting user data to foreign servers in a manner prejudicial to the integrity and defense of India.[24] Given that these applications were overwhelmingly created by Chinese developers and the restrictions were imposed contemporaneously with a border dispute between India and China, media reports suggested that the blocking of mobile applications was a strategic move by the Indian government against Chinese platforms.[25] The provision has also been used to block popular websites

[23] *Chinese Apps Banned in India: India Bans 59 Chinese Apps including TikTok, WeChat, Helo*, The Economic Times (July 29, 2020), https://economictimes.indiatimes.com/tech/software/india-bans-59-chinese-apps-including-tiktok-helo-wechat/articleshow/76694814.cms (last visited Sept. 26, 2020); PUBG Mobile, *117 Chinese Apps Banned in India: Check the Full List*, The Indian Express (Sept. 5, 2020), https://indianexpress.com/article/technology/tech-news-technology/india-bans-pubg-mobile-116-chinese-apps-full-list-6580365/ (last visited Apr. 26, 2022); *Govt Bans 54 Chinese Apps over Security Threat Concerns*, Hindustan Times (Feb. 14, 2022), https://www.hindustantimes.com/india-news/govt-to-ban-54-chinese-apps-that-pose-threat-to-india-report-101644814634095.html (last visited Apr. 26 2022).

[24] Press Information Bureau, *Government Blocks 118 Mobile Apps Which Are Prejudicial to Sovereignty and Integrity of India, Defence of India, Security of State and Public Order*, Press Information Bureau (2020), https://pib.gov.in/pib.gov.in/Pressreleaseshare.aspx?PRID=1650669 (last accessed Apr. 26, 2022).

[25] Sameer Yasir & Hari Kumar, *India Bans 118 Chinese Apps as Indian Soldier Is Killed on Disputed Border*, New York Times (Sept. 2, 2020), https://www.nytimes.com/2020/09/02/world/asia/india-bans-china-apps.html (last accessed Apr. 26, 2022).

such as GitHub (for allegedly hosting terrorism related content), tweets by journalistic organizations and Members of Parliament, and even individuals protesting government policies.[26] On May 1, 2023, following the instructions from Ministry of Home Affairs, the central government banned fourteen apps under Section 69A allegedly on the basis that those apps were used by terrorists in Jammu & Kashmir.[27]

Intermediaries who fail to comply with directions under Section 69A can be fined and imprisoned for up to seven years.[28] While the Blocking Rules generally require that the user who uploaded the disputed content or the intermediary who hosted the content be provided with a notice and hearing,[29] in emergencies, the government has the power to dispense with a notice and hearing for the blocking of content.[30] Further, while blocking orders are required to be reasoned and in writing,[31] the orders themselves are confidential.[32]

In practice, there are few publicly reported instances of the government providing an *ex-ante* hearing to a user or voluntarily disclosing the blocking order.[33] However, where a website owner challenged the blocking of his satirical website under Section 69A, the Delhi High Court directed the MEITY to disclose the blocking order and grant the website owner a *post*-decisional hearing.[34] In 2022, Twitter challenged several blocking orders issued by the Indian government on the grounds that (i) the users whose content was being blocked were not notified, (ii) the content did not satisfy the substantive thresholds for illegality set out under Section 69A, and

[26] Aroon Deep, *Twitter Censors Tweets from MP, MLA, Editor Criticising Pandemic Handling*, MEDIANAMA (2021), https://www.medianama.com/2021/04/223-twitter-mp-minister-censor/ (last visited Apr. 26, 2022); Revathi Krishnan, *Accounts of Prasar Bharati CEO, Caravan, Actor Sushant Singh among Those "Withheld" by Twitter*, THE PRINT (2021), https://theprint.in/india/accounts-of-prasar-bharati-ceo-caravan-actor-sushant-singh-among-those-withheld-by-twitter/596638/ (last visited Apr. 26, 2022); PK Jayadevan & Neha Alawadhi, *Government Blocks over 60 Websites including Github & Sourceforge on Anti-terror Advisory*, THE ECONOMIC TIMES (Dec. 31, 2014), https://economictimes.indiatimes.com/tech/internet/government-blocks-over-60-websites-including-github-sourceforge-on-anti-terror-advisory/articleshow/45704384.cms?from=mdr (last visited Apr. 26, 2022).

[27] Danny D'cruze, *Govt Blocks 14 Messenger Mobile Applications for Spreading Terror*, BUSINESS TODAY (May 1, 2023), https://www.businesstoday.in/technology/news/story/govt-blocks-14-messenger-mobile-applications-for-spreading-terror-379496-2023-05-01#:~:text=The%20Indian%20government%20has%20blocked,the%20Information%20Technology%20Act%2C%202000/ (last visited Feb. 18, 2024).

[28] The Information Technology Act, 2000, § 69A(3).

[29] Blocking Rules, rule 8; Aarathi Ganesan, *Summary: Twitter's Writ Petition before the Karnataka High Court*, MEDIANAMA (2022), https://www.medianama.com/2022/07/223-why-is-twitter-suing-the-indian-government/ (last visited Jan. 10, 2023).

[30] Blocking Rules, rule 9.

[31] The Information Technology Act, 2000, § 69A(1).

[32] Blocking Rules, rule 16.

[33] Apar Gupta, *But What about Section 69A?*, THE INDIAN EXPRESS (Mar. 27, 2015), https://indianexpress.com/article/opinion/columns/but-what-about-section-69a/ (last visited Jan. 10, 2023).

[34] Tanul Thakur v. Union of India WP (Civil) 13037 of 2019, decided on May 11, 2022 (High Court of Delhi).

(iii) blocking orders against entire user accounts (as opposed to specific posts) were disproportionate.[35] On June 30, 2023, the Karnataka High Court dismissed Twitter's challenge to the government's blocking orders. It imposed exemplary costs on Twitter as it considered the case speculative litigation.[36] The court upheld the power of the government to block entire accounts instead of specific tweets and elaborated that such powers were needed as some tweets may have "great propensity to incite anti-national feelings."[37] Between 2018 and October 2023, the central government has sent 13,660 blocking orders to social media platform X (earlier known as Twitter).[38]

5.1.3 *Content Prohibited by Intermediary Guidelines*

Under Rule 3(1)(b) of the Intermediary Guidelines, platforms are required to ensure that their terms of service prohibit users from uploading or sharing a wide range of content including content that is insulting; harmful to children; obscene; infringes any trademark, patent or copyright; threatens public order or the security of India; or violates any Indian law.[39] These categories (cumulatively "Intermediary Guidelines

[35] Ganesan, *supra* note 29.

[36] X Corp v. Union of India WP 13037 of 2022, decided on June 30, 2023 (High Court of Karnataka), https://www.livelaw.in/pdf_upload/wp13710-22-30-06-2023-478944.pdf. (last visited Feb. 18, 2024).

[37] Archit Lohani, *Decoding the Karnataka High Court Ruline: Blocking Accounts vs. Tweets*, MEDIANAMA (July 29, 2023), https://www.medianama.com/2023/07/223-karnataka-high-court-rul ling-blocking-twitter-accounts-tweets/ (last visited Feb. 18, 2024).

[38] *Centre Issued 36800 Blocking Orders to Social Media Platforms Since 2018 under IT Act*, SCROLL.IN, https://scroll.in/latest/1060336/centre-issued-36800-blocking-orders-to-social-media-platforms-since-2018-under-it-act/ (last visited Feb. 18, 2024).

[39] Under Rule 3(1)(b) platforms are expected to prohibit the following categories in their ToS:

- Content that contains a software virus or code that is designed to interrupt, destroy, or limit the functionality of a computer resource;
- belongs to another person and to which the user does not have any right;
- Content that impersonates another person;
- Content that deceives or misleads the recipient about the origin of the message, is misinformation, or is patently false, untrue, or misleading;
- Content that relates to or encourages money laundering or gambling;
- Content that infringes on any trademark, patent, copyright or other proprietary rights;
- Content that is obscene, pornographic, paedophilic, invasive of another user's privacy (including bodily privacy), insulting or harassing of other users on the basis of gender, racially or ethnically objectionable, or promotes enmity between different groups on the grounds of religion or caste with an intent to incite violence;
- Content that is harmful to children;
- Content that threatens the unity, integrity, defence, security, or sovereignty of India, friendly relations with foreign States, or public order, or insults any other nation, or causes the incitement of a serious offence or prevents the investigation of an offence; and
- Content that violates any Indian law.

Prohibited UGC") form the broad umbrella of content that platforms are expected to restrict in their ToS.

Under the Intermediary Guidelines, platforms are legally required to inform their users, at least once a year, that noncompliance with the platform's ToS may result in the removal of noncompliant content or termination of the user's access to the platform.[40] Platforms only lose safe harbor if they fail to remove content after receiving "actual knowledge" of unlawful content (interpreted by the Indian Supreme Court in *Shreya Singhal* to mean a court order) or fail to comply with a government order for removal of content.[41] However, in practice, most large social media platforms will remove most of the above-mentioned categories of content pursuant to their voluntary content moderation activities where they believe such content violates their ToS.

In October 2022, the MEITY amended the Intermediary Guidelines to stipulate that intermediaries "shall make reasonable efforts to cause" their users not to "host, display, upload, modify, publish, transmit, store, update or share" content that constitutes Intermediary Guidelines Prohibited UGC.[42] (As noted above, the Intermediary Guidelines previously merely required platforms to prohibit such content in their ToS.)

Given the recent adoption of this text, there exists some ambiguity over what an obligation to make reasonable efforts to cause users not to publish or transmit Intermediary Guidelines Prohibited UGC involves. A literal interpretation of this language may suggest that the recent amendments change the legal obligation on platforms from – a requirement to include prohibitions against Intermediary Guidelines Prohibited UGC in their ToS – to an obligation to *prevent* users from uploading Intermediary Guidelines Prohibited UGC onto their networks. Such an interpretation may effectively create a strict liability standard for platforms because the hosting of unlawful content by a platform would be a violation of its obligation to prevent users from uploading unlawful content, leading to a breach of the Intermediary Guidelines and consequently a loss of safe harbor. However, this obligation to prevent users is qualified by the expression make "reasonable efforts."

Further, such an interpretation would conflict with Section 79 and other provisions of the Intermediary Guidelines. Section 79(1) of the IT Act expressly provides intermediaries immunity for hosting unlawful content. This immunity would be rendered ineffective if platforms lost this immunity simply upon a user uploading unlawful content onto their network. As Section 79(1) constitutes primary legislation, and the recent amendments amend delegated legislation (the Intermediary Guidelines), the Amendments cannot override the statutory scheme set out in

40 Intermediary Guidelines, Rule 3(1)(c).

41 The Information Technology Act, 2000, § 79(3); Intermediary Guidelines, Rule 3(1)(d); Shreya Singhal v. Union of India (2015) 5 SCC 1 (Supreme Court of India), ¶ 122. *See* discussion *infra*, Section 5.3.1.2.

42 Intermediary Guidelines, Rule 3(1)(b).

Section 79. Similarly, Rules 3(1)(d) and 3(1)(g) of the Intermediary Guidelines expressly state that platforms are only required to remove unlawful content pursuant to a government or court order, or in the case of nonconsensual intimate images, pursuant to a user complaint.[43] Thus, despite the language introduced by the recent amendments suggesting that platforms have to *prevent* users from uploading unlawful content, a holistic reading of Section 79 and the Intermediary Guidelines would suggest that platforms are not required to ensure an absolute prohibition against Intermediary Guidelines Prohibited UGC on their networks but rather simply demonstrate that they have taken certain affirmative steps toward restricting such content.

5.2 PLATFORM RESPONSIBILITY FOR VARIOUS SUBJECT AREAS

A wide range of content is unlawful under Indian law. This includes online content (primarily regulated by offenses in the IT Act), and general application statutes such as the Indian Penal Code, 1860 (IPC),[44] which regulate content whether found on an online or offline medium. Given the wide range of unlawful content in India, social media platforms may be secondarily liable for UGC on their networks that violate Indian law unless they secure safe harbor under Section 79 of the IT Act. This is because civil or criminal proceedings may be initiated against a platform for hosting unlawful UGC unless the platform can demonstrate it qualifies for immunity under Section 79.[45] Section 79 immunity is applicable against both civil and criminal proceedings that may be brought against platforms.

However, platforms can avoid secondary liability for unlawful content by complying with Section 79 and taking down content upon receiving a court or government order.[46] The obligations of platforms to take down content do not change based on the subject matter of the content hosted except in the cases of (i) nonconsensual intimate content (which must be taken down within 24 hours of receiving a complaint)[47] and (ii) rape and child-sex-abuse material (which SSMIs must "endeavour" to proactively identify using automated tools).[48] Outside of these two categories, intermediaries, including social media platforms, are only required to take down

43 Intermediary Guidelines, Rule 3(2).

44 Recently, the Indian Parliament overhauled India's criminal laws by replacing the colonial era laws on criminal activity, criminal procedure, and the law of evidence. The new set of laws are yet to be notified and made operational. *See* Mayank Kumar, *It's Back to the Classroom for Delhi Police Officers to Learn New Criminal Laws, Unlearn IPC, CrPC*, THE PRINT (Jan. 26, 2024), https://theprint.in/india/its-back-to-the-classroom-for-delhi-police-officers-to-learn-new-criminal-laws-unlearn-ipc-crpc/1933652/ (last visited Feb. 18, 2024).

45 Google India Pvt Ltd v. Visaka Industries Ltd (2020) 4 SCC 162 (Supreme Court of India), ¶53; The Information Technology Act, 2000, § 81. There are certain minor carve outs with respect to copyright and patent actions that are not relevant to the present chapter.

46 *See* discussion *infra*, Section 5.3.1.2.

47 Intermediary Guidelines, Rule 3(2). *See* discussion *infra*, Section 5.2.4.

48 Intermediary Guidelines, Rule 4(4). *See* discussion *infra*, Section 5.4.1.

content pursuant to a court or government order.[49] The remainder of this section lists content that is unlawful in India and then sets out the data protection obligations imposed on intermediaries.

5.2.2 *Hateful, Inciteful, and Defamatory Speech*

The IPC criminalizes:[50]

- content promoting enmity between – different religious, racial, linguistic groups,[51] caste or communities, or any two classes of people;[52]
- content intended to outrage religious feelings or beliefs;[53]
- content prejudicial to "national integration";[54] and
- content that is likely to cause "fear or alarm to the public" or incite individuals to breach the public peace.[55]

Indian law recognizes both civil and criminal defamation.[56] Content that intentionally insults, intimidates, or humiliates a member of a Scheduled Caste or a Scheduled Tribe (identified in the Constitution and various statutes), including the use of abuses involving caste names, is also criminalized in India.[57] Section 66A of the IT Act proscribed "grossly offensive" or "annoying" expression online; however, this provision was struck down by the Supreme Court of India in 2015 as an unconstitutionally vague and overbroad restriction on free expression.[58] The Supreme Court has also intervened in the case of Section 124A of the IPC, which criminalizes seditious speech (defined as speech that causes "disaffection towards the government"). In May 2022, while hearing a constitutional challenge to Section 124A, the Supreme Court ruled that Indian authorities should desist from instituting fresh cases during the pendency of the challenge.[59]

49 Shreya Singhal v. Union of India (2015) 5 SCC 1 (Supreme Court of India), ¶ 122.
50 Recently, the Indian Parliament overhauled India's criminal laws by replacing the colonial era laws on criminal activity, criminal procedure, and the law of evidence. The new set of laws are yet to be notified and made operational. Kumar, *supra* note 44.
51 The Indian Penal Code, 1860, § 153A.
52 The Indian Penal Code, 1860, § 505(2).
53 The Indian Penal Code, 1860, §§ 298, 295A.
54 The Indian Penal Code, 1860, § 153B.
55 The Indian Penal Code, 1860, § 505(1).
56 The Indian Penal Code, 1860, § 499; Subramaniam Swamy v. Union of India (2016) 7 SCC 221 (Supreme Court of India), ¶¶66–68.
57 The Scheduled Castes and the Scheduled Tribes (Prevention of Atrocities) Act, 1989, §§ 3(1)(r)–3(1)(s).
58 Shreya Singhal v. Union of India (2015) 5 SCC 1 (Supreme Court of India).
59 S G Vombatkere v. Union of India WP (Civil) 682 of 2021, order passed on May 11, 2022 (Supreme Court of India).

5.2.3 *Platform Conduct during Elections*

Under Section 171G of the IPC, any person who publishes a statement they know or believe to be false with the intention of affecting the outcome of an election may be fined. Further, content that is "patently false or misleading in nature" or situations where a person "knowingly and intentionally communicates any misinformation" falls within the ambit of Intermediary Guidelines Prohibited UGC and platforms must both prohibit such content in their ToS and make reasonable efforts to cause users not to publish and share such content.[60] In April 2023, the government made amendments to the Intermediary Guidelines to insert a clause that obligates intermediaries to make reasonable efforts to not host content that is fake or false and is in respect to any business of the central government. Under this clause, the government will notify a fact-checking unit that will identify and communicate fake, false, or misleading information to be acted upon by intermediaries.[61]

More importantly, Indian elections have a high volume of misinformation being disseminated over private messaging platforms such as WhatsApp.[62] In an attempt to curb this misinformation, the Intermediary Guidelines require messaging platforms to trace the "originator" of messages.[63] This obligation is discussed further in Section 5.4.

While the Election Commission of India's Model Code of Conduct does prescribe certain restrictions on election-related speech,[64] these restrictions are applicable against electoral candidates, and platforms are not held secondarily liable for violations by candidates. Violations of the Model Code of Conduct are typically addressed through non-monetary penalties imposed directly on the candidate (e.g., suspension of campaigning). Similarly, while the use of social media by electoral candidates and political parties is scrutinized by the Election Commission of India, platforms do not have any election-specific obligations under Indian law.

However, in 2019, major online platforms such as Facebook, Google, WhatsApp, and ShareChat (through the Internet & Mobile Association of India) adopted a voluntary Code of Ethics that platforms agreed to adhere to during state and national elections in India.[65] The Code of Ethics has two key commitments. First, the platforms agreed to enforce the "cooling off period" mandated by Section 126 of

[60] Intermediary Guidelines, Rule 3(1)(b).

[61] Intermediary Guidelines, Rule 3(1)(b)(v).

[62] Vidya Narayanan et al., *News and Information over Facebook and WhatsApp during the Indian Election Campaign* (2019), https://demtech.oii.ox.ac.uk/wp-content/uploads/sites/93/2019/05/India-memo.pdf (last visited Feb. 18, 2024).

[63] Intermediary Guidelines, Rule 4(2). *See* discussion *infra* Section 5.4.4.

[64] Model Code of Conduct, ELECTION COMMISSION OF INDIA, https://eci.gov.in/mcc/ (last visited Jan. 10, 2023).

[65] Press Information Bureau, *"Voluntary Code of Ethics" by Social Media Platforms to Be Observed in the General Election to the Haryana & Maharashtra Legislative Assemblies and All Future Elections* (2019), https://pib.gov.in/pib.gov.in/Pressreleaseshare.aspx?PRID=1586297 (last visited Jan. 10, 2023).

the Representation of the People Act, 1951;[66] which prohibits the display of any election related content forty-eight hours prior to polling.[67] This is operationalized by allowing the Election Commission to directly notify platforms of election-related content during the cooling off period, and platforms have committed to take down the flagged content within three hours.[68] The Commission reported that during the 2019 national elections, 909 posts were taken down pursuant to this mechanism, suggesting that the Commission is ultimately only able to flag a small amount of content.[69]

The second key commitment found in the voluntary Code of Ethics is that platforms will only host political advertisements that have been pre-screened in accordance with the Election Commission's regulations.[70] Such pre-screening of political advertisements was previously applicable to television and has been extended to social media through the adoption of this voluntary Code of Ethics. Under the Code, platforms are also required to tag or label political advertisements so that viewers can distinguish between such advertisements from other content on the site.[71]

5.2.4 *Terrorism-related Content*

Section 66F of the IT Act criminalizes "cyber terrorism." This offense primarily pertains to *conduct* involving the unauthorized access to a computer network or the denial of access to a computer network that is likely to cause death, injury, or disrupt essential services, including critical information infrastructure.[72] However, the provision has sporadically been used against *content* on social media platforms, primarily against content that allegedly incites communal violence.[73] Where the provision is used against content, platforms may be held secondarily liable for cyberterrorism subject to their defense of safe harbor.

The Indian government remains conscious of the use of the internet to promote and facilitate terrorism, primarily responding to such situations by directly blocking

66 Internet and Mobile Association of India, *Voluntary Code of Ethics – reg.* (Sept. 23, 2019), https://static.pib.gov.in/WriteReadData/userfiles/IAMAI-ECI%20VCE.pdf [hereinafter IAMAI Code of Ethics].

67 The Representation of the People Act, 1951, § 126(1)(b).

68 IAMAI Code of Ethics.

69 Nalin Mehta, *Digital Politics in India's 2019 General Elections*, 54 Economic and Political Weekly (2019), https://www.epw.in/engage/article/digital-politics-indias-2019-general-elections (last visited Jan. 10, 2023).

70 IAMAI Code of Ethics.

71 IAMAI Code of Ethics.

72 The Information Technology Act, 2000, § 66F.

73 *Three Kashmiri Students Arrested in Agra for Celebrating Pakistan's Cricket Win against India*, Scroll.in, October 28, 2021, https://scroll.in/latest/1009069/three-kashmiri-students-arrested-in-agra-for-celebrating-pakistans-cricket-win-against-india (last visited Jan. 10, 2023); Mukesh Kumar, *Hisar Journalists Say Junk FIR as Cops Look for Colleague*, The Times of India (Apr. 12, 2021), https://timesofindia.indiatimes.com/city/chandigarh/journalists-say-junk-fir-as-cops-look-for-colleague/articleshow/82021430.cms?utm_source = contentofinterest&utm_medium = text&utm_campaign = cppst (last visited Jan. 10, 2023).

content under Section 69A of the IT Act. For example, in 2015, the government blocked thirty-two websites in India, including vinmeo.com, dailymotion.com, and github.com, until they removed content that Indian authorities alleged was ISIS propaganda.[74] The government has blocked YouTube channels, Facebook accounts, and Twitter accounts for allegedly engaging in coordinated disinformation campaigns that threaten national security.[75] These blocked accounts included accounts operated by organizations made illegal under India's primary anti-terrorism statute, The Unlawful Activities (Prevention) Act, 1967.[76] The Central Government has issued directions to 635 URLs from December 2021 till July 2023 for publishing fake news that was against national sovereignty.[77]

5.2.5 *Intimidation, Trafficking, Nonconsensual Intimate Content, Child Pornography, and Sexually Explicit Material*

The publishing of content depicting the private area of a person "under circumstances violating their privacy" is a criminal offense under the IT Act.[78] Under Rule 3(2) of the Intermediary Guidelines, any user can lodge a complaint with an intermediary against content that depicts the user in a state of nudity or committing a sexual act, including content that has been digitally altered to depict the user as such.[79] The intermediary must remove the complained-against content within twenty-four hours and implement a distinct mechanism for such complaints or risk losing safe harbor vis-à-vis this content.[80] In the case of SSMIs, the user must be allowed to track the status of their complaint by being assigned a unique ticket number for their complaint.[81] It is also relevant to note that the IPC criminalizes the publication of content that discloses the identity of victims of sexual violence or rape absent express authorization.[82]

[74] Kim Arora, *Government Blocks 32 Websites to Check ISIS Propaganda*, The Times of India (Jan. 1, 2015), https://timesofindia.indiatimes.com/tech-news/government-blocks-32-websites-to-check-isis-propaganda/articleshow/45712815.cms (last visited Jan. 10, 2023).

[75] Sarvesh Mathi, *MIB Blocks Twenty-Two YouTube Channels for Spreading Fake News*, MediaNama (2022), https://www.medianama.com/2022/04/223-mib-blocks-youtube-channels/ (last visited Jan. 10, 2023).

[76] *Id.*

[77] *Centre Issued Directives to Block 635 URLs since December 2021 for Spreading Fake News: Anurag Thakur*, The Hindu (July 27, 2023), https://www.thehindu.com/news/national/centre-issued-directives-to-block-635-urls-since-december-2021-for-spreading-fake-news-anurag-thakur/article67127248.ece/ (last visited Feb. 18, 2024).

[78] The Information Technology Act, 2000, § 66E.

[79] *See also* Vasudev Devadasan et al., *CCG Working Paper: Tackling the Dissemination and Redistribution of NCII* (2022), https://ccgdelhi.s3.ap-south-1.amazonaws.com/uploads/ccg-ncii-wp-16dec22-fn-332.pdf. Critically analyzing the overbroad nature of Rule 3(2) of the Intermediary Guidelines.

[80] Intermediary Guidelines, Rule 3(2)(b).

[81] Intermediary Guidelines, Rule 4(6).

[82] The Indian Penal Code, 1860, § 228A.

While India does punish extortion,[83] criminal intimidation,[84] online stalking,[85] trafficking,[86] and identity theft,[87] these offenses primarily apply to the conduct of individuals using the internet and are thus unlikely to give rise to content-related liability for platforms. While the draft Trafficking of Persons (Prevention, Protection and Rehabilitation) Bill (2021) punishes the publication of content that promotes trafficking,[88] the draft legislation has yet to be introduced into Parliament. However, India does criminalize the publication of (i) "obscene material" (content that is lascivious, appeals to the prurient interest, or tends to deprave or corrupt persons)[89] and (ii) sexually explicit material.[90] Thus, platforms could, in principle, be prosecuted for hosting obscene or sexually explicit material, with the ultimate imposition of liability being subject to the platforms' claim to safe harbor under Section 79 of the IT Act.

Finally, the possession or storage of child pornography is criminalized in India.[91] Thus, platforms may be prosecuted for hosting child pornography. Further, under the Intermediary Guidelines, SSMIs have a distinct obligation to "endeavor to deploy" automated tools to proactively identify rape and child sexual abuse material.[92] This obligation is discussed in Section 4.1 of the IT Act ("Obligation to detect certain content").

5.2.6 *Content Removals Pursuant to Court or Government Orders*

One of the preconditions to safe harbor under Section 79 of the IT Act is that platforms remove content upon receiving court or government orders.[93] Court or government orders directing content removal are not limited to a specific subject area. Courts may require intermediaries to takedown specific content pursuant to injunctions in defamation[94] or intellectual property suits,[95] the right to be

[83] The Indian Penal Code, 1860, § 383.

[84] The Indian Penal Code, 1860, § 505.

[85] The Indian Penal Code, 1860, § 354D.

[86] The Indian Penal Code, 1860, § 370.

[87] The Information Technology Act, 2000, § 66C.

[88] Ministry of Women and Child Development, *Draft Trafficking in Persons (Prevention, Care and Rehabilitation) Bill, 2021* (June 2021), § 29, https://wcd.nic.in/sites/default/files/DRAFT%20TRAFFICKING%20IN%20PERSONS%20%28PREVENTION%2C%20CARE%20AND%20REHABILITATION%29%20BILL%202021%20%281%29.pdf (last visited Feb. 18, 2024).

[89] The Information Technology Act, 2000, § 67.

[90] The Information Technology Act, 2000, § 67A.

[91] The Protection of Children from Sexual Offences Act, 2012, § 15; the Information Technology Act, 2000, § 67B.

[92] Intermediary Guidelines, Rule 4(4). *See* discussion *infra*, Section 5.4.1.

[93] The Information Technology Act, 2000, § 79(3); Intermediary Guidelines, Rule 3(1)(d).

[94] Subodh Gupta v. Herdsceneand CS (OS) 483 of 2019 decided on September 18, 2019 (High Court of Delhi); Zulfiqar Ahmad Khan v. Quintillion Business Media CS (OS) 642 of 2018, decided on December 14, 2018 (High Court of Delhi).

[95] Jagran Prakashan Ltd. v. Telegram FZ LLC CS (Comm) 146 of 2020, decided on May 29, 2020 (High Court of Delhi); Dept. of Electronics and Information Technology v. Star India Pvt. Ltd.

forgotten,[96] to remove nonconsensual intimate images,[97] or impose broader obligations to coordinate with government authorities to take down certain classes of content pursuant to public interest litigation.[98] Similarly, government orders have been issued against a wide range of content including (as noted above) Chinese mobile applications alleged to have national security implications[99] and the Twitter accounts of media organizations.[100]

5.2.7 *Data Protection Obligations*

As the Indian Supreme Court has ruled that the right to privacy is a fundamental right guaranteed by the Indian Constitution,[101] India has recently passed the Digital Personal Data Protection Act (DPDP) in 2023. The Personal Data Protection Bill was earlier introduced into India's Parliament in 2019 and scrutinized by a Joint Parliamentary Committee, which released its report in December 2021.[102] However, the Bill was subsequently withdrawn in August 2022[103] and replaced by the Digital Personal Data Protection Bill (2022).[104] Subsequently, by way of a fresh bill introduced by the government in Parliament, both houses passed India's first comprehensive data protection legislation in August 2023.[105] The DPDP creates obligations for data fiduciaries[106] and significant fiduciaries, provides rights for data principals,[107]

FAO (OS) 57 of 2015, decided on July 29, 2016 (High Court of Delhi); Snapdeal Pvt. Ltd. v. GoDaddy LLC CS (Comm) 176 of 2021, decided on April 18, 2022 (High Court of Delhi).

96 Jorawer Singh Mundy v. Union of India WP (Civil) 3918 of 2021, decided on April 17, 2021 (High Court of Delhi).

97 X v. Union of India WP (Cri) 1082 of 2020, decided on April 20, 2021 (High Court of Delhi).

98 Sabu Mathew George v. Union of India (2017) 2 SCC 514 (Supreme Court of India) (advertising for pre-natal sex determination procedures); Registrar (Judicial) v. Union Ministry of Communications 2017 SCC Online 25298 Mad. (High Court of Madras) (content related to video games alleged to promote suicide); *In re*: Prajwala Letter dated 18.2.2015 SMW (Cri) 3 of 2015 (Supreme Court of India) (rape videos).

99 *Chinese Apps Banned in India: India Bans 59 Chinese Apps including TikTok, WeChat, Helo, supra* note 23; Yasir and Kumar, *supra* note 25.

100 Krishnan, *supra* note 26.

101 K S Puttaswamy v. Union of India (2017) 10 SCC 1 (Supreme Court of India).

102 *The Personal Data Protection Bill, 2019*, PRS Legislative Research, https://prsindia.org/billtrack/the-personal-data-protection-bill-2019 (last visited Jan. 10, 2023).

103 *Govt Withdraws Data Protection Bill, 2021*, The Economic Times (Aug. 4, 2022), https://economictimes.indiatimes.com/tech/technology/govt-withdraws-data-protection-bill-2021/articleshow/93334281.cms (last visited Jan. 10, 2023).

104 Ministry of Electronics and Information Technology, *Explanatory Note: The Digital Personal Data Protection Bill, 2022* (2022), https://www.meity.gov.in/writereaddata/files/Explanatory%20Note-%20The%20Digital%20Personal%20Data%20Protection%20Bill%2C%202022.pdf (last visited Jan. 10, 2023).

105 Although the law has been notified by way of the president's assent, the law is currently not in operation as different clauses will be operationalized in a phased manner on future dates.

106 The terminology used for data controllers or data processing entities in the Indian DPDP.

107 The terminology used for data subjects or individuals to whom data relates to in the Indian DPDP.

and establishes a specialized adjudicator for resolving disputes related to data protection. It also provides for penalties that can be imposed by the specialized adjudicator for violations of the law. The law is currently not operational and is expected to be implemented in a phased manner in the next few months.[108] Platforms continue to have certain data protection obligations under the IT Act and the Information Technology (Reasonable security practices and procedures and sensitive personal data or information) Rules (2011) (Personal Data Rules). Section 43A of the IT Act requires corporate bodies possessing or handling "sensitive personal data" to implement reasonable security practices. The DPDP repeals section 43A of the IT Act and will become the primary legislation for data protection in India, once it is made operational by the government. The DPDP Act provides a national framework for processing personal data, replacing limited categories of "sensitive data" covered under the Personal Data Rules.

The Personal Data Rules define "sensitive personal data" as including passwords, financial information, sexual orientation, medical records, and biometric information. Entities that collect, store, or handle sensitive personal data must (i) collect such information for a lawful purpose; (ii) disclose to users the fact that information is collected, the purpose for which it is collected, and the intended recipients of the information; (iii) only retain sensitive personal data for the time it is necessary for the purpose collected; (iv) allow users to correct incorrect or deficient information upon request; and (v) provide a grievance redressal mechanism.[109] However, these obligations do not apply to entities that collect personal data "under a contractual obligation with another Indian or foreign company,"[110] and thus, are only applicable to entities that directly collect data from users.[111] If platforms fail to comply with the Personal Data Rules, they may be liable to compensate users for any losses stemming from the disclosure of sensitive personal data.[112]

5.3 ENFORCEMENT OF PLATFORM RESPONSIBILITY

Compliance with the Intermediary Guidelines constitutes a precondition for safe harbor under Section 79 of the IT Act. Therefore, the threat of losing safe harbor

[108] Digital Personal Data Protection Act, 2023, section 1(2).

[109] Information Technology (Reasonable security practices and procedures and sensitive personal data or information) Rules, 2011; Collection & Processing in India – DLA Piper Global Data Protection Laws of the World, https://www.dlapiperdataprotection.com/index.html?t=collection-and-processing&c=IN (last visited Jan. 10, 2023).

[110] Ministry of Communications & Information Technology, *Clarification on Information Technology (Reasonable Security Practices and Procedures and Sensitive Personal Data or Information) Rules, 2011 under Section 43A of the Information Technology Act, 2000* (Aug. 24, 2011), https://www.meity.gov.in/writereaddata/files/PressNote_25811.pdf.

[111] Aditi Chaturvedi, *GDPR and India* (2017). https://cis-india.org/internet-governance/files/gdpr-and-india (last visited Jan. 10, 2023).

[112] The Information Technology Act, 2000, § 43A.

under Section 79, which may lead to platforms being held liable for unlawful UGC on their networks, is the primary method of enforcing platform compliance with the various obligations outlined in the Intermediary Guidelines.

5.3.2 *Defense to Liability*

As noted in Section 5.1, to avail of safe harbor, an intermediary must (i) not initiate the transmission, select the receiver of the transmission, or modify the information contained in the transmission; (ii) comply with the Intermediary Guidelines; (iii) remove content upon receiving "actual knowledge"; and (iv) not aid or abet the commission of an unlawful act on its network.[113]

5.3.3 *Neutrality and Moderation*

The requirement that platforms must not initiate the transmission, select the receiver of the transmission, or select or modify the information in the transmission is analogous to the requirements of neutrality in Article 12 of the European E-Commerce Directive (Mere conduit).[114] Section 79 does not have an express equivalent to Article 14 of the Directive (Hosting), wherein even platforms that are not mere conduits can avail of safe harbor provided they remove content upon receiving actual knowledge. Rather, the text of Section 79 requires intermediaries to be *both* mere conduits *and* remove content upon receiving actual knowledge. However, as noted above, no platform has been denied safe harbor due to its interference with content, and commentators have argued that even hosting platforms should be able to avail of safe harbor under Section 79.[115]

Furthermore, the Intermediary Guidelines, introduced in 2021, clearly state that the removal of any Intermediary Guidelines Prohibited UGC will not amount to a breach of the neutrality required of Section 79.[116] The Guidelines thus recognize and promote voluntary content moderation by platforms. It remains unclear whether the use of recommender systems would violate the conditions of neutrality required by Section 79. On the one hand, recommender systems may amount to selecting the contents of a transmission. However, no court has specifically returned a finding that a platform's recommender system violates the neutrality requirements of Section 79. Similarly, the Indian government has neither suggested that such systems may lead to the loss of safe harbor or attempted to regulate them through the Intermediary Guidelines.

[113] *See supra*, Section 5.1.1.

[114] The Digital Services Act of the European Union contains the exact same language as in the E-Commerce Directive.

[115] Chinmayi Arun & Sarvjeet Singh, NoC *Online Intermediaries Case Studies Series: Online Intermediaries in India*, 11 (2015), https://papers.ssrn.com/sol3/papers.cfm?abstract_id=2566952.

[116] Intermediary Guidelines, Rule 3(1)(d) (third proviso).

5.3.4 *Notice and Actual Knowledge*

Neither Section 79 nor the IT Act defines the term "actual knowledge." Under the previous iteration of the Intermediary Guidelines (adopted in 2011), "actual knowledge" was set out to mean a complaint by another internet user, effectively setting up a traditional notice and takedown regime where platforms were required to remove content pursuant to private complaints.[117] However, in 2015, the Supreme Court of India in *Shreya Singhal v. Union of India* interpreted "actual knowledge" to mean a court order, effectively ruling that intermediaries would not lose safe harbor unless they failed to comply with a removal order by a court or authorized government agency.[118] This shifted the burden of determining illegality from intermediaries to courts and the government and increased the protection afforded to intermediaries as they were no longer legally required to remove content pursuant to private complaints,[119] although they remained free to do so in accordance with their ToS (i.e., voluntary content moderation).

In 2021, the Indian government codified the interpretation in *Shreya Singhal*, noting that platforms are *only* required to take down content pursuant to a court or government order.[120] However, pursuant to Rule 3(2) of the Intermediary Guidelines and the decisions of courts, platforms are nonetheless deemed to have "actual knowledge" and required to remove content pursuant to a private notice in the case of copyright infringing content[121] and nonconsensual intimate images.[122] As discussed above, the legal position again evolved in October 2022, when the MEITY amended the Intermediary Guidelines to stipulate that platforms must make reasonable efforts to cause their users not to host or transmit Intermediary Guidelines Prohibited UGC. The impact of this recent change has been discussed Section 5.1.3.

The October 2022 amendments to the Intermediary Guidelines also stipulate that, where a complaint pertains to a request to remove Intermediary Guidelines Prohibited UGC, the complaint shall be "acted on" and "redressed" within seventy-two hours.[123] The Supreme Court in *Shreya Singhal* expressly disapproved of this approach, noting that platforms receive a high volume of user complaints,

[117] Arun & Singh, *supra* note 115. This notice and takedown regime neither specified a counter-notice system or a put-back (reinstatement) requirement, thus risking legal content being removed at the behest of private complainants.

[118] Shreya Singhal v. Union of India (2015) 5 SCC 1 (Supreme Court of India).

[119] Kyung-Sin Park, *From Liability Trap to the World's Safest Harbor: Lessons from China, India, Japan, South Korea, Indonesia, and Malaysia*, Oxford Handbook of Online Intermediary Liability 250 (Giancarlo Frosio, ed. 2020).

[120] Intermediary Guidelines, Rule 3(1)(d).

[121] The Copyright Act, 1957 § 52(1)(c); The Copyright Rules, 2013, Rule 75; Myspace Inc. v. Super Cassettes Industries Ltd. 2016 SCC Online Del. 6382 (High Court of Delhi); Aradhya Sethia, *The Troubled Waters of Copyright Safe Harbors in India*, 12 Journal of Intellectual Property Law & Practice 398–407 (2017).

[122] Intermediary Guidelines, Rule 3(2).

[123] Proposed Amendments, Rule 3(2)(i).

and this would effectively lead to platforms deciding which complaints were legitimate and which were not, effectively determining what speech was legal and what speech is not.[124] The amendments state that platforms may institute "appropriate safeguards" to avoid abusive complaints by users.[125] However, short time frames to decide complaints against content has been proven to result in platform overcompliance with removal requests.[126]

5.3.5 *Additional Conditions for Safe Harbor in Intermediary Guidelines*

The Intermediary Guidelines also stipulate other conditions platforms must comply with to secure safe harbor, including (i) data retention obligations;[127] (ii) cooperation with law enforcement;[128] reporting of cyber security incidents;[129] and, in the case of SSMIs, (iii) appointing local compliance and grievance officers;[130] (iv) providing users with notice prior to taking down their content pursuant to ToS violations;[131] (v) publishing transparency reports;[132] (vi) endeavouring to proactively detect rape and child-sex abuse material;[133] and, for SSMIs providing messaging services, (vii) identification of the first originator of messages.[134]

5.3.6 *Efficacy of Enforcement*

The IT Act and the Intermediary Guidelines rely on the risk of losing safe harbor as the primary regulatory tool to govern platform behavior, imposing varied obligations (see Sections 3.1.3 and 4) on platforms as prerequisites to safe harbor. However, given that the loss of safe harbor is determined on a case-by-case basis, and the lengthy nature of litigation in India, no platform has definitively been held liable for hosting unlawful content. For example, in 2008, criminal defamation proceedings were instituted against Google for content on its Google Groups platform. Google sought to have the criminal complaint summarily quashed. The issue of whether the charges against Google should be summarily quashed or decided by trial took over a decade to decide, with the Supreme Court ultimately ruling that a trial should be conducted.[135]

[124] Shreya Singhal v. Union of India (2015) 5 SCC 1 (Supreme Court of India).
[125] Proposed Amendments, Rule 3(2)(i).
[126] Arun & Singh, *supra* note 115; Rishabh Dara, *Intermediary Liability in India: Chilling Effects on Free Expression on the Internet*, SSRN Journal (2011), http://www.ssrn.com/abstract=2038214 (last visited Feb. 18, 2023).
[127] Intermediary Guidelines, Rules 3(1)(g)–3(1)(h).
[128] Intermediary Guidelines, Rule 3(1)(j).
[129] Intermediary Guidelines, Rule 3(1)(l).
[130] Intermediary Guidelines, Rule 4(1)(a)–(c).
[131] Intermediary Guidelines, Rule 4(8). *See* discussion *infra* Section 5.4.2.
[132] Intermediary Guidelines, Rule 4(1)(d). *See* discussion *infra* Section 5.4.3.
[133] Intermediary Guidelines, Rule 4(4). *See* discussion *infra* Section 5.4.1.
[134] Intermediary Guidelines, Rule 4(2). *See* discussion *infra* Section 5.4.4.
[135] Google India Pvt. Ltd. v. Visaka Industries (2020) 4 SCC 162 (Supreme Court of India).

This dispute highlights how the nature of litigation in India coupled with the legal resources of platforms may render intermediary liability (i.e., the risk of liability enforced through private lawsuits) a weak regulatory tool to regulate platform behavior. However, there is some evidence to suggest that the government may believe that a loss of safe harbor either for content or noncompliance with the due diligence rules under the Intermediary Guidelines opens up the platform to liability for all content on the platform,[136] with the MEITY having issued Twitter multiple warnings to "comply with the Intermediary Guidelines or be liable to punishment under the IT Act."[137] However, such an understanding would be contrary to both the principles of secondary liability and the text of the IT Act.

Finally, it is also relevant to note that the IT Act applies to "any offence committed outside India."[138] Additionally, the IPC also applies to any offenses that "target computer resources located in India."[139] Thus, both statutes envisage extra-territorial application in certain situations. However, as the primary mechanism to regulate platform conduct is currently Section 79 and the Intermediary Guidelines, which are in the form of prerequisites to safe harbor against lawsuits initiated against platforms in India, India's regime of platform regulation relies on platforms being sued for hosting or transmitting unlawful content and being subject to the jurisdiction of Indian courts when this occurs.

5.3.7 *Additional Enforcement Methods*

In addition to the loss of safe harbor, there exist three methods through which Indian authorities ensure that platforms comply with specific obligations. First, noncompliance with a government direction for content removal under Section 69A of the IT Act is punishable with a prison term of up to seven years and a fine.[140] Similarly, if a platform does not comply with an order of a court, contempt proceedings may be initiated against it.[141] Finally, under the Intermediary Guidelines, SSMIs are required to appoint a Chief Compliance Officer who is a resident in India.[142] This Officer may be held personally liable in any proceedings relating to unlawful UGC on the platform's network if the Officer fails to ensure the

[136] Surabhi Agarwal, *Twitter Has Failed to Comply with Intermediary Guidelines: Ravi Shankar Prasad*, Times of India (June 17, 2021), https://economictimes.indiatimes.com/tech/technology/twitter-has-failed-to-comply-with-intermediary-guidelines-ravi-shankar-prasad/articleshow/83566900.cms?from=mdr (last visited February 18, 2024).

[137] Aashish Aryan & Surabhi Agarwal, *Twitter India Given "Last Chance" to Follow IT Rules*, ETTelecom.com (June 29, 2022), https://telecom.economictimes.indiatimes.com/news/twitter-india-given-last-chance-to-follow-it-rules/92532133 (last visited February 18, 2023).

[138] The Information Technology Act, 2000, § 1(2).

[139] The Indian Penal Code, 1860, § 4(3).

[140] The Information Technology Act, 2000, § 69(3).

[141] Facebook Inc v. Swami Ramdev FAO (OS) 212 of 2019, decided on January 28, 2020 (High Court of Delhi).

[142] Intermediary Guidelines, Rule 4(1)(a).

platform acts with "due diligence" in complying with the IT Act and the Intermediary Guidelines.[143] However, no liability will be imposed on the Compliance Officer without the Compliance Officer being granted a hearing.[144]

5.4 DETECTION AND MODERATION OF UNLAWFUL UGC

The Intermediary Guidelines, compliance with which is necessary for platforms to avail of safe harbor under Section 79, impose certain obligations on SSMIs with respect to content moderation. These obligations are not imposed on ordinary intermediaries (that do not perform social media functions or have less than 5 million Indian users).

5.4.1 *Obligations to Detect Certain Content Using Automated Tools*

SSMIs are required to "endeavour to deploy technology-based measures" to "proactively identify" content that (i) depicts rape or child sexual abuse material or (ii) is *identical* to content that either a court or government order directed be removed.[145] SSMIs are required to disable access to these two categories of content and inform users trying to access this content why the content has been blocked.[146] This best-efforts mandate to use automated tools to detect and remove content is subject to certain safeguards: (a) The action taken by the SSMI must be proportionate to the free speech and privacy interests of internet users;[147] (b) the automated tools used by the SSMI must be subject to "appropriate human oversight" and periodic review of these automated tools;[148] and finally, (c) the automated tools used by the SSMIs are to be evaluated to ensure "accuracy and fairness," guard against "the propensity of bias and discrimination," and determine their impact on privacy and security.[149] While the inclusion of these safeguards is commendable, in the absence of a designated regulator with meaningful oversight and enforcement powers, it is hard to determine whether these safeguards are complied with in practice.

5.4.2 *Responsibilities When Moderating*

Where an SSMI seeks to remove any Intermediary Guidelines Prohibited UGC voluntarily from its platform, Rule 4(8) of the Intermediary Guidelines requires the SSMI to provide the user who uploaded the relevant content a notice explaining the

[143] Intermediary Guidelines, Rule 4(1)(a).
[144] Intermediary Guidelines, Rule 4(1)(a).
[145] Intermediary Guidelines, Rule 4(4).
[146] Intermediary Guidelines, Rule 4(4).
[147] Intermediary Guidelines, Rule 4(4) (first proviso).
[148] Intermediary Guidelines, Rule 4(4) (second proviso).
[149] Intermediary Guidelines, Rule 4(4) (third proviso).

grounds for removal *before* the SSMI removes the content.[150] The user must also be provided with an "adequate and reasonable opportunity to dispute" the removal of their content and seek reinstatement if the content has already been removed.[151] Such disputes must be decided within fifteen days.[152] The Resident Grievance Officer of the SSMI is expected to oversee the dispute settlement mechanism under Rule 4(8).[153]

Despite the Intermediary Guidelines being in operation for more than a year, there is no evidence that SSMIs are complying with this notice and hearing requirement. One potential reason for this could be that the consequence of noncompliance with Rule 4(8), as with any provision of the Intermediary Guidelines, is a loss of safe harbor. In other words, failure to provide notice and hearing under Rule 4(8) could lead to a platform losing its immunity for hosting unlawful content. However, when a platform voluntarily removes content, it is *not* hosting this content and has removed unlawful content *prior* to when it is legally required to do so (i.e., prior to a court or government order). Therefore, it cannot be held secondarily liable for unlawful content and has few incentives to comply with the conditions necessary to avail of safe harbor. Thus, the loss of safe harbor flowing from a breach of Rule 4(8) may be inconsequential to an SSMI where it has already voluntarily decided to not host content.

In October 2022, the MEITY amended the Intermediary Guidelines to allow users to appeal against platform decisions to government-appointed Grievance Appellate Committee(s) (GACs).[154] On January 27, 2023, MEITY notified the establishment of three GACs in India,[155] which run completely online[156] and are face-less in their operation. Beyond the constitution of the three GACs, there isn't any other information in the public domain about their functioning or the decisions made by them.[157] According to Rule 3A(3), a user may appeal against any decision taken by a platform's Grievance Officer,[158] suggesting that a user can both appeal a platform's decision to remove content but also a platform's decision to *not* remove content in response to a user complaint. Appeals must be initiated within thirty days of being notified of the platform's decision,[159] and the GACs shall "endeavor" to decide the appeal within thirty days[160] pursuant to an online dispute resolution

[150] Intermediary Guidelines, Rule 4(8)(a).
[151] Intermediary Guidelines, Rule 4(8)(b).
[152] Intermediary Guidelines, Rule 4(8)(b).
[153] Intermediary Guidelines, Rule 4(8)(c).
[154] Intermediary Guidelines, Rule 3A.
[155] Establishment of Grievance Appellate Committees, Ministry of Electronics and Information Technology, Government of India, https://www.meity.gov.in/writereaddata/files/243258.pdf.
[156] Grievance Appellate Committee, Government of India, https://gac.gov.in/.
[157] On logging-in with an India based mobile number, the online portal does display the number of total appeals files and total appeals disposed of.
[158] Intermediary Guidelines, Rule 3A(3).
[159] Intermediary Guidelines, Rule 3A(3).
[160] Intermediary Guidelines, Rule 3A(4).

mechanism.[161] Each GAC shall consist of three members; two members shall be independent (but appointed by the Indian government), and one member shall be *ex-officio* (their membership of the GAC will be automatic by virtue of the office they hold).[162] GACs may seek assistance from any person having the requisite qualifications or experience in the subject matter being adjudicated.[163]

The creation of the GACs raises several concerns. First, it is unclear how the independence of GAC members will be secured. For example, selection by an independent body, disclosure of conflicts of interests, security of tenure and salary, and oath of office are some traditional methods to secure independence, but the Intermediary Guidelines do not provide for any of these safeguards in relation to the GACs.[164] Such independence is vital to protect the rule of law as the Indian government, or its instrumentalities, may be litigants before the GACs. Second, while the Intermediary Guidelines does contemplate more than one GAC, it is unclear how the GACs will deal with a large volume of appeals. Platforms make millions of moderation decisions every day and even if a small fraction of these are appealed to the GACs, it may create significant state capacity issues. Third, the Intermediary Guidelines do not expressly provide for basic due process safeguards with respect to the operation of the GACs, such as a notification to the person whose content is under dispute[165] or a written, reasoned order that is publicly available. Although there are three GACs currently in operation in India, beyond their constitution, there isn't any other information available about them in the public domain.

Finally, the Intermediary Guidelines (since October 2022) also require intermediaries to respect the constitutional rights of Indian citizens.[166] While an individual has sued to enforce his constitutional free speech rights against a platform's moderation decision (citing the platform's power over public speech), this case is still pending before the Delhi High Court.[167] Under current constitutional doctrine, Indian citizens may not enforce their constitutional free speech rights against private social media platforms.[168]

[161] Intermediary Guidelines, Rule 3A(6).

[162] Intermediary Guidelines, Rule 3A(2).

[163] Intermediary Guidelines, Rule 3A(5).

[164] Vasudev Devadasan & Bilal Mohamed, *Comments to the MEITY on the Proposed Draft for Amendment in Part-I and Part-II of the information Technology (Intermediary Guidelines and Digital Media Ethics Code) Rules, 2021* (2008), https://ccgdelhi.s3.ap-south-1.amazonaws.com/uploads/ccgnlud-comments-draftamendments-itrules2021–6jul22–301.pdf.

[165] *E.g.*, where User 1 complaints against User 2's content, the platform refuses to remove the content, and User 1 appeals to the GAC, the Intermediary Guidelines do not expressly require that User 1 be notified of the proceeding despite it being User 1's content (and consequently free speech rights) in dispute.

[166] Intermediary Guidelines, Rule 3(1)(n).

[167] Shravya Reddy, *Does Twitter Perform Public Functions? The Sanjay Hegde Case*, Bar and Bench (Nov. 13, 2020), https://www.barandbench.com/columns/does-twitter-perform-public-functions-the-sanjay-hegde-case (last visited Jan. 10, 2023).

[168] *See* Constitution of India (1950), art. 12; Ananth Padmanabhan, Rights: Breadth, Scope, and Applicability, Oxford Handbook on the Indian Constitution (Sujit Choudhry, Madhav Khosla

5.4.3 *Additional Obligations on SSMIs*

SSMIs are required to publish reports documenting their voluntary content moderation activities and responses to user complaints.[169] However, an analysis of these reports suggests they reveal more about the *scale* of platform moderation in India than they do about the *quality* of moderation.[170] SSMIs are also required to provide a user with a "demonstrable and visible mark of verification" (akin to Twitter's "blue-tick") if the user voluntarily verifies their account using "any appropriate mechanism" including an Indian mobile number.[171] Finally, as noted above, SSMIs are also required to appoint a Resident Grievance Officer and a Chief Compliance Officer, who are residents in India,[172] and a nodal contact person to facilitate coordination with law enforcement.[173] However, only the Chief Compliance Officer may be held personally liable.[174]

5.4.4 *Obligations on Messaging Platforms*

Rule 4(2) of the Intermediary Guidelines requires SSMIs that provide services "primarily in the nature of messaging" to "enable the identification of the first originator" of content on their platforms when directed by a court or an order passed under Section 69 of the IT Act ("power to issue directions for interception, monitoring, or decryption").[175] Where the first originator of unlawful content is located outside India, whomsoever is the first originator within India shall be deemed to be the first originator with respect to the content in question.[176]

An order directing the identification of an originator under Rule 4(2) may be passed for the purposes of (i) prevention, detection, investigation, prosecution or punishment of an offense and (ii) where such offense is related to the sovereignty, integrity, or security of the Indian State, its relation with foreign States, public order, or any offense relating to rape or sexually explicit material punishable by a prison term of five or more years.[177] Rule 4(2) further states that an identification order shall not be passed where a less intrusive means of identifying the first originator is effective[178] and that the SSMI shall not be required to disclose the contents of any

& Pratap Bhanu Mehta, eds. 2016). *Cf.* Kaushal Kishore v. State of Uttar Pradesh WP (Criminal) 113 of 2016, decided on January 3, 2023 (Supreme Court of India).

169 Intermediary Guidelines, Rule 4(1)(d).

170 Vasudev Devadasan, *Compliance Reports by Social Media Platforms Are Unhelpful*, MEDIANAMA (Apr. 18, 2022), https://www.medianama.com/2022/04/223-transparency-reports-social-media-platforms-unhelpful/ (last visited Feb. 18, 2023).

171 Intermediary Guidelines, Rule 4(7).

172 Intermediary Guidelines, Rules 4(1)(a), 4(1)(c).

173 Intermediary Guidelines, Rule 4(1)(b).

174 Intermediary Guidelines, Rule 4(1)(a).

175 Intermediary Guidelines, Rule 4(2).

176 Intermediary Guidelines, Rule 4(2) (fourth proviso).

177 Intermediary Guidelines, Rule 4(2) (first proviso).

178 Intermediary Guidelines, Rule 4(2) (second proviso).

message or any other information regarding the content originator or any information related to its other users.[179]

Critics of the Rule have pointed out that messaging platforms providing end-to-end-encrypted services cannot trace originators on their platform[180] and that this is beyond the scope of technical assistance platforms are required to provide law enforcement under Indian law.[181] Commentators have also argued that both the methods proposed for the implementation of this requirement (assigning hash values to every unique message and affixing encrypted originator information to messages)[182] are easily circumvented, require significant technical changes to the architecture of messaging services, offer limited investigatory or evidentiary value, and will likely undermine the privacy and security of all users to catch a few bad actors.[183] Facebook and WhatsApp have challenged the legality and constitutionality of Rule 4(2) in the Delhi High Court.[184] As discussed in Section 5.1, the central government has requested these challenges be transferred to the Supreme Court and heard alongside other challenges to the Intermediary Guidelines. Recently, the Indian government suggested that it may make use of Rule 4(2) to ask messaging platforms to identify the first originator of messages carrying deepfakes of Indian politicians. Government officials suggested that such videos could harm electoral integrity in India.[185] In another situation, the High Court of Tripura, the highest state level constitutional court, stayed the application of the Rule for identifying the originator behind the fake message related to the resignation of the Chief Minister of the state of Tripura.[186]

[179] Intermediary Guidelines, Rule 4(2) (third proviso).

[180] Aditi Agarwal, *Traceability and End-to-End Encryption Cannot Co-exist on Digital Messaging Platforms: Experts*, Forbes India (2021), https://www.forbesindia.com/article/take-one-big-story-of-the-day/traceability-and-endtoend-encryption-cannot-coexist-on-digital-messaging-platforms-experts/66969/1 (last visited Jan. 10, 2023).

[181] Vrinda Bhandari, Rishab Bailey & Faiza Rahman, *Backdoors to Encryption: Analysing an Intermediary's Duty to Provide "Technical Assistance,"* SSRN Journal (2021), https://www.ssrn.com/abstract=3805980 (last visited May 1, 2023).

[182] Aditi Agarwal, *supra* note 164; Aditi Agarwal, *Can Traceability and End-to-End Encryption Co-exist? Here's the Legal View*, Forbes India (2021), https://www.forbesindia.com/article/take-one-big-story-of-the-day/can-traceability-and-endtoend-encryption-coexist-heres-the-legal-view/67001/1 (last visited May 1, 2023).

[183] Gurshabad Grover, Tanaya Rajwade & Divyank Katira, *The Ministry and the Trace: Subverting End-To-End Encryption*, 14 NUJS Law Review (2021); Greg Nojeim & Namrata Maheshwari, *Encryption in India: Preserving the Online Engine of Privacy, Free Expression, Security, and Economic Growth*, 17 Indian Journal of Law and Technology 1 (2021).

[184] Facebook Inc. v. Union of India WP (C) 7281 of 2021 (High Court of Delhi); WhatsApp LLC v. Union of India WP (C) 7284 of 2021 (High Court of Delhi).

[185] Aarathi Ganesan, *Govt May Send WhatsApp Traceability Notice over Deepfakes of Politicians Circulating: Report* (Oct. 16, 2023). https://www.medianama.com/2023/10/223-govt-whatsapp-traceability-notice-deepfakes-politicians/ (last visited Feb. 18, 2024).

[186] *Id.*

6

The Last Breaths of Brazil's Marco Civil?

Artur Pericles L. Monteiro[*]

Platform governance and regulation have been salient political issues in Brazil for years, particularly as part of Congress' response to democratic threats posed by former President Bolsonaro. The question became even more important after the January 8, 2023, attempted insurrection in Brasília,[1] which many blame on social media.[2] This includes the newly installed Lula administration. In a letter read at the February 2023 UNESCO "Internet for Trust" global conference, the president, now in his third (nonconsecutive) term in office wrote that the attack on the nation's seats of power was "the culmination of a campaign, initiated much before, and that used, as ammunition, lies and disinformation," which "was nurtured, organized, and disseminated through several digital platforms and messaging apps."[3] The new administration has made platform regulation a policy priority, with regulatory and administrative pushes across the board.

Concerns have also been raised about platforms' decisions and the policy investment in the events preceding the 2022 elections and the January 8 attempted

* I am grateful to Jacqueline Abreu, Leonardo Rosa, Francisco Brito Cruz and Mariana G. Valente for feedback. I am also thankful to Joel Trachtman and Dominik Hofstetter for editing.

[1] Jack Nicas & André Spigariol, *In Brazil Capital, a Frenzied Mob Storms Congress*, New York Times (Jan. 8, 2023), https://www.nytimes.com/2023/01/08/world/americas/brazil-election-protests-bolsonaro.html.

[2] *See, e.g.*, Sérgio Spagnuolo, *Golpismo É Resultado Direto de Inércia Das Redes Sociais* [Coup Mentality Is the Direct Result of Social Media Inertia], Núcleo Jornalismo (Jan. 9, 2023), https://nucleo.jor.br/linhafina/2023-01-09-golpismo-e-resultado-direto-de-inercia-das-redes-sociais/; Constance Malleret, Dan Milmo & Alex Hern, *Pro-Bolsonaro Violence: Experts Highlight Role of Social Media Platforms*, Guardian (Jan. 9, 2023), https://www.theguardian.com/world/2023/jan/09/pro-bolsonaro-violence-social-media-platforms.

[3] Luiz Inácio Lula da Silva, *Letter from the President of the Republic to the Director General of UNESCO*, Presidência da República [Presidency of the Republic] (Feb. 22, 2023), https://www.gov.br/planalto/en/latest-news/letter-from-the-president-of-the-republic-to-the-director-general-of-unesco.

insurrection,[4] particularly given the parallels between the January 8th events in Brazil and the US attempted insurrection on January 6th, 2021, and the apparent disparity in treatment that each case received from providers such as Meta.[5]

It is clear Brazil has been a battleground where proposals for platform responsibility have been advanced – and disputed. This chapter seeks to provide an overview of existing and proposed frameworks and of recent developments that have been testing the established consensus about related law and policy in Brazil.

6.1 THE CURRENT OVERARCHING FRAMEWORK: MARCO CIVIL DA INTERNET

Marco Civil da Internet (Marco Civil), often referred to as the Brazilian internet bill of rights,[6] is the main legislation defining platform responsibility. While the nickname might suggest otherwise, Marco Civil is an ordinary statute: law no. 12 965/2014.[7] Its drafting process, however, was anything but ordinary, following a years-long public consultation held online by the Ministry of Justice, which itself made use of the internet to gather comments and input from numerous civil society organizations and academics.[8] Marco Civil was the result of a complex political

[4] Meta's Oversight Board decided on a case that concerned the January 8th events, ruling to "overturn[] Meta's original decision to leave up a Facebook video which features a Brazilian general calling people to 'hit the streets,' and 'go to the National Congress and the Supreme Court.'" *See Brazilian General's Speech (Case 2023-001-FB-UA)*, OVERSIGHT BOARD.

[5] "Almost three months from January 8th, Meta has told us very little about its actions in advance of the attempted insurrection. In fact, we can't say for certain even what the policy was and when. As criticized as Meta's involvement and response to the Jan. 6[,] 2021 insurrection in Washington, D.C., was, the reaction and publicly-available information on the events in Brasília don't compare." Artur Pericles Lima Monteiro, *Public Comment on Case 2023-001-FB-UA, on Brazil's Election and Attempted Insurrection*, OVERSIGHT BOARD, 1 (Mar. 23, 2023), https://osbcontent.s3.eu-west-1.amazonaws.com/PC-11022.pdf. *See Id.*, 2–4 (noting Meta made substantial policy changes in response to the US crisis, including changes to design and content ranking, and senior executives, including CEO Mark Zuckerberg, were in involved in announcements, whereas in Brazil the company there as a lack of public communication and no comparable policy changes).

[6] *See, e.g.*, Carlos Affonso Souza, Fabro Steibel & Ronaldo Lemos, *Notes on the Creation and Impacts of Brazil's Internet Bill of Rights*, 5 THEORY & PRAC. LEGIS. 1 (2017).

[7] An unofficial English translation of Marco Civil da Internet was published by the Brazilian House of Representatives: THE BRAZILIAN CIVIL FRAMEWORK OF THE INTERNET (Fernanda Belotti Alice trans., 2016), https://bd.camara.leg.br/bd/bitstream/handle/bdcamara/26819/bazilian_frame-work_%20internet.pdf.

[8] *See* Carolina Rossini, Francisco de Brito Cruz & Danilo Doneda, *THE STRENGTHS AND WEAKNESSES OF THE BRAZILIAN INTERNET BILL OF RIGHTS: EXAMINING A HUMAN RIGHTS FRAMEWORK FOR THE INTERNET*, 3–5 (2015), https://www.cigionline.org/sites/default/files/no19_0.pdf (describing the lead-up to Marco Civil and the public consultation); Francisco Carvalho de Brito Cruz, *Direito, Democracia e Cultura Digital: A Experiência de Elaboração Legislativa Do Marco Civil Da Internet* [Law, Democracy, and Digital Culture: The Experience of the Legislative Drafting of Marco Civil da Internet] (2015) (MSc dissertation, University of São Paulo) (on file with the University of São Paulo) (discussing the drafting of Marco Civil from a

process, which included strong opposition from telecommunication companies, broadcasters and copyright holders, and law enforcement officials.[9] It managed to overcome that formidable resistance and was picked up with renewed energy after the Snowden revelations showed President Dilma Rousseff was a target of surveillance by US agencies.[10] Partly because of this unusual constellation of engagement and participation from a wide range of sectors in Brazilian society, Marco Civil has been regarded as if possessing a distinct *political* status.[11] Proposals for amending the statute are often met with concern with perturbing the viable consensus codified into law by Marco Civil.[12]

Under Marco Civil, platforms, like other internet application providers,[13] are only liable for user-generated content if they fail to comply with a court order directing them to make the content unavailable. This was a response to prior case law, which reformers saw as incentivizing removal of content whenever a notice was served. Introduced in the second round of public consultations on the draft bill (i.e., before the bill was introduced in Congress), this safe harbor went beyond the notice-and-takedown model that had been featured in the draft,[14] itself a departure from a more

policy perspective) (in Portuguese); Paulo Rená da Silva Santarém, *O Direito Achado Na Rede: A Emergência Do Acesso à Internet Como Direito Fundamental No Brasil* (2010) (MSc dissertation, University of Brasília) (on file with the University of Brasília) (describing the background, the drafting process and how the public consultation took place).

9 "Telecommunication companies fiercely attacked the net neutrality provisions; broadcasters lobbied against any change that could amount to making copyright more flexible; and public authorities lobbied for longer data retention periods and reduced safeguards and controls in their access to users' data." Luiz Fernando Marrey Moncau & Diego Werneck Arguelhes, The Marco Civil Da Internet and Digital Constitutionalism, in The Oxford Handbook of Online Intermediary Liability 189, 197 (Giancarlo Frosio, ed. 2020).

10 Souza, Steibel & Lemos, *supra* note 6, at 11–12; Moncau & Arguelhes, *supra* note 9, at 197.

11 *See, e.g.*, Nicolo Zingales, *The Brazilian Approach to Internet Intermediary Liability: Blueprint for a Global Regime?*, 4 Internet Pol'y Rev. 1, 7 (2015), http://policyreview.info/articles/analysis/brazilian-approach-internet-intermediary-liability-blueprint-global-regime (emphasis added): "the Marco Civil is known as a 'constitution for the internet' in light of its focus on fundamental rights .... While the prioritisation of fundamental rights is not enshrined in a document with force superior to that of ordinary legislation, as it is usually the case for national constitutions, the fact that the amendment of the Marco Civil does not require a reinforced procedure is of secondary importance for our purposes: *the symbolic value of this law is enormous*[.]"

12 Rossini, Cruz, & Doneda, *supra* note 8, at 7 (citation omitted): "Although there were compromises, the final approved text was mostly the product of the public, multi-stakeholder consultation process. Most – although perhaps not all – stakeholders saw it as a uniquely legitimate piece of law."

13 Art. 5, VII, Marco Civil, defines internet applications as "a set of functionalities which are accessible by a terminal connected to the internet." *Contrast* internet application providers with internet service providers, which fall under the definition in art. 5, V, for "internet connection": "enabling a terminal to send and receive packets over the internet, by the assignment or authentication of an IP address."

14 Souza, Steibel, & Lemos, *supra* note 6, at 10–11 (noting that the safe harbor was introduced at the second round of public consultations).

stringent liability favored in some cases[15] and often regarded as flowing from tort law in Brazil.[16] Under art. 19 of Marco Civil, upon service of "a specific court order," an internet application provider is required to "take the steps" to make the content unavailable, "within the scope and technical limits of its service." Such court orders must include "clear and specific identification" (art. 19, § 2, Marco Civil), which the Superior Court of Justice has interpreted as requiring that plaintiffs provide URLs (uniform resource locators).[17]

There are two carve-outs to this judicial safe harbor in Marco Civil itself: copyright claims and nonconsensual intimate content. Nonconsensual intimate content operates under a notice-and-takedown model, though one provided explicitly by Marco Civil. Internet application providers are liable for harms resulting from such content if they fail to diligently make it unavailable "within the scope and technical limits of its service," as provided by art. 21, Marco Civil, which also requires the notice to include information that enables the "specific identification" of the infringing content, in addition to verification that the request is legitimate (i.e., is made, or authorized, by the victim).

Copyright claims were excluded from the general framework established in art. 19 to overcome the gridlock blocking Marco Civil from advancing in Congress because of intense lobbying from copyright holders.[18] As Marco Civil was debated around the same time copyright reform was a hot topic, the applicable regime was deferred to a later time. That reform never came, however, so the interim rule included in Marco Civil applies to this day. Under art. 31, liability for copyright infringement resulting from user-generated content follows the Copyright Act (law no. 9.610/1998). Courts have still not settled on what the 1998 statute entails for online intermediaries but have leaned toward "the adoption of a notice-and-takedown regime for copyright infringement, following the model established in the United States by the Digital Millennium Copyright Act and in Europe by the e-Commerce Directive."[19]

Marco Civil seemed stable for many years, despite the fact that the Supreme Court had a dormant challenge in its docket since 2017.[20] After the events of January 8, 2023, however, the Supreme Court twice announced a date for ruling

[15] Moncau & Arguelhes, *supra* note 9, at 193–95 (summarizing those cases as endorsing "a common rationale: internet platforms should bear the full risks of illegal activities by their users").

[16] Anderson Schreiber, *Civil Rights Framework of the Internet (BCRFI; Marco Civil Da Internet): Advance or Setback? Civil Liability for Damage Derived from Content Generated by Third Party*, in Personality and Data Protection Rights on the Internet 241, 249 (Marion Albers & Ingo Wolfgang Sarlet, eds. 2022) (describing "the theory of notice and takedown" as departing from "the Brazilian civil liability system").

[17] Clara Iglesias Keller, *Policy by Judicialisation: The Institutional Framework for Intermediary Liability in Brazil*, 1 Int'l Rev. L., Comput. Tech. 11 (2020).

[18] Souza, Steibel, & Lemos, *supra* note 6, at 13.

[19] Moncau & Arguelhes, *supra* note 9, at 200.

[20] S.T.F., Recurso Extraordinário No.1037396, Relator: Min. Dias Toffoli.

on the challenge. As of December 2023, the case is still pending, but many expect that the justices would invalidate or at least significantly reduce protections for providers. This creates pressure for Congress to pass legislation before the Court takes the question of platform governance for itself.

6.2 LIABILITY BEYOND MARCO CIVIL

Marco Civil governs civil liability for user-generated content and on its own terms does not cover other kinds of liability, such as criminal liability. Generally, failure to comply with a court order can lead to charges for noncompliance with a legal order issued by an official (including a court), which, under art. 330 of the Criminal Code, is punishable with imprisonment of up to six months. Prosecution for noncompliance with removal orders is rare. In 2012, a Google executive was arrested in connection with an order to take down a YouTube video,[21] but this was before Marco Civil went into effect. Noncompliance charges when platforms fail to provide data requested by courts are not unheard of, but also not common. A Facebook vice president was held in custody for about twenty-four hours in 2016 when WhatsApp did not provide data a court was seeking.[22]

In general, criminal legislation does not specify liability for online intermediaries or platforms, but scienter requirements applicable to most criminal offenses in Brazil prevent providers from being held liable for criminal content shared by third parties. Child safety legislation does establish a regime for provider liability for child sexual abuse material (CSAM), adopting a notice-and-takedown regime.[23] "In practice, this means that service providers must respond to takedown notices to avoid criminal liability under [*child safety legislation*]."[24]

6.2.1 *Electoral Law*

Electoral law was also interpreted as not directly affected by Marco Civil, and indeed even after its entry into force electoral courts in Brazil sometimes held providers liable for infringements upon notice served by the affected person, party, or coalition.[25] This was both the result of interpreting electoral legislation and of courts

[21] T. C. Sottek, *Google Executive Arrested in Brazil as the Company Resists Orders to Freeze Political Speech on YouTube*, THE VERGE (Sept. 26, 2012), https://www.theverge.com/2012/9/26/3413476/google-brazil-you-tube-arrest.

[22] Brad Haynes, *Facebook Executive Jailed in Brazil as Court Seeks WhatsApp Data*, REUTERS (Mar. 1, 2016), https://www.reuters.com/article/us-facebook-brazil-idUSKCN0W34WF.

[23] *See* art. 241-A of law no. 8.069/1990, the main act for the protection of minors in Brazil.

[24] Moncau & Arguelhes, *supra* note 9, at 201.

[25] Francisco Brito Cruz, Novo Jogo & Velhas Regras 337–39 (2019) (describing the disputes surrounding intermediary liability for electoral law infringements).

issuing regulation.[26] More recently, however, both electoral legislation and its regulation have been adjusted to follow the judicial safe harbor found in Marco Civil.[27]

6.2.1.1 The 2022 Elections and Eleventh-hour Changes

In the most recent presidential elections, while that model was kept in place, the Superior Electoral Court enacted a resolution after the first round and just ten days before the runoff, which it described as aiming to bring more effectiveness to combating electoral dis- and misinformation. When proposing the resolution, Justice Alexandre de Moraes, who had taken office as the court's president in late August 2022, cited a 47 percent increase in "disinformation reports sent to digital platforms" in the twelve days following the first round.[28]

Under resolution no. 23714/2022 (art. 2), "platforms"[29] are required to take down content within two hours when so ordered by the Superior Electoral Court; noncompliance triggers substantial fines (up to 150,000 Brazilian Reais – over 100 times the minimum wage). The same rules apply for takedown orders against accounts and channels found to be engaged in "systematic generation of disinformation," defined as "persistent publication of false or decontextualized information" (art. 4). Previously, orders had to be complied within twenty-four hours, unless exceptional circumstances warranted a tighter deadline (art. 38, § 4, resolution no. 23610/2019). The president of the Superior Electoral Court was also given authority to act *sua sponte*. Under art. 3 of resolution no. 23714/2022, the president can issue removal orders for any content found to be identical to content previously ruled illegal by the Court. Further, the president is empowered to order the temporary ban (for up to twenty-four hours) of a platform after "repeated noncompliance" (art. 5) with orders on the basis of the resolution.

Records of proceedings based on resolution no. 23714/2022 have been sealed, so a full accounting of its impact cannot be established as of now. A few non-sealed records show that a department within the electoral court, AEED (Assessoria Especial de Enfrentamento à Desinformação, roughly the Special Unit for

26 Under the Brazilian Constitution, electoral courts in Brazil discharge "all powers related to the electoral process": "in addition to deciding electoral cases and controversies (rule adjudication), the electoral justice system organises all elections in Brazil (rule application) and has broad regulatory powers (rulemaking)." Virgílio Afonso da Silva, The Constitution of Brazil: A Contextual Analysis 72 (2019).

27 Francisco Brito Cruz et al., Direito Digital Na Era Eleitoral 112 (2017) (noting that as of 2017 the Marco Civil model was adopted by electoral legislation).

28 T.S.E., Processo Administrativo No. 0601570-94.2022.6.00.0000, Relator: Min. Alexandre de Moraes, 20.10.2022, 3, Diário da Justiça Eletrônico (Tribunal Superior Eleitoral) [D.J.E. (T.S.E.), 24.10.2022.

29 The resolution does not define "platforms." Telegram, a messaging app, received an order on the basis of the resolution, as did Facebook, Instagram, Twitter, YouTube, WhatsApp, Gettr, Kwai, and LinkedIn.

Combatting Disinformation), was charged with social media monitoring and presenting the president with a proposal for action under the resolution. In late October 2022, before the runoff, the department compiled a list of over 200 links to social media posts (on Facebook, Instagram, Kwai, Telegram, TikTok, Twitter, and YouTube), grouped under "narratives" (e.g., "unspecified or generalized fraud," or "video points to 55% of the vote for one of the candidates and claims TSE mistake"), alongside engagement figures for the content and the following count for the account. Justice de Moraes issued an order for the removal of only part of the list prepared by the department, 135 URLs in total, which either garnered more than 500 engagements or were posted by users with followings larger than 5,000. In an indication of what the president interpreted as "identical content" for the purposes of art. 3 authority to issue *sua sponte* removal orders – such order suggests it need not be the same material (i.e. video, image, or text), and perhaps not even the same allegations previously adjudicated by the Court.[30] A different report submitted by the AEED instead emphasized that content listed for removal reproduced in total or in part adjudicated as illegal in two full-court cases it specified. Justice Moraes agreed and issued the order.[31]

It is unclear how long the Court sees the resolution to be in effect. Initially, it looked like the regulation would be in force only for the 2022 elections. After the election results were announced, and as Bolsonaro supporters blocked roads in an effort to prevent Lula from being certified as the president-elect, the AEED submitted a report showing a member of Congress' lower chamber, Carla Zambelli, using social media to commend truck drivers who blocked major highways and to reshare videos of road blocks. This led to an order for the blocking of her social media accounts, which was followed by a further order directed at dozens of other accounts that had, according to the Court's finding, shared like content supporting Zambelli. This last order included at least two accounts (with substantial followings) that shared Zambelli's content to express their disapproval of her conduct. One such user had been tweeting his support for the Court's takedown decisions and criticism against Zambelli and Bolsonaro. Another user used his display name on Twitter to announce his vote for Lula. The Court eventually rescinded the order against these accounts in February 2023; the restriction was in effect for three months.[32]

It is still early to assess the impact of these eleventh-hour changes to electoral regulation, and a full accounting might not be possible. The Superior Electoral Court has rejected access to information requests, even on general enforcement figures, placed by the media.[33] We know of at least four orders issued by the

[30] T.S.E., Petição No. 0601776-11.2022.6.00.0000, Relator: Min. Alexandre de Moraes.
[31] T.S.E., Petição No. 0601772-71.2022.6.00.0000, Relator: Min. Alexandre de Moraes..
[32] T.S.E., Petição No. 0601843-73.2022.6.00.0000, Relator: Min. Alexandre de Moraes.
[33] Cf. Renata Galf, *TSE Alega Segredo e Nega Dados Sobre Regra Que Ampliou Seus Poderes Antes Do 2° Turno* [TSE Mentions Classified Information and Denies Data On Rule That Expanded Its Powers Ahead Of Runoff], FOLHA DE S.PAULO (Nov. 12, 2023), https://www1.folha

president of the Superior Electoral Court citing the new resolution as a basis; these orders included content and account takedowns with the two-hour deadline; there have been no reports of temporary platform bans grounded on resolution 23.714/2022. A constitutional challenge filed by the prosecutor-general had a request for stay denied by the Supreme Court, in a 9-2 vote; majority opinions emphasized a need to show deference to the Superior Electoral Court and the importance of curbing electoral disinformation.[34]

6.3 UNCHARTED WATERS: THE LAW OF CONTENT MODERATION

Marco Civil did not address one of the most important questions for platform responsibility today: content moderation. Although it does provide safe harbor from civil liability arising from user-generated content, Marco Civil was not designed to regulate decisions platforms make when removing, restricting, labeling, or deciding not to act on content. Content moderation was not a primary concern in the drafting of Marco Civil; what drove the adoption of the intermediary immunity regime established in art. 19 of the statute was the risk that platforms would be forced to remove content to avoid costly damages awards being entered against them by courts not too protective of freedom of expression.[35]

This makes sense given that the 2014 Marco Civil was enacted prior to the turn toward platform responsibility and away from intermediary liability as the theoretical framework and regulatory toolkit favored by policymakers since 2015.[36] As attention to the impact of content moderation has grown, however, Marco Civil has had little to say. The focus on liability has meant it "provides no scrutiny over the vast majority

.uol.com.br/poder/2023/11/tse-alega-segredo-de-justica-e-nega-dados-1-ano-apos-eleicao-sobre-regra-que-ampliou-poderes.shtml (reporting on the denial of access to information request filed by the reporter and quoting legal experts who criticized the denial and questioned its legality).

34 *See* S.T.F., Referendo da Medida Cautelar na Ação Direta de Inconstitucionalidade No. 7.261, Relator: Min. Edson Fachin, 26.10.2022, Diário da Justiça [D.J. 23.11.2022].

35 Artur Pericles Lima Monteiro et al., *Armadilhas e Caminhos na Regulação da Moderação de Conteúdo* [Pitfalls and Paths in Regulating Content Moderation], InternetLab 8 (2021), https://www.internetlab.org.br/pt/liberdade-de-expressao/armadilhas-caminhos-moderacao/; Bruna Martins dos Santos, *An Assessment of the Role of Marco Civil's Intermediary Liability Regime for the Development of the Internet in Brazil*, Internet Society, Brazil Chapter 27 (2020), https://isoc.org.br//files/Study_on_the_Marco_Civil.pdf ("Marco Civil's focus was on the issue of the moderation of third-party content and not on the autonomous decisions made by applications *vis-à-vis* such content or user behavior in general.").

36 Giancarlo F. Frosio, *Why Keep a Dog and Bark Yourself? From Intermediary Liability to Responsibility*, 26 Int'l J.L. Info. Tech. 1, 32 (2018) ("Intermediary responsibility has become the latest trend in online governance. Terminologically first, it is slowly displacing the notion of intermediary liability. Responsibility of intermediaries is all over the literature and a powerful slogan for policy-makers.").

of online content related disputes,"[37] which are not brought before courts. Clara Keller, a Brazilian scholar, believes this shows how the celebrated internet bill of rights is insufficient, as it lacks mechanisms "to assure a responsive, transparent and human rights aware governance framework."[38]

In fact, what Marco Civil's silence means for content moderation has been contested. Most have pointed to debates in the public consultation and to legislative history as clearly establishing that its intermediary liability regime should be read only as a rejection of a notice-and-takedown model and therefore not as preventing providers from engaging in content moderation.[39]

Prior to 2021, this seemed like the settled interpretation of the law. Yet, in 2021, then-President Bolsonaro adopted provisional legislation[40] that endorsed the opposite interpretation. Enacted on the eve of Brazil's Independence Day, when protests endorsed by the president included calls for ousting and arresting members of the Supreme Court, the legislation dragged content moderation regulation to the center of the political crisis in the country.[41] The explanatory memorandum to the provisional legislation, MP 1068/2021 (which would have amended Marco Civil), advanced the notion that under Marco Civil much of content moderation was illegal because it violated users' free speech rights. The provisional legislation required social media to limit content moderation to a specified list of illegal content, which notably did not include misinformation.[42] The provisional legislation was quickly rejected by Congress, without ever being advanced to a vote, on the

[37] Keller, *supra* note 17, at 13.

[38] *Id.*

[39] SANTOS, *supra* note 34, at 9 ("The absence of specific provisions with respect to the development of content moderation rules by the providers of Internet applications themselves also indicates that the removal of content is not restricted to the existence of a judicial order, and the provider may remove content that deliberately breaches its policies and terms of use"); Keller, *supra* note 17, at 12 (noting under Marco Civil providers "are free to apply their product policies through content moderation, i.e. according to their criteria").

[40] Under the Brazilian Constitution, the president has the authority to issue provisional measures, which are equivalent to statutory law, go into effect immediately, and are then reviewed by Congress. *See* AFONSO DA SILVA, *supra* note 26, at 220–21. Provisional measures cease to have effect if Congress fails to review them within 60 days (this period may be extended once). In that case, Congress may pass a resolution regulating the effects of that implicit repeal during the period it was effective; if Congress fails to pass such a resolution, the provisional measure applies to facts during its effective period.

[41] *See* Artur Pericles Lima Monteiro, *Brazilians Are Desperately Fighting Against Bolsonaro's Digital Tactics*, REST OF WORLD (Dec. 2, 2021), https://restofworld.org/2021/brazil-bolsonaro-social-media/; Artur Pericles Lima Monteiro, Como Não Regular a Moderação de Conteúdo: Lições de Uma Tentativa Fracassada [How Not To Regulate Content Moderation: Lessons From A Failed Attempt], Liberdade de Expressão: Um Conceito em Disputa [Freedom of Expression: A Disputed Concept] 18 (2022).

[42] For a translation of the now-repealed provisional legislation, Artur Pericles Lima Monteiro, *Unofficial English Translation of Brazilian Provisional Measure 1068, on Content Moderation* (2021) (unpublished), https://dx.doi.org/10.2139/ssrn.3922992.

same night when the Supreme Court enjoined its enforcement.[43] Yet other courts have held that Marco Civil precludes content moderation of lawful speech.

Even if that interpretation that outright bars content moderation is rejected, what rights users have against platforms when their content is removed or otherwise restricted is far from a settled question. In contrast to US First Amendment doctrine, which (at least prior to the *NetChoice* cases) is generally regarded as granting editorial rights to platforms,[44] and to an expansive view of the Communications Decency Act that immunizes platforms from content moderation decisions generally,[45] under Brazilian law it would be unusual to claim that platforms have free speech rights – trumping those of users. This is particularly true given that the Brazilian legal system is generally understood to recognize that constitutional rights apply horizontally, that is, between individuals and other persons, not just against the state.[46] Marco Civil itself is evidence that users hold rights, potentially constitutional rights, against providers abridging their freedom of speech or violating their privacy; contractual provisions infringing on such rights are "null and void" under art. 8.[47]

The scope and extent of users' rights against platforms are not defined; one possibility would be to view those rights as equivalent to those individuals hold against the state.[48] This was arguably the view behind the provisional legislation

[43] *See* Jack Nicas, *Bolsonaro's Ban on Removing Social Media Posts Is Overturned in Brazil*, The New York Times (Sept. 9, 2021), https://www.nytimes.com/2021/09/15/world/americas/brazil-bolsonaro-social-media-ban.html; *See* Monteiro, *How Not To Regulate Content Moderation*, *supra* note 41, for a discussion of the grounds adopted by Congress and the Supreme Court in holding the provisional legislation unconstitutional. A bill with the same language the provisional legislation was introduced by the then President shortly thereafter and has seen little movement in Congress since.

[44] *See* Daphne Keller, Who Do You Sue? State and Platform Hybrid Power over Online Speech 17 (2019), https://www.lawfareblog.com/who-do-you-sue-state-and-platform-hybrid-power-over-online-speech (noting that First Amendment rights arguments have "carried the day for platforms in a number of recent cases"). Ashutosh Bhagwat, *Do Platforms Have Editorial Rights?*, 1 J. Free Speech L. 97, 137–38 (2021) (concluding that "under both extant doctrine and first principles, social media firms should be entitled to significant First Amendment 'editorial rights' to control the content that is carried and highlighted on their platforms").

[45] Danielle Keats Citron & Benjamin Wittes, *The Internet Will Not Break: Denying Bad Samaritans § 230 Immunity*, 86 Fordham L. Rev. 401 (2017) (describing the development of the case law, criticizing the immunity as too broad, and advancing language restricting it to "Good Samaritans").

[46] *See* Afonso da Silva, *supra* note 26, at 116 (discussing the "horizontal effects of fundamental rights" in Brazil).

[47] Indeed, before choosing provisional legislation as the instrument for his attempt at regulating content moderation, former President Bolsonaro considered issuing an executive order establishing a similar regime by way of interpreting art. 8 of Marco Civil. *See* Exposição de Motivos Interministerial No. 30/2021 [Interministerial Explanatory Memorandum No. 30/2021], para. 8.

[48] Moncau & Arguelhes, *supra* note 9, at 210 ("While the MCI states that freedom of expression will be protected online, it does not explicitly state that private parties must respect internet users' freedom of expression to the same extent that state actors are bound. However, in article 19 the MCI seems to at least hint in that direction.").

issued by President Bolsonaro – although the provisional legislation did not conform to constitutional limits on speech regulation,[49] employed vague and imprecise concepts,[50] and would have had the effect of co-opting platforms "to stay on the government's good side."[51] A second possibility would be to try to reconcile users' rights with platforms' by admitting that platforms enact (and enforce) their own content policies and grant users due process rights, with judicial review of the justification offered by platforms for content moderation decisions.[52] A third possibility would look beyond fairness in content moderation and to constrain the latitude platforms have in establishing their content policies to restrict protected speech. Court cases where users seek to have their content or accounts reinstated – and prevail on their claims – are common,[53] yet case law has so far not articulated a theory of users' free speech rights against platforms, a question that is ordinarily left unaddressed.

6.3.1 *Regulating Content Moderation with Consumer Law*

Courts often rely on consumer protection law when deciding content moderation cases. Consumer protection has a wide scope in Brazilian law. Especially after the enactment of the 1990 Consumer Protection Code (CDC, after "Código de Defesa do Consumidor," law no. 8078/1990), consumer protection had a transformative impact in the legal system, affecting much of private law, as well as other areas of

49 *See* Monteiro et al., *Pitfalls and Paths in Regulating Content Moderation*, supra note 35, at 20 (arguing that carveouts in the provisional legislation that impermissibly disfavored protected speech, such as nudity).

50 *See* Monteiro, *How Not To Regulate Content Moderation, supra* note 41, at 21–23 (arguing that vagueness in the categories of content that the provisional legislation specified as eligible for content moderation violated applicable freedom of expression law, and would fail the legality test for free speech violations under the American Convention on Human Rights as interpreted by the Inter-American Court of Human Rights).

51 Monteiro, *Brazilians Are Desperately Fighting Against Bolsonaro's Digital Tactics, supra* note 41. "Bolsonaro's legislation entrusted the executive with oversight and enforcement. Considering how vague and controversial the categories of content listed under the legislation were, it would effectively enable the government to co-opt social media." *Id.* (also noting Bolsonaro's record of attempting to prosecute his critics).

52 Matthias C. Kettemann & Anna Sophia Tiedeke, *Back up: Can Users Sue Platforms to Reinstate Deleted Content?*, 9 Internet Pol'y Rev. 11 (2020) (discussing incipient German case law recognizing platform "house rules" including resulting in content removal, provided that "deletion is not performed arbitrarily, and users are not barred from the service without recourse.").

53 *See* Laís Martins, Renata Hirota & Samira Menezes, *Número de Processos Judiciais Envolvendo Redes Dispara Em 2020* [Number of Judicial Cases Involving Platforms Skyrockets In 2020], Núcleo Jornalismo (Sept. 9, 2021), https://www.nucleo.jor.br/reportagem/2021-09-30-redes-sociais-processos-justica-aumento/ (reporting on data obtained through freedom of information requests showing that, in 2020, there were at least 4,100 proceedings where Facebook, Instagram, Whatsapp, Twitter and, Telegram stand as defendants; note that the cases need not be about content moderation).

the law.[54] Consumer protection modifies the application of ordinary legal concepts and provisions, working from the premise that contract law, for example, should apply differently given the highly asymmetrical character of the relationship between a consumer and a provider of (consumer) goods and services. Given that this asymmetry can also be said to be present in the relationship between users and platforms, and considering that Brazilian courts have long held that consumer protection law should apply even for services nominally provided free of charge, it is no surprise that courts have turned to the CDC to adjudicate claims against platforms.

Consumer protection has recently also opened a new avenue for probing content regulation in court. Prosecutors are allowed to bring consumer protection claims, including class actions. A civil investigation often precedes the filing of such claims. In November 2021, a federal prosecutor in Brazil started an investigation into the content moderation practices of Facebook, Instagram, Telegram, TikTok, Twitter, and YouTube, citing misinformation and online violence. The investigation has served subpoenas to the companies for information on their content policies and enforcement mechanisms, including the number of employees working with Brazilian users.[55]

The theory behind the investigation seems to be that platforms are legally liable for harms resulting from insufficient measures to prevent misinformation, particularly COVID-related, and violence online, as that violates users' consumer-protection rights to accurate information and to safety. The prosecutor states this liability would not be covered by the Marco Civil safe harbor given that such measures are incumbent on platforms themselves and do not implicate liability for losses resulting from user-generated content. Although, as noted, Marco Civil has been interpreted as not regulating content moderation, the prosecutor has suggested that the "lack of a minimal content moderation policy" likely "violates constitutional rights." This reading of the law has yet to be tested in court. Invoking consumer protection legislation would entail that consumer protection agencies would have authority over platform content governance. Such agencies often have no insulation from the executive; the head of the federal agency serves at the pleasure of the president.

6.3.2 *School Shootings and Executive Branch Regulation*

Indeed, this was the state of affairs in early 2023, when the then justice minister announced regulation to respond to an outbreak of school shootings,[56] relying on the Consumer Protection Code. Under portaria 351/2023, the consumer protection

[54] For a discussion of consumer protection law and contract law, see Ronaldo Porto Macedo, *Relational Consumer Contracts: New Challenges for Brazilian Consumer Law*, 12 Soc. & Legal Stud. 27, 32–35 (2003).

[55] See Ministério Público Federal [M.P.F.], Inquérito Civil Público 1.34.001.009969/2021-35.

[56] *See* Laís Martins & Collin Binkley, *Brazil's School Violence Mirrors US. Its Reaction Doesn't*, Reuters (Apr. 23, 2023), https://apnews.com/article/brazil-school-violence-guns-attacks-us-51832f5663d9f7e9591d660cce086205b.

department of the justice ministry is empowered to start administrative proceedings against "social media platforms" (a term not defined in the regulation) for failing to uphold a "general duty of safety and care with regard to the dissemination of illicit, harmful and deleterious content, regarding content that encourages attacks against the school environment or conveys apology or incitement to such crimes or their perpetrators" (art. 2). It can request that platforms provide information on their efforts to tackle such content (art. 3), as well as reports on the assessment and mitigation of systemic risks (art 4). In "extraordinary circumstances," the ministry can itself order platforms to adopt "crisis protocols" (art. 7). Additionally, the regulation also creates a database of such illegal content and notes that hashes may be generated to help in the identification of infringing content (art. 6). Such database was to be managed by the department of public safety, which was also given authority to "advise" platforms to block IP addresses to prevent the creation of new accounts with the same IP address "where previous illegal activity" was identified (art. 5, § 2).

The new regulation on school violence prompted criticism, including from the prosecutor overseeing the civil investigation into platforms.[57] In Congress, members of the opposition introduced a resolution (projeto de decreto legislativo 122/2023) that would rescind the order as *ultra vires*. The concern voiced by different actors is that the regulation would allow the government to order content takedowns and regulate platforms directly. That is generally disallowed under art. 19 of Marco Civil (which requires "a specific court order" for content restrictions). The ministry sidesteps that by relying on consumer protection legislation as a source of administrative law authority; again, Marco Civil textually governs *civil* liability for user-generated content.

The regulation also raises further concerns with this mode of platform regulation: lack of transparency in platform–government engagement. Almost a year after the regulation was passed, the government still has not issued any reports or provided data on how it used its newly established regulatory authorities. Any access to information requests were denied access to the systemic risk assessment reports prepared by the companies and to what sort of information the government directed companies to provide under art. 3 of the regulation.[58] Access to case documents was also denied.

The limited information produced in response to the access to information request suggests that the government did not make full use of the authorities created by the regulation – even though that does not say much about its engagement with the platforms, which was kept confidential. The government responded that it had started proceedings against Meta, Google, Twitter, Telegram, Bytedance, and Kwai. It also stated that it had not created the hash database under art. 6, while it had requested the removal of "hundreds of publications, accounts, [and] channels" and

[57] *See* Isabela Cruz, A *Responsabilidade Das Redes Diante de Ataques Em Escolas* [Social Networks' Responsibility in the Face of School Attacks], Nexo (Apr. 13, 2023), https://www.nexojornal.com.br/expresso/2023/04/13/A-responsabilidade-das-redes-diante-de-ataques-em-escolas (news article quoting federal prosecutor Yuri Luz).

[58] Decisão do Ministro nº 205/2023 [Minister Decision No. 205/2023].

shared with platforms "a list of hashtags and the most commonly used images by suspects so that [platforms] could attempt to automate filtering." The government also said that it had not advised platforms to block user IP address under art. 5, § 2, nor had it created the hash database established by art. 6.

6.4 SCOPE AND JURISDICTIONAL QUESTIONS

Another important point for platform responsibility that is also unsettled concerns territorial and extraterritorial scope. The relevant provision of Marco Civil is the subject of an ongoing dispute. It states that any data processing operation shall comply "with Brazilian legislation and the rights to privacy, to personal data protection, and to the confidentiality of private communication and of records" (art. 11, *caput*, Marco Civil). A further provision specifies that this applies to providers not incorporated in Brazil if they "offer services to the Brazilian public or at least one entity in the same business conglomerate is established in Brazil" (art. 11, § 2, Marco Civil). There are two contrasting views on what this entails for overseas providers, one more expansionist, the other more restrictive.

The more expansionist interpretation of the scope of Marco Civil featured in a recent high-stakes case, which led to an order for blocking access to Telegram nationwide, which was rescinded before it was implemented. Supreme Court justice Alexandre de Moraes had been unsuccessful in serving the app with orders directing it to disable accounts and remove content from public channels and to provide data related to the accounts. The accounts belonged to supporters of President Bolsonaro who are the targets of an investigation, opened by the Supreme Court itself, looking into a possible conspiracy to defame members of the Court and organize attempts to have them forcibly removed. Authorities elsewhere had likewise failed to reach Telegram, informally or through legal service.[59] Telegram had been sent official notices from the Court through its publicly listed email accounts but never acknowledged receipt. The Court also served a Brazilian firm representing the app on intellectual property matters. When all that failed, the order for the ban of the app until it complied with outstanding orders was entered, on March 17, 2022.[60]

59 Janosch Delcker, *Germany Takes on Telegram to Fight Extremism*, DEUTSCHE WELLE ("In April 2021, the German government sent two letters to the company's operational headquarters in Dubai ... The company never replied.") (Jan. 19, 2022), https://p.dw.com/p/45kFo; Morgan Meaker, *Germany Has Picked a Fight with Telegram*, WIRED (Feb. 3, 2022), https://www.wired.com/story/germany-telegram-covid/ (describing how the Germany Federal Office of Justice had failed to serve Telegram, even after requests for legal assistance to the United Arab Emirates, where Telegram is incorporated).

60 Other authorities had discussed similar measures. *See Brazil Electoral Court Could Ban Telegram App for Not Fighting Fake News*, REUTERS (Jan. 20, 2022), https://www.reuters.com/technology/brazil-electoral-court-could-ban-telegram-app-not-fighting-fake-news-2022-01-20/.

The Court relied on a Marco Civil provision that subjects noncompliance with personal data protection provisions of the statute to a range of sanctions, including suspension and ban of "activities implicating operations falling under art. 11." It directed internet service providers to block connections to Telegram and for Apple and Google to "prevent users from using the app" and remove it from their respective app stores; all those to whom the order was addressed were given five days to comply. Surprisingly, even though the order was initially sealed, it also warned anyone attempting to "technologically circumvent" the ban to carry on "communicat[ing] with the Telegram [app]" of "criminal and civil liability" and established a 100,000 reais daily fine. This seemed to refer to the use of proxy servers or virtual private networks (VPNs) to bypass blocking by internet service providers.

None of this was ever implemented because Telegram eventually responded. On his Telegram public channel, Telegram CEO Pavel Durov cited "an issue with emails going between our telegram.org corporate addresses and the Brazilian Supreme Court" and "apologize[d] to the Brazilian Supreme Court for our negligence." Stating that they had "found and processed" the "takedown request," Durov "ask[ed] the Court to consider delaying its ruling for a few days at its discretion to allow us to remedy the situation by appointing a representative in Brazil and setting up a framework to react to future pressing issues like this in an expedited manner."[61] In response, the Court found that Telegram had not complied with all outstanding orders but gave the app additional time to do so, while it also conditioned lifting the nationwide ban on the appointment of a local representative. Telegram had also been ordered to report on "all the steps taken to fight disinformation and fake news." After further communication from Telegram, including with the appointment of a representative, the Court was satisfied Telegram had complied and eventually rescinded the order.[62]

The interpretation favored by Justice Moraes in the Telegram ban case contrasted with that endorsed by another member of the Supreme Court in an ongoing case connected to the 2016 ban of WhatsApp, which the Supreme Court itself had stayed.[63] In ADPF 403, which concerns the constitutionality of blocking messaging apps, Justice Rosa Weber concluded that sanctions such as those adopted against WhatsApp in 2016 (and later Telegram, in 2022) went beyond what *Marco Civil* provided, which in her view limited the suspension or ban of a provider's operations to infringements of provisions related to data protection and the confidentiality of

[61] Pavel Durov (@Durov), TELEGRAM (Mar. 18, 2022), https://t.me/durov/180.

[62] *See* Jack Nicas, *Brazil Lifts Its Ban on Telegram After Two Days*, NEW YORK TIMES (2020), https://www.nytimes.com/2022/03/20/world/americas/brazil-telegram-bolsonaro.html.

[63] Luciana Magalhães, *Brazil's Supreme Court Lifts Block on WhatsApp*, WALL STREET JOURNAL (2016), https://www.wsj.com/articles/court-orders-block-to-whatsapp-chat-service-in-brazil-1468952805; For a discussion of that case and preceding orders blocking access to WhatsApp, *see* Jacqueline de Souza Abreu, *Disrupting the Disruptive: Making Sense of App Blocking in Brazil*, 7 INTERNET POL'Y REV. 1 (2018), http://policyreview.info/articles/analysis/disrupting-disruptive-making-sense-app-blocking-brazil.

communications. That is, only for violations of users' privacy rights would providers be subject to a suspension or ban. This represents a narrower view of the extraterritorial scope of Marco Civil.

The courts have not discussed what is meant by "offering services to the Brazilian public" under art. 11, § 2, Marco Civil; although this could be read as any services accessible by users in Brazil, a similar provision in the European Union's General Data Protection Regulation (art. 3(2)) has been interpreted by the European Data Protection Board as requiring targeting of residents of the EU, for example, accepting payment in a currency of a EU member-state, operating under a top-level domain level of a EU member-state (e.g., ".de"), or mentioning dedicated addresses or phone numbers to be reach from an EU country, among other factors.[64]

While the Supreme Court has not yet addressed the territorial scope of Brazilian law under art. 11 of Marco Civil, an answer has been suggested in an April 2023 opinion on whether Brazilian officials can directly request data from foreign providers or must go through mutual legal assistance treaties or other judicial assistance procedures. The Court argued that when "the specific circumstances of art. 11 of *Marco Civil da Internet* and art. 18 of the Budapest Convention [on Cybercrime]" are present, the data can be requested directly. In *obiter dicta*, the rapporteur's majority opinion takes the view that art. 11 of Marco Civil establishes that "providers … must submit to [Brazilian] national legislation,"[65] implying "all legislation." The rapporteur did, however, caveat that art. 11 of Marco Civil would be addressed directly in ADPF 403 and its sister case, ADI 5527, which are pending.[66]

6.5 THE "FAKE NEWS BILL"

In 2020, as the pandemic took over Brazil and many were concerned with COVID-related mis- and disinformation, including notably from the president's social media,[67] Congress started considering the "fake news bill," as Senate bill no. 2630/2020 came to be known. The bill has changed considerably since it was introduced and cleared the Senate in July 2020, undergoing two substantive revisions, in late 2021 and early 2023.

[64] *See* European Data Protection Board, *Guidelines 3/2018 on the Territorial Scope of the GDPR (Article 3)* 17–18 (2019), https://edpb.europa.eu/sites/default/files/files/file1/edpb_guidelines_3_2018_territorial_scope_after_public_consultation_en_1.pdf (describing factors for determining the extraterritorial scope of the GDPR).

[65] S.T.F., Ação Declaratória de Constitucionalidade No. 12, Relator: Min. Gilmar Mendes, Feb. 23, 2023, 38.

[66] *Id.* at 25.

[67] *See* Julie Ricard & Juliano Medeiros, *Using Misinformation as a Political Weapon: COVID-19 and Bolsonaro in Brazil*, 1 HARV. KENNEDY SCH. MISINFORMATION REV. 3 (2020) ("President Bolsonaro's recurring statements about COVID-19 have become one of the main vectors of misleading content."); Monteiro, *Brazilians Are Desperately Fighting Against Bolsonaro's Digital Tactics*, *supra* note 41 ("When the pandemic hit Brazil, Bolsonaro mirrored former U.S. President Trump's approach in downplaying the seriousness of Covid-19.").

At one point, it would have made disinformation illegal and created a traceability mandate for messaging apps. From April 2023, the bill was modified to combat disinformation by curbing the undisclosed use of bots in social media, requiring disclosure of adverts and boosted content, and increasing transparency over content moderation. Instead of traceability, the bill would provide for a data preservation procedure applicable to messaging apps. It would create due process requirements for content moderation and demand information on content moderation processes and decisions.

While the 2021 draft was mostly focused on due process, transparency, and self-regulation, the revised version takes a different approach. Introduced just days before a vote was to be held on the bill, the April 2023 draft changes the intermediary liability regime established in Marco Civil, creating secondary liability for harms (a) resulting from ads or (b) where providers fail to abide by their duty of care obligations in the duration of crisis protocols.

The duty of care obligations are related to content "that may constitute" several categories of criminal offenses, including newly introduced crimes against the rule of law, terrorism, crimes against minors or their apology, and racial discrimination. It also includes references to violence against women and violations of the public health law. It is not often clear when the elements of the relevant criminal offenses are present when it comes to social media content.

Crisis protocols can be activated when systemic risks resulting from a provider's services are "imminent," the provider has been negligent toward such risks, or their response is deemed insufficient. The protocols can last for thirty days, with thirty-day extensions possible if there is a "persistence of imminent risks." Providers will be given a list of "relevant aspects" that mitigation measures must address, which suggests they will have to come to decide which measures to adopt themselves.

The bill does not specify any agency for enforcement, which allows the president to assign to any executive department the powers and delegated regulation established by the bill. This includes BRL50 million fines "per infringement" and a temporary suspension from operating in Brazil. The agency that will be responsible for overseeing the bill was a major point of dispute between the government, the opposition, and the platforms.

Platforms opposed the bill. Google published a blog post, which it featured just below the Google Search home search box in Brazil, arguing the bill would give "broad powers to a governmental body to rule what Brazilians can see on the internet."[68] Telegram messaged Brazilian users a statement that claimed the bill would give "censorship powers to the government." Both provoked energetic responses from Supreme Court Justice Alexandre de Moraes, who issued *sua sponte*

[68] Marcelo Lacerda, *Como o PL 2630 Pode Piorar a Sua Internet*, Blog Google Brasil (Apr. 27, 2023), https://blog.google/intl/pt-br/novidades/iniciativas/como-o-pl-2630-pode-piorar-a-sua-internet/.

orders against them. Google was directed to take down the blog post; Meta and Spotify were also directed to take down all "ads, texts, and information" referring to the bill as "the censorship bill" (as its detractors call it) or pay hourly fines of BRL150,000.[69] Telegram, which had messaged Brazilian users with its statement, was ordered to remove it and to distribute a text prepared by Justice Moraes that denounced "patent and illicit disinformation" perpetrated by Telegram; failure to comply would trigger a 72h ban and an initial fine of BRL500,000.[70] The companies complied. At the request of the prosecutor-general, Justice Moraes also launched a criminal inquiry against Google and Telegram executives, citing crimes against the rule of law,[71] among others.[72]

As of December 2023, the bill was still pending. The government's congressional leadership attempted to overcome gridlock by working on another bill, Bill no. 2370/2019, a proposal for broad copyright reform, to which the "publishers' rights" component of the fake news bill would be attached. Under that proposal, providers would be required to compensate news media for using "journalistic content." If providers and media companies failed to agree on terms, the bill would create mandatory arbitration. That bill also did not advance, however, because of a dispute on an unrelated copyright question – the compensation streaming services would owe to artists.[73]

6.6 ADDENDUM

As this chapter went to press, X was unavailable in Brazil, as a result of an order issued by Justice Moraes.[74] To prevent circumvention, the order initially went as far as imposing a general ban on the use of VPNs in the country. Moraes subsequently revised this, but his order still would still fine anyone who used the platform, in a departure from the principle that court decisions are only binding on the parties. The order against X was entered over its noncompliance with account takedown

[69] *See* S.T.F., Inquérito No. 4781, Relator: Min. Alexandre de Moraes, order of May 2, 2023.

[70] Id., order of May 10, 2023. The full text of the statement, since deleted, is transcribed in the order.

[71] In his order launching the inquiry, Justice Moraes cited art. 359-L of the Criminal Code, which creates the criminal offense of "attempting, with the use of violence or serious threats, to abolish the rule of law, by preventing or limiting the discharge of constitutional powers." *See* S.T.F., Inquérito No. 4933, Relator: Min. Alexandre de Moraes, order of May 12, 2023.

[72] Kari Paul, *Brazil Receives Pushback from Tech Companies on "Fake News" Bill*, GUARDIAN (May 3, 2023), https://www.theguardian.com/world/2023/may/03/alphabet-google-fake-news-law.

[73] *See* João Gabriel & Thiago Resende, *Câmara Adia de Novo Votação de Projeto de Direitos Autorais diante de Divergências* [House Postpones Vote On Copyright Bill After Disagreement], FOLHA DE S.PAULO, August 15, 2023, https://www1.folha.uol.com.br/poder/2023/08/camara-adia-de-novo-votacao-de-projeto-de-direitos-autorais-diante-de-divergencias.shtml.

[74] S.T.F., Petição No. 12.404, Relator: Min. Alexandre de Moraes, Order of Aug. 30, 2024.

orders. The court escalated to a national blocking of the services after X publicly announced that it would not comply with the takedown commands and closed its Brazilian offices. When that also impeded service of process to X, Justice Moraes additionally directed the company to appoint a representative in Brazil, which it did not. The order blocking X, therefore, identifies as grounds both noncompliance with account takedown orders and with the appointment of a representative order. While I cannot at this stage offer a full-fledged discussion of the blocking of X, the latter point is important as it relates to the discussion of the territorial scope of Marco Civil (Part IV).

Justice Moraes grounded his order on an interpretation of Civil Code provisions on foreign companies "operating" in Brazil.[75] The order adopts categorical language when it speaks of the requirement to appoint a representative; it does not cabin its interpretation to the particular case. Given that, the implication would seem to be that any internet application provider whose services are available in Brazil must also appoint a representative. It is unclear whether Justice Moraes would be willing to go to such an extent. This is a novel interpretation of Brazilian legislation pertaining to internet application providers. Indeed, Justice Moraes himself did not rely on it even when he issued the ban on Telegram for essentially the same reasons.[76]

From that perspective, the X blocking order reveals that Marco Civil might be eroded even if it is not repealed or held unconstitutional. The protracted questions about how to construe its territorial application clauses would be made irrelevant.

And it is not just the Civil Code provisions on foreign companies that might change the framework. Adding to the consumer protection inroads described above, in 2024, the Justice Ministry's consumer protection department, Secretaria Nacional do Consumidor, also announced draft rules on data access for researchers and transparency reports by platforms.[77] Perhaps more importantly, the Superior Electoral Court issued wide-ranging regulations ahead of the 2024 municipal elections.[78] Such regulations seem to recreate a notice-and-takedown regime for certain categories of content, although there is a push to interpret the language of the provision (art. 9-E) as requiring a court order. More fundamentally, the rules introduce a duty of care for "notoriously false or decontextualizing facts" that might compromise "electoral integrity." The duty of care provision (art. 9-D) requires application providers to, at a minimum and among others, adapt their content policies, publish transparency reports, and conduct risk assessment and mitigation.

[75] Art. 1.134, *caput*, CÓDIGO CIVIL [C.C.] [CIVIL CODE].

[76] See *supra* Part IV.

[77] Pedro Nakamura, *Senacon cria regras para transparência de dados e anúncios nas redes* [Senacon Creates Rules for Social Media Data and Ad Transparency], NÚCLEO JORNALISMO (Jul. 31, 2024), https://nucleo.jor.br/curtas/2024-07-31-senacon-regras-apis-bibliotecas-plataformas.

[78] T.S.E., Resolução No. 23.732, de 27 de Fevereiro de 2024, Diário da Justiça Eletrônico (Tribunal Superior Eleitoral) [D.J.E. (T.S.E.) de 4.3.2024.

6.7 CONCLUSION

Brazil's Marco Civil was once seen as a model. It was something of a national icon for which Brazilians took pride. Its main provision on content created an immunity for providers that was passed in response to findings of liability that were seen as encouraging overblocking. Like other jurisdictions, Brazil opted for a governance model that mostly neutralized courts. Now, like other jurisdictions, Brazil is considering a different approach. While questions about its central provisions remain unanswered ten years on, the whole edifice might either soon be supplanted by new legislation or significantly reconfigured by the Supreme Court. Even if it is never formally repealed, it is already no longer the guiding star it once was for swathes of Brazilian law. Instead, areas of the law once thought subdued by Marco Civil seem on the verge of unseating it as a governance model.

7

International Dimensions of Infectious Disease Control

Applications to Platform Responsibility

Mark Jit and Dominik K. Hofstetter[*]

7.1 INTRODUCTION

An online platform can be understood as a digital service that facilitates interactions such as the transmission of information between multiple distinct but interdependent sets of users who interact through the platforms.[1] While the terminology of platforms commonly refers to the online media space, platforms can also exist elsewhere. Indeed, there are striking analogies to the field of infectious disease epidemiology. In this space, infections are analogous to information that can be spread from person to person, while routes of transmission (such as aerosols, food, and sexual contact) are analogous to online platforms that spread information. The spread of information more generally, which includes disinformation, misinformation, and other harmful content,[2] on online platforms and the spread of infectious agents through transmission routes both require a source and a target, and both spread faster the more people are "infected." Information thus thrives, much like infectious diseases, from a platform's greater reach.

* We would like to express particular thanks to the editors, Joel P. Trachtman and Bhaskar Chakravorti, for their initiative, guidance, and comments.

1 *See* OECD, What Is an "Online Platform"?, An Introduction to Online Platforms and Their Role in the Digital Transformation 19 (2019), https://www.oecd-ilibrary.org/content/component/19e6a0f0-en (last visited Jan. 2, 2024).

2 For the purposes of this chapter, misinformation is false or inaccurate information that is spread, regardless of an intent to mislead, while disinformation is misinformation that is intentionally spread (*see, e.g., Topic: Misinformation and Disinformation*, American Psychological Association, https://www.apa.org/topics/journalism-facts/misinformation-disinformation (last visited Dec. 27, 2023); *Misinformation versus Disinformation, Explained*, The Foundation for Individual Rights and Expression, https://www.thefire.org/research-learn/misinformation-versus-disinformation-explained (last visited Dec. 27, 2023). Both categories of information, as well as further harmful online content, all bear risks for users of online platforms and societies at large, as is the case with infectious disease agents.

The key difference is that infections require physical proximity or intersections between individuals or routes of transmission to spread, while information can spread electronically from afar. These are not new concepts; analytical models of information spreading like an infection date back at least to the 1950s.[3]

Like information disseminated through online platforms, infectious diseases can cross international borders as they track the movement of people (and sometimes animals and goods). Hence, their control and management have major implications for international relations, and international law. An example is the continuing COVID-19 pandemic, the largest recent global infectious disease-related crisis in terms of both health and economic impact. It has had profound effects on international travel, trade, migration, and political relations, some of which are likely to have long-term implications.[4] Yet COVID-19 is only one of a series of major international infectious disease threats over the last few decades that have shaped the international political, economic and legal framework related to global health. In 2005, following the 2002–2004 severe acute respiratory syndrome (SARS) outbreak, the World Health Organization (WHO) revised its international health regulations (IHR) to allow for the declaration of a public health emergency of international concern (PHEIC): "an extraordinary event which is determined … to constitute a public health risk to other States through the international spread of disease and … to potentially require a coordinated international response."[5] Since then, the WHO has declared a PHEIC six times: in 2009 (influenza A/H1N1), twice in 2014 (polio and Ebola), in 2015 (Zika), in 2018 (Ebola), and in 2020 (SARS-CoV-2).

Pandemics are usually triggered by a spillover event, during which a pathogen is transmitted from an animal reservoir population to a human host, and subsequently adapts to efficient transmission within human populations, as was the case for influenza pandemics as well as SARS and SARS-CoV-2. Such spillover events may happen increasingly frequently due to climate change, biodiversity loss, and encroachment of human settlements on animal habitats. Other infectious disease outbreaks may be triggered by the weakening of control measures such as vaccinations and quarantines that have kept infections under control, as a result of internal or external conflict and political unrest. Once an infection emerges, it can spread rapidly across internal and external borders due to global connectivity and travel. A recent example is the measles outbreak in Venezuela sparked by internal political

[3] Luís M. A. Bettencourt et al., *The Power of a Good Idea: Quantitative Modeling of the Spread of Ideas from Epidemiological Models*, 364 Physica A: Statistical Mechanics and its Applications 513 (2006).

[4] Packiaraj Thangavel, Pramod Pathak & Bibhas Chandra, *Covid-19: Globalization – Will the Course Change?*, 26 Vision 7 (2022).

[5] Article 1, World Health Organization, *International Health Regulations. Third Edition* (2005), https://www.who.int/publications-detail-redirect/9789241580496 (last visited Jan. 2, 2024).

and economic turmoil,[6] which in turn spread to neighboring parts of Brazil and led to the reversal of a hard-won certification of measles elimination in the Americas.

The periodic occurrence of pandemic events has shed a spotlight on the functioning of the legal and regulatory framework at play in global health and infectious disease control, at both domestic and international levels. While the necessity and relative benefits of international coordination may have been evident for a long time, regulatory fragmentation, lack of implementation of international agreements on the domestic level, and disagreement on the allocation of resources appear to shape current pandemic responses across the globe. The primary instrument in the global health repertoire is the IHR administered by the WHO, which provides a platform for multi-country cooperation in infectious disease control. The IHR is meant to provide the international community with an overarching legal framework that defines Member States' rights and obligations in handling public health events and emergencies that have the potential to cross borders.[7]

Drawing on the analogy between the spread of infectious diseases and the spread of information across online platforms, this chapter looks to lessons from global health governance to formulate suggestions for the governance of online platforms and their content moderation practices.

To this end, we will first examine the rationale for international cooperation in infectious disease control, as well as review the history of the global health governance framework and uses of the IHR during the COVID-19 pandemic and previous PHEICs. We will then assess the suitability of the IHR and current global health governance framework in controlling the "platforms" of transmission. Finally, we return to our analogy with online platforms and rely upon lessons from the infectious disease control space, to formulate recommendations for the global governance of online platforms.

7.2 RATIONALES FOR MULTILATERAL COOPERATION IN INTERNATIONAL INFECTIOUS DISEASE CONTROL

An early shared recognition of the need for States to cooperate beyond their national borders in identifying, preventing, and controlling infectious disease outbreaks has largely shaped the current governance framework around international health and, more specifically, infectious disease control. While rationales for cooperation in this area have notable historical origins dating back to the nineteenth century, this

6 Alberto E. Paniz-Mondolfi et al., *Resurgence of Vaccine-Preventable Diseases in Venezuela as a Regional Public Health Threat in the Americas*, 25 EMERG. INFECT. DIS. 625 (2019).

7 *See* Article 2 International Health Regulations (2005) Third Edition [hereinafter IHR] providing, "the purpose and scope of these Regulations are to prevent, protect against, control and provide a public health response to the international spread of disease in ways that are commensurate with and restricted to public health risks, and which avoid unnecessary interference with international traffic and trade."

chapter will emphasize the contemporary rationale for multilateral cooperation, best expressed in the language of externalities.

7.2.1 *Historical Origins of Cooperation in Infectious Disease Control*

The similarities in the context and mechanisms of transmission between infectious diseases, on the one hand, and information across platforms, on the other, are reflected historically. Indeed, the history of public health and infectious disease control from an international perspective finds one of its earliest links in the history of the International Sanitary Conferences (ISCs) that took place between 1851 and 1938. The catalyst for these ISCs was a growing awareness of the global spread of diseases and the need for coordinated responses.

At the time of the first ISC in 1851, the transmission of diseases between distant places was not a new phenomenon in the dismal and overcrowded conditions of the industrial revolution. However, technological advances and the revolution in transportation at the time allowed diseases to suddenly travel at an unprecedented speed.[8] The speed and volume of international travel has continued to increase exponentially since then. The effect of this was particularly evident throughout the COVID-19 pandemic and the remarkable speed at which an initial outbreak in Wuhan was able to reach countries around the world within days.

The substantial increase in the speed of transmission of infectious disease can be likened to the unparalleled speed at which information nowadays spreads across online platforms. Various studies have assessed the parameters that influence the volume and speed of this online information spread.[9] For instance, negative information (e.g., in tweets) appears to spread faster than positive or neutral information.[10] Moreover, information transmission patterns in the aftermath of an emergency or crisis event demonstrate the differences between information transmission routes (e.g., mobile phone data vs. tweets) and the information (and misinformation) that can be spread through each transmission route.[11] The evolution of online information spread tracks the analogous developments that led to

[8] Valeska Huber, *The Unification of the Globe by Disease? The International Sanitary Conferences on Cholera, 1851–1894*, 49 Hist. J. 453, 455 (2006); World Health Organization, *The First Ten Years of the World Health Organization* (1958).

[9] *See* overview in, Didier Henry, Erick Stattner & Martine Collard, Information Propagation Routes between Countries in Social Media, Companion of The Web Conference 2018 on The Web Conference 2018 – WWW '18 1295 (2018), http://dl.acm.org/citation.cfm?doid=3184558.3191569 (last visited Jan. 5, 2024).

[10] *See* Nasir Naveed et al., *Bad News Travel Fast: A Content-Based Analysis of Interestingness on Twitter*, Proceedings of the 3rd International Web Science Conference 1 (2011), https://dl.acm.org/doi/10.1145/2527031.2527052 (last visited Jan. 5, 2024).

[11] *See, e.g.*, James P. Bagrow, Information Spreading during Emergencies and Anomalous Events, Complex Spreading Phenomena in Social Systems 269 (Sune Lehmann & Yong-Yeol Ahn, eds. 2018), http://link.springer.com/10.1007/978-3-319-77332-2_15 (last visited Jan. 5, 2024).

rapid and wide infectious disease spread in the nineteenth century. An identical awareness of the risks of a rapid spread of infectious disease is thus necessary in the online information space.

While awareness of the risk of infectious disease spread grew, participants at the first ISC disagreed on the specifics of infectious disease control. For instance, most doctors involved at the first ISC agreed that cholera was a problem that transcended national boundaries and that international cooperation was thus needed to tackle it. If both cholera and its prevention were international concerns, a solution could thus not come about on a solely national basis.[12] Despite vague agreement on the need for collective action, disagreement on the causes of infectious diseases and suitable control mechanisms posed insurmountable barriers to actual international agreement at the ISCs for many years to come.[13] With regard to online platforms, representatives from most countries would likely agree that certain forms of online information (e.g., dis- and misinformation or harmful content) pose considerable risks and challenges for their societies. At the same time, much like with early disagreements at the first ISC, properly defining what each country considers to be such harmful content, and then deciding on how to combat this, may at first appear to be an impossible task.

And yet the earliest ISCs offer hope if we can consider them as attempts at an inte rnationalization of global health governance. They provided a forum for the management of differences, between different countries and different scientific stances, but also, they would later evolve into the main platforms for discourse and gradual harmonization and standardization in this field.[14] So, while an international forum that addresses the risks that come with the spread of harmful content online may at first not appear a feasible endeavor, it may lay the foundation for internationalization, harmonization, or, at the very least, international (and high-level) discussions on the matter.

7.2.2 *Contemporary Rationales for Multilateral Cooperation*

The motivation for multilateral cooperation in infectious disease regulation has only strengthened since the initial and rudimentary desire to create an international forum to discuss global health, particularly with the creation of the WHO and increasing interconnectedness of the globe. It can best be described in the economic language of externalities.[15] Externalities are benefits or costs of an activity that fall on third parties. For instance, externalities involved in goods transactions do not fall on either producers or consumers of the good. Here, we are particularly interested in inter-countries externalities that fall on populations of third countries.

[12] Huber, *supra* note 8, at 457.

[13] *See* Norman Howard-Jones, *The Scientific Background of the International Sanitary Conferences* (1975), 99.

[14] *See, e.g.*, Howard-Jones, *supra* note 13; World Health Organization, *supra* note 8.

[15] Mark Jit et al., *Multi-Country Collaboration in Responding to Global Infectious Disease Threats: Lessons for Europe from the COVID-19 Pandemic*, 9 The Lancet Regional Health – Europe 100221 (2021).

Positive externalities involve benefits falling on third parties. For instance, activities to control infection in one country (such as vaccination and quarantine) can also prevent spread to others. The best example is eradication of an infectious disease, which requires cooperation of every country in the world before any country can enjoy the full benefits. Similarly, control of an infection at its source can save considerable resources in controlling it after it has spread to other countries. Economists have also proposed the concept of the "caring externality" – people appreciate and derive utility from knowing that other people (including those in other countries) are living healthy lives.[16]

However, negative externalities can also occur in infectious disease control. For instance, during a pandemic there may be a limited supply of goods needed to prevent and treat illness (such as vaccines, antivirals, and personal protective equipment), so consumption of these goods by one country reduces supply and raises prices for others. Countries may respond to the identification of a pathogen in a country by curtailing international travel from that country, which may have negative economic consequences on the country. Consumption of antibiotics may help prevent bacterial infections but may also cause antibiotic resistance, a global negative externality.

In the absence of externalities, individuals or countries acting in their own self-interest will achieve the most globally efficient outcome, though not necessarily the most equitable. This is usually no longer the case when externalities are incorporated. So, at least in theory, multilateral collaboration can seek "win-win" cooperative optimum conditions across actors and countries and thus can enhance global welfare. Indeed, essential determinants of global health (e.g., pathogens, air, food, and water) are not solely confined to national borders. Instead, threats to these determinants can spread to adjacent countries, regions, and even continents. Controlling the determinants of global health can thus only be achieved by international cooperation and global governance.

The same language of externalities can be applied to the spread of information through online routes of transmission. The benefits from one state's attempts to control harmful content may be reaped by many other countries. That being said, since such content may originate in any country and then spread "virally" across the globe, its "eradication" would require the cooperation of every country in which such information or content may be hosted. Moreover, as with infectious disease agents, controlling or preventing the creation or spread of dis- and misinformation and harmful content at its source would likely free up considerable content moderation and law enforcement resources in the other affected countries. On the other hand, negative externalities may be observed in instances where private enterprises, that is, online platforms, have limited content moderation resources to commit to controlling harmful content. If an online platform commits such resources to one

[16] A. J. Culyer, *The Nature of the Commodity "Health Care" and Its Efficient Allocation*, 23 Oxford Economic Papers 189 (1971).

geographic region, this may come at the expense of a different region, where the shortage of content moderation resources would entail a greater "virality" of the information at issue. Moreover, any efforts at content moderation within one country (or by an intervening third country) inevitably raise free speech concerns. Thus, when applied to the spread of information online, the language of externalities describes a strikingly similar picture as with infectious diseases.

7.3 MECHANISMS OF REGULATORY CONTROL

Several types of multilateral interventions involve regulatory control. The most obvious category is "command and control regulations" that prohibit activities with negative externalities (such as international travel) or mandate activities with positive externalities (such as vaccination). Regulatory regimes could include alignment of national regulations on private actors, such as regulating sales of medical interventions by private manufacturers and regulating movement by individuals.

Such regulations could be replaced with "Pigouvian" taxes and subsidies. Resource pooling can be thought of as a type of Pigouvian tax/subsidy – that is, a financial transfer from the beneficiaries to the producer of a positive externality (subsidy) or from the producer to the victims of a negative externality (tax). Examples of positive externalities that may be deemed worthy of a subsidy could include herd protection from vaccination, caring externalities to achieve greater equity, and economies of scale when countries collaborate to produce sufficient supplies of medical equipment.

The IHR provide a common framework and broad guidelines to implement such control regulations and Pigouvian taxes. Namely, the IHR provide guidelines on interventions at points of entry (Part IV), the design of public health measures (Parts V and VIII), standards for health documents (Part VI), and permissible charges (Part VII). The guidelines account for a state's desire to implement measures it deems necessary while emphasizing the need to prevent negative externalities and reinforce positive ones. State parties' agreement on the IHR can be understood as the States' recognition of the benefits of multilateral coordination in devising measures to detect, contain, and prevent infectious diseases.

7.3.1 *Evaluating the International Framework on Infectious Disease Control*

As previously outlined, the first ISC was convened in Paris in 1851.[17] While most representatives disagreed on the cause of cholera and the best methods of disease prevention, subsequent iterations of these conferences finally led to the 1892 adoption of the International Sanitary Convention on the control of cholera and the

[17] Michael McCarthy, A *Brief History of the World Health Organization*, 360 THE LANCET 1111 (2002); *See also*, N. Howard-Jones, *The World Health Organization in Historical Perspective*, 24 PERSPECTIVES IN BIOLOGY AND MEDICINE 467 (1981).

1897 convention that addressed the plague. While international health governance was initially fragmented across a number of regional organizations, the 1945 UN Conference on International Organizations in San Francisco voted to establish a new international health organization and only a year later the International Health Conference in New York approved the Constitution of the WHO. Since its coming into force in 1948, the WHO largely guided by its Constitution and decisions of its principal body, the World Health Assembly, was involved in wide-ranging disease prevention and control efforts across the globe.

As a governance forum, States provided the WHO with a number of authorities to develop global health law. The World Health Assembly, which consists of delegates of WHO Member States, has in turn codified evolving regulations to coordinate international action to prevent, detect, and respond to pandemic threats. Specifically, the WHO constitution provides the WHO with authority to develop international law on public health matters by adopting conventions (Article 19), regulations (Article 21), and recommendations (Article 23). Despite these vast authorities, the WHO has been reluctant to exercise its Article 19 authority and has instead made use of Article 21 in formulating the IHR to address infectious disease control. This in turn left a number of global health threats unaddressed.[18]

The IHR, adopted as an Article 21 regulation containing legally binding standards that designate specific actions that must be taken by Member States and provide the primary legal agreement relating to the threat of infectious diseases. Beyond these binding standards, certain States have also negotiated nonbinding frameworks to advance aspects of health security. The Pandemic Influenza Preparedness (PIP) Framework enables better coordination of international information and research sharing for pandemic influenza strains, by bringing together the WHO, Member States, and non-state actors, such as pharmaceutical companies.

The governance of infectious disease control is also informed in part by the practices of the WHO's constituent bodies. As the principal decision-making body of the WHO, the World Health Assembly serves as the "norm-creator".[19] The WHO Executive Board, the Secretariat, the Director-General, the Emergency Committee, and the WHO Regional Organizations all serve to contribute to expedient and efficacious decision-making in times of health emergencies. The bodies broaden the involved expertise and voices beyond those represented in the World Health Assembly and introduce technical expertise. Thus, the practice and the degree to which these bodies are considered to be acting within or without their constitutional mandates informs the success and legitimacy of the global health law framework as a model for international governance.

[18] Benjamin Mason Meier et al., *The World Health Organization in Global Health Law*, 48 J. Law. Med. Ethics 796, 797 (2020).

[19] Pedro A Villarreal, The World Health Organization's Governance Framework in Disease Outbreaks: A Legal Perspective, The Governance of Disease Outbreaks: International Health Law: Lessons from the Ebola Crisis and Beyond 263 (2017).

Despite the existing norms and framework to address infectious diseases, countries acted on their own or at best regionally for much of the response to the COVID-19 pandemic, from border control to vaccine distribution. This has led to calls for and negotiations surrounding a pandemic treaty.[20] In the wake of the COVID-19 pandemic and increasing risk factors for future pandemics, there is a need to assess whether the current international regulatory regime is fit for purpose and sufficient. Early proposals for a pandemic treaty[21] recognized gaps in the scope of the IHR, specifically as it relates to the production of and access to necessary equipment, medicines, and vaccines. Moreover, unlike the IHR, a pandemic treaty could aim primarily at preventing the outbreak of the next pandemic, rather than solely responding to an existing outbreak.[22] These calls were underlined by the Independent Panel on Pandemic Preparedness and Response (IPPPR) appointed by the WHO Director-General, to examine how COVID-19 became a global health crisis. In a background paper on the international law relating to pandemic preparedness, the IPPPR found that a "Framework Convention – Protocol approach" could allow for the most beneficial governance reforms of the existing system.[23]

Such an agreement has been in the works since the end of 2021, and on October 16, 2023, the world received a first glimpse of the complete draft negotiating text. Most recently in November 2023, the 194 Member States of the WHO began deliberating on the concrete text in Geneva. The discussions on the draft pandemic treaty highlight the differences in States' positions, which often reflect differences in capacities and resources to identify and respond to disease outbreaks. For example, while industrialized countries want to focus more on prevention and information-sharing, developing countries emphasize the need for equitable access to vaccinations, medicines, and other resources to form the core of such a Pandemic treaty. As is usually the case at the WHO, any agreement will need to be reached by consensus. The question of whether States will agree on working toward resilient health systems, benefit sharing, outbreak surveillance cooperation, and equitable sharing of resources thus depends on States' willingness and ability to strike compromises.[24]

20 John Zarocostas, *Countries Prepare for Pandemic Treaty Decision*, The Lancet, Nov. 27, 2021, at 1951.

21 Ironically, the content of a potential pandemic treaty has been the subject of substantial dis- and misinformation on various online platforms. The disinformation includes claims that the treaty would threaten national sovereignty and that the WHO could deploy troops to enforce vaccine mandates and digital passports. While all of these claims have been authoritatively debunked, their spread has sowed public mistrust toward any such pandemic accord (see Ahmed Soliman et al., *WHO Pandemic Accord: Full Adherence to the Principle of Sovereignty*, 402 The Lancet 1322 [2023]).

22 Jorge Vinuales et al., *A Global Pandemic Treaty Should Aim for Deep Prevention*, 397 The Lancet 1791 (2021).

23 Alexandra Phelan & Priya Pillai, *International Health Law in Perspective – Background Paper* 16 (2021).

24 Kerry Cullinan, *Draft Pandemic Accord: IP Waivers And Benefits For Sharing Pathogen Information Are In – For Now* (Oct. 17, 2023), https://healthpolicy-watch.news/draft-pan

7.3.2 *An International Framework to Provide Guidelines for Platform Responsibility*

In the infectious disease control space, the IHR provide a common framework and broad guidelines for States to realize various regulatory goals. Likewise, the online platform space could benefit from a multilateral instrument that could provide broad guidelines for States to consider when attempting to establish or adapt rules relating to platform responsibility. As in the infectious disease space, guidelines that fulfill the role of a framework agreement could account for a State's desire to implement measures it deems necessary while emphasizing the need to prevent negative externalities and reinforce positive ones. State parties' agreement on a multilateral instrument could, similar to the infectious disease space, be understood as the participating States' recognition of the benefits of multilateral coordination in devising measures to detect, contain, and prevent the spread of dis- and misinformation and other harmful content. That being said, the feasibility of such a multilateral agreement is a question that hinges on the prospect of reconciling the interests of the various actors in the online platform space.

7.3.3 *Key Actors in International Coordination Mechanisms*

International cooperation around infectious diseases relies on cooperation between multiple public and private actors to agree and implement mechanisms for coordination. Historically, the key platforms have been inter-governmental, with the WHO playing the leading role in setting international norms and standards on health. While the WHO has extensive technical and field staff, its decision-making is vested in the World Health Assembly, an annual forum in which each WHO Member State has an equal vote.

However, the WHO faces multiple challenges to playing this leadership role. The greatest challenge is financial. The WHO's budget from membership dues has steadily declined in real terms since the 1990s, so it is increasingly reliant on voluntary contributions from governments and private donors.[25] This creates a situation where the WHO's agenda can be largely dictated by external donors, which limits its strategic maneuverability and its ability to lead initiatives that require large financial resources.[26] A second challenge is that while the World Health Assembly has a mandate to set global health standards, it lacks legal mechanisms to enforce compliance. Indeed, neither the WHO Constitution, nor any specific

demic-accord-ip-waivers-and-benefits-for-sharing-pathogen-information-are-in-for-now/ (last visited Jan. 3, 2024).

[25] Srikanth K. Reddy, Sumaira Mazhar & Raphael Lencucha, *The Financial Sustainability of the World Health Organization and the Political Economy of Global Health Governance: A Review of Funding Proposals*, 14 Globalization and Health 119 (2018).

[26] Villarreal, *supra* note 19, at 267–68.

agreements such as the IHR or framework agreements such as the WHO Framework Convention on Tobacco Control (FCTC) contain provisions granting investigation or enforcement powers to any WHO body, nor any equity obligations.[27]

Even the proposed text of the pandemic treaty lacks proper commitment to an independent accountability mechanism designed to promote compliance with its content. The pandemic agreement draft does contain commitments on States' self-reporting on their pandemic prevention, preparedness, and response efforts. However while the Conference of the Parties, made up of State delegates that govern the agreement's implementation, has reserved the option to assemble an "implementation and compliance committee," some have argued that even this language falls short of what would be required to hold States accountable and achieve treaty compliance.[28]

Consequently, the global health governance space created by the WHO's limitations is filled by a range of government-linked and private actors. These range from initiatives from individual countries (e.g., the United States President's Emergency Plan For AIDS Relief or PEPFAR), to charities associated with individuals (e.g., the Bill & Melinda Gates Foundation), to nongovernmental organizations (e.g., Médecins Sans Frontières), to public-private partnerships (e.g., Gavi, the Vaccine Alliance), to for-profit organizations (e.g., pharmaceutical companies and health consultancies).[29]

These actors shape international cooperation around infectious diseases through the interaction of their complementary and conflicting objectives. Most of these actors ostensibly have a common objective of improving health. For the WHO, this objective is explicitly stated in Article 1 of its constitution,[30] although as stated, the WHO is ultimately governed by national actors who may pursue different objectives. Nonprofit actors like health charities also pursue this goal but often within more narrow arenas, for example, improving vaccine uptake or reducing HIV burden globally. Furthermore, many of these actors at least in theory take leadership from

[27] The IHR Review Committee on COVID-19 notably concluded that while the IHR were not deficient, strong accountability and enforcement mechanisms would have been necessary, as IHR implementation by States and by the WHO throughout the COVID-19 pandemic was lacking (Preben Aavitsland et al., *Functioning of the International Health Regulations during the COVID-19 Pandemic,* 398 The Lancet 1283 [2021]).

[28] Susanna Lehtimaki et al., *Where There Is a Will, There Is a Way: Independent Assessment of Member State Compliance with the Pandemic Agreement,* 12 The Lancet Global Health e18 (2024).

[29] Jeremy Youde, Contemporary Global Health Governance Actors, Global Health Governance in International Society (Jeremy Youde, ed. 2018), https://doi.org/10.1093/oso/9780198813057.003.0005 (last visited Januart 7, 2024); Benjamin Mason Meier & Matiangai V. S. Sirleaf, Global Health Landscape: The Proliferating Actors Influencing Global Health Governance, Global Health Law & Policy: Ensuring Justice for a Healthier World (2023).

[30] World Health Organization, *Constitution of the World Health Organization* (1995), https://apps.who.int/iris/bitstream/handle/10665/121457/em_rc42_cwho_en.pdf (last visited June 29, 2022).

the WHO on technical and normative issues. For instance, Gavi, the Vaccine Alliance, procures and funds vaccines for the world's poorest countries, but candidate vaccines in its portfolio have to first be identified by the WHO. Finally, for-profit actors promote health as a means to an end (revenues from sales of health-related goods). Hence, they have an interest in international norms around infectious disease interventions.[31]

The fragmented landscape of actors in international infectious disease management demonstrates the type of cooperation challenges that attempts at international online platform responsibility governance also face. With regard to online platforms, however, the stated goals of private platform operators and those of public officials and nongovernment organizations in different countries may diverge even more heavily than in the infectious disease space. While private and non-state initiatives in global health benefit from general leadership and technical guidance by the WHO, an equivalent multilateral body with similar standing is clearly missing in the online platform responsibility space. Instead, private corporations will heavily tailor their content moderation practices according to the attitudes and visions of the States that exercise direct or indirect regulatory jurisdiction over their platforms, ultimately further fragmenting the governance landscape for online platforms.

7.4 CHALLENGES AND SOLUTIONS TO ACHIEVING OPTIMUM INTERNATIONAL REGULATORY COOPERATION

Despite the existence of a formal institution charged with global health governance and the IHR, the COVID-19 pandemic brought to light critical flaws that exist in the global health law framework related to infectious diseases.[32] It also highlighted the fundamental challenges that prevail when trying to coordinate collective action in global health.

7.4.1 *Challenges to International Regulatory Cooperation*

A primary problem is that individual States may not necessarily benefit from participating in such agreements until all partner States agree to collaborate.

[31] On the reallocation of the exercise of public authority away from public institutions toward semi public and private entities, in part due to the need for greater resources and functional specialization, *see, e.g.*, Mateja Steinbrück Platise, The Changing Structure of Global Health Governance, The Governance of Disease Outbreaks. International Health Law: Lessons from the Ebola Crisis and Beyond (2017).

[32] For an evaluation of the performance of the IHR during the COVID-19 pandemic, *see, e.g.*, Aavitsland et al., *supra* note 27; Hu Zhang, *Challenges and Approaches of the Global Governance of Public Health Under COVID-19*, 9 FRONTIERS IN PUBLIC HEALTH (2021), https://www.frontiersin.org/article/10.3389/fpubh.2021.727214; Anne Bucher, George Papaconstantinou & Jean Pisani-Ferry, *The Failure of Global Public Health Governance: A Forensic Analysis*, BRUEGEL 18 (2022).

Furthermore, actors (such as politicians) negotiating such agreements for their States may have aims that do not perfectly coincide with even the self-interest of their populations as a whole. Hence, reaching the globally optimal solution may require unreasonable amounts of time and political capital. Such solutions are not easily achieved under the time pressure associated with infectious disease outbreaks, and the urgency of providing resources such as materials, expertise, drugs, and vaccines to populations most in need. Consequently, even if most actors agree, in principle, with its overarching goals, outcomes of international agreements often fall short of achieving optimal solutions. This point is most prominent in critiques of the IHR (and even the proposed pandemic treaty), as they provide aspirational guidelines, but time and again miss the mark in terms of compliance and accountability (Ebola, MERS, COVID-19).[33]

A further challenge in engendering international support for multilateral collaboration is that the benefits of such cooperation are often abstract, diffuse, and time-lagged. For instance, internationally agreed travel protocols during a pandemic can strike a balance between protecting the global economy and preventing infection spread. Similarly, agreement to pool medical resources such as drugs and vaccines across countries can enable supplies to be directed to populations at greatest need, as well as contribute to global eradication efforts. However, these aims are less immediate than nationalistic solutions such as closing borders to all infected countries and competing to obtain the greatest share of medical resources.

Finally, even when norms acquire legal standing, international bodies such as the WHO lack mechanisms to create adequate incentives for adherence or sanction noncompliance, beyond the threat of international opprobrium. For example, while the IHR impose a "reciprocal responsibility," calling on all nations to detect, report, and contain public health threats in ways that are "commensurate with and restricted public health risks, and which avoid unnecessary interference with international traffic and trade,"[34] many countries during COVID-19 continued to enforce strong travel restrictions long beyond the point that it was epidemiologically sensible to do so.[35] While some consider the IHR's obligations legally binding, there is much ambiguity and uncertainty as to its enforcement capabilities. The language of the IHR mostly speaks in "shall" terms, which make it difficult to describe a potential breach. Moreover, the consequences of such a breach are not delineated nor is the dispute settlement mechanism apt for potential State-to-State claims that may arise.[36]

[33] *See, e.g.*, David P. Fidler, *The Case against a Pandemic Treaty | Think Global Health*, Council on Foreign Relations (2021), https://www.thinkglobalhealth.org/article/case-against-pandemic-treaty (last visited Jan. 3, 2024).

[34] Art. 2, International Health Regulations.

[35] Timothy W. Russell et al., *Effect of Internationally Imported Cases on Internal Spread of COVID-19: A Mathematical Modelling Study*, 6 The Lancet Public Health e12 (2021).

[36] Susan L Erikson, The Limits of the International Health Regulations: Ebola Governance, Regulatory Breach, and the Non-Negotiable Necessity of National Healthcare, The

This ambiguous framework leads to descriptions of the IHR as empowering the WHO to control and lead the conduct of Member States, all while lacking the power to adopt measures enforceable as law. In other words, the IHR are binding but not enforceable as law.[37]

7.4.2 *Solutions and Examples of International Regulatory Cooperation*

A partial solution to bridge the challenges described above is to establish international standards or norms that have widespread agreement across countries because they are rooted in commonly shared legal and ethical principles. These norms then serve as heuristics to guide any international coordination.

For instance, global health governance essentially presupposes that the protection and promotion of health is not merely an issue of a person's country of residence but also has a strong transnational dimension, which is why the "right to health" is recognized in a number of international instruments.[38] The WHO Constitution envisages in its Preamble, that "the enjoyment of the highest attainable standard of health is one of the fundamental rights of every human being without distinction of race, religion, political belief, economic or social condition. The health of all peoples is fundamental to the attainment of peace and security and is dependent upon the fullest co-operation of individuals and States. The achievement of any State in the promotion and protection of health is of value to all."[39] Hence all WHO Member States have in principle endorsed a universal "right to health," which has also found its way into other international legal obligations and undertakings.[40] Such a norm then provides the argument for resource pooling to enable all populations to access available medical technology on the basis of need. Without such a norm, the case for resource pooling might be difficult to communicate since the costs of infection control (buying and delivering vaccines, responding to

Governance of Disease Outbreaks. International Health Law: Lessons from the Ebola Crisis and Beyond 355–59 (2017).

37 Pia Acconci, *The Reaction to the Ebola Epidemic within the United Nations Framework: What Next for the World Health Organization?*, 18 Max Planck Yearbook of United Nations Law Online 405 (2014).

38 A. Katarina Weilert, The Right to Health in International Law – Normative Foundations and Doctrinal Flaws, The Governance of Disease Outbreaks: International Health Law: Lessons from the Ebola Crisis and Beyond (2017).

39 Preamble, World Health Organization, *supra* note 30.

40 Indeed, the realization of the right to health is closely dependent upon the attainment of other human rights, such as the right to food, housing, work, education, human dignity, life, nondiscrimination, equality, privacy, access to information, and free movement. As a result, a number of other international conventions and protocols deal with various facets of the right to health: *see, e.g.*, Universal Declaration of Human Rights (Dec. 10, 1948) G.A. Res. 217 (III) A, art. 25, providing that provides that everyone "has the right to a standard of living adequate for the health and well-being of himself and of his family"; International Covenant on Economic, Social and Cultural Rights (Dec. 16, 1966) 993 U.N.T.S. 3, art. 12, providing the most comprehensive provision on the right to health in international human rights law.

outbreaks) fall on specific countries while the benefits (less infection spread overall, more equitable health distribution) are diffuse and time-lagged.

As a result, such basic norms provide important guidance that can be rapidly operationalized in crisis situations. For example, when COVID-19 vaccines became available in 2020, the WHO endorsed a values framework that included principles such as global and national equity as well as human well-being. This enabled the COVAX Initiative, a global collaboration to procure and supply COVID-19 vaccines to the world, to establish principles for vaccine distribution such as seeking to ensure that high-risk populations in every country had access to the primary series of vaccines first.

However, equitable distribution of vaccines globally has been stymied by other issues besides distribution, such as production, procurement, and local delivery. During the pandemic, nationalistic trade policies, differences in purchasing power between countries, variations in national regulatory frameworks, and complex procedures to move key vaccine inputs across borders prevented efforts to ensure equitable vaccine distribution.[41] So in practice, while individual countries have used mechanisms consistent with WHO principles (such as distribution of vaccines according to vulnerability, rather than to willingness to pay), distribution between countries has nonetheless disadvantaged countries with fewer resources to produce and procure vaccines. Any set of broad guidelines is thus only as robust and valuable as the wider legal, political, and economic context allows it to be.

7.5 LESSONS FROM INFECTIOUS DISEASE CONTROL

Given the large between-country externalities involved in infectious disease interventions, there should be large net health and economic gains to be made globally by multilateral cooperation in this area. However, the global infectious disease control landscape has become extremely complex and fragmented, with convening, governance, financing, action, and advocacy roles often split between different public and private actors pursuing their own agendas. The stated agendas can range from pursuing national self-interest (State representatives), improving global health within a given timeline (private charities), advocating for increasing funding in a certain health area (nongovernmental organizations), through to maximizing shareholder value (pharmaceutical companies). Hence there is no guarantee that all these actors are able to cooperate to pursue the theoretical optimum cooperative solution.

Consequently, a pragmatic route has been to identify broader norms and standards that are acceptable across all actors. These norms can then be used to identify

[41] Indermit Gill & Michele Ruta, *Why Global Vaccine Equity Is the Prescription for a Full Recovery*, Brookings (Feb. 11, 2022), https://www.brookings.edu/blog/future-development/2022/02/11/why-global-vaccine-equity-is-the-prescription-for-a-full-recovery/ (last visited Jan. 2, 2024).

low-hanging fruit where international agreement is easier to achieve. For instance, one of the great successes of international coordination was the eradication of smallpox through vaccination in 1980. This achievement was possible because it was feasible both technically (a cheap and effective vaccine existed, and humans were the only host of the smallpox virus) and politically (both the United States and the Soviet Union found common cause in eradicating smallpox).[42] This then enabled international cooperation toward eradication of other infections such as polio, measles and trachoma.

Indeed, the eradication or prevention of specific diseases may provide the most viable room for negotiation and subsequent cooperation. A similar rationale may help inform discussions on international coordination in the realm of content moderation and online platform governance.

7.6 DERIVING RECOMMENDATIONS FOR PLATFORM RESPONSIBILITY REFORMS

In 1978, French historian Emmanuel Le Roy Ladurie suggested that the world had historically become a "marché commun des microbes" (a "common market of microbes"), as large epidemic outbreaks followed established trade routes and troop movements.[43] Online platforms have since become "digital town squares," with information, including dis- and misinformation and other harmful content, following even faster and more interconnected routes of transmission. Indeed, much like in the infectious disease space, the responses to global "outbreaks" of dis- and misinformation and harmful content appear to be equally complex and fragmented. For this reason, this chapter relies on the lessons from infectious disease control highlighted above to make recommendations in the domain of online platform responsibility.

The principle of achieving low-hanging fruit first to build trust and momentum toward more challenging (but still achievable) goals extends to the real of online platforms. The low-hanging fruit in the digital social media space may include regulation to prevent the dissemination of material that virtually all actors can agree is undesirable, such as images of sexual exploitation of minors or harmful and incorrect medical advice, as well as technical instructions that enable the construction of weapons of mass destruction. The feasibility of such a consensus can be derived from equivalents in infectious disease control that include disease eradication and prevention of the spread of emerging infections at the source, since these activities have a clear goal, definable end, and easily identifiable benefits for all

[42] D. Henderson, *Smallpox Eradication – a Cold War Victory*, 19 World Health Forum 113 (1998).

[43] Emmanuel Le Roy Ladurie, *Un Concept: L'Unification Microbienne Du Monde (XIV°–XVII° Siècles)*, 23 Schweizerische Zeitschrift für Geschichte 627, 629 (1973).

countries. Yet, as the early historical experiences in international health governance have taught us, agreement on what constitutes such low-hanging fruit in the online information space and, more importantly, the definition of its causes and origins, will inevitably prove contentious. This means that States and other involved actors would have to agree on the lowest common denominator in this realm, as a starting point in their attempts at international cooperation. Progress beyond the low-hanging fruit is more challenging for two main reasons.

Firstly, while there may be consensus on the desirability of some goals, there may be disagreement over how the cost of reaching them is shared. Examples include the cost of moderating undesirable content on online platforms (and the cost of adverse publicity from unpopular moderation decisions), which may be analogized to the cost of vaccination development and production in the infectious disease space. Such activities need to be accompanied with appropriate mechanisms for resource sharing so that costs of the activities are equitably borne and are commensurate with the benefits. This rationale must also extend to the equal investment of content moderation resources across online platforms' global presence to ensure that "out-breaks" of disinformation are not relegated to regions of the world that may not be at the top of online platforms' market priorities lists.

Secondly, there may not even be consensus on the relative desirability of goals. The harms from lack of infection control (people dying as infectious diseases spread) are almost universally accepted as bad, while the harms from the spread of disinformation are more contested and often a matter to be judged in the "eye of the beholder" or in this case, "disseminator." What may be "political speech" to one platform user is "hate speech" to another, and vice versa. What one State may consider interference in its electoral system, another State may disavow or label as an information campaign aimed at building oppositional political capital. Needless to say, achieving international agreement on what content may be deemed harmful and thus worthy of removal from online platforms poses a far greater challenge than agreeing on infectious diseases that should be prevented and cured. However, as with infectious diseases, the far-reaching consequences of harmful online content still necessitates efforts to find common ground in regulating such content, at the very least between like-minded nations.

Third, both nationally and internationally, resources to control infections and harmful content on social media (such as vaccines, staff, and systems to enforce content moderation) are largely private goods (rivalrous and excludable). Conversely, the goods from better control (such as better information leading to people making more welfare-enhancing choices) are largely public goods (non-rivalrous and non-excludable) or at least club goods (non-rivalrous and excludable). As a result, both a national and international framework that addresses platform responsibility and content moderation must take this into account and create appropriate incentives that shape online platforms' resource allocation decisions.

8

Platform Responsibility Reforms

Lessons from International Financial Regulation

Federico Lupo-Pasini

8.1 INTRODUCTION

The global nature of online platforms makes their regulation very complex and challenging. Such complexity arises from the difficulty of regulation to capture the cross-border effects of online platform's activities.[1] The asymmetry between the national reach of law versus the global scope of the market is not a problem unique to internet platforms. As we saw in the other contributions in this book, global health governance and corporate tax suffer from similar challenges.[2] Other examples include competition policy, international trade regulation, and climate regulation, just to name a few. When problems are global, only international cooperation can address them in a satisfactory way.[3] In many of those areas, political, social, or economic barriers stand in the way of global Pareto optimal solutions. Yet, there are examples in international regulation that show that under certain conditions, global cooperation is indeed feasible and can bring a long-lasting positive regulatory equilibrium. International banking regulation is one such example.[4]

In this chapter, I will draw a parallel between international financial regulation and platform regulation. In many ways, banks and platforms share similar issues.

[1] There is a vast scholarship on the challenges of internet jurisdiction. *See* Teresa Scassa & Robert Currie, *New First Principles: Assessing the Internet's Challenges to Jurisdiction* (2010) 42 (4) GEORGETOWN J. OF INT'L L. 1018; Joel Reidenberg et. al, *Internet Jurisdiction: A Survey of Legal Scholarship Published in English and United States Case Law* (Fordham Law, Legal Studies Research Paper No. 2309526, 2013). On the international jurisdictional aspects of platforms governance, *see* Dan Jerker & B. Svantesson, Internet Jurisdiction and Intermediary Liability, Oxford Handbook of Online Intermediary Liability (Giancarlo Frosio, ed. 2020); Bertrand de La Chapelle & Paul Fehlinger, Jurisdiction on the Internet: From Legal Arms Race to Transnational Cooperation, Oxford Handbook of Online Intermediary Liability (Giancarlo Frosio, ed. 2020).

[2] *See* Chapters 7 and 9.

[3] *See* Joel. P. Trachtman, The Economic Structure of International Law (2008).

[4] On the problems of cooperation in financial regulation, see Federico Lupo-Pasini, The Logic of Financial Nationalism (2017).

They both operate in a global market and tend to produce harmful effects from their activities: systemic risks and harmful content, respectively. When banks started to expand significantly in global markets in the 1980s, bank supervisors were confronted with very similar challenges to what platform regulators are facing right now. Their answer was to entrust one organization, the Basel Committee on Banking Supervision, with the task of hosting the regulatory dialogue that eventually led to a common regulatory framework – the Basel Capital Accord, also known as Basel I, II, and III.[5] While not all the conditions that underpinned the success of the Basel Accord can be replicated for internet platforms, it is nonetheless helpful to rely on this experience as a potential guide for platform regulators across the globe.

8.2 THE RATIONALE FOR REGULATORY ACTION

Before we venture into the complex discussion on the international regulation of global banks and internet platforms, which will occupy a large part of this chapter, we need to explain what these two regimes have in common from a regulatory perspective. Banks and platforms share two critical regulatory problems. First, they both exist and operate in a network. Second, they both generate harmful effects from their activities. In this section, I will explain how financial regulation has tackled the negative externalities of banks' activities and draw a parallel with the regulation of platforms.

8.2.1 *Understanding Banking and Platform Networks*

Banks and platforms operate in an ecosystem – the financial system and the internet, respectively – where they are forced to interact with third parties to provide their services. Both organizations are structurally connected to a broad network of users, suppliers, clients, and other entities without which they cannot function.

Bank balance sheets give an excellent idea of how interconnectedness operates in banking.[6] On the liability side, banks borrow in many ways from various parties. They take deposits from retail customers. They issue multiple forms of debt securities such as secured or loss-absorbing bonds from institutional and retail investors. They borrow short-term from repo lenders (a service sometimes offered by other banks) and money market funds. They assume potential derivatives liabilities with

[5] International banking regulation is a very complex and multifaceted subject, given the structure of modern commercial banks that operate as investment firms and commercial lenders. In this chapter, I will discuss the prudential regulation of banks, whose centrepiece is capital and liquidity regulation. For more information on this topic, *see* Simon Gleeson, Gleeson on the International Regulation of Banking (2018).

[6] John Armour et al., Principles of Financial Regulation 284–87 (2016); Nicholas Arregui, Mohamed Norat, Antonio Pancorbo & Jordi Scarlata, *Addressing Interconnectedness: Concepts and Prudential Tools* (IMF Working Paper WP/13/199, International Monetary Fund, 2013).

various traders. In addition, they receive financing in the form of equity from their shareholders, which take the enterprise risks of investing in the bank and the rewards if the bank makes profits. On the asset side, banks invest their money (which originates from the various sources described above) in many ways. They lend to retail and commercial customers by issuing loans and mortgages. They pledge debt securities as collateral for other operations (including short-term financing for other financial institutions). They also invest in markets by purchasing various financial instruments or gold and hold some deposits at the central bank. This very quick snapshot of banks' activities shows that banks are legally and financially intertwined with a myriad of different actors – mostly, other financial institutions – in a way that make each of them inherently co-dependent. Yet, operating into the financial system is fundamental for banks, as it reduces transaction costs and expands the pool of capital available.[7]

Internet platforms also operate in a network – the internet – and rely on interconnectedness, albeit very differently.[8] Indeed, platforms rely on third-party app developers or influencers to create the content that is, in turn, offered to end users. In most cases, including Twitter, Instagram, or Facebook, end users are at the same time active generators of content as well as passive consumers of content. More importantly, platforms are often connected to maximize their users' network effects. For instance, Instagram feeds can be shared through WhatsApp, Twitter, Pinterest, and other platforms. The same is true with most other apps like TikTok or YouTube – thus expanding further the network effects that the platform can rely on. This particular business model is facilitated by a specific regulatory approach that favors interconnectivity and interoperability as the dominant norms.[9] Finally, like banks are linked to their depositors, also apps are linked to the final users who provide indirect inputs into the functioning of the platform.

8.2.2 *Externalities*

Being part of a network would not be a problem if it wasn't because both banks and platforms are structurally prone to generate harmful effects through their activities. This creates a regulatory problem as these harmful effects negatively impact the entire network where the firm operates. In other words, without regulation, the business models of banks and platforms would make them inherently unable to perform their functions in a socially efficient way. In economics, this problem is described as an externality. This concept defines the indirect costs (negative

7 IMF, Understanding Financial Interconnectedness (2010); IMF , Understanding Financial Interconnectedness – Supplementary Information (2010).

8 Martin Peits & Paul Belleflamme, The Economics of Platforms (2021).

9 Niels ten Oever, The Metagovernance of Internet Governance, Power and Authority in Internet Governance Return of the State? (Blayne Haggart, Natasha Tusikov & Jan Aart Scholte, eds. 2021).

externalities) or benefits (positive externalities) that a third party receives due to another party's particular activity.[10]

When it comes to banking, the main problem has always been to tame the excessive proclivity of banks to take risks and, on a broader level, to ensure that financial losses are not transferred across the financial system.[11] Unfortunately, banks cannot avoid taking risks. Indeed, their funding and operational model is based on borrowing short term and investing long term. While banks try to minimize financial losses by adopting internal models that calculate their various credit, market, and operational risks, they cannot eliminate them. Risk is a necessary part of finance that banks have to live with.[12]

Crucially, despite taking risks, banks do not fully internalize the financial costs of their activities. Indeed, the accounting mechanics of bank balance sheets means that a financial loss on the asset side (the bank's investments) is inevitably met by a loss from the liabilities side. In other words, the loss would be taken by one of the bank's various creditors. When financial losses are too high, the insolvency of a bank would create a cascade of negative spillovers to all the bank's creditors and, progressively, to the entire financial system. We define this as "systemic risk."[13]

Platforms' activities can also produce externalities, both positive and negative.[14] Depending on whether they are open access or on subscription, platforms' network effects enhance the platform's value for every additional user they attract. This means that platforms are provided incentives to attract users and content producers to expand their networks. Yet, the more a platform successfully expands its usership and increases the audience, the higher the chance that harmful content will be drawn due to the platform's increased ability to disseminate content. Sometimes, the same content can become viral thanks to particular algorithms and recommendation systems. Harmful content can be considered a negative externality of platforms' activities as it negatively affects some users.

[10] Steven Shavell, Foundations of Economic Analysis of Law 77–101 (2004).

[11] Armour et al., *supra* note 6, at 57–59.

[12] *Id.*, at 289.

[13] Steven Schwarcz defines systemic risk as "the risk that (i) an economic shock such as market or institutional failure triggers (through a panic or otherwise) either (X) the failure of a chain of markets or institutions or (Y) a chain of significant losses to financial institutions, (ii) resulting in increases in the cost of capital or decreases in its availability, often evidenced by substantial financial-market price volatility." *See*, Steven L. Schwarcz, *Systemic Risk*, 97 The Georgetown Law Journal 193, 204 (2008); *See also* Viral V. Acharya, A *Theory of Systemic Risk and Design of Prudential Bank Regulation*, 5 Journal of Financial Stability 245 (2009); Douglas W. Diamond & Philip H. Dybvig, *Bank Runs, Deposit Insurance, and Liquidity*, 91 Journal of Political Economy 401 (1983); Jean-Charles Rochet & Jean Tirole, *Interbank Lending and Systemic Risk*, 28 Journal of Money, Credit and Banking 733–34 (1996); Franklin Allen & Douglas Gale, *Financial Contagion* 1–2 (C.V. Starr Center for Applied Econ., Research Report No. 98-33, 1998).

[14] Yassine Lefouili & Leonardo Madio, *The Economics of Platform Liability*, 53 Eur. J. of Law & Econ. 319, 324 (2022).

Ultimately, much like banks have an incentive to take on more significant risks to improve profitability, platforms have an incentive not to police content to protect their network. Harmful content for platforms is much like market or credit risk for banks. It is a by-product of the firm's activities and business model that cannot be easily eliminated. In the case of platforms, harmful content is a structural element of the platforms' business model, which relies on network effects as its primary driver of profit. Given platforms' inherent need to attract users and producers, policing content is arguably a barrier to growth. It would limit the potential expansion of the platform to new users and producers.

8.2.3 *Regulating Externalities*

Regulating externalities requires striking a trade-off between the need to guarantee the maximum profitability for the firm, on the one hand, and the protection of third parties' interests, on the other.

In banking, regulating negative externalities has been achieved through various policies. First, banks are screened before being given a licence to operate – thus, before being admitted into the financial system – and monitored by supervisory agencies through various means. Second, banks must finance their operations through loss-absorbing instruments, including capital and subordinated bonds that can be converted into equity if the bank's losses pass a certain threshold. In addition, they must keep a portion of their funds liquid to meet a sudden surge in creditors' withdrawals. Third, banks must restrict their investment choices by not concentrating on a few assets. All these tools reduce the freedom of maneuver of banks and, with that, their profitability to a certain extent.[15]

Regulating platforms' externalities is perhaps more challenging as the regulation of internet platforms has been historically based on two fundamental pillars: openness and freedom. Notwithstanding this, if demand for a more interventionist approach arises, liability rules could be used to restrain the harmful effects of free speech. According to Lefouili and Madio, liability rules may be socially desirable when the interests of the platform to police itself and the interests of the society are not aligned.[16] This could be because of externalities and excessive market power arising from the quasi-monopolistic nature of some platforms.[17]

The decision is not straightforward, as liability rules might also reduce platforms' profitability and innovation. This largely depends on how they are designed. The rules on platform liability can be intended as a spectrum from lenient (no liability)

[15] Whether capital reduces banks' profitability is an old debate in economics. For an argument in support of capital as the primary source of funding see, Anat Admati and Martin Hellwig, The Bankers' New Clothes: What's Wrong with Banking and What to Do About It (2013).

[16] Lefouili & Madio, *supra* note 14, at 323.

[17] Xinyue Hua & Kathryn Spier, *Product Safety, Contracts, and Liability*, 51 The RAND Journal of Economics (2020).

to strict (strict liability). Each choice will have a cost on the firm and the consumers. From a regulatory perspective, a strict liability regime might reduce the attractiveness of platforms – very much like adopting very high capital adequacy standards for banks might reduce the bank's profitability. There are different potential explanations for this. First, a strict liability regime would inevitably lead to higher litigation costs and increased fines. The threat of litigation would then translate into over-policing by platforms eager to avoid penalties and prolonged court battles. Second, the increased need for platforms to divert financial and human resources to police content would increase firms' operating costs and reduce their profitability. This will then increase the costs of using the platform for consumers.[18]

8.3 THE CHALLENGES OF REGULATING FIRMS IN GLOBAL MARKETS

The regulation of externalities in banks and platforms is made astonishingly more complicated by the global nature of their networks. Regulating firms operating in a global market presents unique challenges. Regulators need to factor in two additional elements when designing rules: the presence of foreign firms and users and the challenge of foreign regulators with different regulatory objectives.

8.3.1 *Global Markets in Banking and Internet Platforms*

Since the 1970s, banks and capital markets have progressively internationalized.[19] Many Western and Asian banks now operate regionally or, in some cases, globally through branches and subsidiaries. Those local entities are themselves very connected with the local market. They raise debt and, sometimes, capital locally and invest in the local economy. Capital markets also operate globally. Corporations can list in foreign stock exchanges and issue foreign-denominated debt. Investment funds and global banks also sell various instruments to clients abroad with minimal regulatory barriers.[20]

Global financial interconnectedness brings many benefits, but it also means that a problem in one part of the global financial system can quickly spill out beyond national boundaries. We define it as "global systemic risk."[21] The first manifestation of global systemic risk was during the string of banking crises in the 1980s and early 1990s. Still, it was during the 2008 global financial crisis – at the very height of

[18] Lefouili & Madio, *supra* note 14, at 324.

[19] Emilios Avgouleas, Governance of Global Financial Markets: The Law, the Economics, the Politics 35–54 (2012); Rawi Abdelal, Capital Rules: The Construction of Global Finance (2007).

[20] IMF, *supra* note 7.

[21] Globalization and Systemic Risk (Douglass Evanoff et al., eds. 2009); Roger W. Ferguson Jr., International Financial Stability (2007).

financial globalization – that we witnessed how global systemic risk truly operates. The collapse of several financial institutions in the US triggered a chain reaction that immediately impacted European banking and capital markets.[22]

The structure of the internet is somehow very similar, as it developed over the years as a fundamentally global network. Interconnectivity brings substantial benefits as it allows platforms to reach economies of scale, increase network effects, and spur innovation. Platforms or apps developed in one country can be immediately launched and made accessible to users across the globe. This is possible due to the inherently stateless nature of the internet, where the technical specifications in systems like iOS or Android are often more important than the local regulatory requirements. While firewalls and other barriers to access specific platforms exist and are often applied to censor content, these barriers are an exception to the norm. Yet global interconnectivity dramatically increases the reach of negative externalities sometimes produced by platforms as many more users – often with different cultural and political sensitivities to content – can be impacted.

8.3.2 *Regulatory Trilemma*

The next question is how to approach regulating globally active and interconnected firms. This section discusses the main theoretical approaches in the financial regulation literature.

Much like the internet, the global financial system is built upon a dangerous asymmetry between the global scope of financial markets and the national scope of economic policies.[23] Unlike other areas of international economic policy that rely on an international organization to set binding rules and solve interstate disputes,[24] international finance has historically operated through nonbinding agreements. Without an international organization competent to develop a common rulebook, each country is free to regulate and police firms operating in its jurisdiction. In an interconnected market, national control over financial policies creates two main challenges.

First, globally active firms can practice regulatory arbitrage and force national regulators to compete in designing rules that appeal to firms as opposed to regulations tailored to the need of the local market. If the cross-border provision of services is possible, firms would exploit regulatory loopholes and relocate to jurisdictions with minimal regulatory or business constraints. This would place regulators

[22] The collapse of Lehman Brothers in August 2008 – which was back then the most international US financial institution – almost immediately sent a funding shock to all its European subsidiaries. As these were connected to the local markets, they created a contagion across the local financial system. In turn, the financial crises in various European countries created a systemic shock into the real economy, which ultimately affected the fiscal balance of a few European countries.

[23] Lupo-Pasini, *supra* note 4.

[24] The classical example is international trade, where rules are set and adjudicated at the World Trade Organization.

between a rock and a hard place, as they have to strike a delicate balance between the need to design rules that respond to local economic needs or attitudes – be these stringent prudential rules or very lenient free speech laws – and the need to maintain the competitiveness of national firms against foreign firms.

If regulations are too rigid, regulators risk that firms relocate to a different jurisdiction where the regulatory compliance costs are lower, thus putting the remaining firms at a competitive disadvantage. Conversely, if regulations are too lenient, regulators might not respond to the local regulatory needs. As I will explain in Section 8.4, this was the main problem that banks faced with regard to capital adequacy regulation in the 1980s. The regulatory dichotomy between competitiveness and national interest is made more complicated by the option of a third choice: autarchy. In other words, if regulators are unwilling to tailor their rules to the demand of the global market, they adopt a protectionist stance and close their market to foreign-based firms.

Second, when foreign firms conduct business on a cross-border basis while regulated by their home rules,[25] host regulators cannot address the negative externalities those firms produce in the host regulator's market.[26] For example, imagine a bank headquartered in Country A (subject to Country A's rulebook) with substantial operations in Country B through a network of branches. Country B's supervisor (the host) will not be able to control the bank's solvency and risk position, which might create risks for local creditors. The same example could be easily used for an internet platform subject to its home country's rule. If the home rules allow for harmful speech that has a detrimental impact on host users, there is little the host regulator can do other than adopt a protectionist stance that blocks the platform. In both cases, the only option for the host regulator is to prevent the foreign firm from operating in the host territory.

Several political science, economics, and legal scholars have successfully analyzed the challenges of global regulation. The most important contributions are regulatory race theories, transnational regulatory network theories, and dominance theories.[27] Schoenmaker's *Financial Trilemma* illustrates very well the complexity of international regulatory design in international banking (Figure 8.1).[28] The trilemma posits that an interconnected financial system cannot achieve at the same time: (1) national sovereignty over financial policies, (2) an optimum level of global financial stability (essentially, the absence of cross-border externalities), and (3) meaningful financial integration. States have to give up one of them.

25 In banking, this would occur when the bank operates abroad through branches or subsidiaries. Internet platforms operate cross-border by simply offering their services and products to customers located in foreign jurisdictions.

26 In international banking, the "home supervisor" is the supervisor/regulator where the bank is headquartered. In contrast, the "host supervisor" is the supervisor/regulator in the foreign jurisdiction where the bank operates through branches or subsidiaries.

27 I will discuss some of those theories in Section 8.4.

28 Dirk Schoenmaker, Governance of International Banking: The Financial Trilemma (2013).

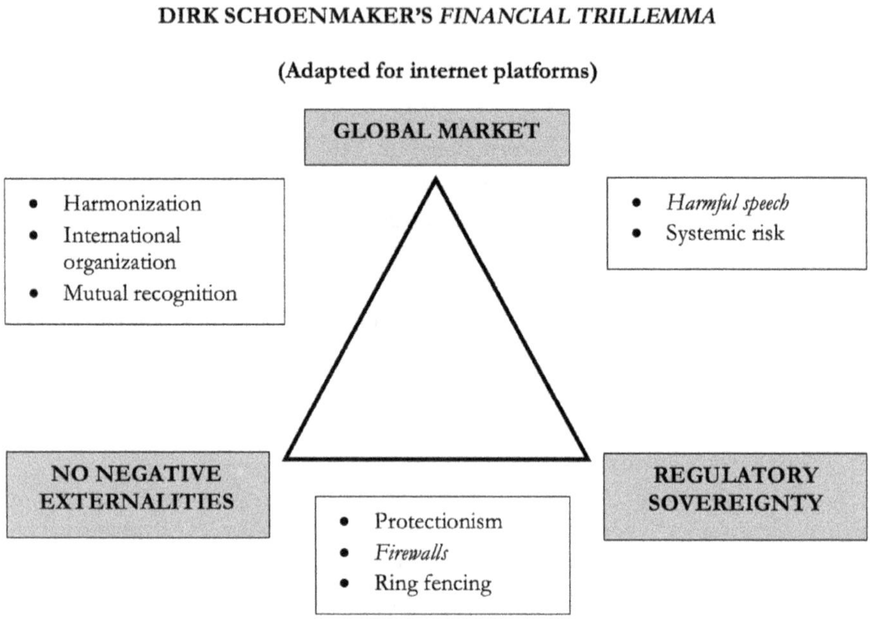

FIGURE 8.1 Dirk Schoenmaker's *Financial Trilemma* (adapted for internet platforms).

According to Schoenmaker's theory, if countries maintain financial integration and national control over financial policies, they will inevitably suffer instability as foreign regulators refuse to cooperate. Alternatively, if they want to achieve a globally stable financial system, they have two options. One option is to relinquish the power to set financial policies. This can be done in many ways, from regulatory harmonization to mutual recognition or even creating a global institution tasked with setting international rules. The opposite option is the reduction of financial integration. This alternative can also take many shapes and forms. The easiest option is to ask foreign banks to incorporate locally through subsidiaries, thus giving up their freedom to move assets across the consolidated global banking group. The most drastic option is a return to Bretton Woods–like financial system in which there is no capital mobility and financial systems operate only within national lines.

The problem of cross-border negative externalities plays out slightly differently with internet platforms. The policing of platforms allows for a higher margin of control and flexibility by national regulators compared to what we see with banking. For instance, a national regulator might opt to restrict speech that is destabilizing internally but to allow speech that is destabilizing externally. Notwithstanding this, it is helpful to use the trilemma analogy as it gives a sense of the broader cooperation trade-offs with which internet regulators have to grapple.

Regulators unwilling to sacrifice their regulatory freedom and eager to protect local users against harmful speech originating from foreign-based internet platforms will have no option but to react. They can do so in many ways. One drastic option would be to erect firewalls or other protectionist measures that reduce local access to foreign platforms. This, however, would hurt consumers not affected by harmful content. A milder option would entail the regulation of foreign platforms according to the local liability regime. Thus, foreign platforms would be required to comply with local platform content rules requiring the takedown of harmful content or the imposition of penalties for breaches of content policy. Foreign platforms would face the choice of either adapting to the host country's regulatory and legal requirements or else renouncing to enter the host country's market if the cost of compliance is deemed too high. At the same time, regulators must assess the risks of harmful speech from foreign platforms if they want to maintain an open internet and regulatory sovereignty. The best solution is to agree on a common global framework, which reduces regulatory competition and, at the same time, maintains the benefits of interconnectivity and openness.

After illustrating the choice regulators need to confront, the next step is to assess how cooperation can be achieved. International cooperation in financial regulation has been through various ups and downs in the last four decades. While cooperation in certain areas of financial regulation was successful, for instance, in the prudential regulation of banks, in others, it failed dramatically. In Section 8.4, I will look at the most successful experience in regulatory cooperation in finance: the harmonization of bank prudential rules in the Basel Accord.

8.4 REGULATORY HARMONIZATION

When banking integration took off in the 1980s, regulators in the UK and the US were confronted with the problem of how to maintain the competitiveness of their local banks against Japanese banks, which were subject to more lenient prudential rules. The critical issue was the application of capital adequacy requirements.

8.4.1 *The Basel Accord*

Bank regulators in the United Kingdom and the United States, the two most globally active banking systems in the 1980s, adopted capital adequacy rules as part of their prudential rulebook.[29] They required locally supervised banks to fund their assets with a minimum amount of 3 percent to 5 percent of capital.[30] The rules were eventually harmonized between the two jurisdictions through a bilateral supervisory agreement. When global bank activity took off in the 1980s, US and UK banks found themselves

[29] The banking sector highly contested capital adequacy rules as they allegedly increased banks' funding costs and reduced profitability. *See* ADMATI and HELLWIG, *supra* note 8.

[30] Rules varied according to jurisdiction, type of bank, and calculation methods. For the US, *see* Joseph Haubrich, A *Brief History of Bank Capital Requirements in the United States*, Economic Commentary 2020-05 – Federal Reserve Bank of Cleveland (2020).

at a disadvantage against foreign competitors – especially Japanese banks – which did not apply the same prudential standard. In a few years, cheaper funding costs allowed Japanese banks to acquire a substantial market share in the US.

The issue for Western regulators was how to strike a balance between the need to protect the stability of their financial systems while at the same time maintaining the competitiveness of local firms. Regulators were caught between a rock and a hard place as they were confronted with a choice between the risks and the benefits of financial globalization. The option of withdrawing licences to foreign banks was not feasible, as the economy was booming, and local industries needed fresh cash from foreign banks. US and UK regulators had a binary option: either to lower their capital requirements to align them with Japanese banks or convince the Japanese regulator to accept a common regulatory standard. Negotiations took place within the Basel Committee on Banking Supervision (BCBS), a regulatory network for bank regulators from G10 countries.[31] Ultimately, under the peer pressure from BCBS members and the open threats by the US to withdraw the licence to Japanese banks, Japanese regulators caved in.

The agreement to implement a common capital adequacy standard for banks was finalized in 1988 and adopted not long after that. It was enshrined in a supervisory agreement, the Basel Accord – also known as Basel I. The Basel Accord went through substantial iterations, especially after the 2008 global financial crisis, and it is now in its third version.[32] Unlike international treaties, the Basel Accord is a soft agreement. Thus, the agreement is voluntary, and it only offers a template, albeit a very detailed one, that national regulators are free to adapt and tweak to the specificities of their financial system. The agreement sets a minimum standard that national regulators can improve, as some did.[33] While there were problems in implementing Basel I and II, the latest version has been widely adopted by BCBS members with a reasonable degree of uniformity. At present, Basel III is the industry standard for bank prudential regulation.[34]

8.4.2 *Explaining Cooperation*

The Basel Accord has been widely studied in the legal, political science, and economics literature.[35] Two questions, in particular, are essential for the

[31] Charles Goodhart, The Basel Committee on Banking Supervision: A History of the Early Years 1974–1997 (2011).

[32] Daniel K. Tarullo, Banking on Basel: The Future of International Financial Regulation (2008).

[33] For instance, Switzerland has historically adopted a regulatory capital ratio that is higher than that required by the Basel Accord.

[34] Simon Gleeson, The International Regulation of Banking: Capital and Risk Requirements (2013).

[35] David Andrew Singer, Regulating Capital: Setting Standards for the International Financial System (2007); Bryce Quillin, International Financial Co-Operation Political Economics of Compliance with the 1988 Basel Accord (2008); Tarullo, *supra* note 32.

comparative analysis of the international regulation of platform responsibility: why was harmonization obtained? And how was compliance with the agreement achieved?

The binary option between harmonization and regulatory competition has been subject to extensive scholarly analysis.[36] In the earlier literature on international finance, a debate ensued about whether regulatory differences would lead to a race to the bottom or the top in financial regulation. Political scientists such as Cerny argued that the push from the financial sector to maintain competitiveness would lead to a dangerous de-regulatory drive.[37] Conversely, Romano argues that regulatory harmonization forces firms to adopt similar strategies, which might increase systemic risk if they do not work.[38] Regulatory diversity would boost innovation and force regulators to compete for the best regulatory framework. Ultimately, the Basel Accord showed that harmonization could be achieved, although only in Basel III the regulatory playing field was leveled up to a stringent standard.

As a subordinate question, it is interesting to see why an agreement was reached on the prudential standards adopted by Western regulators and not on the Japanese prudential rules. Political economy scholars such as Keohane and Kapstein argued that cooperation could be achieved because all national regulators agreed that low capital requirements would put their financial systems at risk of instability.[39] In his analysis of the Basel Accord, Singer similarly argues that national regulators had little choice but to strike an international deal due to the severe risks of financial instability that lax capital requirements would bring.[40]

Hence, cooperation was the easiest choice. Other scholars, including Simmons and Drezner, have tried to explain this outcome as a result of market dominance by the United States and the United Kingdom.[41] According to their theories, the

[36] Daniel W. Drezner, *Globalization, Harmonization, and Competition: The Different Pathways to Policy Convergence*, Journal of European Public Policy 841 (2005); Junji Nakagawa, International Harmonization of Economic Regulation (2012); Andrew T. Guzman, *International Regulatory Harmonization*, 3 Chicago J. Int'l. Law 271, 278 (2003).

[37] Philip Cerny, *Globalization and the Changing Logic of Collective Action*, 49 Int'l. Org 595 (1995)

[38] Roberta Romano, *Empowering Investors: A Market Approach to Securities Regulation*, 107 Yale L.J. 2359 (1998); Roberta Romano, *For Diversity in the International Regulation of Financial Institutions: Critiquing and Recalibrating the Basel Architecture*, 31 Yale J. of Reg. 1 (2014); Roberta Romano, *Against Financial Regulation Harmonization: A Comment* (Yale Law & Economics Research Paper No. 414, Nov. 20, 2010) available at SSRN: https://ssrn.com/abstract=1697348.

[39] Ethan B. Kapstein, Governing the Global Economy: International Finance and the State (1994); Ethan B. Kapstein, *Resolving the Regulator's Dilemma: International Coordination of Banking Regulation*, 55 Int'l. Org. 323 (1989).

[40] Singer looks at the incentives of regulators to level up the standards and proposes a model based on the domestic pressure faced by regulators in light of exogenous shocks to financial stability or international competitiveness. *See* David Andrew Singer, *supra* note 35.

[41] Daniel W. Drezner, All Politics Is Global: Explaining International Regulatory Regimes 135–37 (2008); Beth A. Simmons, *The International Politics of Harmonization: The Case of Capital Market Regulation*, 55 Int'l. Org. 589, 601–5 (2001).

dominance of big financial centers would act as a magnet for smaller centers, which are compelled to align their rules if they want to access foreign markets. While dominance theories cannot be extended to the entire set of financial regulations, they help explain the Basel Accord.[42] Indeed, Japan was practically coerced into agreeing to the standard under the threat of its banks being denied market access in the US – back then, the most lucrative market for international banks.

A more recent stream of scholarship looks at why cooperation is maintained given the non-binding nature of the Basel Accord. Transnational Regulatory Network (TRN) theories explain cooperation by examining the institutional structures underpinning the design and implementation of financial standards.[43] According to these theories, regulators participating in the network are compelled to comply with the standards due to pressure from different sources, including fellow regulators, the industry, and international organizations. In this regard, it is interesting to see how the IMF and the World Bank have consistently monitored compliance with the Basel Accord in their periodical financial sector assessment reports.

8.5 LESSONS FOR PLATFORM RESPONSIBILITY FROM THE BASEL ACCORD

The experience with negotiating the Basel Accord and its subsequent implementation can offer some insights into what is needed to achieve an international agreement that is sustainable in the long term.

8.5.1 *The Importance of Regulatory Networks*

Firstly, the Basel Accord benefited from an already existing and well-functioning Transnational Regulatory Network, the BCBS, which was set up precisely to discuss and address common regulatory issues. Banking regulators from G10 countries had already cooperated successfully within that network to address the supervision of cross-border banks, an issue that caused various banking crises in the 1970s and early 1980s.[44] It is without a doubt that the positive experience in successful cooperation

42 Stavros Gadinis, *The Politics of Competition in Financial Regulation*, 49 Harvard Int'l L.J. (2008).

43 Andrew Moravcsik, A *New Statecraft? Supranational Entrepreneurs and International Cooperation*, 53 Int'l. Org. 267, 269–70 (1999); Kal Raustiala, *The Architecture of International Cooperation: Transgovernmental Networks and the Future of International Law*, 43 Va. J. Int'l L. 1, 5 (2002); Pierre-Hugues Verdier, *Transnational Regulatory Networks and Their Limits*, 34 Yale J. Int'l L. 113 (2009); Chris Brummer, Soft Law and the Global Financial System: Rulemaking in the 21st Century 63–67 (2012); Anne Marie Slaughter, A New World Order 36–61 (2004).

44 The Basel Committee on Banking Supervision was created in 1974 to address the allocation of supervisory powers of cross-border banks between home and host supervisors. The first supervisory standard issued by the BCBS was the Basel Concordat.

with the Basel Concordat and the familiarity between national regulators helped to get another agreement on the ground.

Moreover, as correctly argued by network and institutional theories, national regulators faced heavy peer pressure to find a common standard that would work for the global banking industry. Putting up a fight to resist an agreement that most members saw as a positive advancement to safeguard financial stability would have put Japanese regulators in a very awkward position within the BCBS. Given the widespread consensus among regulators that capital adequacy rules were fundamental for guaranteeing financial stability, national regulators were under heavy pressure to adopt the standard as they did not want their banking system to be perceived as risky and unstable.[45]

Internet platforms, unfortunately, do not benefit from the presence of an established regulatory network like the BCBS. Internet governance is split across a few different organizations, such as the Internet Governance Forum or the Internet & Jurisdiction Policy Network, and a few other private sector organizations, such as the Internet Corporation for Assigned Names and Numbers (ICANN) or the Internet Society. The absence of a single catalyst of regulatory debate could make cooperation more difficult, as regulators might not feel the institutional and peer pressure they would otherwise experience if all regulatory actions on internet governance converged into one single regulatory network.

8.5.2 *Dominant Markets*

Secondly, there was an apparent power asymmetry between those financial regulators that wanted an agreement, the US and the UK (eventually followed by European G10 regulators), and those who resisted it, Japan.[46] In the 1980s, the US was the most significant banking market in size and business opportunities. The UK was not as big, but its capital market was well developed, and its banks were active globally. On the other hand, the Japanese market was very attractive but difficult to penetrate for foreign banks. Japanese banks needed market access to Europe and the US more than European and US banks needed access to the Japanese market. Thus, the threat by the United States to suspend the licence of Japanese banks that were not subjected to adequate prudential standards was seen as a clear danger by the burgeoning Japanese banking industry.

In this light, a global deal on the regulation of harmful speech could probably be pushed if enough pressure was coming from US regulators and the European Commission, as they oversee the two biggest markets for platforms. Both

[45] Simmons, *supra* note 41, at 602.

[46] Also, some European G10 countries (Germany and France) initially opposed the agreement. Still, they immediately agreed once they feared that they would be perceived as somehow inferior by the broader banking industry. *See* Kapstein, *supra* note 39, at 340–41.

jurisdictions, in different ways, play a prominent role in regulating the digital economy. The United States, as a host of the biggest internet companies in the world and a massive market in itself, is centrally placed to regulate digital platforms. The European Union, while less central in developing successful startups, has nonetheless acquired a major role as a global regulator due to its uncompromising stance in leveling up the regulatory playing field in data privacy and hate speech.[47] Following Simmons and Drezner's theories of regulatory dominance, once the two regulatory powers agree to a common standard, it would be difficult for smaller markets not to adjust to it.[48]

On the contrary, a division between US and EU regulators would probably make harmonization impossible. Unfortunately, this outcome might be inconceivable given the different interests at stake. One player, the US, has a clear incentive to promote innovation and guaranteeing a fertile ground for the development of new start-ups. This might lead to a softer stance on platform responsibility. On the other hand, the EU is historically more sensitive to the protection of consumers, which might push it toward a stricter approach to harmful content. Predicting whether such divisions can be healed as they were in banking regulation is challenging. Much depends on the economic development of the two markets over time and the degree of global integration achieved by platforms. Yet, as I show in Section 8.5.3, adopting a more flexible approach in the initial regulatory standard might help to get the two regulators progressively closer.

8.5.3 *The Flexibility of Soft Law*

Thirdly, the history of the Basel Accord clearly shows that regulatory standards have become increasingly stringent and more detailed. Basel I was only 30 pages long and was very basic in its approach. If we compare it with the latest version, Basel III, which extends to hundreds of pages if we also include the annexes, we can see an apparent trajectory toward increased precision and detail. The initial vagueness and flexibility of the standard allowed national regulators to accommodate the agreement to the specificities of their banking system. It also helped regulators sell the deal to local politicians and the local banking industry.

Notwithstanding this, it is essential to remember that Basel I, and especially Basel II, were considered one of the reasons for the regulatory failures that led to the global financial crisis in 2008. The excessive flexibility in calculating banks' risk-weighted assets allowed banks to bypass the capital ratio set as the agreement's primary objective, enabling them to increase their leverage. This element is widely recognized as the key reason for banks' excessive risk appetite and fragility during the 2008 financial crisis.

47 *See* Anu Bradford, The Brussel Effect (2012).

48 Simmons, *supra* note 41; Drezner, *supra* note 41.

In this light, it would be recommendable to work on a platform responsibility framework that is flexible enough to entice reluctant regulators to join in while progressively working to strengthen it once regulators and the industry have become used to it. For instance, the EU, US, and other national regulators could agree to work on an outcome-based framework that simply sets the basic principles and the final regulatory targets while maintaining flexibility in achieving them. This would allow national regulators to tweak the standards to the local needs and legal framework. It would arguably make the negotiation easier and faster. Over time, the framework could be improved and more detailed in its prescriptions.

8.5.4 *Compliance*

From a cooperation perspective, complying with international regulatory standards is much easier than in other areas of regulation, like cross-border banking resolution, where the incentives to defect are very high. Thus, the main hurdle is to reach a common position. Regulatory convergence confronts regulators with a very challenging initial task of accommodating different regulatory preferences and goals. Sometimes states want to achieve regulatory coordination with other states because they know this will bring more significant individual benefits than unilateralism. Still, they might fight over which alternative is best. Yet, states have few incentives to change once a common position is reached.[49] This explains why there has been no public attempt by national regulatory authorities to exit the Basel Accord. Two reasons explain why compliance with the Basel Accord worked.

First, the Basel Accord was immediately perceived as a fundamental regulatory tool by international financial organizations and the broader regulatory community. Backed by a widespread consensus among economists, no regulator raised doubt as to the effectiveness of capital adequacy measures in preventing financial instability. The IMF, the World Bank, and the OECD list the Basel Accord as one of the essential elements in the prudential regulatory framework and look for its adoption as part of their engagement with their members. The institutional pressure coming from international organizations helped to extend its adoption beyond G10 countries.

Secondly, it is essential to highlight that once the agreement was reached, there was pressure from the broader financial industry to implement the standards. Hedge funds, banks, investment funds, rating agencies, and other market players shared the common belief that capital adequacy rules were necessary to guarantee financial stability. Therefore, regulators faced much market pressure to adopt the standards as part of their prudential toolbox if they wanted to attract foreign capital.

[49] *See* Pierre-Hugues Verdier, *Transnational Regulatory Networks and Their Limits*, 34 Yale J. of Int'l L. 113 (2009); Chris Brummer, *How International Financial Law Works (and How It Doesn't)*, 99 Georgetown L J. 257 (2011); Chris Brummer, *Why Soft Law Dominates International Finance and Not Trade*, 13 J. of Int'l Econ. L. 623 (2010).

8.6 WHEN COOPERATION IS MORE DIFFICULT

The experience with the Basel Accord is somehow an unmatched success in international financial cooperation. As I explained earlier, various factors conspired to make cooperation easier. However, many other critical regulatory problems in international finance did not lead to optimal cooperation solutions, despite causing substantial negative externalities. Historically, cooperation has been challenging in many areas, including money laundering, securities regulation, over-the-counter (OTC) derivatives, central counterparties, and resolution and insolvency of cross-border financial institutions. More recently, national regulators are struggling to cooperate on cryptocurrencies and sustainable finance, the two key regulatory areas of contemporary finance.

Despite its allure and simplicity, harmonization is perhaps the most challenging cooperation solution. However, there are other regulatory options besides harmonization. In Section 8.6.1, I will briefly discuss two of them, extraterritoriality, and mutual recognition. I will do so by looking at the regulation and clearing of OTC derivatives.

8.6.1 *OTC Derivatives*

Markets, like banks, are also very susceptible to creating negative externalities. One problem, for instance, is the use of non-centrally cleared OTC derivatives. Without proper regulation, OTC derivatives can expose traders to substantial losses.[50] Without central clearing, traders cannot gauge the actual trading position of their counterparty, thus taking excessive risks. In a global market where derivatives trading often has a cross-border dimension, achieving a regulatory playing field is fundamental. Managing derivatives risks would prevent globally active foreign firms from creating global systemic spillovers. Not surprisingly, given OTC derivatives' havoc created during the 2008 global financial crisis, the 2009 Pittsburgh G20 put their regulation at the forefront of the regulatory agenda.[51]

The regulation of OTC derivatives is quite complex. Derivatives markets involve multiple actors other than the trading parties involved in the bilateral deal, including trade repositories, clearing agencies, and trading platforms. It also requires a vast array of regulatory interventions, from margin requirements to trade reporting requirements or the supervision of central counterparties, just to mention a few. Despite the push from national regulators, the Financial Stability Board (FSB), the

[50] *See* Dan Awrey, *Split Derivatives: Inside the World's Most Misunderstood Contract*, 2 YALE J. ON REG. 495 (2019).

[51] At the 2009 Pittsburgh summit, G20 leaders agreed to tackle the question of OTC derivatives and proposed that "all standardized OTC derivative contracts should be traded on exchanges or electronic trading platforms, where appropriate, and cleared through central counterparties by end-2012 at the latest. OTC derivative contracts should be reported to trade repositories. Non-centrally cleared contracts should be subject to higher capital requirements." G20 Leaders' Statement: The Pittsburgh Summit (Sept. 24–25, 2009).

International Organization of Securities Commissions (IOSCO), and other organi–ations, regulatory coordination has not been achieved on many critical regulatory issues. This does not mean that cooperation did not work at all. In many areas, there have been substantial improvements compared to 2008. Yet we are far from seeing the same regulatory playing field we achieved with capital adequacy regulation, where rules were substantially harmonized.[52] Instead, regulatory cooperation takes place through bilateral agreement on mutual recognition and the extraterritorial application of local laws.

8.6.2 *Mutual Recognition*

Mutual recognition is a possible solution to coordination problems that cannot be solved through harmonization. In a Mutual Recognition Agreement (MRA), two national regulators agree to determine each other's regulatory frameworks as substantially similar. Through the MRA, each national authority permits the partner's firms to access the domestic market without complying with local regulatory requirements. Firms must only comply with their home regulatory framework and can operate in a foreign market subject to home rules. In securities regulation, a mutual recognition agreement allows firms authorized and supervised in a foreign country to operate or transact in the host-country jurisdiction without the host country's approval, provided that the home country does the same with the host country's firms.[53] Some regulatory challenges with OTC derivatives were solved through MRAs, including the regulatory spat between the US Commodity Futures Trading Commission (CFTC) and the European Securities and Markets Authority (ESMA) over the recognition of foreign derivatives clearing regimes.[54]

Mutual Recognition was one of the driving forces behind the creation of the European Single Financial Market in the 1980s/1990s through its ability to promote financial integration without intruding on states' regulatory sovereignty.[55] This quality explains why recognition is considered an excellent approach to solving regulatory cooperation problems. In a world where policy coordination can only be achieved through lengthy multilateral negotiations, assigning the burden of regulating a financial institution or individual transaction to a single authority is the easiest way to promote efficient financial integration. The simple fact that countries do not need to engage in lengthy negotiations to agree on an identical regulatory regime, as

[52] IOSCO, Market Fragmentation & Cross-Border Regulation (2019); John Kiff et al., *Applying the Central Clearing Mandate: Different Options for Different Markets* (IMF Working Paper 22/14, 2022).

[53] Pierre-Hugues Verdier, *Mutual Recognition in International Finance*, 52 Harvard Int'l L.J. 55 (2008).

[54] European Commission Press Release IP/16/281, European Commission and the United States Commodity Futures Commission: Common approach for transatlantic CCPs (Feb. 10, 2016).

[55] Matteo Ortino, *The Role and Functioning of Mutual Recognition in the European Market of Financial Services*, 56 The Int'l and Comp. L. Quarterly 309 (2007).

is the case with harmonization, speeds up negotiations and arguably favors the signing of new agreements.

In this light, mutual recognition could be a useful tool for international cooperation on platform regulation if the main regulatory objective is to integrate the market. First, mutual recognition agreements can be structured as bilateral deals but later expanded to plurilateral agreements. This would allow two regulators with similar, but not identical, approaches to free speech or data sharing to mutually allow the partner's platforms to access their market without changing domestic law. Platforms would also be provided incentives to expand across borders as they would not be subject to two regulatory compliance requirements.

Yet, if not properly arranged, mutual recognition might entail substantial risks if the home regime is not up to the host country's standards, does not share the same regulatory goals, or has the incentive to externalize risks to the host country. This is why TRNs such as the FSB or the BCBS exert a vital role in setting minimum regulatory standards. In securities regulation, regulators are often more wary of the risks of giving access to firms authorized under a weak regulatory regime. In a mutual recognition agreement, regulators provide recognition to a foreign regime only after having conducted a compatibility test that ensures the similarity of regulations. Thus, in cross-border securities regulation, recognition usually levels up the regulatory playing field and operates only between partners with similar regimes. This ensures that no "firm can escape regulation" and no "dangerous" transactions can occur in a shared market.

The main risk associated with a mutual recognition solution in platform regulation is lowering consumer protection standards. If the host country's laws on free speech and harmful content were more rigid than the home's, the host country's users would be less protected against harmful content originating from the foreign platform as rules on content would follow the platform's home country's standards. Given that the regulation of harmful content is much closer to consumer protection than listing rules, it is more difficult to imagine that mutual recognition could be a solution for the regulation of harmful content. Very rarely do countries regulate consumer protection standards through mutual recognition. In conflict of laws, the law applicable to consumer protection issues is typically the laws of the consumer's jurisdiction, not the company's. This is because, in many jurisdictions, the European Union, above all, consumer protection is given primacy over other objectives.

8.6.3 *Extraterritorial Regulation*

The last possible option, albeit the most disruptive, is to extend local laws' reach to activities in another jurisdiction. This protects the jurisdiction that adopts this approach against the negative externalities from foreign firms. Extraterritoriality is a well-known regulatory instrument in finance, which has been used by US, UK, and EU regulators to address the risks in capital markets.[56] It is also used extensively by many jurisdictions for financial crime – such as corruption and money laundering – as it tackles actions that are often committed abroad but impact the local market.

Extraterritoriality is not a single clear-cut approach as it can be tailored according to the specific conditions of the market. The most common use of extraterritorial jurisdiction in finance is linking domestic law to local contact points. These contact points could be local firms or individuals affected by the foreign action or firms and national citizens operating abroad. The US Dodd-Frank Act, for instance, puts under the reach of US law any financial entity that (1) has transacted with a US counterparty, (2) enjoyed a financial guarantee provided by a US entity, or (3) has entered into a derivatives transaction with a counterparty that was guaranteed by a US entity. In the European Union, the European Market Infrastructure Regulation (EMIR) requires that clearinghouses authorized in a third country "comply with legally binding requirements which are equivalent to the requirements set out in EU law to be used by European firms.[57] Sometimes, the jurisdiction of securities regulators is extended to all activities that "have a direct and significant connection with activities in, or effect on, commerce in the United States," as in the Dodd-Frank Act.[58]

If protecting content users is the main regulatory objective, extraterritoriality is, undoubtedly, the best option. The extraterritorial reach of local content rules would protect local users against harmful content disseminated by a foreign platform. This would be the case if "users" were the contact point for applying local laws. Thus, in this case, it would be sufficient for specific content to reach users for the foreign platform to be subject to the final users' laws. This approach would be much closer to current regulatory practice when the main objective is to protect consumers.

Yet, the regulatory trade-offs associated with extraterritoriality are opposite to those related to mutual recognition. While extraterritoriality is better for protecting local consumers, it is much worse for market integration. Indeed, platforms located in countries with more liberal harmful content rules might be deterred from entering a market whose content rules would subject the platform to substantial litigation costs. Ultimately, firms are the primary victims of this situation as extraterritoriality increases market fragmentation. Indeed, firms must comply with multiple regulatory requirements for every jurisdiction they are linked to. We saw this with the

56 When capital markets integration took off in the 1980s, regulators in key financial centers – especially the US – had to grapple with the issue of how to treat a foreign company seeking access to the local markets. The SEC answered by requiring foreign firms listing in the US to comply with local rules, subject to a few exemptions. *See* Howell E. Jackson, *Substituted Compliance: The Emergence, Challenge, and Evolution of a New Regulatory Paradigm*, 1 J. FIN REG. 169, 172 (2015).

57 EMIR, art. 25(6).

58 Dodd-Frank Wall Street Reform and Consumer Protection Act §722(d).

regulation of OTC derivatives, which is still subject to numerous national regulatory requirements.[59] Moreover, extraterritoriality is perceived as an undiplomatic way to regulate commercial affairs. While it protects the jurisdiction that adopts it, it also reduces the regulatory sovereignty in the jurisdiction whose firms are targeted.

8.7 CONCLUSION

This chapter looked at the experience in regulating international banks and capital markets to draw lessons that could be applied to the regulation of online platforms. The history of the Basel Accord shows that regulating cross-border externalities is not impossible, notwithstanding the obvious political challenges. A few elements make cooperation easier: establishing a forum where national regulators and industry can discuss a common regulatory approach would make negotiations easier. Coordination between two dominant markets could pull the rest of the world toward the agreed regulatory standard. Finally, a light and flexible regulatory standard would make its adoption easier politically and enable the regulatory framework to develop organically.

When regulatory harmonization is not possible, other approaches can be considered. But they would come with substantial political and social costs. Mutual recognition of regulation between two or more countries would permit platforms to provide services to another country's consumers while subjecting them to their home country's rules. However, local consumers/users would not be protected under this model. Indeed, they would be subject to the regulatory approach of the country where the platform is headquartered. This makes this solution unlikely unless all countries share a common interest in pushing for the internationalization of their own domestic online platforms.

When the protection of local users is the main objective, the extraterritorial application of national laws to regulate the activities of foreign online platforms is the best solution. If a platform promotes harmful content, it could be subject to regulatory or civil action by the consumers of the country where its action was considered harmful. Yet, extraterritoriality comes with substantial costs, as it could block the international growth of online platforms, reduce cross-border data flows, and lead to tit-for-tat retaliatory action.

59 IOSCO, Market Fragmentation & Cross-Border Regulation (2019).

9

The International Tax Regulatory Approach as a Model for Platform Content Moderation

Carlo Garbarino

9.1 THE GLOBAL SCOPE OF THE TAX PROBLEM

This chapter examines the global regulatory issues concerning international taxation with particular attention to recent developments, in order to generate proposals for means of addressing platform content moderation issues at both the rule-making stage and the rule-application stage. We therefore provisionally assume that a potentially correct analogy between international tax regulation and platforms content regulation can be based on the fact that policy issues in areas are engendered by the prominent role that platforms – intended as "a foundation technology or set of components used beyond a single firm and that brings multiple parties together for a common purpose or to solve a common problem"[1] – have assumed in the new models for conducting business. We will subject this assumption to critical analysis.

We therefore surmise that there is a similarity between the "opportunistic" platform-generated profits diversion that will be described in this chapter and "immoderate" platform content use and develop an analogical argument based on this similarity: since the two situations are similar, if it is true that the international community should establish regulatory structures that "moderate" the opportunistic use of new technological platforms that artificially divert profits away from taxation, then it is also probably true that the same international community should establish regulatory structures that "moderate" the use of new technological platforms that artificially distort information.

It is essential to remark here the first phenomenological resemblance between the tax regulatory problem and the regulatory problem of content moderation: non-state actors through platforms access, manage, and regulate flows of capital and similarly

[1] Annabelle Gower & Michael Cusumano, *Defining Software Ecosystems: A Survey of Software Platforms and Business Network Governance* (2004), http://slingerjansen.files.wordpress.com/2009/04/definingsecos.pdf.

manage flows of information, designing new imaginary gateways for both capital and information that exploit regulatory differentials. So, in both cases there is the need for a regulatory response both at international and domestic level.

We can therefore argue that there is a striking "homology" between capital and information. Homology is not just a phenotypic similarity in the current aspects but a more profound similarity of two phenomena over time because they have a common origin.[2] In social sciences, homology is a situation in which different human beliefs, practices, or artifacts share similarities due to genetic or historical connections. Here, in the discussion of regulatory options about profit diversion (based on capital) and content moderation (based on information), the homology is the underlying similarity between capital and information that in platform economy tend to be merged, becoming a hybrid constituted by intangible information, defined here as "computational capital."

The upshot is that policies that counteract aggressive tax strategies that rely on fully mobile capital may be considered, in a broad sense, a potential model for policies for platform content moderation that rely on fully mobile computational capital. Therefore, one can hypothesize that tax regulatory approaches may be of potential interest for platform content moderation in spite of the fact that, as we will see, they have not so far proved entirely successful.

The chapter will begin by explaining the scope of the global tax problem (Section 9.1) and then address the related regulatory process at two levels. At a first descriptive level, the chapter will detail the process and institutional structures by which policies have been actually developed as well as their shortcomings (Section 9.2). At a second deeper explicatory level, the chapter will attempt to flesh out the phenomenology of actual platform operation and its global tax implications (Section 9.3). The chapter will conclude suggesting possible lessons that can be learned from tax regulation for platform responsibility rules (Section 9.4).

Let's start with explaining the scope of the global regulatory tax problem. The international tax framework based on treaties established in the twentieth century aimed at preventing double taxation in case of reciprocal investments among countries. This framework appeared to be relatively stable until a novel issue emerged: countries unilaterally reduce their effective tax rates to attract capital, thereby affecting the mobile capital base determining what has been defined as "tax competition," that is a race-to-the-bottom of tax rates, a competition among States to attract investments.[3] Under these competitive constraints, capital is invested in jurisdictions where the tax rates are lower.

[2] In evolution, homology is the similarity of the structure, physiology, or development of different species of organisms based upon their descent from a common evolutionary ancestor.

[3] *See, for example*, Michael P. Devereux, Ben Lockwood & Michela Redoano, *Do Countries Compete over Corporate Tax Rates?*, 92 J. PUB. ECON. 1210 (2008); Joel Slemrod, *Are Corporate Tax Rates, or Countries, Converging?*, 88 J. PUB. ECON. 1169 (2004).

Bilateral tax treaties do not address tax competition because they do not include tools to limit the decisions of key players about the location of investment and are just aimed at preserving the Westphalian sovereignty of the Contracting States. The consequence is that tax treaties do not provide tools for multilateral cooperation and governance in respect to tax competition so that there is the need to devise new regulatory tools.[4]

The tax predicament, however, not only rests on a competition among States but also on the fact that multinational enterprises (MNEs) pursue action plans that thoroughly exploit tax differentials. We will see in detail what is the actual operation of platforms currently used by MNEs (Section 9.3), but one initially should be aware of the fact that, in a "classic" sense based on corporate legal concepts, MNEs respond to central management and control, relying on foreign controlled companies and chains of companies ("units") that are coordinated under global tax strategies, even if they might be decentralized in terms of markets. By contrast, individual states only rely on local control of a territory for tax purposes. MNEs can thus be fittingly denominated "Global Actors" because they enter an asymmetric game in which the other actors are states, that is, local actors.

So, there is an additional dimension of tax competition that goes beyond a conflict-game among states leading to race-to the-bottom of tax rates: private actors such as MNEs intermediate between the state where they are based (the home state) and the states where they market their products or services (the host states) to reduce or eliminate taxation.[5] This goal is pursued through top-down "aggressive tax strategies."

These strategies deployed by Global Actors are difficult to be defined in simple terms because they have reached a level of staggering complexity that cannot be recounted here but are in essence based on the "separate unity principle" accepted by virtually all corporate tax systems. This principle is derived from corporate limited liability and recognizes the separate nature of the units belonging to a Global Actor.

Under this principle, a Global Actor that is truly an integrated economic concern on a planetary scale is instead viewed tax-wise as a cluster of separate units, each unit being subject to taxation in the jurisdiction where it operates. Thus, it is possible for Global Actors under a centralized strategy to attribute profits or losses to those separate units of the appropriate jurisdictions: profits will flow to low-tax jurisdictions, costs will be deducted in high-tax jurisdictions, and losses will flow to profitable units to offset their profits.

4 Philipp Genschel & Thomas Rixen, Settling and Unsettling the Transnational Legal Order of International *Taxation*, Transnational Legal Orders (Terence C. Halliday & Gregory C. Shaffer, eds. 2015).

5 Rosanne Altshuler & Harry Grubert, *The Three Parties in the Race-to-the-bottom: Host Governments, Home Governments and Multinational Companies*, 7(3) FLA. TAX REV. 153 (2005).

The result is that Global Actors tend to be subject to a global effective rate that is lower than the weighted algebraic sum of the nominal rates of the different countries where they operate, and this leads to a situation where they operate in a sort of "meta-nation" ideally located in between the home state and the host state, not defined by traditional state boundaries.

This engenders a regulatory-tax arbitrage in which Global Actors are asymmetrically confronted by the limited reach of territorial states. This is a new brand of a geopolitical architecture in which states and non-state organizations such as Global Actors access, manage, and regulate the intersection of territory and flows of capital, and, in so doing, design new imaginary gateways for a fully mobile capital that segregates profits in jurisdictions which offer lower rates under the constraint of tax competition.

In the tax world this regulatory-tax arbitrage has been defined as "base erosion and profit shifting" (BEPS). The base erosion component of BEPS is that deductions are made in high-tax countries, so that the national tax base of these high-tax countries is reduced by the subtraction of tax-deductible costs. The profit shifting component of BEPS is that these sums that are deducted are paid to entities of the same group located in low-tax countries, triggering a transfer of gross revenues to those countries.

The structural feature of BEPS comes from these two complementary components: there is a de-coupling of tax-deductible costs (artificially located in high-tax jurisdictions) and gross revenues usually of a mere financial nature and detached from actual operation (artificially located in low-tax countries, often defined as "tax havens" or "offshore financial centers"). In the context of content moderation, there is a similar arbitrage since platforms can be established in low-regulation jurisdiction, and yet offer services in high-regulation jurisdictions.

A burgeoning literature[6] attempts to showcase the basic techniques of BEPS aggressive strategies[7] that rely on the manipulation of the remuneration of debt (interest) or intangibles (royalties or other fees) within the different units of Global

[6] *See, for example*, Ana P. Dourado, *The Base Erosion and Profit Shifting (BEPS) Initiative under Analysis*, 43 Intertax 2 (2015); Reuven S. Avi-Yonah & Haiyan Xu, *Evaluating BEPS*, 10 Erasmus L. Rev. 3 (2017); Philip Baker, *Is There a Cure for BEPS?*, 5 Brit. Tax Rev. 605 (2017); Yariv Brauner, Assessing BEPS: Origins, Standards, and Responses – The United States Report for the 2017, 102A IFA Cahiers de Droit Fiscal International (IFA, ed. 2017); Yariv Brauner, *BEPS: An Interim Evaluation*, 6 World Tax J. 10 (2014); Allison Christians, BEPS and the New International Tax Order, 2016 B.Y.U. L. Rev. 1604 (2016); Stephen E. Shay & Allison Christians, Assessing BEPS: Origins, Standards, and Responses, 102A IFA Cahiers de Droit Fiscal International (IFA ed., 2017).

[7] Harry Huizinga, Luc Laeven & Gaetan Nicodeme, *Capital Structure and International Debt Shifting*, 88(1) J. Fin. Econ. 80 (2008); Harry Huizinga & Luc Laeven, *International profit shifting within multinationals: A multi-country perspective*, 88 J. Pub. Econ. 1149 (2008); Kimberly A. Clausing, *The Revenue Effects of Multinational Form Income Shifting*, Tax Notes (2011), http://ssrn.com/abstract=2488860 (last visited Mar. 3, 2024); Dhammika Dharmapala, *What Do We Know about Base Erosion and Profit Shifting? A Review of the Empirical Literature*, 35 Fiscal Stud. 421 (2014).

Actors.[8] Manipulation of intra-group transfer prices is also an important profit-shifting channel for Global Actors through the tax-induced management within MNEs of debt, intangibles, or intra-group services.[9]

Another group of techniques that involve BEPS are those in which Global Actors are capable of achieving "double exemption" as a result of regulatory gaps or through complex techniques denominated "hybrid mismatches," which take advantage of the differences of tax systems. Profits may even escape all forms of taxation: this situation has been defined as "stateless income/profits"[10] and can be restated as "stateless capital" in light of the fact that income/profits are generated from a fully mobile capital. Stateless capital challenges the foundation of the taxing powers of states anchored to a territory.

It is essential to remark here the second phenomenological resemblance between the tax regulatory problem and the regulatory problem of content moderation: if there is stateless capital, then equally there can be "stateless information" in the sense that both terms – stateless capital and stateless information – directly point to the fact that both capital and information escape the regulatory reach of states. Of course, this resemblance does not imply that content moderation should be proprietary to one or more individual states to the detriment of others, but some form of standard must be achieved.

9.2 THE INTERNATIONAL POLICY RESPONSE

These situations of reduced or nil taxation of MNEs[11] epitomized in the BEPS acronym have been addressed by the OECD/G20 Action Plan (the BEPS Project), which unfolded in 2013–17, leading to the release of fifteen reports in 2014–15[12] and

[8] Dhammika Dharmapala, *Base Erosion and Profit Shifting: A Simple Conceptual Framework*, 12 (4) CESifo DICE Report 8–14 (2015).

[9] *See, e.g.*, Aaron Flaaen, *The Role of Transfer Prices in Profit-Shifting by U.S. Multinational Firms: Evidence from the 2004 Homeland Investment Act* (FEDS, Working Paper No. 2017-055, 2017).

[10] Edward D. Kleinbard, *Stateless Income*, 11(9) Fla. Tax Rev. 699 (2011); Yariv Brauner, *What the BEPS*, 16(2) Fla. Tax Rev. 55 (2014).

[11] OECD, *Measuring and Monitoring BEPS, Action 11 – 2015 Final Report* (2015), https://www.oecd-ilibrary.org/docserver/9789264241343en.pdf?expires = 1622326728&id = id&accname = guest&checksum = 08D70B8C3A37A999E2B44D6217C9D41C (last visited May 29, 2023). *See also* Ernesto Crivelli, Ruud A. de Mooij & Michael Keen, *Base Erosion, Profit Shifting and Developing Countries*, 72(3) Finance Archive 268 (2016); Fatih Guvenen, Raymond J. Mataloni Jr., Dylan G. Rassier & Kim J. Ruhl, *Offshore Profit Shifting and Domestic Productivity Measurement* (NBER, Working Paper No. 23324, 2017).

[12] OECD, Action Plan on Base Erosion and Profit Shifting (2013), available at http://dx.doi.org/10.1787/9789264202719-en; OECD, *Part 1 of a Report to G20 Development Working Group on the Impact of BEPS in Low Income Countries* (2014), http://www.oecd.org/tax/part-1-of-report-to-g20-dwg-on-the-impact-of-beps-in-low-income-countries.pdf (last visited Mar. 3, 2024).

to the modification of the OECD Commentary and Model in 2017,[13] followed in 2018–22 by the Inclusive Framework (the Inclusive Framework) initially with an Interim Report,[14] then by proposing revised "*nexus rules*" (Pillar One)[15] and different types of "profit allocation rules" (Pillar Two),[16] and finally by advancing a comprehensive proposal together with a program of work.[17]

This section will detail at a first descriptive level the process and institutional structures by which policies have been actually developed as well as their shortcomings.

The fifteen Actions of the initial 2013–17 BEPS Project can be divided into three main areas: global disclosure rules, guidelines for national tax policies, and modifications of tax treaties. These BEPS measures were expected to become applicable via changes to bilateral tax treaties or through changes in domestic laws, so the purpose of the BEPS Project was to facilitate through soft law a complex implementation process both at an international and domestic level. The problem is that these OECD BEPS measures were not introduced through a multilateral legal instrument and therefore were not binding (except for those eventually included in BEPS-modified tax treaties).

In addition, the 2013–17 BEPS Project was affected by other structural flaws. First, the OECD was trying to forge consensus about complex rules to be implemented by states based on the idea that profits should be taxed where economic activities are performed and value is created.

The consensus should instead have been about direct constraints on the behavior of Global Actors; without such consensus, the BEPS situation was basically tolerated in the name of Westphalian tax sovereignty. Second, the 2013–17 BEPS Project

[13] OECD, Action Plan on Base Erosion and Profit Shifting, at 52.

[14] OECD, Tax Challenges Arising from Digitalisation – Interim Report 2018: Inclusive Framework on BEPS (2018), https://www.oecdilibrary.org/docserver/9789264293083en.pdf?expires=1622298762&id=id&accname=guest&checksum=CB32D91D859CDD529F0D74B6B024F180 (last visited May 29, 2023)

[15] OECD, Tax Challenges Arising from Digitalisation – Report on Pillar One Blueprint: Inclusive Framework on BEPS (2020) (last visited Mar. 3, 2024).

[16] OECD, Tax Challenges Arising from Digitalisation – Report on Pillar Two Blueprint: Inclusive Framework on BEPS (2020), https://www.oecd-ilibrary.org/docserver/abb4c3d1en.pdf?expires=1622298926&id=id&accname=guest&checksum=BFEE294C4D66E061298F3043EC6AE31E (last visited May 29, 2023). *See also*, *Fair Taxation of the Digital Economy*, European Commission (2018), https://ec.europa.eu/taxation_customs/business/company-tax/fair-taxation-digital-economy_en (last visited Mar. 3, 2024).

[17] *Statement on a Two-Pillar Solution to Address the Tax Challenges Arising from the Digitalisation of the Economy* – October 8, 2021, OECD, Paris, www.oecd.org/tax/beps/statement-on-a-two-pillar-solution-to-address-the-tax-challenges-arising-from-the-digitalisation-of-the-economy-october-2021.htm. *Programme of Work to Develop a Consensus Solution to the Tax Challenges Arising from the Digitalisation of the Economy, OECD/G20 Inclusive Framework on BEPS*, OECD, Paris, www.oecd.org/tax/beps/programme-of-work-to-develop-a-consensus-solution-to-the-tax-challenges-arising-from-the-digitalisation-of-the-economy.htm (last visited Mar. 3, 2024).

failed to focus on the fact that aggressive tax strategies of MNEs exacerbate the negative effects of tax competition impinging on the powers of states. Third, the 2013–17 BEPS project preserved the single entity principle and thus did not hinder the capability of MNEs to shift around deductions, profits, and losses to the units located in appropriate jurisdictions.

In conclusion, in the initial 2013–17 BEPS Project, there was a certain amount of international cooperation in discussing policies, but there was no plan of an institutional architecture that could ensure adequate multilateral governance.[18]

The BEPS Project at OECD level was continued by the 2018–23 Inclusive Framework, which focused on "nexus rules" (Pillar One) and profit allocation rules (Pillar Two).[19] After initial hesitation, the policy process of the Inclusive Framework was kickstarted in 2021 by the proposal by the United States of a "global minimum tax" in which individual home countries undertake the ethical and political obligation to tax their own multinationals on global profits in a kind of defensive alliance.[20] In addition to the global minimum tax administered by home countries of MNEs based on OECD Pillar Two, market jurisdiction can of course adopt rules that protect their territorial tax prerogatives on the basis of OECD Pillar One.

If a global minimum tax proposed by the United States and other countries is agreed at the international level, each individual state will participate in a cooperative framework by unilaterally subjecting multinationals based in that home state to a minimum rate of tax (15 percent or more) on global profits. In this sense, the global minimum tax is a country-by-country extraterritorial tax.

Thus, the global minimum tax is *not* a systemic international mechanism to allocate profits of multinationals among countries but simply the alignment of home states unilaterally taxing their own multinationals. Each home state undertakes the responsibility to tax its own multinationals on the basis of extraterritorial legislative jurisdiction while host states remain free to exercise their tax power on profits sourced in their territory.

This is a promising basis for an analogy between international taxation and content moderation in terms of potential policy strategies. If regulation by the home state appears to be a "dominant strategy" in international taxation in the specific sense of game theory, that is, a strategy that is superior no matter what the other players do, then the same could be true in respect to content moderation. In that context, therefore, the home states of the main platforms should, in theory, adopt a dominant strategy by undertaking the obligation to regulate these platforms converging to basic principle through multilateral agreements. Once platforms are subject

[18] Itai Grinberg, Breaking Beps: The New International Tax Diplomacy (2015); Ruth Mason, *The Transformation of International Tax*, 114.3 Am. J. Intl. Law 353–402 (2020).

[19] *See*, *supra* notes 14 and 15.

[20] US Department of Treasury, *Made in America Tax Plan* (2021), https://home.treasury.gov/system/files/136/MadeInAmericaTaxPlan_Report.pdf (last visited Mar. 3, 2024).

to common rules agreed by home states of the Global Actors owning such platforms, the policies of host states will be, to a certain extent, irrelevant insofar as they impose lower limitations.

The salient point here is that in international taxation, home state regulation is a dominant strategy because it ensures the collection of taxes irrespective of what other states do; while in content moderation, home state dominant strategies appear more problematic because the policy issue is not just in terms of collection, but it involves complex cultural and semantic problems of what content moderation should be.

A global minimum tax does not require fully inclusive multilateralism but can be pursued through so called minilateralism, a word and a concept suggested by Moises Naim in 2009:[21] when it is difficult to reach broad consensus, the most effective move is the inclusion of the smallest possible number of countries needed to have the largest possible impact on solving the problem of profit shifting. The same principle could apply in content moderation.

It should be clear from the outset that the OECD is *not* currently endorsing a global minimum tax. The term "global minimum tax" is often used in a generic way to denote the efforts of the international community to tax multinationals, but this term has an exact meaning that specifically comes from the US proposal of a "country-by-country minimum tax." So a "global minimum tax" is a tax unilaterally imposed by each home state through extraterritorial legislative jurisdiction on the multinationals that are based in that state (i.e., when the ultimate parent company is resident there). To consider a simple example: the United States already imposes a kind of global minimum tax on the worldwide income of its citizens; this tax could be extended to multinationals based in the United States, and the same would respectively occur in other home states.

The OECD is *not* currently endorsing such a global minimum tax but rather is pursuing something different: an Inclusive Framework based on a pervasive consensus of more than 130 countries on a very detailed agenda that establishes a *mechanism to allocate profits of multinationals among countries*. This is an ambitious idea of establishing thoroughly common criteria to allocate profits but is not a country-by country minimum tax "US style." The OECD/G20 Inclusive Framework has in fact continued in its search of a global consensus about common rules trough a "two-pillar solution" based on Pillar One and Pillar Two.[22]

With regard to the reallocation of taxing rights to market jurisdictions (Pillar One), the OECD has defined as "in-scope companies" affected by the changes that are now negotiated the multinationals with global turnover above 20 billion euros

[21] Moisés Naím, Minilateralism, 173 Foreign Policy 135 (2009).

[22] OECD, *Statement on a Two-Pillar Solution to Address the Tax Challenges Arising From the Digitalisation of the Economy* (July 1, 2021), https://www.oecd.org/tax/beps/statement-on-a-two-pillar-solution-to-address-the-tax-challenges-arising-from-the-digitalisation-of-the-economy-july-2021.pdf (last visited Mar. 3, 2024).

and profitability above 10 percent (i.e., profit before tax/revenue). Extractives and regulated financial services are excluded.

There will be a new special purpose nexus rule permitting allocation of so called "Amount A" to a market jurisdiction when the in-scope multinational derives at least 1 million euros in revenue from that jurisdiction. Revenue will be "sourced" to the end market jurisdictions where goods or services are used or consumed. To facilitate the application of this principle, detailed source rules for specific categories of transactions will be developed.[23]

"Source" is a term of art in international taxation since its inception and indicates the establishment of criteria that indicate where specific items of income are actually generated, created, or located. This idea implies that it is possible to identify the structural features of economic activities on the basis of which allocating rules are capable of attributing taxing powers to the so called source state. Although commentators have criticized the idea of being able to pinpoint the actual source of income in the context of a globalized/digitized economy, the OECD is still advocating this idea, with the added complication that the proposed criteria are overly complex, presenting critical problems in terms of actual implementation.

There is also a so-called Amount B to allocate profits to market countries that reflects in-country baseline marketing and distribution activities in those countries that will be applied on the basis of the arm's length principle, which will be simplified and streamlined.[24] In-country baseline marketing and distribution activities are those typically developed by local units (such as agents, distributors, and affiliated companies) in the relevant markets to carry out the core minimally required business presence of multinationals and therefore a commensurate amount of income must be attributed to such units to reflect those baseline marketing and distribution activities.

By contrast, Pillar Two consists of two interlocking domestic rules (together the Global anti-Base Erosion Rules [GloBE] rules): (i) an Income Inclusion Rule (IIR), which imposes a top-up tax on a parent entity in respect of the low taxed income of an entity of the group; and (ii) an Undertaxed Payment Rule (UTPR), which denies deductions or requires an equivalent adjustment to the extent the low tax income of an entity of the group is not subject to tax under an IIR.

In addition, a treaty-based rule (the Subject to Tax Rule, STTR) allows source jurisdictions to impose limited source taxation on certain related party payments subject to tax below a minimum rate. The STTR will be creditable as a covered tax under the GloBE rules. The GloBE rules will apply to multinationals that meet the

[23] Where the residual profits of an in-scope multinational are already taxed in a market jurisdiction, a marketing and distribution profits safe harbor will cap the residual profits allocated to the market jurisdiction through Amount A.

[24] The OECD has announced that during 2022 a text of a Multilateral Convention and Explanatory Statement to implement Amount A of Pillar One will be released, to be followed by a high-level signing ceremony for the Multilateral Convention.

750 million euros threshold as determined under BEPS Action 13 (country by country reporting). OECD guidelines for a minimum effective tax on multinationals (Pillar Two) have been thereafter released at the end of 2021.[25]

These OECD guidelines of 2021 were followed closely by the proposal of an EU Directive, which was finally adopted at the end of 2022,[26] which introduces a minimum EU 15 percent tax rate that will apply to any large group, both domestic and international, including in the financial sector, with combined financial revenues of more than €750 million a year and with either a parent company or a subsidiary situated in an EU Member State.

The effective tax rate is established in each Member State by dividing taxes paid by the entities in that Member State by their income. If the effective tax rate for the entities in a particular jurisdiction is below the 15 percent minimum, then the Pillar Two rules are triggered and the group must pay a top-up tax to bring its rate up to 15 percent, which applies irrespective of whether the subsidiary is located in a country that has signed up to the international OECD/G20 agreement. The calculations will be made by the ultimate parent entity of the group unless the group assigns another entity.

If the global minimum rate is not imposed by a non-EU country where a group entity is based, Member States will apply the Undertaxed Payments Rule, which is a backstop rule to the primary Income Inclusion Rule. It means that a Member State will effectively collect part of the top-up tax due at the level of the entire group if some jurisdictions where group entities are based tax below the minimum level and do not impose any top-up tax. The amount of top-up tax that a Member State will collect from the entities of the group in its territory is determined via a formula based on employees and assets.

The last phase of the process is currently under way and reveals major criticalities of the OECD approach: the OECD in fact, at the World Economic Forum in Davos in May 2022, has admitted that its two-pillar project will not be implemented in 2023, as announced. One of the reasons for the impasse is certainly the sheer complexity of the guidelines proposed by the OECD, but there is also a structural reason, that is, the fact that the OECD is trying to reach an over-inclusive consensus (more than 130 countries) on a hyper-detailed agenda and at the same time is lacking a strategic vision: the attention is focused on technical details but there is a lack of

[25] OECD, *Tax Challenges Arising from the Digitalisation of the Economy – Global Anti-Base Erosion Model Rules (Pillar Two): Inclusive Framework on BEPS*, Paris (2021), https://www.oecd.org/tax/beps/tax-challenges-arising-from-the-digitalisation-of-theeconomy-global-anti-base-erosion-model-rules-pillar-two.htm. OECD, *Tax Challenges Arising from the Digitalisation of the Economy – Commentary to the Global Anti-Base Erosion Model Rules (Pillar Two)*, Paris (2021), https://www.oecd.org/tax/beps/tax-challenges-arising-from-the-digitalisation-of-the-economy-global-anti-base-erosion-model-rules-pillar-two-commentary.pdf.

[26] Proposal for a Council Directive on ensuring a global minimum level of taxation for multinational groups in the Union {SWD (2021) 580 final} COM (2021) 823 final, finally approved as Council Directive EU 2022/2523 on December 14, 2022 (GU L 328/1 del 22.12.2022).

institutional design. This reflects the depth versus breadth debate about policies and governance in international relations literature, also forming the basis for the concept of minilateralism.

In light of this impasse, the global minimum tax initially proposed by the United States in 2021 and then endorsed by other countries actually appears to be the only effective way to address the root of the problem: if the home states adopt a dominant strategy and tax the global profits (i.e., domestic + foreign) of MNEs based in those home states irrespective of what other host states do (tax or exempt), there will be no tax arbitrage because there will at least be a minimum tax rate (15 percent or more) in the home states, so that aggressive tax strategies that shift profits to lower tax jurisdictions will be futile.

So, to develop the potentially correct analogy that compares platforms and taxation, "global minimum moderation" should be pursued through a kind of "essential harmonization" with mutual recognition of minimum standards or criteria. This could be the platform analog of "global minimum taxation."

As mentioned, the OECD has not fully adopted the proposal of a global minimum tax but has introduced very complex arrangements that jeopardize the establishment of an international tax regime that would trigger a paradigm shift toward cooperative multilateralism. Pillar One advances profit allocation rules to protect market jurisdictions and Pillar Two only proposes optional recapture rules (the so called top-up tax) for taxing foreign profits if subject to lower rates, but this is just a fallback option, and, in addition, countries are not obligated to adopt it.

The lack of an explicit will of the OECD to push for a real global minimum tax is a failure of its initial "inclusive" proposal. It is, however, still possible that countries freely adopting the global taxation minimum standard will form "defensive alliances" against tax competition and profit shifting through multilateralist geopolitical compacts inspired by minilateralism,

As a matter of fact, in 2022–23, several countries autonomously began to implement Pillar Two through different types of country-by-country minimum taxes. At this stage, there is no explicit minilateralist pact among those countries, but their moves are an indication that minilateralism is beginning to work in the tax arena.

Thus, minilateralism could also work in the platform context of content moderation on the basis of its potential capabilities that have been described in international relations literature. These minilateral compacts in fact are a well-known form of institutional design because they aim at putting together a sufficient number of players to address a policy issue, without the need to strive in the direction of unattainable forms of unanimity or full coordination, often prone to free ride problems.

For example, even in the context of global warming – a typically global problem that requires a global coordinated response – minilateralist solutions have been propounded. Minilateralist solutions do not present the problems of the current over-inclusive proposals to introduce a mechanism of binding rules because they are based on the incentives of each actor to participate. Minilateral compacts in fact initially operate in a framework that has been defined by international relations literature as an "international regime." International regimes are identified in the literature as "sets of implicit or explicit *principles*, *norms*, *rules*, and *decision-making procedures* around which actors' expectations converge in a given area of international relations."[27]

These principles, norms, rules, and procedures prescribe certain actions and proscribe others, so they imply obligations, even though these obligations are not enforceable through a hierarchical legal system. Thus, this definition adopts a conception of regimes as social institutions rather then sets of binding legal prescriptions.

Minilateral compacts have several main advantages. First, they do not imply the detailed rules through formal international agreements as they only require the participating home states to extend a minimum to Global Actors based in those states on their global operation. Second, cooperation is pursued among countries genuinely sharing the common policy subjecting multinationals to regulation. Third, it is more likely that a compact is formed for effective change on clearly identified measures when the number of participating actors is not over-inclusive. Finally, minilateral compacts initially operating as international regimes facilitate the eventual achievement of more inclusive cooperation and thus are the basis for subsequent binding international agreements. These advantages of minilateralism could potentially apply to international tax regulation and content moderation.

Specifically, in tax minilateralism, the states that are the most capable of taxing multinationals on global profits act together with the states that are most vulnerable. It is also possible that states cluster in different compacts on the basis of geopolitical criteria in a kind of "polycentric cooperation." In a scaling down of the current inclusive approach, the OECD could, acting as an orchestrator, thus become the venue of one or more minilateral compacts. A similar institutional dynamic could also be activated in content moderation, possibly through the orchestration of an international organization.

Minilateralism could also be seen as the "club of the powerful," for example, in tax matters developing countries often balk at the strategy of a core of home states taxing their MNEs globally, claiming that it would only be in the interest of OECD capital-exporting countries. It should, however, be clear that such a strategy would not limit the tax prerogatives of other countries, such as BRICS or developing countries: these countries obviously retain their right to tax multinationals under OECD Pillar One or otherwise, irrespective of the fact that multinationals will be taxed in their home states.

[27] Stephen D. Krasner, *Structural Causes and Regime Consequences: Regimes as Intervening Variables*, International Regimes 1(2) (Stephen D. Krasner ed., 1983) (emphasis added).

Similarly, in content moderation, regulation by home states simply ensures application of a minimum standard but does not exclude regulation by host states. It is worth mentioning that in the context of content moderation platforms often have limited moderating resources and so focus those resources in highly regulated jurisdictions such as the US or EU, as opposed to low regulated jurisdictions; but when a minimum standard is ensured in home states, moderating resources can be internally distributed within the Global Actor on the basis of opportunity and efficiency, rather than on the basis of level of regulation.

At the end of the analysis of the global policy process developed in this section, it is essential to remark a third phenomenological resemblance between the regulatory problem of content moderation and the tax regulatory problem: if it is true that we conceive of a minimum standard in a minilateral setting – at least initially – through which individual home countries undertake the ethical and political obligation to tax their own multinationals on global profits in one or more defensive alliances, we could conceive of a minimum standard through which individual home countries undertake the ethical and political obligation to moderate platform content.

The alternative regulatory model – both for global taxation and content moderation – is to pursue an inclusive consensus on a very detailed agenda to be enforced through formal multilateral treaties: in that context, if consensus on detailed rules cannot be achieved and pinned down in binding rules, resort must be made to guidelines and soft law, which can prove to be ineffective.

9.3 TAX IMPLICATIONS OF GLOBAL PLATFORMS

After having described in Section 9.2 the process and institutional structures by which policies have been actually developed as well as their shortcomings, this section will attempt, at a deeper level, to explicate how and why actual platforms' operation have relevant global tax implications and possibly what inferences or comparisons may be drawn from the tax regulatory world to content moderation.

I anticipate that these structural implications point to a potential problem of "intractability" for tax regulation of Global Actors. I define as "intractability" the conundrum or cul-de-sac in which state actors would find themselves if they exclusively rely on their territorial prerogatives to tax profits that are deemed to be located "somewhere," while they are essentially located "anywhere."

So, the point I make here is that to overcome the problem of intractability the only feasible way appears to be a multilateral approach based on the individual extraterritorial jurisdictions of state actors willing to participate in an alliance that sets certain minimum standards on the taxation of global profits.

Aggressive tax strategies described in Section 9.2, when considered at the deeper explicatory level of this section, should be viewed as being foundationally based on technological constructs that rely on the "extraction" and use of data through platforms. This "data extraction" is explained as follows: platforms rely on raw data to generate knowledge and to achieve that goal, raw data is recorded and organized to be usable by the corporate legal owners of platforms, the Global Actors. In the extraction process raw data consists of information about facts of the world, while knowledge consists of explanation and use of such facts.

Therefore, for Global Actors the raw material that must be extracted is the data, the source of this raw material are the activities of users on platforms, and the organization of such data is the knowledge accumulated by Global Actors. Platforms extract, analyze, and use the increasingly large amounts of data that are recorded as a form of computational capital to make profits.

Once the new business models became wholly based on such technology aimed at the extraction and use of data through platforms, it came as a natural result that aggressive tax strategies were molded by their technological base of data extraction and thus morphed into brand new structures significantly different from the previous ones based on legal arrangements. At the same time, however, the traditional corporate form of Global Actors essentially remained unchanged and based on the separate unity principle described in Section 9.1, which allows base erosion and profit shifting. So Global Actors "own" platforms in the traditional corporate sense but through them pursue aggressive tax strategies that are different from preceding ones.

In a very general sense, these new aggressive tax strategies exploit to the maximum extent the potential of data to generate through platforms new types of profits that are not taxable. We generally denominate these new business models as the "digital economy," alluding to the fact that the traditional industrial economy based on production and distribution of goods and services now relies on new information technology that improves that production and distribution. This is only a partial dimension of the new reality: what in effect happens in such a "digital economy" is structural reliance on global platforms to expand the reach of traditional profitability in an "extractive mode" that leads to the accumulation of so called big data. Massive new expanses of potential data are in fact now accessible so that data itself has become a fundamental resource to be extracted, as much as oil and other natural resources in the past.

For example, Google initially limited itself to use data to pivot advertising revenues away from traditional media, but then platform data acquired primary importance for many other Global Actors as data analysis is itself generative of data in a continuous feedback loop. The result is that data serves a whole range of functions across different industries ranging from technology (Google, Facebook, and Amazon), dynamic start-ups (Uber, Airbnb), manufacturing (GE, Siemens), agribusiness (John Deere, Monsanto), and so on. The common denominator is that data mainly generates new markets and products and cost reductions of revenue-making activities, therefore leading to more revenues and higher profitability.

Aggressive tax strategies exploit "platforms" to extract data, but what exactly are platforms in this context and how are they used taxwise? Platforms are IT infrastructures that enable two or more groups to interact. Therefore, platforms are intermediary technological frameworks that not only bring together different users (customers, advertisers, service providers, producers, suppliers, even physical objects)[28] but also provide tools that enable these users to build their own products, services, and marketplaces. For example, Apple and Microsoft enable developers to build and sell new apps to users, while Google provides a platform for advertisers and content providers to target people searching for information.

So corporate owners of platforms became intermediaries vis-a-vis users to generate new products and profits,which could not be generated through traditional methods. There are several characteristics of platform content that have a connection with profit-generating activities and aggressive tax strategies aimed at diverting such new profits away from taxes. These brand-new characteristics of platforms are the following, each of them generating an asymmetry between Global Actors and taxing States: (1) intermediation and positional asymmetry, (2) network effects and growth asymmetry, (3) complementary strategies and per-capita asymmetry, and (4) neutrality and strategic asymmetry:

First, platforms provide the infrastructure to intermediate between different groups and therefore Global Actors who own platforms do not have to build a marketplace nor even necessarily maintain a physical presence in certain market jurisdictions. For example, Google relies on online search activity, Facebook on social networking, Uber shifted urban private transportation into an online platform. This is the key to the advantage of platforms over traditional business models, which require physical presence in market jurisdictions.

The disappearance of physical presence is also a competitive advantage of platforms owned by Global Actors over taxing States and results in a positional asymmetry: while Global Actors owning platforms do not need to position themselves on a geographical space, tax regulators traditionally need geographical space to detect profit-generating activities and assert jurisdiction.

Second, platforms are based on network effects: the more numerous the users who use a platform, the more valuable that platform becomes for all other users and for the owner of the platform. For example, Facebook has constantly increased its social networking platform and Google improves search algorithms through the increased use online. This implies that platforms are capable of rapidly scaling up their operation by relying on preexisting infrastructure and incurring low marginal costs of production, so that there are few natural limits to the growth of

[28] Annabelle Gawer, Platform Dynamics and Strategies: From Products to Services, Platforms, Markets and Innovation (Annabelle Gawer, ed. 2009).

platforms. The result is another type of asymmetry, namely a growth asymmetry: while Global Actors relying on platforms are innately bound to expand on a global scale, tax regulators are limited by their local geographical space.

Third, platforms use complementary strategies: for example, one division of the Global Actor reduces the price of a service or good (even providing it for free) and generates losses, while another division increases prices to offset these losses generating profits. To pursue these strategies, platforms increase the number of their users at a global scale by offering services that often are not directly priced. For example, Google notably started as a completely free service but then began to make profits through advertising and then through a host of services.[29]

The result is that there is another type of asymmetry, a per-capita asymmetry: while Global Actors relying on platforms do not cater to a population that is identified by the allegiance to state territory, tax regulators inherently need to interface directly with a locally settled population that exhibits an ability to pay taxes that are linked to the use of local indivisible services and public goods.

Finally, platforms present themselves as neutral spaces for users to interact but in fact pursue deliberate strategies in terms of product and service development, marketplace interactions, and so on. The typical example is Facebook, which epitomizes the evolution of online social networks presenting its the platform as a free forum when in reality it is a tool to collect valuable data. This strategy is also used by many industrial players as a complement to their core business.

The result is that there is another type of asymmetry, a strategic asymmetry: Global Actors portray themselves as neutral and transparent platforms but deploy strategies that are not visible to users and to tax regulators; by contrast, tax regulators necessarily use and announce policies and regulations that are thoroughly visible in the public-civic space to Global Actors.

In addition to these four basic characteristics/asymmetries of platforms, there are also different types of platforms depending on the specific activities that Global Actors perform: advertising platforms, cloud platforms, industrial platforms, product platforms, and lean platforms.

Advertising platforms (e.g., Google, Facebook), extract information on users and then use the products of that process to sell advertising and for other uses. Cloud platforms (e.g., AWS, Salesforce), which own the hardware and software of digital-dependent businesses and are renting them out as needed. Industrial platforms (e.g.,

[29] Shoshana Zuboff, The Age of Surveillance Capitalism: The Fight for a Human Future at the New Frontier of Power 233–90 (2019).

GE, Siemens), build the hardware and software necessary to transform traditional manufacturing into internet-connected processes that lower the costs of production and transform goods into services. Product platforms (e.g., Rolls Royce, Spotify), generate revenue by using other platforms to transform a traditional good into a service and by collecting rent or subscription fees on them. Finally, lean platforms (e.g., Uber, Airbnb), which reduce their ownership of assets to a minimum and profit by reducing costs.[30]

The four characteristics – asymmetries of platforms (intermediation and positional asymmetry, network effects and growth asymmetry, complementary strategies and per-capita asymmetry, neutrality and strategic asymmetry – are thus combined within different types of platforms (advertising, industrial, product, and lean platforms) generating different and specific tax strategies that cannot be recounted here in detail.

What are then the tax implications of global platforms? In a general sense, intermediation and positional asymmetry significantly limit host-States' tax enforcement power for the lack of physical presence, typically a fixed place of business in the form of a permanent establishment (PE) or through a dependent agent, so called agency PE. Network effects and growth asymmetry attribute to Global Actors flexibility and resilience unattainable by state actors, while complementary strategies and per-capita asymmetry create vast opportunities for regulatory tax arbitrage. Finally, neutrality and strategic asymmetry create a gap between the opacity of strategies of Global Actors and the forced transparency of tax regulators.

The upshot is that Global Actors using platforms have the capability of escaping local state tax enforcement, are much more flexible than States in implementing advantageous strategies, rely on regulatory arbitrage, and are capable of pursuing aggressive tax strategies that are opaque to tax regulators. The practical result is that for each individual Global Actor, there is a combination of platform-based features that is the signature of that player. In addition, these features are entirely proprietary to that player and very opaque to the outside, with the consequence that the "formula" of the aggressive tax strategy of each individual Global Actor is fiercely guarded against intrusions by tax regulators.

The capability of tax regulators to "pierce through" the unique "formula" of "opportunistic" platform use would be tantamount to the dismantling of aggressive tax strategies, but this achievement is, at the current stage, highly unlikely. This deficiency points to what I consider a problem of intractability, that is, the impossibility of a territorial approach, which poses the need to strive for a multilateral (initially minilateral) approach based on the global reach of regulatory states aggregating in minimum standards compacts.

It is essential to highlight at this point that there is a fourth resemblance between the tax and content moderation regulatory problem as they are both affected by this

[30] Nick Srnicek, Platform Capitalism 17–55 (2017).

intractability problem: if it is true that from a territorial perspective, BEPS involving the strategies described above is not readily tractable, then it is probably true that content moderation is not tractable exclusively from a territorial perspective as it relies on similar strategies. So, in both cases, minilateral minimum standards should be pursued. Of course, the intractability of content moderation is, in addition, caused by various factors that are not relevant for tax policy.

9.4 POSSIBLE LESSONS FOR PLATFORM RESPONSIBILITY

As tax regulatory approaches can potentially be of interest for platform content moderation, we draw in this section a few conclusions to suggest possible lessons for platform responsibility rules. In doing that, I would like to make three clarifications about differences between the tax regulatory problem and the content moderation problem.

First, while the tax regulatory problem, by definition, involves a top-down exercise of sovereign powers to limit the opportunistic use of global platforms that leads to regulatory arbitrage by corporate actors, the content moderation problem involves a delicate balance between the exercise of sovereign powers and the protection of freedom of speech in many cases of individual citizens that access and use global platforms.

Second, in the international tax arena, a balance is pursued to ensure that each item of income is taxed at least once but no more than once, while in content moderation, a balance could be pursued to ensure that common principles are established once and for all, but this goal is much more difficult. In international taxation, a "follow the money" principle decides the game: once the home state has ensured collection of global profits of multinationals that are subject to its responsibility, the game is over and taxation is secured. This is not necessarily true in content moderation, where complex issues are at stake and national policies may overlap.

Third, from a strictly *semantic perspective*, the two problems appear different: tax regulation does not look at the meaning of information but strives to tax profits that arise from the use of data/information by platforms, while content moderation inevitably looks at the meaning of information to moderate it.

In spite of these three differences, our analysis has demonstrated that in both tax regulation and content moderation platforms managed by Global Actors have an impact on the perception of reality by users and influence their behavior. A platform – which is a technology that brings multiple parties together for a common purpose or to solve a common problem – is in fact a standards-based system that at the same time (i) distributes interfaces among users through remote coordination and (ii) centralizes the integrated control of interfaces and users through that same coordination. As a result, platforms distribute some form of autonomy to the edges of their networks while standardizing the conditions of communications.

Interfaces appear obvious and transparent to users, but the internal architecture of the platforms remains unknown to them and constitutes the medium through which strategies are developed by Global Actors. As Bratton notes:

> The dominant contemporary genre of *Interface*, the graphical user interface, is an interactive visual diagram that presents a visually coherent image of otherwise discontiguous and opaque processes and flows. Some emerging technologies, such as augmented reality, superimpose interfacial elements directly into the *User's* perceptual field, with the capability of articulating the significance of people, places, and things according to the program of different imagined communities. *This collapse of the metaphorical space between perceived object and its interpretation, especially when paired with messianic political theologies, can engender forms of cognitive fundamentalism* (emphasis added).[31]

Interfaces are representations, in a broad sense "images": Jean Baudrillard, a postmodern French philosopher, had anticipated during the 1980s this idea of representations or images as a means of concealing this absence of reality that characterizes this current cognitive fundamentalism, calling such representations "*simulacra*."[32] He envisaged successive phases of the modes of representation in which signs become increasingly empty of representational meaning and indeed the apex of this process is reached when users access certain existing platforms through their interfaces.

Baudrillard so described the "image" in a process that starts from faithful representation of external reality to the dissolution of it:

> These would be the image:
> It is the reflection of a basic reality.
> It masks and perverts a basic reality.
> It masks the absence of a basic reality.
> It bears no relation to any reality whatever: it is its own pure simulacrum.[33]

So essentially the "immoderation" of content generated within platforms is in most cases a lack of representational meaning for the users tethered to a precise platform's strategy, what Bratton defines as "forms of cognitive fundamentalism." In addition, "immoderation" of content is also the result of deliberate and controlled distortion of reality when strategies are willfully pursued through "echo-chambers," "trolls," and other techniques to influence users in the most diversified contexts.

These innate platform constraints on the representational function of content point to the need of a regulatory regime that relies on rules on procedural accountability that include, for example, common principles for the "notice-and-takedown"

[31] Benjamin H. Bratton, The Stack: On Software and Sovereignty 299 (2016).
[32] Jean Baudrillard, Selected Writings (Mark Poster, ed. 1988).
[33] Jean Baudrillard, The Precession of Simulacra, Art After Modernism Vol. 1, 170 (Brian Wallis, ed. 1984).

procedure and the strengthening of the cooperation with public authorities.[34] Such a regime of course would not exclude traditional types of moderation that depend on some sort of semantic control, such as automated moderation, pre-moderation or post-moderation, reactive moderation, and distributed moderation.[35]

These rules on procedural accountability for content moderation are somehow similar to the basic obligation of Global Actors owning platforms to report all their global profits at least in one state, their home state, and therefore to be accountable/pay taxes on those profits. So, in both tax regulation (dealing with capital) and content moderation (dealing with information), the common regulatory problem is how to subject to procedural accountability inappropriate outcomes of platforms that strategically control computational capital.

At the beginning of the chapter, I argued that there is a homology between capital and information that in a platform economy tend to be merged, becoming a hybrid computational capital; and the chapter has foregrounded three forms of resemblance between the tax regulatory problem and the regulatory problem of content moderation. First, non-state actors access, managem and regulate through platforms flows of capital and similarly flows of information exploiting regulatory differentials, so that there is the need of regulatory alignment in both cases. For example, the host state may be lenient on content moderation in comparison to the home state of the Global Actor owning the platform (or the other way around), thus there can be conflicting/overlapping policies.

Second, since both capital and information escape the regulatory reach of States, some form of common standard must be achieved in both cases. For example, a platform may escape the regulation on content moderation by both the host state and the home state of the Global Actor owning the platform, so that a common regulative approach is required so that it establishes at least a minimum standard of procedural accountability to minimize regulatory arbitrage.

Third, such common standards can be achieved only if individual home States of Global Actors owning platforms assume together the ethical and political obligation to moderate profit diversion as well as immoderate use of platform content through procedural accountability, in light of the fact that the alternative regulatory model would be to pursue an inclusive consensus on a very detailed agenda, a task that is quite hard in the context of content moderation and that is proving unsuccessful in the tax world.

[34] This is the approach used in the EU with the Regulation (EU) 2016/679 of the European Parliament and of the Council of 27 April 2016 (General Data Protection Regulation) – available at: https://eur-lex.europa.eu/eli/reg/2016/679/oj – entered into force on May 25, 2018 repealing the preexisting Data Protection Directive.

[35] This is the approach used in the EU with the Digital Services Act (Regulation (EU) 2022/2065 – available at https://eur-lex.europa.eu/eli/reg/2022/2065/oj – which updates existing EU legislation regarding illegal content, transparent advertising, and disinformation. *See, e.g.*, Alexandre De Streel ET AL., Online Platforms' Moderation of Illegal Content Online: Law, Practices and Options for Reform (2020).

This homology between capital (leading to "opportunistic" platform-generated profit diversion) and information (leading to "immoderate" platform content use) points to the fact that information extracted by platforms becomes a hybrid computational capital and therefore to the need of regulatory structures that reduce excessive opportunism and immoderation in the use of this computational capital by platforms.

This leads to a final conclusion about the regulation of computational capital: as we have assessed that there is an intractability problem of both profit diversion and content moderation when addressed exclusively from a territorial state perspective, in both cases multilateral minimum standards should be pursued. These standards should rest on a country-by-country assumption of responsibility by States to regulate Global Actors based in those countries, initially in a minilateral forum creating an international regime that does not necessarily require formal international agreements, to be possibly extended in a more inclusive format that may contemplate formal agreements.

10

Drawing Lessons from Efforts at Moderating Extremism

Farah Pandith and Simone Lipkind[*]

10.1 INTRODUCTION

During the summer of 2023, as interest in AI technology skyrocketed, so did the public's fear of its implications. Pew's August 2023 poll found that 51 percent of those surveyed were more concerned about AI than excited about it, marking not only a majority of respondents but also a 51 percent jump from 2021, when Pew had first polled Americans on this AI question.[1] A 2023 Reuters poll found that 61 percent of Americans believed AI could threaten civilization.[2]

Much of the fear of AI revolves around a future doomsday-scenario in which the technology becomes as smart as humans and then turns against us on its own accord. But what about bad actors and subsets of society that may already be working to wield AI against their fellow humans? Tristan Harris, an ethicist, has sounded the alarm on Silicon Valley's overly rosy perception of AI's ability to democratize access and specifically warned against the dangers of unqualified democratization.[3] Unqualified democratization, introduced to a world teeming with hate and extremism, makes for an ominous mix. The technology is new, but the threat is old, and the past offers insights into how extremists leverage technological advancements for their own nefarious purposes. This chapter will delve into the intricacies of violent

[*] Mitakshi Lakhani '24, candidate for Masters in Law and Diplomacy at the Fletcher School of Law and Diplomacy at Tufts University, contributed to the development of this chapter.

[1] A. Tyson & E. Kikuchi, *Growing Public Concern about the Role of Artificial Intelligence in Daily Life*, Pew Research Center (Aug. 28, 2023), https://www.pewresearch.org/short-reads/2023/08/28/growing-public-concern-about-the-role-of-artificial-intelligence-in-daily-life/ (last visited Feb. 18, 2024).

[2] A. Tong, *AI Threatens Humanity's Future, 61% of Americans Say: Reuters/Ipsos Poll*, Reuters (May 17, 2023), https://www.reuters.com/technology/ai-threatens-humanitys-future-61-americans-say-reutersipsos-2023-05-17/ (last visited Feb. 18, 2024).

[3] Tristan Harris, *AI Myths and Misconceptions, Your Undivided Attention*, Center for Humane Technology (May 11, 2023), https://www.humanetech.com/podcast/ai-myths-and-misconceptions (last visited Feb. 18, 2024).

extremism, its historical evolution and visible amplification through online disinformation, and the critical need for a whole-of-society approach to combat these threats.

10.2 DEFINING VIOLENT EXTREMISM

One must define violent extremism before attempting to speak about its union with disinformation. "Violent extremism" essentially involves threats or behaviors indicating a movement toward violence. As J. M. Berger, a writer and researcher focused on extremism, argues, there are extremist activities that can lead to violence without being violent themself, such as "segregation, laws against interracial marriage, and employment bans."[4] Beyond the actual violence, violent extremism includes preparation, organization, and motivation, involving law enforcement. Ideologically, it stems from religious, political, or ethnic grounds, which have been growing since the tragedy of 9/11. In today's context, we are discussing non-state actors using an "us versus them" ideology that assumes, "the success of 'us' is inseparable from hostile acts against 'them,'"[5] but various ideologies can lead to destructive actions, posing a worrisome threat.

Countering violent extremism (CVE) is a new strategy that emerged after 9/11. It aims to dismantle ideology's appeal and hinder non-state actors' recruitment by strengthening communities against extremist ideas, promoting alternative identities, and establishing social, mental, and cultural support systems. Crucially, CVE is non-kinetic – it does not rely on military action against radicalized individuals.

10.3 A HISTORICAL TIME LINE OF VIOLENT EXTREMISM IN THE DIGITAL AGE

Starting in the 1980s and '90s, websites and blog posts emerged as platforms for spreading hateful ideologies, but there was minimal effort from the private or public sector to regulate or take down such content. The novelty and absoluteness of publishing their ideology on a website gave violent extremists like StormFront and Al Qaeda the legitimacy they craved. Extremists discerned early on that the power to persuade goes to those who can reach the most people, and communicating your point of view on a scale not previously possible gave violent extremists what they most desired: possible ideological soldiers. Through the 9/11 era, and even for some time afterwards, Al Qaeda leveraged the internet, as well as various mediums like videotapes and CDs, to disseminate sermons and spread their ideology. It was a form of communication, and it was powerful. It created ripple effects and acted as a

4 Julia Simms, *Are We Talking About Extremism All Wrong?*, New America (Sept. 27, 2018), http://newamerica.org/weekly/are-we-talking-about-extremism-all-wrong/ (last visited Feb. 16, 2024).

5 J. M. Berger, Extremism (2018).

precursor to the "shares" we see now. This method of communication helped create a brand and a powerful emotional response. Indeed, it facilitated radicalization and significant new opportunities for organizations like Al Qaeda. But there were limitations. It was a static one-way communication tool.

The shift from stagnant websites to interactive social media platforms marked another pivotal milestone, not just in the platforms themselves but also how extremist groups utilized them. The transition to two-way communication on platforms like Facebook and YouTube transformed the landscape, allowing for the engagement necessary to create communities that provided intellectual and emotional support. This shift, post-9/11, was exemplified by video posts of Bin Laden on platforms like YouTube, which gave groups like al Qaeda the opportunity to foster emotional connections in a way they could not before on static websites. What is powerful here is the lift off from an individual who has some ideas, to a larger group of people who can *act* on these ideas after. Thus, there was now a new dimension to ideological affinity.

Furthermore, Facebook, YouTube, and Google, through their fast-changing algorithms, started shaping online behavior – creating a rapid, addictive cycle. With single searches triggering millions of results, these platforms' frictionless pace prevented (and continues to prevent) thoughtful absorption, pushing users in directions influenced by emotional responses to content, regardless of their rational instincts. These manipulative code nuances, nudging users oblivious to their intent down unforeseen rabbit holes, were unprecedented and society was not trained to recognize their subtle pull. Users could find themselves exposed to extremist content after a single innocuous search.

The 2005–6 Danish Cartoon Crisis acted as another flashpoint altering the landscape of digital extremism. Satirical cartoons of the Prophet Muhammad drawn in Denmark sparked an unforeseen global phenomenon.[6] The cartoons' virality showcased digital spaces' unprecedented force multiplier effect. What happened in Copenhagen resonated in Kabul, creating an interconnectedness that was previously unimaginable and highly consequential. Three years after the cartoons' initial publication, Al Qaeda bombers attacked Denmark's embassy in Pakistan killing six and injuring dozens.[7] Five years later, a Somali axeman tried to kill one of the Danish cartoon artists in his own home.[8]

The advent of the so-called Islamic State, also known as ISIS, marked another paradigm shift in extremists' exploitation of digital tools for international influence.

6 C. S. Smith & I. Fisher, *Firestorm over Cartoon Gains Momentum*, New York Times (Feb. 2, 2006), https://www.nytimes.com/2006/02/02/international/europe/firestorm-over-cartoon-gains-momentum.html (last visited Feb. 18, 2024).

7 *Dead after Pakistan Embassy Blast*, CBS News (June 3, 2008), https://www.cbsnews.com/news/6-dead-after-pakistan-embassy-blast/ (last visited Feb. 18, 2024).

8 *Somali Charged in Attack on Cartoonist*, NBC News (Jan. 2, 2010), https://www.nbcnews.com/id/wbna34662389 (last visited Feb. 19, 2024).

ISIS leveraged the digital domain to reshape extremist narratives and emerged as online superstars. Their mastery of this "new" human landscape was pivotal, creating a brand through content like their *Dabiq* magazine. The magazine, with its slick design, served as a powerful recruitment tool, helping the group attract members from far beyond Iraq and Syria. Al Qaeda's *Inspire* magazine, which also attracted a wide online readership, took a different approach, acting more as a manual for adherents, instructing them on various aspects of violent extremism, including bomb-making. The Boston Marathon bombers, Tamerlane and Dzhokhar Tsarnaev (twenty-six and nineteen years old, respectively, in 2013) claimed they used this digital content as a guide in their attack, marking a critical juncture in understanding extremist instruction manuals' impact in the digital era.[9] These online resources facilitated both far-reaching recruitment efforts on behalf of a distant caliphate and lone wolf homeland attacks.

The transition to encryption ushered in yet another new challenge – smaller platforms, not just major social media players – emerged as potent threats, serving as sanctuaries for those banned from larger platforms, allowing them to continue their activities.[10] In 2016, the rise of QAnon showcased the power of misinformation and conspiracy theories, even on relatively unknown sites. Originating from platforms like 4Chan and Telegram, QAnon, the theory that "a group of Satan-worshipping elites who run a child sex ring are trying to control our politics and media,"[11] initially seemed too absurd to be taken seriously. This analysis was further compounded by gender biases that underestimated a group with so many female adherents.[12] Critically, these smaller platforms were also encrypted allowing users to raise money, spread their ideology, organize, and plan in a way that initially went undetected by authorities. The QAnon fringe movement gained momentum during the Trump era by exploiting these smaller, ungoverned spaces to both eventually infiltrate mainstream networks and maintain a way of communicating with their audiences in the event they were banned from those larger, more mainstream platforms. Their example would prove to be essential learning for how the online space was

9 On April 15, 2013, Tamerlan and Dzhokhar Tsarnaev detonated two homemade pressure cooker bombs near the finish line of the Boston Marathon killing three and injuring hundreds. *See Unclassified Summary of Information Handling and Sharing Prior to the April 15 2013 Boston Marathon Bombings*, United States Department of Justice (Apr. 10, 2014), https://oig.justice.gov/reports/2014/s1404.pdf (last visited Feb. 14, 2024).

10 Jacob Ware, *The Third Generation of Online Radicalization*, George Washington University Project on Extremism (June 16, 2023), https://extremism.gwu.edu/third-generation-online-radicalization (last visited Feb. 19, 2024).

11 J. Rose, *Even If It's "Bonkers," Poll Finds Many Believe QAnon and Other Conspiracy Theories*, NPR.org (Dec. 30, 2020), https://www.npr.org/2020/12/30/951095644/even-if-its-bonkers-poll-finds-many-believe-qanon-and-other-conspiracy-theories (last visited Feb. 18, 2024).

12 M. Bloom, F. Pandith & J. Ware, *Female Extremists in QAnon and ISIS Are on the Rise. We Need a New Strategy to Combat Them*, NBC News (Dec. 11, 2020), https://www.nbcnews.com/think/opinion/female-extremists-qanon-isis-are-rise-we-need-new-strategy-ncna1250619 (last visited Feb. 18, 2024).

changing. This evolution in technique involving linking profiles across platforms marked a paradigm shift in the dissemination of extremist ideologies. This dynamic shift underscores the imperative to comprehend the evolving stages of technology and their profound impact on human interaction.

In 2017, the Burmese military triggered the Rohingya Genocide through a years-long campaign of misinformation, lies, and conspiracy propaganda on Facebook.[13] This tragic event served as a stark revelation, illustrating the profound impact achievable not only by terrorist organizations or extremist movements but also by state actors themselves employing digital platforms.

Two years later, the 2019 Christchurch attack, live-streamed and accompanied by an advanced coordinated online presence of memes, hashtags, and crowdsourcing, showcased extremists' nuanced understanding of online communication.[14] The strategic adaptation of words and images aimed to attract more followers, utilizing platforms like Facebook for engagement, and the shared manifesto, with disturbing parallels to Oslo killer Anders Brevik's, prompted the Christchurch Call, a commitment from governments and online service providers to eliminate terrorist and violent extremist content online in order to prevent further such attacks.[15] Five years later, such attacks are still too common.

In summary, the internet initially offered simplistic one-way interactions. Although primitive compared to current technology, this advancement was a milestone nonetheless allowing regular individuals to share content in unprecedented way. The next stage involved two-way interaction. The subsequent wave introduced encryption, empowering smaller platforms to take ownership and provide refuge for malicious actors. Understanding these stages is imperative, as they unveil differences in human interactions with technology. Some involve static absorption of information, others incorporate emotional engagement, while the third stage is

[13] In 2017, Myanmar's security forces embarked on a campaign in the country's western region under the pretext of restoring security. The campaign killed 6,700 Rohingya in the first month alone and would go on to displace hundreds of thousands in what UN Secretary-General Antonio Guterres has labeled as an ethnic cleansing attempt. *See* Eleanor Albert & Lindsay Maizland, *The Rohingya Crisis*, Council on Foreign Relations (Jan. 23, 2020), https://www.cfr.org/backgrounder/rohingya-crisis. (last visited Februart 18, 2024). Leading up to the campaign, Myanmar's military had as many as 700 people tasked with spreading anti-Rohingya propaganda on Facebook. *See also* Paul Mozur, *A Genocide Incited on Facebook, with Posts from Myanmar's Military*, New York Times (Oct. 15, 2018), https://www.nytimes.com/2018/10/15/technology/myanmar-facebook-genocide.html.

[14] In March of 2019, Brenton Tarrant killed 51 people at a mosque and Islamic center in Christchurch, New Zealand. New Zealand authorities eventually uncovered that Tarrant had visited alt-right websites, posted alt-wing content on his Facebook page, and donated money to alt-right groups outside of New Zealand. *See Christchurch Massacre: Inquiry Finds Failures ahead of Attack*, BBC News (Dec. 8, 2020), https://www.bbc.com/news/world-asia-55211468 (last visited Feb. 19, 2024).

[15] *Christchurch Call Story*, Christchurch Call, https://www.christchurchcall.com/about/the-christchurch-call-story (last visited Feb. 19, 2024).

characterized by clandestine interactions in ostensibly secure spaces.[16] The comfort, ease, and safety of these encrypted spaces pose a substantial challenge to national security, as activities ranging from fundraising to spreading ideologies can transpire beyond the purview of authorities.

Undoubtedly, recounting pivotal moments when digital technology became a conduit for propagating violent extremism is disheartening. They serve as a stark reminder that we are consistently lagging behind in our efforts to address these issues, playing catch-up instead of leading the way. In the internet's nascent days, policymakers underestimated its potential for harm and consequently lacked the regulatory framework needed to navigate its wild and uncharted terrain. Opportunistic actors, spanning from human traffickers to extremists, seized the chance to establish their operations online. The digital age, in a manner of speaking, democratized terrorism – making it accessible to anyone anywhere – dismantling barriers and enabling the localized dissemination of ideologies.

10.4 EXTREMISM WITHOUT BORDERS

Even though America chooses to define violent extremism with the artificial parameters "international" and "domestic," ideology has no borders. We understand and have witnessed how important, and far-reaching, inspiration can be. It moves people into action regardless of whether that inspiration comes from a region that is different from yours. The universal desire for identity and affiliation transcends cultural disparities and physical borders. Extremist ideas and techniques seamlessly traverse online landscapes, impacting movements across continents.

In regions as disparate as India, Kenya, and Japan, cultural norms have undergone transformation due to the pervasive influence of online platforms. Japan had QAnon marches happening in its streets, even though we thought QAnon was a distinctly American phenomenon. Yet it was making sense to some Japanese young people. The conspiracy theory was taking root in a country extremely different from the United States. But the rage of the "us vs them," or plausibility of the outrageous conspiracy, or belief in a human hierarchy can still have local meaning in unexpected places, regardless of the specifics of what skin color or religion, for example, are desirable within a specific country. The current epoch, characterized as the "Rage Era," exhibits global ramifications affecting politics, campaigns, and the dissemination of disinformation. Previously unimaginable, America's role as a source of inspiration for online branding and organizational strategies for ideological movements like the Far-Right holds significance, with these ideas disseminating to various corners of the world. There will likely soon come a time when the United States is designated a state sponsor of terror.

[16] *Supra*, note 10.

The convergence of lifestyle dynamics with their impact on discourse and identity expression, especially among the youth, through social media, adds another layer of complexity to this global phenomenon. Observing the interplay between the creativity exhibited by the youth in expressing themselves and the negative forces compelling them in specific directions is indeed a captivating phenomenon. This intricate dynamic, unfolding on a global scale, demands a nuanced understanding of how these elements shape narratives and influence societies across the world. The intertwining of marketing tools and tactics with ideological and personal branding has transformed into a lifestyle choice. This extends beyond online platforms to influence various aspects of individuals' lives, from their clothing choices to the news sources they prefer and even the tattoos they display.[17] The dynamic surge we observe in nations, especially in response to American trends, highlights the adaptability and amplification of these ideologies globally.

The exploration of rules, norms, and the evolving dynamics of lifestyle choices provides valuable insights into the complex tapestry of global influences shaping the narratives of our time. The examination of the "developing" world's role in propagating violent extremism through digital means, the global dissemination of extremist ideas, and the intertwining of lifestyle dynamics with ideological expressions illuminates the intricate challenges faced by societies worldwide. As we navigate this complex landscape, a nuanced understanding of the interconnected nature of these phenomena is crucial for developing effective strategies to counteract the influence of extremist ideologies on a global scale. Far too often, our responses have failed to adequately take these complexities and nuances into account.

10.5 PREVIOUS ATTEMPTS AT MITIGATING ONLINE HARMS

There was widespread concern after 9/11 that as large online platforms evolved, they could serve as both a haven and recruiting system for extremists; but social media companies still failed to establish a standard for user protection. It was only after 2013, amid the rise of ISIS, that companies and policymakers began to address the issue seriously. Finally, some of the biggest tech companies involved publicly recognized the significance of their platform to extremists.[18]

The government realization struck with urgency, acknowledging that extremists were exploiting these platforms for recruitment globally. Approximately 40,000 individuals from across the globe were recruited by ISIS to the so-called

[17] Farah Pandith, How We Win: How Cutting-Edge Entrepreneurs, Political Visionaries, Enlightened Business Leaders, and Social Media Mavens Can Defeat the Extremist Threat (2019).

[18] S. Higham & E. Nakashima, *Why the Islamic State Leaves Tech Companies Torn between Free Speech and Security*, Washington Post (July 16, 2015), https://www.washingtonpost.com/world/national-security/islamic-states-embrace-of-social-media-puts-tech-companies-in-a-bind/2015/07/15/0e5624c4-169c-11e5-89f3-61410da94eb1_story.html (last visited Feb. 18, 2024).

Caliphate,[19] and many of these individuals were radicalized online. Governments mounted pressure on tech companies, urging them to act. Although this was a welcome step, the government's initial response was to remove specific content, which ultimately proved ineffective as bad actors adapted, circumventing tracking systems and manipulating hashtags. Consider *Mein Kampf*, once confined to the realm of print, now perpetually accessible online. The dissemination of its ideology and its influence on nefarious actions exemplify the lasting impact of online content. Once something exists online, it is almost impossible to remove it completely or permanently. Even though an individual's, and the US government's, first instinct is often "take content down!" this strategy does not work for long and misses that social media platforms have emerged as colossal information repositories fundamentally reshaping the landscape. This metamorphosis has not only revolutionized the interconnection of ideas but also introduced enduring challenges with far-reaching consequences. The videos of America-born Al Qaeda Islamic "scholar" Anwar Alawlaki continued to radicalize individuals for years after his death despite repeated attempts to block them, underscoring the persistence of ideologies and the internet's pivotal role in recruitment.

As the US government shifted from a predominantly content removal focused policy, it pressured tech companies to act on algorithms enabling harmful content. Terms of service became a focal point, with diverse platforms having different standards. The US government emphasized not just ethical behavior but companies' responsibility to national security. However, aligning private-sector incentives with the nation's need to counter extremists posed challenges. Tech companies began modifying terms of service and algorithms but with misaligned incentives regarding the nation's need to curb extremism. This dualistic dynamic impacted the speed and nature of responses, entangling legal, moral, and ethical considerations in the quest for a solution. Silicon Valley's response lacked innovation and proactivity, because it was primarily driven by bottom-line considerations. Efforts like Facebook's Oversight Board[20] and the Global Internet Forum to Counter Terrorism (GIFCT)[21] were steps

[19] Lila Hassan, *Repatriating ISIS Foreign Fighters Is Key to Stemming Radicalization, Experts Say, but Many Countries Don't Want Their Citizens Back*, PBS (Apr. 6, 2021), https://www.pbs.org/wgbh/frontline/article/repatriating-isis-foreign-fighters-key-to-stemming-radicalization-experts-say-but-many-countries-dont-want-citizens-back/ (last visited Feb. 19, 2024).

[20] "The purpose of the board is to promote free expression by making principled, independent decisions regarding content on Facebook and Instagram and by issuing recommendations on the relevant Meta content policy. When fully staffed, the board will consist of 40 members from around the world that represent a diverse set of disciplines and backgrounds. These members will be empowered to select content cases for review and to uphold or reverse Facebook and Instagram content decisions. The board is not designed to be a simple extension of Meta's existing content review process. Rather, it will review a select number of highly emblematic cases and determine if decisions were made in accordance with Meta's stated values and policies." Oversight Board, https://www.oversightboard.com/ (last visited Feb. 18, 2024).

[21] "The Global Internet Forum to Counter Terrorism (GIFCT) is an NGO designed to prevent terrorists and violent extremists from exploiting digital platforms. Founded by Facebook, Microsoft, YouTube and X (formerly Twitter) in 2017, the Forum was established to foster

taken to self-govern and foster collaboration. However, the pace of change remained (and continue to remain) unsatisfactory. As threats continued to spiral, civil society gained prominence, fueled by citizen activism and concerns about technology's impact on minors. The challenge extended beyond content removal, requiring a systemic overhaul.

While mechanisms like GIFCT aimed at containing bad actors' influence, the broader landscape demanded more. The lack of a clear champion among tech companies and the absence of substantial proactive measures highlighted the need for a fundamental reboot of the American approach to what had become a mainstream utility. So stuck was the discourse around online harms that it was almost impossible to think creatively or to apply common sense changes to social media's daily functions.

Addressing online harms demands an innovative, comprehensive approach. Companies, lawmakers, and citizens must collaboratively navigate the challenges posed by extremist content. Facebook's Oversight Board and GIFCT demonstrate attempts at self-regulation, but the pace of change remains a concern. US politics and legislative stalemate make it almost impossible to make any kind of change, even if one is talking about protection of vulnerable children as young as Gen Alpha.

This multifaceted challenge involves not only preventing harmful content but also reducing the appeal of its underlying extremist ideologies. It will require something from all of us.

10.6 PATHS FORWARD

The battle against online extremism in its many current and future iterations requires a comprehensive, scaled, multigenerational funded, whole-of-society approach. Policymakers, tech companies, nongovernment organizations (NGOs), and citizens all need to work together, addressing issues of identity and belonging and other causes of radicalization, implementing effective regulations, and fostering a digital environment that prioritizes the well-being of society over individual interests. Behavioral change requires attention to the entire societal eco-system and the patience to stick with a strategy beyond short political cycles. The challenges are vast, but with strategic collaboration and forward-thinking initiatives, it is possible to mitigate the spread and dangers of online extremism. The following elements can decrease these harms:

technical collaboration among member companies, advance relevant research, and share knowledge with smaller platforms. Since 2017, GIFCT's membership has expanded beyond the founding companies to include over two dozen diverse platforms committed to cross-industry efforts to counter the spread of terrorist and violent extremist content online." *About*, Global Internet Forum to Counter Terrorism, https://gifct.org/about/ (last visited Feb. 18, 2024).

Redefining the Government's Role: Governments, despite their regulatory power, have limitations in combating extremism. The need for collaboration between tech companies, governments, and NGOs becomes evident here. To make a real difference, society needs a multipronged strategy that involves various sectors and targets different audiences. Policymakers, corporate pioneers, civil society leaders, and regular citizens must collaborate.

While governments can use regulation to influence the online space, designate terrorist groups, and impede funding flows, NGOs often take on the crucial task of preventing the appeal of extremist ideology. They actively engage in preventing the radicalization process by addressing the appeal of extremist ideologies. Local NGOs bring unique legitimacy, insight, and acumen to deploy effective initiatives. However, their efforts are hindered by the scale of the issue; NGOs are relatively small compared to the magnitude of the problem. Governments should do more than just acknowledge the importance of local initiatives and empower civil society by providing support in terms of grants and resources.

A government is best suited to implement incentives for stakeholders whose priorities are not always inherently aligned with the government's own. Analogous to the guardrails in physical spaces, the digital realm requires well-defined standards and laws. Governments should play a proactive role in establishing and enforcing regulations that are better, broader, and forward leaning. Learning from the European Union's Digital Service Act,[22] which imposes stricter requirements and penalties for

[22] The Digital Services Act is the most important and most ambitious regulation in the world in the field of the protection of the digital space against the spread of illegal content, and the protection of users' fundamental rights. There is no other legislative act in the world having this level of ambition to regulate social media, online marketplaces, very large online platforms (VLOPs) and very large online search engines (VLOSEs). The rules are designed asymmetrically: Larger intermediary services with significant societal impact (VLOPs and VLOSEs) are subject to stricter rules. After the Digital Services Act, platforms will not only have to be more transparent, but will also be held accountable for their role in disseminating illegal and harmful content. Amongst other things, the DSA:

1. Lays down special obligations for online marketplaces in order to combat the online sale of illegal products and services;
2. Introduces measures to counter illegal content online and obligations for platforms to react quickly, while respecting fundamental rights;
3. Protects minors online by prohibiting platforms from using targeted advertising based on the use of minors' personal data as defined in EU law;
4. Imposes certain limits on the presentation of advertising and on the use of sensitive personal data for targeted advertising, including gender, race and religion;
5. Bans misleading interfaces known as "dark patterns," and practices aimed at misleading.

Stricter rules apply for very large online platforms and search engines (VLOPs and VLOSEs), which will have to:

1. Offer users a system for recommending content that is not based on profiling;
2. Analyse the systemic risks they create: Risks related to the dissemination of illegal content, negative effects on fundamental rights, on electoral processes and on gender-based violence or mental health.

data privacy violations, could serve as a model for the United States to follow. As explained by Christoph Busch in Chapter 3, the Digital Services Act will not replace the EU's Terrorist Content Online Regulation (TCO Regulation), which went into effect in 2022. Under the TCO Regulation, platforms may be required to remove specified "terrorist content" within specific timeframes. As Busch explains, "national authorities have the power to issue 'removal orders' requiring hosting service providers to remove or disable access to terrorist content in all EU Member States 'as soon as possible and, in any event, within one hour of receipt of the removal order.'"

Encouraging positive behavior and rewarding responsible conduct might too be a method worth exploring more deeply. Carrots, in the form of benefits or rewards, could motivate companies to prioritize ethical practices, aligning their interests with societal well-being. Historically, the issue has been complicated by many things, including the pace of technology and the age of US lawmakers, most in the legislative branch are not digital natives,[23] which impacts the way they use and understand social media. This often results in their inability to identify exactly what they want tech companies to do outside of change the algorithms, which will cause companies to lose money and an overall weakness in the government's ability to make the case to regular citizens about online harms. The US government has approached this issue by first trying to convince then force tech companies to change. But one could look at this issue not just with a stick in hand, but also a carrot. Early implementation of incentives for technology companies, such as tax benefits offsetting the loss in revenues due to algorithm changes, could have mitigated the spread of extremist content. The delay in implementing these incentives allowed extremists to exploit the online space, underscoring the importance of timely and effective measures.

There are also a myriad of opportunities for more effective partnerships between governments and private sector tech companies in the fight about societal manipulation. One example: Can AI, in its predictive capacity, help us recognize key opportunities to avert potential harm? The interconnectedness of extremist ideologies poses a formidable challenge. AI, by deciphering patterns, could offer insights. Consider the Christchurch shooter – could AI have detected signs across various online platforms, creating a digital flag for governments? The potential for AI to act as a preemptive tool in preventing attacks is an enticing prospect worth exploring. The current policy landscape often sticks to familiar tools without embracing novelty. Unlike other fields that adapt to new devices, policy tends to rely on

In the context of the Russian invasion of Ukraine, involving grave and widespread violations of the human rights of the Ukrainian people, and the particular impact on the manipulation of online information, the Digital Services Act introduces a crisis response mechanism. This mechanism will make it possible to analyse the impact of the activities of VLOPs and VLOSEs on the crisis and rapidly decide on proportionate and effective measures to ensure the respect of fundamental rights." *EU Digital Services Act*, https://www.eu-digital-services-act.com/ (last visited Feb. 18, 2024).

[23] G. Skelley, *Congress Today Is Older Than It's Ever Been*, FiveThirtyEight (Apr. 3, 2023), https://fivethirtyeight.com/features/aging-congress-boomers/ (last visited Feb. 19, 2024).

traditional methods while expecting different outcomes. The key to fostering trust lies in collaborative efforts, innovative thinking, and a willingness to experiment with different approaches rather than clinging to established ways under the assumption that existing knowledge alone can guide decision-making. This requires cooperation among key stakeholders, domestically and internationally.

Collaborating on a Global Scale: Hate and extremism, as borderless issues, demand a global response. However, the current global efforts have been weak, characterized by outdated solutions, small-scale programs, and a lack of creativity. Meanwhile, "us versus them" ideologies have proliferated across border and bridged the domestic-foreign divide.

Policymakers need to collaborate on a global scale, thinking differently, scaling programs, and creating innovative, bold solutions that suit the purpose of countering extremism. Multilateral organizations are a critical tool. We have come together on natural or humanitarian disasters in the past with many different nations pitching in, bringing in tools and insights. We sprint into action when an earthquake or a tsunami or a fire happens. Nations that do not like each other find ways to work together. But we still do not have those systems in place in an effective way on issues of extremist ideology.

Likewise, we have come together on hard power in the past – fighting a common enemy. We have alliances and treaties and other mechanisms to discuss and coordinate. We share hardware and knowledge and information sharing through diplomatic and military channels among governments has improved greatly since 9/11. But even though nations now understand the risk environment better because of this coordination and partnership, on the innovation side we are still behind. There is so little that is out of the box thinking. We keep doing what we have been doing and we are not getting ahead of the threat due in part to the lack of willingness to share and adopt best practices globally, particularly regarding societal aspects.

Unfortunately, nations do not extensively share information on societal aspects of challenges including extremism. There is a need for increased interest in human behavior, fostering learning from other countries, as it intricately ties to online dynamics. The EU stands out in comprehending and addressing these societal impacts more effectively. While Americans discuss the issue, there is a notable gap in translating discussions into actionable measures.

If you are talking about hard power everyone knows what that means. Ideology is far more wiggly and squishy. It makes people uncomfortable and they do not know how to handle it. Multilaterals can make a difference not just by sharing best practices, but by really scaling the innovation piece. There are examples of governments who have decided that they are going to go hard on this issue. The EU is not waiting for the tech companies to tell them what to do. They are saying society comes first! We are going to protect our citizens, and toward that end, companies must abide by our definition of the public good. They show us a roadmap of what new policy can do. There are other non-technology related examples as well. Take the Danes and their successful recycling culture – they ingrained it into society and incentivized the population effectively.[24] Exploring such successes and understanding the underlying factors can inform strategies for behavioral change in the American context.

This is not the first time that humans have been faced with a difficult problem or a common threat that extends beyond their borders. Have there been other moments in time in human history when people from other parts of the world understood a threat and all came together and said, "Our security is interconnected. What are we going to do about it now that we have not done before" Yes, there have been. And we know firsthand that kind of response has taken place when the realm was science, for example. During the pandemic (while it took what seemed like forever but was actually remarkably fast) we found a vaccine for COVID-19 by sharing data and working together in unprecedented ways across borders. We also troubleshot ways of increasing societal buy-in for things like mask wearing and social distancing. What would it mean to apply these resources and this thinking to the extremist threat we all face? What would it mean not to forsake the exploration process but to know when to solidify an approach and move fast because we have consulted a diverse group of stakeholders? Leading without lagging demands this and a better understanding of what is coming next.

Imagining and Forecasting the Future: In the aftermath of 9/11, there was a mad scramble to address the immediate threats without much contemplation on the evolving nature of extremist prowess. We missed the opportunity for deep early ideation and exploration, which could have better prepared our nation for subsequent versions of extremist ideologies or the possibility that old hatreds would reemerge through new variants. We also missed the types of tools that could be deployed and the cultural changes that were a consequence of the new threat environment. Today's challenges draw from old and new tools, various demographics of digital natives, and limited scaled systems to deal with the current landscape.

Disinformation is a type of weapon. We need to respond to disinformation just as if an adversary had a new kind of missile, or tank, or gun. We need to develop a robust analysis of this weapon's potential to do harm.

In the realm of extremism, adept predictions require cultural intelligence. Cultural intelligence is a tool that aids in assessing communities, recognizing cultural shifts, and understanding what is important to specific demographics. One needs to know the reasons *why* a particular demographic acts in a particular way, not just that they are producing a particular type of action. Each generation responds differently, and policymakers should be clear on the nuances within varying societies because it can help build critical knowledge about preventative

[24] *Record-Breaking Year for Danish Recycling: 92 Per Cent of Bottles and Cans Returned for Recycling*, State of Green, Apr. 1, 2020, https://stateofgreen.com/en/news/record-breaking-year-for-danish-recycling-92-per-cent-of-bottles-and-cans-returned-for-recycling/ (last visited Feb. 18, 2024).

posturing going forward. When that cultural intelligence is not used at all in policymaking, in how we think about this threat, we miss a huge opportunity to succeed. As technology and society entwine, a cultural shift emerges – one to which bad actors are acutely attuned. Shaping culture becomes a potent weapon in the hands of violent extremists, reshaping beliefs, identities, and actions. We all understand how important culture is in general, and we should be applying that element to the work of defeating extremists as well.

Focusing on Digital Literacy: Online misinformation and digital extremism are addictive, and therefore digital literacy and hygiene should be prioritized, just as we prioritize responses to other addictive substances. This is imperative, especially for the three generations of digital natives: Millennials, Gen Z, and Gen Alpha. The understanding of how these generations are manipulated needs to be highlighted. Finland sets an example by teaching digital literacy in kindergarten, recognizing the importance of individuals comprehending manipulated content.[25] This emphasis on digital education can create a more discerning online population that questions and critically evaluates the information they encounter on an almost 24/7 basis. By preparing youth in this way, we make it harder for bad actors to win them over to their ideological armies.

10.7 A CAUSE FOR HOPE

Optimism emerges in these younger generations in the form of Gen Alpha, Gen Z, and Millennials, digital natives who are better attuned to the intricate workings of technology through better grasp of digital literacy and cybersecurity. Their potential solutions, combined with policymakers accepting the need for change, could pave the way for a more secure online environment.

While data may not conclusively support the claim, younger generations appear more tech-savvy, discerning fact from fiction. They grasp concepts like deepfakes,[26] CGI,[27] and AI,[28] understanding their presence in daily life. This familiarity might

[25] E. Mackintosh, *Finland Is Winning the War on Fake News. What It's Learned May Be Crucial to Western democracy*, CNN (May 17, 2019), https://edition.cnn.com/interactive/2019/05/europe/finland-fake-news-intl/ (last visited Feb. 19, 2024).

[26] A deepfake is an image, video, or audio recording that has been generated or altered by machine learning, specifically deep learning, technology. Deepfakes are hyper realistic and can convincingly "depict someone appearing to say or do something that they in fact never said or did." *Science & Tech Spotlight: Deepfakes*, Government Accountability Office, last modified Feb. 20, 2020, https://www.gao.gov/products/gao-20-379sp.

[27] CGI, or computer-generated imagery, refers to "the creation of still or animated visual content using imaging software." *Definition: Computer-generated imagery (CGI)*, TechTarget, https://www.techtarget.com/whatis/definition/CGI-computer-generated-imagery (last visited Jan. 30, 2024). In the context of violent extremism, CGI poses a threat similar to deepfakes.

[28] AI, or artificial intelligence, refers to "a machine-based system that can, for a given set of human-defined objectives, make predictions, recommendations or decisions influencing real or virtual environments." *Artificial Intelligence*, US Department of State, https://www.state.gov/artificial-intelligence/ (last visited Jan. 30, 2024).

empower them to question the authenticity of, for instance, a talking bear on the back porch or a deep fake of President Joe Biden admitting to various crimes. This technological gap affects all generations, but the younger demographics seem more attuned to the ongoing changes.

Every generation faces transformative communication technologies. For Gen Alpha, the internet and AI represent only the latest chapter. While unique, it follows a historical pattern. The crucial message for these digital native generations is that they have agency. Lessons from past technological shifts can empower them to shape a future when responsibility and action lie with individuals who demand more from all of us.

Similar questions arose in the past when new technologies, such as the telephone or radio broadcasts, reshaped the human experience. Each generation witnesses transformative advancements that alter their connection to the world. Understanding this continuum is critical.

Considering the multitude of examples demonstrating how technology can shape societies for better or worse over time, the question arises for digital natives: Could this be the moment for your generation to participate actively? Directly addressing today's challenges requires a collective effort that goes beyond the expectation of external interventions. It is a call to embrace agency, whether one is an entrepreneur, educator, government employee, or any other profession. Society's rules are not dictated by external forces; we collectively shape them. The current challenges arise from a lack of societal responsibility to tackle complex issues, emphasizing the need for immediate action.

The imperative is to act now rather than adopting a passive stance. Reflecting on the example of David Hogg, a Gen Z gun control activist who transformed a personal experience into a commitment to work on gun reform, underscores the impact of individual agency.[29] Waiting for older generations to enact sweeping laws may not be the most effective approach for the moment we find ourselves in. All over the world, youth are activating a new era of empowerment and standards on issues like the environment, human rights, equity, democracy and freedom. Instead of standing by, Gen Z is proactively pursuing the changes they envision for the world.

They are not the first generation to want a more fair, more peaceful world, but they have a leg up on generations before them. The data, insights, and speed of information give them a unique and powerful moment even though challenges may persist. While imperfection is inevitable, the application of lessons learned over the last two decades can mitigate harm and bring us forward into a different era where AI, cultural intelligence, and human dedication across sectors can make the threat of violent extremism less viable.

[29] David Hogg, *March for Our Lives* (Jan. 31, 2024), https://marchforourlives.com/david-hogg/ (last visited Feb. 19, 2024).

Waiting for change has not produced protection for any of us. Bad actors like the White Supremacist group Attomwaffen are already working on luring in Gen Alpha.[30] The moment is now to accelerate the application of lessons learned over two decades and build stronger, more resilient communities online. The question is, will we use this moment or squander it?

30 Helen Young, *Extremists Use Video Games to Recruit Vulnerable Youth. Here's What Parents and Gamers Need to Know*, THE CONVERSATION, November 9, 2022, https://theconversation.com/extremists-use-video-games-to-recruit-vulnerable-youth-heres-what-parents-and-gamers-need-to-know-193110.

11

Policy Approaches to Defining and Enforcing Responsibilities for Online Platforms

Josephine Wolff

In 1996, when the United States Communications Decency Act was passed, including the Section 230 provisions that protect online service providers from being held liable for most content posted on their platforms by users, the five most visited websites on the internet were AOL, Webcrawler, Netscape, Yahoo, and Infoseek.[1] By August 2023, the list of the five most visited websites in the world consisted entirely of companies that had not even been founded in 1996, when Section 230 was adopted: Google, YouTube, Facebook, Wikipedia, and Twitter.[2] Critics of Section 230's liability protections for online platforms point out how much the online landscape has shifted in order to argue that the law was written without any understanding of the new types of platforms that would emerge on the Internet and the impacts they would have. Supporters of Section 230, by contrast, point to these new platforms as evidence of the law's success, arguing that websites like YouTube, Facebook, and Twitter could never have existed without the protections enshrined in Section 230 because their developers would otherwise have faced crushing liability risks. What's clearly true is that the dominant platforms of the modern internet look very different from the ones that were most popular at the time that Section 230 was passed, and that these newer platforms are now giving rise to a wide range of very different policy approaches around the world. Whether the emergence of these platforms is viewed as a positive consequence of an unexpectedly prescient liability regime underpinned by Section 230, or a negative consequence of a disastrously lax approach to platform liability, there is no question that they are now subject to an increasingly complicated – and growing – set of public policies that alternately target specific types of platforms, specific types of content, and specific types of liability in the context of a variety of different, competing policy priorities.

[1] Comscore, *A Look Back in Time … at the Most Visited Web Domains of 1996!* (July 21, 2011), https://www.comscore.com/Insights/Blog/A-Look-Back-in-Time-at-the-Most-Visited-Web-Domains-of-1996 (last visited Mar. 3, 2024).

[2] Semrush, *Top Websites: Most Visited Websites in the World, August 2023*, https://www.semrush.com/website/top/ (last visited Mar. 3, 2024).

At the heart of this proliferating set of platform policies and proposals is not just the global growth of the internet since 1996 – though that has, of course, driven many more countries to take an interest in regulating online platforms – but also the fact that the individual platforms themselves now serve many more functions than they used to, ranging from providing access to news and information to providing encrypted messaging systems to selling cloud storage. This means that the types of content hosted on each of these platforms are more varied, the groups of people using them are more diverse, and the threats they pose are much more numerous and difficult to predict and disentangle. Accordingly, online platform regulation now involves multiple different strands of policy focused on different types of responsibilities for different types of platforms – a stark contrast to the one-size-fits-all approach of Section 230, which granted liability protections with a fairly broad brush to all "interactive computer services," with the exception of some criminal and intellectual property-related claims.

This chapter aims to build on the comparative country chapters as well as the generative chapters authored for this volume and the underlying project, by breaking down and disentangling some of the different policy debates and goals surrounding online platform responsibility. Identifying these different threads in the technology policy domain allows for a more granular discussion of which, if any, of these goals might lend themselves to some greater degree of international coordination, and whether there is potential for global governance solutions around certain issue areas related to online platforms. Similarly, separating out different policy concerns is useful for considering the implications of the generative chapters about banking regulations and taxation. As the authors of those chapters discuss, none of those areas offers a perfect analogy to the problems posed by online platforms, but each of them may still have something to offer by way of insight with regard to particular facets of online platform regulation.

This chapter is structured as follows. Section 11.1 reviews key themes of the comparative chapters with the goal of identifying different policy goals related to online platforms along three different types of obligations: responsibilities to target particular categories of unwanted content, responsibilities for platforms that wield particularly significant influence, and responsibilities to be transparent about platform decision-making. Section 11.2 considers which of these policy goals present the greatest opportunities for international coordination and agreement and which of them actually require such coordination in order to be effectively implemented. Finally, it considers what lessons can be drawn from existing policy efforts for how to foster greater coordination around areas of common interest related to online platforms.

11.1 GOALS OF ONLINE PLATFORM POLICY MAKING

The goals of regulating platform providers and their responsibilities have evolved and expanded considerably since the passage of Section 230. Jeff Kosseff traces the history and motivations of Section 230 to identify the primary goals that policymakers had in mind when authoring those early protections for online platforms and finds that one of the main reasons Congress passed that section of the law was to enable websites to be able to perform content moderation without facing additional liability for doing so. Kosseff explains that prior to the passage of Section 230, many US courts held that websites that had reason to know about content posted on their platforms could be held liable for it. So, when the dial-up service provider CompuServe was sued because an online newsletter it distributed contained allegedly libelous material, a court dismissed the case in 1991 on the grounds that the company had no way of knowing about that material. But when CompuServe's competitor Prodigy was later sued for comments made on one of its financial bulletin boards, a court found that it had opened itself up to greater liability than CompuServe by voluntarily hiring moderators to review posts on its platform and enforce user conduct rules.[3]

The Prodigy case attracted the attention of then-US Representatives Chris Cox and Ron Wyden, Kosseff explains, and in 1995 they introduced a bill that would later turn into the core of the Section 230 protections, with the intention – according to the law itself – of "promot[ing] the continued development of the Internet and other interactive computer services and other interactive media" as well as "remov[ing] disincentives for the development and utilization of blocking and filtering technologies that empower parents to restrict their children's access to objectionable or inappropriate online material."[4] Kosseff notes, "From the relatively sparse legislative history, it is clear that Section 230's drafters had two primary goals. First, they wanted to ensure that the nascent commercial Internet was unburdened from regulation and litigation. Second, they wanted to encourage online providers to moderate as they (and their users) saw fit."[5]

These aims – especially the goal of encouraging internet innovation and development – were not uncommon priorities for regulators during the late 1990s and early 2000s, even outside of the United States. Indeed, the template laid out by Section 230 of enacting broad liability protections for online service providers and carving out a couple specific exceptions was echoed in Brazilian policy, which provided safe harbor for platforms covering all content besides copyright claims and nonconsensual intimate content (as well as anything a court explicitly ordered them to remove), as Artur Pericles L. Monteiro's chapter points out.[6] Similarly, Indian platform policy has for many years also revolved around the promise of liability protections for platforms except in the case of two types of content: nonconsensual

[3] Jeff Kosseff, The Twenty-Six Words That Created the Internet (2019).

[4] 47 U.S.C. § 230, Protection for private blocking and screening of offensive material.

[5] Testimony of Jeff Kosseff Before the Senate Committee on Commerce, Science & Transportation, available at: https://www.commerce.senate.gov/services/files/444EFF87-84E3-46DB-B8DB-24DC9A424869 (last visited Mar. 3, 2024).

[6] *See* Chapter 6.

intimate content and rape and child sex abuse materials.[7] However, not all countries took this model as their basis for shaping platform liability. Christoph Busch's chapter describes how the European Union's E-Commerce Directive – a precursor to the Digital Services Act – took exactly the approach that led to the difference in treatment of CompuServe and Prodigy by dictating that only platform operators that were not playing any "active role" in determining which content was permitted on the platform were protected from being held liable for hosting that content. The Digital Services Act (DSA) also provides platforms with liability protections conditional on the platform not knowing about the illegal content they host, but it adds a "Good Samaritan rule" that aims at the same goal as Section 230: permitting providers to conduct moderation activities and self-initiated investigations without losing their liability protections.[8]

11.1.1 *Content-Specific Carve-Outs*

These twin goals of promoting the online economy and enabling online platforms to moderate user-generated content without facing additional legal burdens for doing so were important in shaping the platform policies of many countries – but not all. In China, as Jufang Wang's chapter points out, online platforms have instead been assigned "primary responsibility" for the content that users post on their servers and are therefore required to constantly monitor and moderate that content.[9] The policy goal motivating this model is presumably control over the types of information being shared via online platforms, and while China takes a particularly strong stance in prioritizing that as their top policy aim with regard to platforms, almost all of the countries that have passed platform-related regulations have made it a priority to force platforms to police certain types of content proactively. Most of these priorities have emerged as targeted carve-outs from broad platform liability protection laws, such as the exemptions in Section 230 for criminal liability and copyright-related claims, or for copyright and nonconsensual intimate content in Brazil, or for nonconsensual intimate content and rape and child sex abuse materials in India.

By carving out specific categories of content that platforms could be held liable for, countries could offer fairly broad liability protections, reducing the burden on online service providers to monitor everything, while still maintaining a few core priorities for certain types of content that were of particular concern. Unsurprisingly, these priorities varied by country – but they have also changed and evolved over time, alongside the growth and evolution of the online platforms themselves. In the 1990s, the existence of popular peer-to-peer file-sharing websites like Napster, as well as a robust music and film industry with a significant lobbying presence in

7 *See* Chapter 5.
8 *See* Chapter 3.
9 *See* Chapter 4.

Washington, DC, meant that liability for illegal sharing of copyrighted material was a particular concern in the United States, leading to the Section 230 exemption for copyrighted material. The policies established by Brazil and India, developed later on and in the context of very different political climates, prioritized liability for nonconsensual intimate content. And US regulators, in revisiting the protections of Section 230 in recent years in light of concerns about online sex trafficking, misinformation, and censorship, have introduced proposals that target the liability protections for a variety of other categories of content, including inaccurate information, political speech, and advertisements. Of these myriad proposals, only one significant carve out to the Section 230 protections has actually been enacted in the United States – the controversial Stop Enabling Sex Traffickers Act (SESTA) and Allow States and Victims to Fight Online Sex Trafficking Act (FOSTA), both passed in 2018, which exempted federal and state sex trafficking laws from Section 230's liability protections.[10] SESTA/FOSTA caused many websites, including Craigslist, Reddit, and Facebook, to stop hosting online advertisements for sex work or other sexually explicit content for fear of any resulting liability, leading critics of the law to allege that rather than helping crack down on sex trafficking, it had only made sex work more dangerous and difficult.[11]

Other countries have similarly introduced specific carve-outs to their liability protections that center on specific types of content. For instance, Busch describes the provisions governing "terrorist content" in the European Union, and Monteiro describes the proposed Brazilian policy that would have made platforms legally liable for misinformation posted on their platforms.[12] As Jhalak Kakkar, Shashank Mohan, and Vasudev Devadasan demonstrate, India has similarly introduced a variety of content-specific liability policies, including ones for terrorism-related content and election-related content.[13] Interestingly, India's approach to regulating liability protections for platforms has hinged in some cases not just on the type of content but also the technical transmission mode and format of that content. Specifically, Indian regulators have taken aim at end-to-end encrypted messaging platforms in their 2021 Intermediary Guidelines and Digital Media Ethics Code by requiring platforms to "enable the identification of the first originator" of any message – something that is technically infeasible under end-to-end encrypted systems.[14] This intersection of platform liability policy with encryption policy

[10] H.R.1865 – Allow States and Victims to Fight Online Sex Trafficking Act of 2017, https://www.congress.gov/bill/115th-congress/house-bill/1865/text; S.1693 – Stop Enabling Sex Traffickers Act of 2017, https://www.congress.gov/bill/115th-congress/senate-bill/1693/text.

[11] David McCabe & Kate Conger, *Stamping Out Online Sex Trafficking May Have Pushed It Underground*, New York Times (Dec. 17, 2019), https://www.nytimes.com/2019/12/17/technology/fosta-sex-trafficking-law.html

[12] *See* Chapters 6 and 3, respectively.

[13] *See* Chapter 5.

[14] Intermediary Guidelines and Digital Media Ethics Code, https://egazette.nic.in/WriteReadData/2021/225464.pdf (last visited Mar. 3, 2024).

highlights how intertwined the various areas of internet policy have become in light of the many different functions that online platforms now perform. By targeting specific types of content and imposing additional obligations and liability on platforms related to those categories, regulators can sometimes strike a balance between the broad goals that motivated Section 230, as well as other early platform policies and the specific policy priorities that revolve around particularly controversial or volatile issues or types of content. However, unless these carve-outs are very narrowly targeted, they can sometimes backfire with platforms choosing to over-zealously remove content they fear may open them up to greater liability, as in the case of SESTA/FOSTA and some US digital copyright protections, or finding that the technical implementation of their services is incompatible with the requirements for their liability protections, as in the case of the Indian Intermediary Guidelines.

Notably, most of these carve-outs focus on types of information that regulators want to discourage platforms from leaving up by imposing additional liability on them if that content is not removed. However, carve-outs to liability protections can also work in the opposite way: requiring platforms *not* to take down certain types of content or be liable for its removal. For instance, in September 2021, Brazilian President Jair Bolsonaro temporarily banned social media companies from removing content related to the country's 2022 elections, including his own posts claiming that he would win the election unless the voting machines were compromised. The Brazilian ban forbade platforms from removing any content that did not involve nudity, drugs, or violence and required them to obtain court orders before being permitted to remove any other types of content from their platforms.[15] Carve-outs of this nature reverse the motivation for policies like Section 230, aiming to disincentivize content moderation by increasing the potential liability associated with proactively moderating online posts, rather than encouraging that voluntary moderation activity by providing liability protections for it.

11.1.2 *Platform-Specific Liability Regimes*

Both of the policy goals that motivated Section 230 – promoting development of the internet economy and protecting platforms that choose to engage in voluntary content moderation – have shifted somewhat over the course of the past decade, though neither has disappeared. As the online economy has grown and the major digital platforms have become more established, regulators' fears of inhibiting the continued development of the internet have receded somewhat, at least in countries where there is sufficient internet penetration and infrastructure. In the United States, for instance, it is no longer plausible to argue that without broad liability

[15] Jack Nicas, *Brazil's President Bans Social Networks From Removing Some Posts*, New York Times (Sept. 9, 2021), https://www.nytimes.com/2021/09/09/world/americas/bolsonaro-social-networks.html (last visited Mar. 3, 2024).

protections for online platforms there will be no successful platforms, especially given how many resources the most successful of those companies now have to put toward compliance. However, there is still considerable concern in many countries with developed tech sectors that they may fall behind other countries or fail to innovate as quickly and successfully as their competitors. So, the policy goals that now motivate the preservation of regulations like Section 230 and analogous laws in other countries center on the importance of innovation and protecting new and emerging technologies and companies from high barriers to entry. Facebook or Google might be able to afford to comply with onerous liability regimes, advocates for broad liability protections now argue, but newer, smaller companies won't be able to, so any attempt to impose more liability on platforms will only serve to further entrench the existing dominant platforms and hinder innovation and competition from new entrants.

Whether or not these concerns are warranted, they have yielded a newer style of platform regulation in recent years – one that focuses specifically on the largest platforms, carving up the ever-growing landscape of online intermediaries to pin additional responsibilities on only the largest and most influential platforms. Busch describes the DSA Level 4 due diligence obligations that apply only to "very large online platforms" (VLOPs) and "very large online search engines" (VLOSEs) that have more than 45 million average monthly users in the EU. These obligations include conducting risk assessments and independent annual audits of DSA compliance at their own expense, granting researchers and regulators access to data related to systemic risks, publishing their terms and conditions in the official languages of every country where they offer their services, making the "main parameters" used by their recommender systems "clear and accessible," and more frequent transparency reports (every six months instead of every year). The rationale for these additional obligations is explained in the Act itself, which states that it "sets asymmetric due diligence obligations on different types of digital service providers depending on the nature of their services and their size" because "certain substantive obligations are limited only to very large online platforms, which due to their reach have acquired a central, systemic role in facilitating the public debate and economic transactions" and "which are prone to the highest levels of risks for the EU society and economy." By contrast, the DSA states, "very small providers are exempt from the obligations altogether."[16] Even the lowest level of DSA obligations exclude all "micro" and "small" enterprises, or all enterprises with fewer than fifty employees and annual turnover of less than 10 million Euros.[17]

[16] Regulation (EU) 2022/2065 of the European Parliament and of the Council of 19 October 2022 on a Single Market For Digital Services and amending Directive 2000/31/EC, http://data.europa.eu/eli/reg/2022/2065/oj.

[17] Article 2(3), Commission Recommendation 2003/361/EC of May 6, 2003, concerning the definition of micro, small and medium-sized enterprises, 2003 O.J. (L 124) 36, 39.

In its Intermediary Guidelines, India similarly defines a category of "significant social media intermediaries" (SSMIs) that have more than 5 million users in India. These SSMIs, like VLOSEs and VLOPs, have additional obligations under the Guidelines, including being required to appoint a Chief Compliance Officer as well as a contact for 24/7 coordination with law enforcement officials, to publish monthly compliance reports, and to identify the originator of all messages sent via its platform.[18] In contrast, the United States and China have largely avoided imposing different obligations to larger or smaller platforms, choosing instead to regulate all online service providers consistently, perhaps in part because they are home to some of the largest platform companies who most strenuously object to being the subject of additional responsibilities. The goals of policy approaches tailored to the size of platforms are generally to impose requirements and obligations that are proportional to the resources of individual platforms, thereby placing the greatest burden of compliance on the companies that are both best able to shoulder that burden and also most likely to have the greatest impact on the largest number of users. In other words, like Section 230 and its successors, these policies are partly motivated by a desire to encourage innovation – and not discourage the creation of new online start-ups by requiring them to undertake onerous compliance regimes – and also partly motivated by a desire to encourage as much proactive content moderation as possible from the companies that can afford it.

11.1.3 *Transparency Obligations*

A final category of policy approaches to platform responsibility center on transparency obligations of the online platforms. These include the DSA provisions requiring platforms to disclose "policies, procedures, measures and tools used for the purpose of content moderation," the transparency reports detailing how many complaints SSMIs received each month and how many pieces of content they removed that are mandated by India's Intermediary Guidelines, or the proposed Brazilian fake news bill that would require platforms to disclose sponsored online content. In the United States, many of the largest platform providers publish transparency reports about the quantity of content they take down and who they receive takedown requests from; however, these reporting mechanisms are largely voluntary. In many cases, this reporting activity dates back to the transparency reporting that several tech platforms began doing in the wake of the Edward Snowden leaks to try to reestablish trust with their users by providing them with as much information as they were legally allowed to about when they turned over user data or otherwise complied with government orders. Legislative proposals that would require more transparency around online advertisements have not met with much success in the United States, though the Federal Trade Commission does require

[18] Ministry of Electronics and Information Technology, S.O. 942(E) (Notified on Feb. 25, 2021).

the labeling of ads and sponsored content on many platforms for consumer protection purposes.[19] In China, platform transparency reports are less common, according to Wang, but companies like TikTok that are trying to maintain a global user base publish them in order to align with expectations for Western platforms.[20]

The goals of these transparency requirements range from informing users about the nature of the content they view on these platforms – in particular whether someone is paying to show it to them and, if so, whom – to helping users understand the rules and mechanisms for content moderation. The emphasis of what, precisely, must be made transparent and to whom is dictated by the primary concerns of the regulators in question. For instance, in the DSA, EU regulators prioritize transparency around recommender systems and automated content moderation because of their concerns that automation will render these systems too difficult for users to comprehend. In India, the emphasis is on revealing how much content is removed and why, due to concerns about over-zealous or insufficient moderation (or both). In Brazil and the United States, meanwhile, transparency proposals for platforms often intersect with concerns about misinformation and aim to mitigate the impact of information on platforms by forcing disclosures about when someone has paid, or been paid, to post that content so that users have more context in which to evaluate the information they are exposed to.

11.2 OPPORTUNITIES FOR INTERNATIONAL COOPERATION AND LEARNING FROM OTHER DOMAINS

The motivations for online platform–related policymaking span a wide range of policy goals from encouraging innovation to supporting content moderation of unwanted content, preventing the removal of desired online content, and better informing users about when content is removed and why, as well as the nature of the content they are viewing. Reconciling all of these policy goals is a challenge even within the borders of one country, much less at the international level, because some of these goals are directly at odds with each other, like encouraging voluntary moderation to reduce unwanted content and insisting platforms can't remove most forms of content without a court order to reduce unwanted censorship of political speech by platforms. For the major platforms operating across multiple countries, there might be value in greater international harmonization of the rules governing some of these areas, but to a large extent the platforms themselves have been a primary instrument of such harmonization by implementing some of the same sets of community guidelines for acceptable content or disinformation labeling practices

19 FTC, *FTC Releases Advertising Disclosures Guidance for Online Influencers* (Nov. 5, 2019), https://www.ftc.gov/news-events/news/press-releases/2019/11/ftc-releases-advertising-disclosures-guidance-online-influencers (last visited Mar. 3, 2024).

20 *See* Chapter 4.

across all of the jurisdictions in which they operate. Indeed, for platforms like Facebook, when content moderators decide whether or not to remove flagged posts, they first check whether a post violates the company-wide Community Standards for content and only refer to the laws governing the jurisdiction where the user appears to be located if the content passes that first test. In other words, while platforms still expend time and resources complying with diverse, uncoordinated national laws, they have attempted in many cases to focus more of their resources on implementing a single, company-wide set of rules for content moderation that takes precedence over different national laws.

11.2.1 *International Cooperation*

Given how culturally- and context-specific rules and ideas about illegal speech, misinformation, and censorship are, it is difficult to imagine how countries would reach any clear consensus on the right way to regulate these issues or why it would be beneficial for them to do so when global platforms are, on the whole, able to tailor moderation practices to different national versions of their platforms. For instance, many large platforms, including Facebook and Google, maintain different country-specific versions of their websites for users that can be tailored to the domestic laws of that country. So, when a user visits one of these websites, they will be automatically directed to the version that corresponds to and adheres to the local laws of the country where their connection and device appears to be located, based on information like their IP address, their self-identified home address, and other device and connection information. This data is collected and analyzed not just to enable platforms to comply with domestic laws but also so they can target users with ads based on their location. In other words, the analysis of where a user is does not add a significant burden for the platform beyond what they would do anyway to provide location-based ad targeting.

This automatic redirection to different versions of a service can be reasonably effective – though the determinations made about where a user is geographically using location information are not always correct – but it does not actually prevent people in one country from accessing another country's version of the same platform. Therefore, one downside of this approach is that it leaves unwanted content available on other countries' instances of those same platforms – meaning that it is often still accessible to people even in the country where it has ostensibly been removed if they are willing to put in some effort to locate it. On the other hand, this can also be viewed as an advantage of the geofencing approach to content moderation: one country's rules about what platforms may or may not host online need not dictate the content available to other people in other places.

Indeed, just as US-based platforms and tech companies like Apple are sometimes criticized for acceding to the demands of other countries, especially China, about what content and software to offer users, Wang's case study of TikTok makes clear that the reverse is also true: China-based platforms hoping to attract a global user base feel pressure to comply with standards and expectations of users and governments in other countries. This represents, in a sense, a certain sort of international standardization: multinational platforms segment their online presence by country and apply the national laws of each country to the specific instance of their platform aimed at that audience, directing users to the appropriate version of the site based on the location of their IP address while still allowing them to deliberately navigate to other versions. Wang's example of TikTok publishing transparency reports to align with Western companies indicates that this approach extends even beyond the companies' online presences to their other activities and public facing releases. While enforcing different rules and policy measures for different national versions of a platform is certainly not the same as reaching international consensus on these measures, it is no small thing that so many countries have accepted this approach as a satisfactory implementation of their domestic laws (there are of course notable exceptions of countries that instead choose to block entire platforms rather than allow tailored, local versions). This widespread acceptance of a highly imperfect system of implementation and enforcement is, itself, an impressive feat of international coordination.

Unsurprisingly, the areas where there have been the most successful efforts toward international cooperation on specific policy goals and measures are those where there is widespread agreement about what types of information are illegal or unwanted. For instance, platforms and law enforcement officials around the world coordinate on efforts to remove child sexual abuse materials, working from a shared database of image and video hashes. Similarly, there has been considerable international coordination around the policing and removal of copyrighted content on online platforms. This coordination has been possible not just because there are well aligned laws on these issues in many countries but also because the platforms themselves have not had to worry about alienating large swaths of their user bases by removing these classes of content. Political content and disinformation, by contrast, has been trickier to coordinate internationally and also – not unrelatedly – harder to moderate in ways that don't infuriate large groups of users.

Interestingly, several large platforms have taken more proactive steps to moderate disinformation around public health topics, including the COVID-19 pandemic, than they have to remove disinformation concerning political candidates or topics. In large part, this seems to stem from the perception within the platforms that there is clear, agreed-upon expert consensus on issues relating to topics like COVID-19 that they can use to distinguish disinformation but no way to assemble an unbiased expert panel to make similar distinctions around political information. This points to another possible opportunity for international cooperation around nonpolitical disinformation campaigns that might allow for more shared strategies and standards for what types of content should be removed from online platforms through consultation with international groups of experts.

11.2.2 *Lessons from Financial Regulation*

The generative chapters in this volume propose possible parallels between platform regulation and global governance schemes for other domains. Having disentangled some of the different policy goals surrounding platform responsibility-focused policies, it is perhaps useful to consider which of these parallels are most relevant to different aims. For instance, Federico Lupo-Pasini proposes in his discussion of international financial regulation that one of the lessons tech regulators might draw from the Basel Accord is that "regulatory standards became increasingly stringent and more detailed" over time. In that context, he suggests, it might make sense for policymakers "to work on a platform responsibility framework that is flexible enough to entice reluctant regulators to join in while progressively working to strengthen it once regulators and the industry have become used to it."[21]

This is an approach that seems best aligned with the areas where there is broad consensus around a rough policy goal but no clear agreement about the correct implementation. For instance, the policy efforts driving more transparency around how platforms moderate content and who pays for content on those platforms might be susceptible to a framework of this sort, whereby countries agree to promote some degree of reporting or transparency for platforms (as many of them already do) and then gradually arrive at a more standardized, specific set of transparency requirements over time. This approach also gives companies and regulators more time to figure out what types of reporting and transparency related to recommender systems and automated content moderation are helpful and understandable for a general audience.

It's less clear whether the lessons drawn from financial regulation about who will advocate for international policy efforts will apply to online platforms, however. Lupo-Pasini points out that in the case of the Basel Accord, "there was pressure from the broader financial industry to implement the standards. Hedge funds, banks, investment funds, rating agencies, and other market players shared the common belief that capital adequacy rules were necessary to guarantee financial stability. Therefore, regulators faced much market pressure to adopt the standards as part of their prudential toolbox if they wanted to attract foreign capital."[22] Many of the policy goals related to online platform responsibilities do not have a strong lobby in the private sector – indeed, the one that did (protecting copyrighted material and keeping infringing content off online platforms) was carved off into its own set of policies in the late 1990s and has been much more rigorously enforced than most other policy efforts in this space. The policy goals of promoting moderation, requiring platforms to remove unwanted user content, preventing platforms' from removing user content, placing additional due diligence burdens on the largest platforms,

[21] *See* Chapter 8.
[22] *Id.*

and imposing transparency requirements on platforms all have no strong support from the online platforms or any other powerful private sector coalition. Potentially, industry stakeholders might seek greater international harmonization of rules in these areas in order to reduce the need for them to customize moderation practices and national versions of their services to different jurisdictions, but so far it is not clear that this is a priority for the big platforms. Many of them have to employ separate teams to build and moderate individual national versions of their services anyway due to the differences in language, so more harmonization of rules might not actually provide such substantial relief from the burdens of trying to provide a service to people in countries all over the world.

Moreover, while at least some of these broad policy goals are held by many governments, unlike in the lessons drawn from international tax efforts, there are no clear financial incentives for governments to push these policy priorities forward, much less for them to work together to do so. Policy measures like the EU's DSA, which allows regulators to issue fines of up to 6 percent of global annual turnover for companies that violate the Act, could potentially generate some income for the governments imposing them. However, these types of penalties in EU technology regulations are often seen as a means for the EU to extract money from the primarily US-based major tech companies and can thereby actually serve to discourage cooperation between the United States and Europe. This suggests that at least in some cases, reaching greater international cooperation on platform-related policies may necessitate governments giving up some of the financial incentives that might otherwise help motivate the passage of such policies in a strictly domestic or regional context.

12

Why Global Platform Governance Is a Sham

Daniel W. Drezner

12.1 INTRODUCTION

Fifteen years ago in *All Politics Is Global*, I developed a typological theory of global economic governance.[1] My argument was that globalization had not transformed international relations but merely expanded the arenas of contestation to include policy arenas that had previously been the exclusive province of domestic politics. In my model, global governance structures and international law were intervening variables; what truly mattered was the distribution of preferences among the great powers, defined as jurisdictions with large markets that allowed governments to be rule-makers rather than rule-takers. When great power coordination was achieved, then effective governance would be the outcome. When great power coordination was not, then global governance would exist in name only.

Quite a lot has changed in the last fifteen years. Despite widespread commentary about de-globalization in the wake of Trump, Brexit, and the COVID-19 pandemic, metrics like the DHL Global Connectedness Index[2] demonstrate that the online exchange of information and data has continued to accelerate. If anything, the work-from-home trend in the advanced industrialized democracies has boosted the data intensity of the modern global economy. Demands for greater content moderation across myriad platforms have concomitantly increased as well. Can any standards be negotiated at the global level?

For reasons I will spell out below, my theory in *All Politics Is Global* was pessimistic about such an outcome. In reviewing the drafts of the other generative

[1] Daniel W. Drezner, All Politics Is Global: Explaining International Regulatory Regimes (2007).

[2] Steven A. Altman & Caroline R. Bastian, *DHL Global Connectedness Index 2022: An in-depth report on the state of globalization*, NYU Stern School of Business, Center for the Future of Management, DHL Initiative on Globalization (Feb. 2023), https://www.dhl.com/content/dam/dhl/global/delivered/documents/pdf/dhl-global-connectedness-index-2022-complete-report.pdf (last visited Mar. 3, 2024).

and comparative chapters in this volume, that suspicion has only been reinforced. At the current moment, the likeliest result will be a hypocritical system of "sham governance." Under this system, a few token agreements might be negotiated at the global level. Even these arrangements, however, will lack enforcement mechanisms and likely be honored only in the breach. The regulatory center of gravity will remain at the national level. Changes at the societal and global levels over the past fifteen years only reinforce the dynamics that lead to that outcome.

The rest of this chapter is divided into four sections. Section 12.2 summarizes the arguments I made in *All Politics Is Global* and why that model would predict a sham governance outcome. Section 12.3 considers how international relations has changed over the past fifteen years in ways that undercut or reinforce the model's conclusions. Section 12.4 considers how changes in the political economy of the internet could undercut or reinforce the model's conclusions. Section 12.5 looks at where we are now and where we might be headed.

12.2 A GENERAL TYPOLOGY OF GLOBAL ECONOMIC GOVERNANCE

Regulatory coordination across borders is commonly represented as a simple coordination game, sometimes referred to as "battle of the sexes."[3] In this game structure, actors are better off if they coordinate to arrive at the same outcome than if they do not. The content of any coordination agreement can have distributional implications, however, which leads to the bargaining problem in world politics. States want to reach agreement, but they would prefer to reach agreement on regulatory standards closest to their preexisting status quo. This creates incentives for governments to obtain a first-mover advantage, writing the rules before any other actor. Of course, such an approach, if pursued by multiple actors, risks an outcome of no coordination. The question regulators and negotiators must consider is how much the added benefit of international coordination exceeds the adjustment costs of any agreement that forces a change in the domestic policy compact.

In *All Politics Is Global*, I made three addendums to this standard coordination problem. First, not all actors are equal in this standard-setting game. Domestic market size is a powerful source of bargaining power in regulatory coordination. Large markets act as a global attractor for multinational corporations. This endows large-market jurisdictions with greater leverage in translating their domestic standards into global standards.[4] Because multinational corporations tend to prefer policy certainty and uniformity across borders, they will have the incentives to adopt the

[3] The original parable involved a couple trying to decide whether to take a vacation at the beach or in the mountains.

[4] A partial exception to this rule is when leaders attempt to use international negotiations to shift the domestic status quo. *See* Locating the Proper Authorities (Daniel W. Drezner, ed. 2002); Henry Farrell & Abraham Newman, Of Privacy and Power (2019).

preferences of their largest customer, thereby acting as an amplifier of that jurisdiction's preferences.[5]

If one market is truly hegemonic and desiring of high standards, the result can be akin to what American political economy scholars call "the California effect" and what Anu Bradford calls "The Brussels Effect" – a race to the top in standards.[6] If the hegemonic actor is more libertarian in its approach to regulation, the result can be akin to what American political economy scholars call "the Delaware effect" and international political economy scholars call the "race to the bottom." When there is no hegemonic actor, however, the question of regulatory standards is a matter of international bargaining.

Second, when there is a great power concert over the content of regulatory standards, there will be effective coordination at the global level. In the first decade of this century, the only large-market jurisdictions of sufficient size were the United States and European Union. When those two jurisdictions reached an agreement on standards, the only variation in the outcome would be the precise global governance process. In a world in which most jurisdictions are on the same page, the harmonized global governance outcome would usually be a mix of private orders (like ICANN) and universal-membership international governmental organizations (IGOs) like the International Telecommunications Union (ITU). When the great powers are in agreement but there is resistance from the Global South or other weaker actors, the outcome is one of club governance. Club-membership IGOs such as the Organization for Economic Cooperation and Development (OECD) or G-20 will set the standards and then use a mix of cajoling and coercion to bring smaller jurisdictions into line. This was how the G-7 countries were able to create the Financial Action Task Force (FATF) and institute a stringent, global anti-money laundering standard.[7]

Finally, and most importantly, at the most basic level the battle of the sexes game is not always the correct description of standard-setting. The coordination game always assumes that an outcome of coordination is a Pareto-improvement over an outcome of no coordination. There are some issue areas, however, where the adjustment costs are so high that this condition does not hold. When adjustment costs are prohibitively high, the equilibrium outcome is no agreement.

For example, as an occasional international traveler, I am keenly aware of the potential benefits of coordination for electrical outlets – no more travel plug converters! That said, because electrical grids were created prior to the current era of globalization, the adjustment costs for any country that had to shift those

5 *See*, on this point, Nikhil Kalyanpur & Abraham Newman, *Mobilizing Market Power: Jurisdictional Expansion as Economic Statecraft*, 73(1) Int'l. Org. 1 (2019).

6 Anu Bradford, The Brussels Effect – How the European Union Rules the World (2020).

7 Beth Simmons, *The International Politics of Harmonization: The Case of Capital Market Regulation*, 55(3) Int'l. Org. 589 (2001); Drezner, *supra* note 1; Julia Morse, The Bankers' Blacklist (2021).

standards would be massive.[8] These adjustment costs vastly outweigh the inconvenience of buying the occasional adapter when crossing borders.

On online content moderation and regulation, I predicted in *All Politics Is Global* that there would no bargaining core, even between the United States and the European Union. Different cultural histories meant that what was considered taboo in one society would be tolerated in another one. Indeed, as the other chapters in this volume demonstrate, the great powers hold rather divergent preferences on content moderation. As Eric Goldman (Chapter 2) noted in his discussion of the American approach to content regulation, "many categories of speech that are regulated internationally may be Constitutionally protected in the United States and thus subject to little or no government restrictions." As for the broad immunity provisions contained in the 1996 Communications Decency Act, he observed, "[the immunity of] Section 230(c)(1) is a globally unique policy. No other country has adopted a legal rule like it."[9] Indeed, this standard stands in marked contrast to the European Union's E-Commerce Directive or India's Information Technology Act.[10] This is before one factored in the disparate policy preferences of autocratic and democratic governments. I therefore concluded: "Countries have wildly divergent preferences to which Internet content should be regulated .... For this issue, there is no bargaining core among governments. The predicted outcome would be the unilateral use of national regulations to bar undesired content, and the creation of sham standards at the global level."[11]

12.3 WHAT A LONG STRANGE FIFTEEN YEARS IT'S BEEN

It has been nearly twenty years since I developed my model for global governance. That is an appreciable period in the history of international relations and an eon in the history of the internet. What have been the key changes in the world that would affect my prediction?

On the international relations side of the ledger, there have been three significant shifts. The first is that the number of great powers has expanded. China's economy is now the largest in the world if one measures GDP using purchasing power parity; even if one uses market exchange rates China is projected to eclipse the United States and European Union sometime in the next decade. In 2009, the G-20, which included all the BRICS economies, supplanted the G-7 and was officially

[8] *See*, Tim Büthe, *The Power of Norms; the Norms of Power: Who Governs International Electrical and Electronic Technology?*, WHO GOVERNS THE GLOBE? (Deborah D. Avant, Martha Finnemore & Susan K. Sell, eds. 2010).

[9] *See* Chapter 2.

[10] *See* Chapters 3 and 5.

[11] DREZNER, *supra* note 1, at 95. *See also*, Daniel W. Drezner, *The Global Governance of the Internet: Bringing the State Back In*, 119(3) *Pol. Sci. Quarterly* 477 (2004).

designated "the premier forum for our international economic cooperation."[12] China's ever-increasing market size has had the predicted gravitational effect on multinational corporations. Any truly global economic governance now requires Chinese buy-in.

As Jufang Wang's chapter demonstrates, China's regulatory preferences are sharply at odds with those in Europe or the United States. China's definition of "harmful content" is much more expansive than in Western societies. It includes – but is not limited to – "smearing national heroes and martyrs" and "sabotaging China's national unity or religion policies."[13] Chinese preferences for platform responsibility and content moderation are therefore far more restrictive than any standards promulgated by American or European authorities. The probability of harmonized or club governance in this issue area becomes even more remote.

A second significant shift has been the ongoing democratic recession. Whether one looks at Freedom House, Polity, or other metrics, the results are similar: over the past fifteen years the world has become less free.[14] This is due to a combination of factors. Authoritarian leaders in places like Russia and Iran have swept aside any countervailing institutions while enhancing the state's coercive apparatus. In many democracies, populist leaders have hollowed out institutional checks, political opposition, and legal limits on executive power. The reasons for the democratic recession are unimportant for this analysis. What is important is that an increasing number of anocracies and autocracies will possess policy preferences on content moderation and regulation that more closely resemble China than the United States or European Union. India's penal code, for example, criminalizes "content intended to outrage religious feelings of beliefs" and "content prejudicial to 'national integration.'" That sounds far more similar to Chinese standards than European standards.

The third trend is the blowback from US security allies with respect to Edward Snowden's revelations in 2013 about US covert surveillance. Snowden revealed that the United States had taken advantage of its network centrality to surveil key allies' email and phone communications. Although this monitoring did not extend to social media, the revelations of US hypocrisy forced many key allies to adopt countermeasures that did have ramifications for social media.[15] This US surveillance highlighted the ways in which the United States could exploit weaponized interdependence in online networks.[16] In particular, the United States could exploit

[12] G20 Leaders Statement: The Pittsburgh Summit (Sept. 25, 2009), http://www.g20.utoronto.ca/2009/2009communique0925.html (last visited Mar. 3, 2024).

[13] *See* Chapter 4.

[14] *See* Larry Diamond, *Facing Up to the Democratic Recession*, 26(1) J. OF DEMOCRACY 141 (Jan. 2015); Larry Diamond, *Democratic Regression in Comparative Perspective: Scope, Methods, and Causes*, 28(1) DEMOCRATIZATION 22 (2021).

[15] Henry Farrell & Martha Finnemore, *The End of Hypocrisy: American Foreign Policy in the Age of Leaks*, 92(6) FOREIGN AFFAIRS 22 (2013).

[16] Henry Farrell & Abraham Newman, *Weaponized Interdependence: How Global Economic Networks Shape State Coercion*, 44(1) *Int'l. Security* 42 (July 1, 2019).

the "panopticon effect" of network centrality to collect data and metadata about social media users. As the chapter by Artur Pericles L. Monteiro demonstrates, key US allies seized on the Snowden revelations to call for greater data sovereignty – that is, for social media firms like Google, Facebook, and Twitter to keep personal user data within a jurisdiction's national boundaries.[17] Such a move enables these jurisdictions to legislate questions of data privacy with minimal concerns about great power responses.

12.4 FROM WEB 1.0 TO WEB 2.0

On the political economy side of the ledger, the most significant shift has been from a Web 1.0 to Web 2.0 architecture. Web 1.0, which roughly characterizes the first fifteen years of internet commercialization, was a "read-only" venue, in which a small number of providers generated content for a much larger audience. The consumption of internet content was relatively passive. Even the small number of content providers are fragmented, however. The industrial organization of Web 1.0 limited the market power of any internet service provider relative to its competitors. Therefore, conversations about platform moderation and regulation made little sense, since there were no platforms of any appreciable size beyond, perhaps, AOL.

The transition to Web 2.0 led to a much more interactive online experience. The introduction of social media enabled a more participatory experience for users. The economics of social media, however, made Web 2.0 radically different from Web 1.0.[18] The quality of social media is primarily a function of quantity; as the size of the network increases, so does the consumer utility. This creates a structure of natural monopolies, in which giants like Apple, Facebook, Google, or TikTok dominate certain spheres of Web 2.0. Also-rans like Friendster, MySpace, Yahoo, or Vine quickly receded from view. Content regulation and moderation shifted from an internet-wide discussion to more focused questions about corporate culture within the firms that hosted the dominant platforms.

At the same time, the primary revenue source for Web platforms raised thorny questions about data privacy. As one review essay famously noted, the users of social media provide the value-added for these platforms in supplying the raw data that these platforms can exploit for commercial purposes.[19] This gives Web 2.0 winners a powerful incentive to resist any official restrictions to be placed on their platforms. Because these companies prove to be natural monopolies, they also have the resources to wage political fights against any such regulations. This does not mean that Web 2.0 monopolies can always thwart regulatory outcomes; the actions of the Chinese censorship regime, the European Commission's Competition Directorate,

[17] *See* Chapter 6.

[18] *See*, on this point, Hal Varian & Carl Shapiro, Information Rules: A Strategic Guide to the Network Economy (1998).

[19] John Lanchester, *You Are the Product*, 39(19) London Review of Books 3 (Aug. 17, 2017).

and even the US Federal Bureau of Investigation falsify this claim. It is more accurate to state that these firms can use the threats of political voice and market exit to apply some constraints on these regulatory efforts. As Google's litigation strategy in India reveals, "the nature of litigation in India coupled with the legal resources of platforms may render intermediary liability (i.e., the risk of liability enforced through private lawsuits) a weak regulatory tool to regulate platform behavior."[20]

Beyond the lobbying advantage, Web 2.0 providers also possess a massive informational advantage over potential regulatory actors. Simply put, the financial remuneration for working at a large platform firm like Facebook or Google vastly outweighs working for the state. This means that the allocation of human capital will be heavily skewed toward the platform provider in any negotiation or litigation with either legislative or regulatory actors. The imbalance in skilled personnel makes it harder for the elected officials to pass the requisite laws and regulations. In some instances, members of legislatures have demonstrated such radical ignorance about the nature of online platforms that they lack the requisite knowledge to ask informed questions.

Even if elected officials were more tech-savvy, it is far from clear whether they could craft effective regulation of online platforms. Ordinary models of regulation assume imperfect information between the producer and the regulator. The growing complexity of the online sector, however, exacerbates that information asymmetry even more. Political science models demonstrate that as the complexity of the relevant business sector increases, the regulatory outcomes will be increasingly biased toward those preferred by the firms.[21] This holds for sectors like pharmaceuticals and commercial aviation; it likely holds for Web 2.0 as well.

12.5 THE PRESENT AND THE FUTURE

All of the trends discussed in Sections 12.3–4 reinforce the likelihood of a sham governance outcome for content moderation and platform regulation. The rise of China makes the possibility of great power agreement on any substantive content moderation extremely unlikely. China's treatment of Google and other US-based platforms demonstrate its hostility to Western modes of content regulation. US resistance to a Code of Conduct for Cyberspace, as promoted by Russia and China, speaks to this lack of consensus between the great powers.[22] In recent years, China has also grown more comfortable in using its market power to pressure

[20] *See* Chapter 5.

[21] Nolan McCarty, *The Regulation and Self-Regulation of a Complex Industry*, 79 *Journal of Politics* 1220 (2017).

[22] Jeffrey Lantis & Daniel J. Bloomberg, *Changing the Code? Norm Contestation and US Antipreneurism in Cyberspace*, 32 Int'l. Relations 149 (2018).

Western multinationals.[23] Indeed, Chinese officials may well view their "Great Wall" approach to online content as an implicit industrial policy for Chinese internet providers, allowing the likes of TikTok, Huawei, and Weibo to compete with Facebook, Samsung, and Google on the global stage. This only increases the incentive for Chinese public policy preferences to diverge from the West. Rising geopolitical tensions over Taiwan and the South China Sea will further decrease the likelihood of cooperation. A great power concert over platform moderation is a nonstarter.

The growth of more illiberal autocracies increasing the number of states that might share Chinese regulatory preferences hints at a possible rival standards outcome. China and the OECD economies could promulgate two competing sets of content moderation standards and try to cajole or coerce the rest of the world to their standard. The alienation of many US allies to Washington's hypocrisy, however, makes even this kind of agreement unlikely. The United States and European Union already have disparate policy preferences over content regulation; the festering lack of trust from the Snowden affair will make agreement that much more difficult to achieve. Similarly, China's myriad overreaching and "wolf warrior" diplomacy will make even autocratic leaders wary of permitting too much Chinese control over cyberspace.[24]

Finally, over time, the dominant platforms have acquired sufficient lobbying resources and political influence to dramatically raise the costs of additional regulation. The libertarian origins of Silicon Valley permeate the entire sector, causing these firms to be reflexively hostile to additional regulation. Some platforms have ratcheted up self-regulation in an effort to forestall additional government intrusion. In this political environment, the only possible remaining outcome is one of sham governance, in which content-free nostrums are agreed upon at the global level and barely implemented at the national level.

Indeed, this largely matches current descriptions of internet governance. A recent Council on Foreign Relations task force report concluded that while the United States aspired to create an open, global internet, that ideal no longer bore any resemblance to reality:[25]

> The utopian vision of an open, reliable, and secure global network has not been achieved and is unlikely ever to be realized. Today, the internet is less free, more fragmented, and less secure.

[23] Peter Harrell, Elizabeth Rosenberg & Edoardo Saravalle, *China's Use of Coercive Economic Measures*, Center for a New American Security (June 2018); Victor Cha & Andy Lim, *Flagrant Foul: China's Predatory Liberalism and the NBA*, 42(4) The Washington Quarterly 23 (2019).

[24] Daniel W. Drezner. *The Song Remains the Same: International Relations after COVID-19*, 74 (S1) Int'l. Org. E18 (2020).

[25] Adam Segal & Gordon Goldstein, *Confronting Reality in Cyberspace: Foreign Policy for a Fragmented Internet* 2, Council on Foreign Relations, Independent Task Force Report No. 80 (July 2022).

> Countries around the world now exert a greater degree of control over the internet, localizing data, blocking and moderating content, and launching political influence campaigns. Nation-states conduct massive cyber campaigns, and the number of disruptive attacks is growing ....
>
> Malicious actors have exploited social media platforms, spread disinformation and misinformation, incited disparate forms of political participation that can sway elections, engendered fierce violence, and promoted toxic forms of civic division.

Could this change in the future? Further technological innovation could rejigger the distribution of policy preferences. The claimed evolution from Web 2.0 to Web 3.0 – in which, as with Substack, the user could exercise more autonomy and ownership over content creation – could lead to a redistribution of benefits and responsibilities that makes content regulation easier. That said, most of the salient trends suggest an even further fragmentation of platform regulation. In theory, a massive scandal could create a policy window that would prompt additional regulation. In practice, Facebook's myriad scandals have not led to any meaningful change in content regulation. This suggests that Web 2.0 monopolies still possess the requisite political power to act as effective veto players. On the international relations side of the ledger, rising geopolitical tensions will act as a further deterrent to effective global standards.

The rise of populist nationalism within the advanced industrialized democracies will also have debilitating effects on the ability to regulate. As Goldman warns in his memo, "online speech freedoms have become inextricably intertwined with partisan politics, which creates irreconcilable conflicts."[26] In many instances, populists exploited disinformation campaigns via online platforms to obtain greater political influence; they will stoutly resist efforts to regulate that political tool. Furthermore, by definition, populists dislike technocratic methods of regulation, perceiving them to be a tool of elites that constrain political power. Populism and political polarization both erode the rule of law, enervating effective regulation. Populism also emboldens private actors to litigate against the state, hopeful that a new government will countermand the orders of the previous government.[27]

The increase in data localization will enable a more heterogenous set of platform moderation policies to emerge. Multinational firms will find it harder to claim that they are beyond the scope of national regulation. Given ongoing trends in international relations and the industrial organization of the internet, however, there will not be any substantive global governance on this issue for the next generation.

[26] *See* Chapter 2.

[27] Daniel W. Drezner, *The Death of the Democratic Advantage?*, 24(2) Int'l Studies Rev. viac017 (2022).

13

The Disinformation Paradox

Why Regulating Online Content at Home May Make Matters Worse in the World

Bhaskar Chakravorti

13.1 INTRODUCTION

Proponents of social media and digital platforms more broadly point to the idea of societal well-being advanced through interconnectivity and collective access to vast troves of user-generated content. Individual users can discover content – ranging from deep wisdom to shallow banalities to everything else in between. Each participant on a platform can draw upon insights from anywhere in the world; conversely, in principle, a single user's voice can reach well beyond their immediate circles. There are so many striking examples of such collective sharing of content, from the experience of humanity communing digitally through a shared period of physical isolation during the COVID-19 pandemic to receiving news and updates about unfolding events, wars, elections, or sports. Our IDEA 2030 research by The Fletcher School's Digital Planet program, in collaboration with Equiception, a research firm, conducted an analysis of content on digital platforms during the first seven months of 2020 and parsed the emotional states of citizens in messages posted on digital platforms across eight democracies during an unprecedented time when many democratic civil liberties were suspended. The research revealed a surprising similarity of sentiment, primarily of positivity – presumably in solidarity during a period of collective adversity. This shared experience may have helped many get through one of the most extraordinary periods of uncertainty and anxiety for citizens everywhere of the kind that few had experienced in their lifetimes.[1]

Digital platforms had been designed with the objective of sharing in mind. The founder and CEO of Meta (formerly Facebook), Mark Zuckerberg, famously wrote in the opening of his 2012 Founder's Letter: "Facebook was not originally created to

[1] Auret van Heerden, Bhaskar Chakravorti, Ravi Chaturvedi & Ravi Sreenath, *Inclusive Crisis Management by Governments: Using Digital Ethnography and Sentiment Analysis as a Sensing Function and Policy Tool*, IDEA 2030, Digital Planet, The Fletcher School, Tufts University (Oct. 2021), https://sites.tufts.edu/digitalplanet/files/2021/Sentiment-Analysis-During-the-Pandemic.pdf (last visited Feb. 18, 2024).

be a company. It was built to accomplish a social mission – to make the world more open and connected." The high-minded vision and the imperatives of running a company aside, it is now clear that the very openness and connectivity of digital platforms can cut both ways. Harmful content – whether it is disinformation or false, misleading, and inaccurate information and news, hate speech, conspiracy theories, and posts planted for purposes of political or commercial gain or inciting violence or with the potential of undermining institutions – represents a classic negative externality as the outcome of the open and connected nature of digital platforms. While we can recognize the social ills of harmful content, its moderation is hard. The reason comes down to a single critical factor: the misalignment of incentives. It is this misalignment that gives rise to a "disinformation paradox," where attempts to regulate harmful content could give rise to even more of it. This chapter explores this phenomenon and possible resolutions.

The chapter is organized as follows. Section 13.2 highlights the role of incentives in inhibiting adequate self-moderation of content by digital platforms. This means that public oversight and regulation is needed as a corrective measure. In Section 13.3, I shall argue that even such public oversight and regulation is fraught with challenges and may give rise to unintended consequences that could result in making the disinformation problem worse across the world. Ironically, once again, incentives are at the root of the problem. Section 13.4 outlines additional factors in play stemming from the dynamic nature of the industry that add to the complications of effective content moderation. The Sections 13.5–6 offer alternative approaches to addressing the problem and their limitations.

13.2 INCENTIVE INCOMPATIBILITY AND THE PROBLEM OF UNDER-MODERATION OF CONTENT BY DIGITAL PLATFORMS

Mark Zuckerberg's company has been in the news repeatedly for its inability to moderate the content that it helps disseminate to every corner of the world. In her October 5, 2021, testimony before Congress, former Facebook employee and whistleblower Frances Haugen made a strong case for public oversight and regulation of digital platforms. She asserted that the products of her former employer (now known as Meta Inc.), "harm children, stoke division and weaken our democracy."[2]

Clearly, Zuckerberg or any of the other founders of the major digital platforms did not intend to get to such an outcome. To understand how the platform he created might have gotten to this point, we must appreciate the disinformation chain responsible for the outcome. The chain originates with the creator of content and ends with the user who views the content at the other end. The originator of the

[2] *Whistleblower Says Facebook's Choices Are "Disastrous" for Children, Democracy*, Wall Street Journal (Oct. 5, 2021), https://www.wsj.com/livecoverage/facebook-whistleblower-frances-haugen-senate-hearing (last visited Feb. 19, 2024).

content may have their own reasons for creating it. In the intermediate stages of the chain, there are other users who share, endorse, and comment on the original thereby passing it along to an even larger body of users. In parallel, the platforms and their algorithms and recommender systems determine what content users encounter. At every stage in this chain, in principle, harmful content could be flagged, blocked, or de-prioritized – but it isn't. Instead, it is more likely to be amplified. The reason is that the incentives of participants involved in the disinformation chain are misaligned with appropriately moderating such content.

Users who create disinformation have different incentives – from innocent mischief to political – driving the urge. Similarly, those who share it help propagate it for different reasons; often, it is precisely because disinformation can be edgy and there is an expectation that it will command greater engagement, which is what users want from their posts. In many instances, the users in the chain may not even know that are passing along disinformation. The platforms, for their part, often cite the sheer scale of the problem as their biggest challenge in catching disinformation. In fact, Mark Zuckerberg has noted:[3]

> We have a responsibility to keep people safe on our services. That means deciding what counts as terrorist propaganda, hate speech and more. We continually review our policies with experts, but at our scale we'll always make mistakes and decisions that people disagree with.

No doubt, the difficulties of content moderation at scale are considerable, given that tens of billions of posts – and a billion stories alone across the Meta platforms – are created every day.[4] That said, there is another, more structural reason as to why this is hard: attempts to moderate harmful content would run counter to the platform company's commercial interests and the incentives offered to key employees. Content of any kind leads to user engagement, which, in turn, can be monetized by selling spots to advertisers. Product managers at Facebook, for example, have compensation structures that are tied to getting users to maximize their time and engagement on the platforms. Indeed, these incentives work: platforms, such as those owned by Meta, have been successful at extending the time and engagement by users. Furthermore, both go up when the content is harmful. A study by researchers at New York University and the Université Grenoble Alpes found that disinformation generated six times the volume of engagement as did posts from

3 Mark Zuckerberg, *The Internet Needs New Rules. Let's Start in These Four Areas*, Washington Post (Mar. 30, 2019), https://www.washingtonpost.com/opinions/mark-zuckerberg-the-internet-needs-new-rules-lets-start-in-these-four-areas/2019/03/29/9e6f0504-521a-11e9-a3f7-78b7525a8d5f_story.html (last visited Feb. 19, 2024).

4 Facebook Earnings Call, Q4, 2018, https://www.facebook.com/business/ads/stories-ad-format# (last visited Feb. 19, 2024).

trustworthy news and information sources.[5] In turn, this greater engagement and time spent on the platform pays off for the company because over 97 percent of the company's revenues are derived from advertising, which increases with exposure.[6] Even if there were concerns about the content, procedures at the platforms are optimized to put such concerns aside. For example, user interactions that were once analyzed by engineers are increasingly being analyzed by algorithms that create personalized feedback loops for tweaking and tailoring each user's news feed to keep pushing up their engagement.[7] Simultaneously, hiring content moderation teams costs money and do not generate revenue. During times when business slows, such cost centers are among the ones that get cut. We saw this play out across multiple platforms. The most extreme case was the company formerly known as Twitter, which decimated its content moderation teams – both in-house employees and outside contractors – after the takeover by Elon Musk. As a result, there was a spike in the volume of harmful content on the platform. This also has the effect of driving advertisers and some users away, thereby cutting into revenues, but Twitter – now called X – has not made many changes in response.[8] Indeed, the entire process of how content is circulated on the platform is caught in a vicious cycle of incentives incompatible with appropriately moderating harmful content.

There is, thus, an inherent contradiction in platforms self-moderating content. Self-moderation systems and rules will be incomplete or are likely to be self-serving or ad hoc. This is a classic example of market failure and calls for regulators or lawmakers to step in. However, external oversight and regulation is vulnerable to its own incentive incompatibility challenge.

13.3 INCENTIVE INCOMPATIBILITY AND MODERATION OF CONTENT BY REGULATORS

The chapters in this book authored by Eric Goldman, Cristoph Busch, Jhalak Kakkar et. al, Jufang Wang and Artur Pericles cover the state of content moderation regulation across a wide range of jurisdictions – US, EU, India, China, and Brazil – and the varying states of such regulations across them. As the chapters collectively

5 Laura Edelson et al., *Understanding Engagement with Us (Mis)Information Sources on Facebook*, Association For Computing Machinery (Nov. 2021), https://lig-membres.imag.fr/gogao/papers/news-interactions-imc2021.pdf (last visited Feb. 19, 2024).

6 *Meta Reports Fourth Quarter and Full Year 2021 Results*, Meta Investor Relations (2021), https://investor.fb.com/investor-news/press-release-details/2022/Meta-Reports-Fourth-Quarter-and-Full-Year-2021-Results/default.aspx (last visited Feb. 19, 2024).

7 Karen Hao, *Facebook Whistleblower Hearing: Frances Haugen Testified before Senate Panel*, MIT Technology Review (Mar. 11, 2021), https://www.technologyreview.com/2021/03/11/1020600/facebook-responsible-ai-disinformation/ (last visited Feb. 19, 2024).

8 A. Counts & E. Nakano, *Twitter's Surge in Harmful Content Keeps Advertiser Away*, Time (July 19, 2023), https://time.com/6295711/twitters-hate-content-advertisers/ (last visited Feb. 19, 2024).

highlight, there is no harmonization across these jurisdictions, China being the most stringent about its rules and the US the least at the federal level, with the EU as an early mover to put the most holistic set of laws in place to create the guardrails for the digital economy.

Moreover, the state of regulation itself is constantly in flux as the regulators respond to political pressures and platforms respond to the regulatory actions. In some jurisdictions, the regulations and restrictions are being legally challenged by the platforms; the lawsuit by Twitter against the government of India is one such example.[9] In other instances, the government went so far as to block platforms altogether, as was the case in Russia after its invasion of its neighbor, Ukraine.[10] For their part, the platforms themselves have adopted aggressive tactics to build leverage in their negotiations with governments and regulators, knowing fully well how reliant users are on the platforms themselves. This was the case in Australia, in March 2021, when Facebook caused significant havoc by blocking Australian users from news pages to preempt legislation that would make Facebook pay for news content.[11] After five days of chaos in the country, the Australian Parliament caved in.[12]

All of these differences and shifting boundaries of regulatory reach means that a platform that operates in a global market must conform to a highly fragmented set of regulations. The fragmentation is not just because of the lack of standardization across countries. In a jurisdiction, such as the US, the regulations are uneven across states. While there has been little movement at the federal level, several states have taken more activist positions. Consider the law AB 587, enacted in California, on September 14, 2022.[13] The law requires that each social media company above a certain size, "must provide detailed description of content moderation practices used by the social media company for that platform, including how automated content moderation systems enforce terms of service of the social media platform and when these systems involve human review."[14] The penalties for violating the rules appear small when compared to the revenues of the social media companies: the company

[9] K. D. Singh & K. Conger, *Twitter, Challenging Orders to Remove Content, Sues India's Government*, New York Times (July 8, 2022), https://www.nytimes.com/2022/07/05/business/twitter-india-lawsuit.html (last visited Feb. 19, 2024).

[10] D. Milmo, *Russia Blocks Access to Facebook and Twitter*, The Guardian (Mar. 4, 2022), https://www.theguardian.com/world/2022/mar/04/russia-completely-blocks-access-to-facebook-and-twitter (last visited Feb. 19, 2024).

[11] K. Hagey, M. Cherney & J. Horwitz, *Facebook Deliberately Caused Havoc in Australia to Influence New Law, Whistleblowers Say*, Wall Street Journal (May 5, 2022), https://www.wsj.com/articles/facebook-deliberately-caused-havoc-in-australia-to-influence-new-law-whistleblowers-say-11651768302 (last visited Feb. 19, 2024).

[12] *Id.*

[13] Assembly Bill No. 587, California Legislative Information (2021–22), https://leginfo.legislature.ca.gov/faces/billTextClient.xhtml?bill_id=202120220AB587 (last visited Feb. 19, 2024).

[14] *Id.*

is liable for a civil penalty not to exceed $15,000 per violation per day, but they can add up to a much larger political and regulatory liability. Besides California, there are parallel actions being taken elsewhere by lawmakers on the other end of the political spectrum: Florida and Texas are two major states attempting to pass legislation that would have an impact on online content moderation. In June 2021, the 11th Circuit Court of Appeals blocked major provisions of a Florida law that would penalize social media companies for blocking a politician's posts. The court cited infringement of the companies' First Amendment rights as the argument for its decision.[15] As for Texas, the US Court of Appeals for the 5th Circuit upheld its law that would prevent social media companies from blocking or taking down posts based on the poster's political ideology.[16]

It is notable that the state of California is among those leading the charge on setting content moderation regulations in place, given the technology industry's economic significance to the state. Supporters of such laws would argue as follows:[17]

> Efforts by social media companies to self-police [problematic] content have been opaque, arbitrary, biased, and inadequate. While some platforms share limited information about their efforts, the current lack of transparency has exacerbated concerns about the intent, enforcement, and impact of corporate policies, and deprived policymakers and the general public of critical data and metrics regarding the scope and scale of online hate and disinformation. Additional transparency is needed to allow consumers to make informed choices about the impact of these products (including on their children) and so that researchers, civil society leaders, and policymakers can determine the best means to address this growing threat to our democracy.

Meanwhile, not everyone agrees that a law such as AB587 is the answer. Eric Goldman offers a forceful critique.[18] He argues that AB587 amounts to censorship by placing regulators in the middle of the editorial process and second-guessing the platforms' editors; moreover, he is concerned that it places too heavy a burden on the platforms – up to more than 161+ different statistical disclosures and reporting systems that are incompatible with those required elsewhere and will impose

[15] Cat Zakrzewski, *Federal Judge Blocks Florida Law That Would Penalize Social Media Companies*, Washington Post (June 30, 2021), https://www.washingtonpost.com/technology/2021/06/30/florida-social-media-law-trump/ (last visited Feb. 19, 2024).

[16] Cat Zakrzewski, *5th Circuit Upholds Texas Social Media Law*, Washington Post (Sept. 16, 2022), https://www.washingtonpost.com/technology/2022/09/16/5th-circuit-texas-social-media-law/ (last visited Feb. 19, 2024).

[17] *Bill Analysis – AB-587 Social Media Companies: Terms of Service (2021–22)*, California Legislative Information, https://leginfo.legislature.ca.gov/faces/billAnalysisClient.xhtml?bill_id=202120220AB587 (last visited Feb. 19, 2024).

[18] E. Goldman, *A Short Explainer of Why California's Mandatory Transparency Bill (AB 587) Is Terrible*, Technology & Marketing Law Blog (Aug. 9, 2022), https://blog.ericgoldman.org/archives/2022/08/a-short-explainer-of-why-californias-mandatory-transparency-bill-ab-587-is-terrible.htm (last visited Feb. 19, 2024).

substantial extra costs. Goldman is concerned that, in the end, the information will not result in meaningful action that benefit users.

Considering such arguments both for and against such laws, the California law and similar laws from other states are destined for further debate and appeals. Eventually, they are likely to wind up in the Supreme Court. From the perspective of the platforms, all of this adds uncertainty on top of fragmentation.

Given differing demands from regulators in different jurisdictions and the changing nature of the legal landscapes from country to country and, in countries such as the US, from state to state, the social media companies will, no doubt, make choices in terms of where to allocate from their shrinking reservoir of content moderation efforts and resources. These resource allocation decisions are crucial as there is no globally deployable algorithmic solution that can moderate content worldwide, do it consistently, and at scale. According to UCLA's Sarah T. Roberts, author of *Behind the Screen: Content Moderation in the Shadows of Social Media*, "if you talk to actual industry insiders who will speak candidly and who are actually working directly in this area, they will tell you that there is no time that they can envision taking humans entirely out of this loop."[19] According to a study by the Transatlantic Working Group at the University of Pennsylvania's Annenberg Public Policy Center, algorithms are neither reliable nor effective in content moderation for many reasons: the absence of context, potential for bias, linguistic barriers, etc.[20] Moreover, content creators have also become creative about the way they can bypass automated blockers and filters through "algospeak": code words, mis-spellings, and veiled language to avoid algorithms that detect blocked hashtags and keywords. In some instances, the algorithm may over-correct; an example arose in the case of the Israel-Hamas war where many Palestinian posts were blocked as they referenced – not necessarily in support of – controversial topics or banned organizations. This means that there is no easy way to automate content moderation and the process must involve human intervention. Moreover, the content moderation workforce is not globally fungible; to be effective in any given geography, it must be trained in local languages, colloquialisms, locally relevant dog whistles, coded language, mores, and contexts.

Content moderation, in other words, requires platforms to allocate a budget to the activity, and the size and allocation of the budget would, naturally, follow the push and pull of regulators. Among the many revelations in Frances Haugen's testimony to Congress, 87 percent of Facebook's global content moderation budget was dedicated to identifying disinformation solely in the US, leaving 13 percent for all others. Notably, at the time of Haugen's testimony, 52.5 percent of Facebook's

[19] Z. Mack, *Why AI Can't Fix Content Moderation*, The Verge (July 2, 2019), https://www.theverge.com/2019/7/2/20679102/content-moderation-ai-social-media-behind-the-screen-sarah-t-roberts-vergecast (last visited Feb. 19, 2024).

[20] E. Llansó et al., *Artificial Intelligence, Content Moderation and Freedom of Expression*, The Transatlantic Working Group (Feb. 26, 2020), https://cdn.annenbergpublicpolicycenter.org/wp-content/uploads/2020/06/Artificial_Intelligence_TWG_Llanso_Feb_2020.pdf (last visited Feb. 19, 2024).

revenues (data from the first quarter of 2021) came from outside the US and Canada and 90 percent of users of Facebook were from outside the US.

To get a sense of how out of proportion the budget allocation was, consider the fact that besides the US, Facebook's own team had placed Brazil and India in its "tier zero" of highest priority of countries to monitor for hate speech and elections-related harmful content. Germany, Indonesia, Iran, Israel, and Italy were in next-highest priority: tier one.[21] The differences in terms of content moderation resources allocated were significant and notable in the disproportionality of the allocation. For the higher priority countries, Facebook's community standards were available in local languages, there were AI classifiers to detect hate speech and disinformation in these languages, and a larger team of human moderators deployed. In the rest of the world, few of these amenities were available: there were fewer translations, AI classifiers, or fact checkers; in some cases, none were available, even though the potential for harm was high.

As demands for regulatory enforcement of content moderation increase in the US and states take the lead in imposing different regulations on the platforms, the incentives for the companies are clear: to dedicate a disproportionate amount of content moderation resources to the US. In addition, the EU has taken on a more activist regulatory position. Its Digital Services Act contains more rigorous content moderation requirements and calls for greater transparency about the content on digital platforms. The Act also requires labeling of promoted content so users can place it in context. No doubt, the EU too will garner a significant share of content moderation resources.

In addition to the regulatory demands, there are economic incentives driving the resource allocation decisions of platforms. Consider the case of Meta and the origins of its revenues. The US and Canada generated $50.25 of revenue per user as compared to $15.64 in the next-highest market, Europe, and an average of $9.82 worldwide.[22] It is no wonder that Meta allocates resources disproportionately in favor of the US.

In the meantime, the technology sector itself has to contend with economic pressures and there is a need to keep costs under control. As the regulatory pressures in the US and EU add up, combined with the fact that the economic returns are so much more attractive in these markets, the rational decision for digital platforms would be to over-allocate content moderation resources in these jurisdictions at the expense of the rest of the world. The consequence of these decisions is a sobering one: with fewer resources allocated to content moderation, particularly in the developing world, the volume and intensity of disinformation is likely to only

21 Casey Newton, *Facebook's Leaked Tier List: How the Company Decides Which Countries Need Protection*, The Verge (Oct. 25, 2021), https://www.theverge.com/22743753/facebook-tier-list-countries-leaked-documents-content-moderation (last visited Feb. 19, 2024).

22 *Facebook's Average Revenue per User as of 2nd Quarter, 2022, by Region*, Statista, https://www.statista.com/statistics/251328/facebooks-average-revenue-per-user-by-region/ (last visited Feb. 19, 2024).

increase – with potential for greater harm as many of the institutional safety nets present in the US and EU may be absent in these other parts of the world. Regulation in the global north, unintentionally, has a spillover effect on the global south by shifting the presence of harmful content from the north to the south. At the heart of this dynamic, once again, is the incentive system that drives the decision-making in the digital platforms: resource allocation decisions are driven by a combination of market and regulatory forces.

This is, in essence, what I would characterize as the "disinformation paradox": the desire to regulate content in one part of the world leads to less content moderation elsewhere; since the "elsewhere" is the larger user base with fewer institutional safeguards and users with fewer options for fact-checking or seeking alternative sources of news and information, the volume and intensity of disinformation elsewhere could be greater and the net impact on the world could be worse than the status quo.

13.4 SHIFTING INDUSTRY STRUCTURE, POLITICAL DYNAMICS, AND THEIR IMPACT ON CONTENT MODERATION

The imperatives that drive content moderation resource allocations also have roots in the changes in the digital industry structure and the political drivers that affect the platform companies. It is natural, as I have done so far, to center the discussion on content moderation using the example of the predominant platform company, Meta, whose issues in many ways are quintessential to those of the wider industry. That said, there are several other digital platforms that must contend with challenges that are idiosyncratic to their own circumstances. These idiosyncratic elements also influence how these platforms respond to the call for content moderation. Consider the examples of two sets of platforms, the first includes prominent ones, such as TikTok and X, formerly Twitter, and the second includes newer entrants in the industry that are positioned as havens for free-speech and, in some ways, free of content moderation responsibilities.

13.4.1 *TikTok*

If there is any platform that is giving Meta a run for its money, across all its platforms, it is TikTok, the video sharing app. TikTok is notable not only because it has been the most-downloaded app in recent years but has the potential for greater harm from hosting unmoderated content. Its users skew younger (it is more popular among Gen Z users than Instagram), representing a particularly vulnerable demographic, which often becomes a highly prized target of disinformation creators. TikTok holds the distinction of being the most engaging of all social media apps in the US – by far: an average user spends over ten minutes per session, which is twice that of the next most engaging app, Pinterest.[23] This, too, makes it a haven for manipulating users

[23] *Most Popular Social Media Apps in the US, as of September 2019, by Average User Session*, STATISTA, https://www.statista.com/statistics/579411/top-us-social-networking-apps-ranked-by-session-length/ (last visited Feb. 19, 2024).

through content. Moreover, TikTok is very popular in the developing world where institutional and regulatory safeguards are under-developed: besides the US at number one, it is striking to note that Indonesia, Brazil, Mexico, Russia, Vietnam, the Philippines, Thailand, Turkey, and Saudi Arabia constitute the remaining nine countries in the top ten of TikTok users.[24] Next, consider the format of TikTok, which itself is another contributor to the challenges: content moderation is inherently hard because it is more difficult to filter video than it is to sort through textual content. On top of this, disinformation creators have found ways of bypassing roadblocks through deliberate misspellings of hashtags or innuendo, and other hacks of the moderation systems.

TikTok's influence is now so widely felt that even the search engine powerhouse, Google, is turning to it for inspiration and new ideas as it finds a growing proportion of Gen Z users are turning to TikTok for search and away from Google.[25] This means that TikTok is encroaching into territory that is well beyond that of social media and is under even greater scrutiny from both industry competitors and lawmakers.

But TikTok has another – more structural – organizational problem to contend with: it is owned by China-based ByteDance. With geopolitical tensions rising between the US and China, American policymakers have concerns about the ByteDance connection and the potential data vulnerability this represents as the company might give the Chinese government access to US user data. Others worry that TikTok itself could become a tool for content manipulation by Chinese officials. TikTok management is, of course, walking a fine line as the US is its most valuable market. This means, much like Meta but for reasons that extend into the geopolitical, it is likely to devote its limited content moderation resources disproportionately to the US. Particularly because the platform and its Chinese holding company is in the crosshairs of US lawmakers, we should expect it to tend to the squeaky wheels in the US. Thanks to both business and political pressures, the rest of the world should expect to be left under-resourced for content moderation by TikTok. Indeed, a Mozilla Foundation report finds that TikTok has become the force to reckon with for fueling disinformation and hosting "some of most dramatic disinformation campaigns" in countries such as Kenya.[26]

13.4.1 X, *Formerly Twitter*

For some platforms, content moderation rules are ad hoc and their organizations and processes haven't kept up with the evolving needs and the circumstances in

[24] *Which Countries Use TikTok the Most? TikTok User Data for 2022*, TikTok U.S. Data Security, https://www.houseofmarketers.com/which-countries-use-tiktok-the-most-tiktok-user-data-for-2022/ (last visited Feb. 19, 2024).

[25] *Google Borrows from TikTok to Keep Gen Z Searching*, WIRED (Sept. 28, 2022), https://www.wired.com/story/google-borrows-from-tiktok-to-keep-gen-z-searching/ (last visited Feb. 19, 2024).

[26] *From Dance App to Political Mercenary*, Mozilla Foundation, https://assets.mofoprod.net/network/documents/From_Dance_App_to_Political_Mercenary.pdf (last visited Feb. 19, 2024).

which content is produced. X is an interesting case in point. While it is a highly influential platform, its user base is small relative to the Meta platforms or TikTok or YouTube, and the company often flies underneath the radar as much of the external scrutiny is on the behemoths. Recently, the spotlight turned on the platform because of the saga of Elon Musk staging and then reneging on a takeover of the company and then finally completing the acquisition. Twitter, as X used to be known, had struggled to introduce new features and innovations on its platform and its management has been under pressure to roll out new features. When it does, it seems the features run the risk of exacerbating disinformation problems. Prior to the Musk acquisition, in an explosive revelation, Twitter's former head of security Peiter "Mudge" Zatko alleged that its Spaces feature suffers from very poor content moderation. "About half of Spaces content flagged for review was in a language that the moderators did not speak, and there was little to no moderation happening," according to Zatko's whistleblower complaint filed with the US Securities and Exchange Commission, the Federal Trade Commission, and the Justice Department.

What was even more damning was that Twitter executives were, reportedly, aware of the potential for abuse but refused to slow the roll-out of Spaces, despite its use by white nationalists, Taliban supporters, and anti-vaxxers, each being notorious for their reliance on creating and spreading harmful content. Employees who raised concerns were told that given the volume of conversations and multiplicity of languages, the technology necessary to properly moderate Spaces simply did not exist.[27]

For another "innovation" on Twitter that could complicate the process of content moderation, consider the Edit Tweet feature: it lets users edit their posts for a fixed time period after posting. This feature could open the door to harmful content as miscreants could edit in language after a harmless tweet has gone out and has been retweeted and circulated. The edit could allow disinformation creators to bypass the initial content moderation screens and gain a wide audience.

The biggest blow to the platform's content moderation capabilities came after Elon Musk's acquisition. The Fletcher School's Digital Planet found that hate speech and toxic narratives have surged in the weeks immediately after the takeover. The analysis focused on three hateful narratives: anti-Semitism, anti-LGBTQ+ rhetoric, and racial/ethnic hate speech, and found a marked increase in all three narratives.[28] Subsequently, Elon Musk, the owner of the platform himself contributed to harmful speech directed at Yoel Roth, the person who had been responsible for Trust and Safety on the platform after Roth had been fired by Musk. Roth was forced to flee his home after he received

[27] Aisha Malik, *Twitter Ex-security Head Says the Social Network Has "Deficient Moderation" for Spaces*, TechCrunch (Aug. 23, 2022), https://techcrunch.com/2022/08/23/twitter-mudge-deficient-moderation-spaces/ (last visited Feb. 19, 2024).

[28] *Hate Speech on Elon Musk's Twitter: Under Musk, Hate Speech Is Rising*, Digital Planet (Dec. 8, 2022), https://digitalplanet.tufts.edu/musk-monitor-under-musk-hate-speech-is-rising/ (last visited Feb. 19, 2024).

death threats as a direct outcome of Musk's posts. It is hard to find a more egregious example of under-moderation of content by digital platforms anywhere.

The dismantling of content moderation at X has had consequences. The platform run afoul of the EU's Digital Services Act, it has received a stern rebuke from Thierry Breton, the European commissioner who oversees the law, and advertisers have fled the platform in droves.

13.4.3 *Niche Players Championing Free Speech*

The heightened scrutiny of the major platforms has created a market entry opportunity for newer platforms that can cater to the needs of niche groups, disinformers, and others who wish to fly under the radar. Consider platforms such as BitChute, Odysee, and Rumble that had grown as the major incumbent platforms instituted more content rules. The newer platforms were positioned in the market as champions of free speech and, as a result, had become concentrators of disinformation, from conspiracies to hate speech. In an increasingly polarized climate in countries like the US, such platforms have gained an audience quickly. According to data from digital intelligence firm Similarweb, BitChute's online traffic grew 63 percent in 2021; it commanded an audience more than double that of MSNBC.com at that time.

To add to the regulatory challenges, it is not just classic social media platforms where harmful content could find a home. Twitch, the Amazon subsidiary, where users gather to watch skilled gamers play popular games, such as Fortnite and Minecraft, has become open territory for predators who pursue young users to exploit them. The moderation rules at Twitch have not succeeded in stopping children from broadcasting their presence and blocking predators.[29]

13.5 POTENTIAL SOLUTIONS

The earlier discussion highlights the difficulties of effective content moderation either initiated by the companies themselves or by activist regulators. In fact, regulatory activism could make the problem worse globally. This raises the question: What are possible alternative routes to a solution?

Consider some options.

13.5.1 *Letting Regulators Focus on What's Best for Their Own Jurisdictions*

This appears to be the default approach based on the actions that have been taken thus far. As discussed earlier, a regulator in a substantive market, such as the US or

[29] C. D'Anastasio, *Child Predators Use Amazon's Twitch to Systematically Track Kids Who Stream*, BLOOMBERG (Sept. 21, 2022), https://www.bloomberg.com/graphics/2022-twitch-problem-with-child-predators/?cmpid = BBD092222_TECH&utm_medium = email&utm_source = newsletter&utm_term = 220922&utm_campaign = tech&leadSource = uverify%20wall (last visited Feb. 19, 2024).

EU, could take actions that have a spillover effect on other jurisdictions by increasing the amount of disinformation in these latter regions, thereby giving rise to the disinformation paradox.

The complication is that it is hard to imagine that lawmakers and regulators in the parts of the world where disinformation spillover occurs will sit still. They are likely to respond by setting up their own restrictions and regulations and, like their US and EU counterparts, likely to do so without regard for the potential for harm to those on the outside. The regulators put their own regulations and restrictions in place for both defensive and offensive reasons. The defensive action is understandable as these jurisdictions feel there is insufficient content moderation occurring in their jurisdictions, so they feel the need to step in. The offensive action could be because governments around the world see platforms as powerful mechanisms for shaping political narratives; hence regulating and exerting control over them becomes important for existential reasons.

The collective outcome is that regulators across the world engage in a noncooperative game and are trapped in a cycle of mutually reinforcing "beggar-thy-neighbor" actions tantamount to a classic prisoners' dilemma problem. We can also think of this situation as a tragedy of the commons, where authenticity of information as a public good is under threat. Everyone is worse off because the platforms are left balancing competing regulations and rules, making them less effective in moderating content overall. Misinformation content creators take advantage of the fragmentation and lack of coordination across regulatory regimes to do their mischief. The costs of content moderation to the platforms go up and their incentives are to pare back content moderation resources to the extent they can.

To make matters worse, some governments are likely to utilize the window of opportunity created by this lack of discipline across the world and use the regulatory cudgel to shape narratives and, potentially, get into the disinformation business themselves or stifle action that promotes the spread of authentic information. A case in point is India, where Alt News, a leading fact-checking organization on issues ranging from child kidnapping rumors to anti-Muslim rhetoric, ran afoul of the administration that was keen on pushing its own version of the facts. One of the founders of Alt News was jailed and has charges pending against him with accusations against him being leveled by the ruling BJP party.[30] In other instances, countries, such as Nigeria, blocked Twitter altogether. In other circumstances, analysts argue that in countries, such as Kenya, where, historically, there were no content moderation rules in place, the abundance of disinformation will provide governments the excuse to impose strict censorship and shut down entire platforms, leading to outright censorship. As the author of the Mozilla Foundation report on disinformation on TikTok in Kenya noted, "If the platforms don't get their act

[30] Suhasini Raj, *In India, Debunking Fake News and Running into the Authorities*, New York Times (Sept. 22, 2022), https://www.nytimes.com/2022/09/22/world/asia/india-debunking-fake-news.html (last visited Feb. 19, 2024).

together, they become convenient excuses for authoritarians to clamp down on them across the continent . . .. And we all need these platforms to survive. We need them to thrive."[31]

13.5.2 *Regulatory Coordination*

There are several – imperfect – resolutions to the tragedy of the commons problem in other contexts. To consider their application in the current situation, in essence, we need the regulators in the various jurisdictions to get to a "cooperative" outcome where they harmonize or coordinate on the demands placed on the platforms. In addition to the benefits of harmonizing regulation and setting standard guidelines, such coordination by regulators and lawmakers across jurisdictions also helps build up their collective bargaining power vis-à-vis the major platforms. Such rebalancing of bargaining power can help avoid situations such as the experience of Australian lawmakers noted earlier, where Meta simply used its market power to force the lawmakers to acquiesce.

In antagonistic settings, such cooperative outcomes have arisen out of threats of noncooperation, involving a commitment to punishing any deviation from the cooperative outcome. This does not appear to be desirable or practical in the international regulatory context as it doesn't seem practical for regulators to punish other regulators or even to threaten them implicitly. Alternatively, we can consider a solution involving explicit coordination among regulators. There is a precedent for such actions in other international contexts where there is a risk of a tragedy of the commons: consider the examples of agreements over trade and monetary policies, energy use and GHG emissions reduction, public health measures, international security alliances, among many others.

Such international coordination could work if there were sufficient guarantees that all or most regulators would achieve their objectives from a coordinated solution. As has been noted in the analyses of the effectiveness of international coordination in other contexts, such coordination fails when:

- Different countries come to the table with fundamentally different models in mind which leads to a breakdown in communication. As Jeffrey Frankel has noted in his analysis of coordination over international trade and monetary policy, when two players sit down at the board, "they are unlikely to have a satisfactory game if one of them thinks they are playing checkers and the other thinks they are playing chess."[32]

[31] Neha Wadekar, *Why Dangerous Content Thrives on Facebook and TikTok in Kenya*, Washington Post (July 31, 2022), https://www.washingtonpost.com/world/2022/07/31/kenya-meta-tiktok-facebook-disinformation/ (last visited Feb. 19, 2024).

[32] Jeffrey Frankel, *International Coordination*, Faculty Research Working Paper Series, RWP-16-002, Harvard Kennedy School (Jan. 2016), https://www.hks.harvard.edu/research-insights/research-publications (last visited Feb. 19, 2024).

- Different countries make assumptions about why the other parties wish to coordinate and these assumptions are based on their own models, which could be wrong and sets the coordinated agreement up for failure.
- Each country has its own set of internal political dynamics to attend to and there are interest groups with differing agendas that destabilize the cross-country agreements.
- Countries vary significantly in their interests in regulating versus letting the market do the job.
- Agreements are harder as there are more countries at the table and there are significant asymmetries across the needs and interests and the relative market and political power of the countries.

Each of these factors is present in the case of coordinating over content moderation. In the increasingly fractured and politicized world of managing online content, the chances of such misperceptions are high, especially when it is clear that the platforms only have a limited set of resources to go around.

13.5.3 *Extending a Regulator's Reach beyond the Jurisdiction*

Can a regulator hold a platform accountable for content moderation in geographies that are not part of its jurisdiction? In theory, this could be a way in which the regulators in the US or the EU could anticipate the emergence of harmful content elsewhere, especially in the most vulnerable parts of the world, and put their leverage to good use while mitigating the unintended consequences of vulnerable jurisdictions being starved of content moderation resources.

One solution is to have lawmakers in regions such as the US and the EU pass laws to regulate not only the content hosted by the platforms but also on the investments that platforms make on content moderation and how these resources are deployed across the world. For instance, platforms could be required to maintain a certain threshold of content moderation staff for countries in proportion to the number of users and the level of disinformation risk there.

While these ideas have merits, there are several problems to consider.

One is the obvious problem of going against self-interest. If it is common knowledge that there is only a limited amount of content moderation resources to go around, then there is a potential zero-sum game between such resources being deployed in the regulator's home jurisdiction versus elsewhere. By holding platforms responsible for content elsewhere, the regulator runs the risk of thinning out resources to moderate content that affects the constituency that the regulator cares about the most – in its own jurisdiction.

A second problem is best illustrated by the example of California's AB 587, which provides a useful parallel. The California law extends its reach beyond the state and requires disclosures from entities and users from outside of California, including from foreign countries. This opens up the possibility of potential conflicts with a multitude of laws and restrictions that may be incompatible with those proposed for California. As Eric Goldman has argued, this can create several "Dormant Commerce Clause" problems: he cites the example of a recent New York law that defines "hateful conduct" and specific requirements for dealing with it, which may not coincide with what California requires, or the disclosure requirements in Texas that are structured differently from those in California. When such differences are added across numerous jurisdictions, Goldman argues, the law would place an undue burden on the platform.[33]

It is conceivable that a similar argument could be applied to any regulation that affects content moderation beyond the regulator's jurisdiction and would result in an undue burden on the platform leading to an impractical solution or an unenforceable task for the regulator. The burden is likely to increase as one considers the reality that this concern extends not just to multiple states in the US but to multiple countries.

13.5.3 *Algorithmic Solutions*

In theory, the most equitable way to catch disinformation without skewing resources in the direction of the most powerful nations is by relying on automated systems that can reliably monitor and filter content worldwide. Algorithms can, in principle, perform linguistic or graphic or visual analysis, for example, and flag problematic content. Text can be interrogated for word vectors, word positioning, and connotation or reverse engineer images to catch harmful content or deepfakes. If algorithms could in the future catch most of the harmful content increases, the dilemmas highlighted here are significantly lessened as the reliance on a limited pool of human content moderators is reduced.

But, as I noted earlier, we are too far from that future. With algospeak, even simple workarounds such as misspelling hashtags or introducing punctuation marks can help disinformation get around filters and blocking systems. Moreover, there is an entire arsenal of coded language and dog whistles that vary by context, language, and culture that allow the bad stuff to slip through. It would take a long time before enough data can be collected to train algorithms to reliably recognize all such bypassing tricks and hacks.

Moreover, an over-reliance on algorithms developed in the West can create its own biases and inequities as these systems fail to recognize codes from parts of the world that are far away from the hubs where such AI-powered tools are being

[33] E. Goldman, *California Seems to Be Taking the Exact Wrong Lessons from Texas and Florida's Social Media Censorship Laws*, TECHDIRT (June 23, 2022), https://www.techdirt.com/2022/06/23/california-seems-to-be-taking-the-exact-wrong-lessons-from-texas-and-floridas-social-media-censorship-laws/ (last visited Feb. 19, 2024).

developed. To appreciate the difficulties, consider an example from Kenya, where a narrator in a video clip mimicked a detergent commercial and spoke of "detergents" to eliminate "madoadoa," an innocuous word meaning a spot to be removed from a piece of clothing. In reality, the word "madoadoa" in this context referred to members of Kamba, Kikuyu, Luhya, and Luo tribes and was inciting viewers to violence against them. To make matters worse, these code words shift over time and younger users are constantly developing fresh colloquialisms and neologisms, especially for sensitive topics, which would make the search for the algorithmic solution a task of Sisyphean proportions.

There is one area where one could hold out hope for algorithmic solutions. As more harmful content gets created by other algorithms, using generative AI, it is conceivable that the process of training such "bad" AI could be reverse engineered to then train "good" AI, which becomes better at catching the bad stuff.

That said, it is hard to see a future where humans are taken out of the loop altogether. Humans will be present at the creation of content. The need for and reliance on human moderators will never go away. Ironically, much of the labor for such moderation will continue to be drawn from the countries where labor is cheap and plentiful – and these are the countries that are most at risk of disinformation being rampant. It is also hard to see a future without the role of regulators taking a more active stance on content moderation. But they need to go beyond demanding that there ought not to be harmful content disseminated within their jurisdictions, as the Digital Services Act does. As noted earlier, lawmakers need to be pressed to require that platforms maintain a minimum threshold of content moderation staff for countries in proportion to the number of users and an objective evaluation of the level of disinformation risk in these countries.

13.6 IN CONCLUSION: A CASE FOR BETTER DIGITAL HYGIENE

In closing, I would like to offer a very different approach to the solution as a complement to the ideas presented earlier. While this approach in no way takes care of the problem, it is important to pay attention to an important piece of the disinformation puzzle – by taking the spotlight off of platform responsibility but pointing it at the other end: on user responsibility. There is a need for investment in better education and global standards in "digital hygiene." Much like reading, writing, social studies, and even personal hygiene, the ability to use the internet in productive ways and sort authentic information from disinformation ought to be codified and integrated into curricula in schools across the world. We have done very little in this arena since the bulk of the efforts has been directed at policing or regulating content on the platforms.

If we accept that disinformation or harmful content will never be eliminated, possibly for all the reasons discussed in this chapter, we must invest in ways to mitigate the damage wherever possible and limit its power in ways that can be shared universally. Driving on highways, for example, always carries a degree of risk, which is why we emphasize road safety rules and inculcate better driving habits. In combination with the introduction of new technologies that aid automotive safety, this will lead to fewer crashes. My final recommendation would be to apply similar principles to the problem of content moderation and invest in the area of user education and to institutionalize it in schools across the world. No matter what else is done to regulate content moderation or holding platforms to account, educated digital consumers represent the best – and most inclusive – defense against the scourge of disinformation.

14

Platform Responsibility

An International Legal Synthesis

Joel P. Trachtman[*]

14.1 INTRODUCTION: COMPARATIVE REGULATION, CONFLICTS OF REGULATION, AND COOPERATION IN REGULATION

This chapter is intended to analyze the needs and possibility for international cooperation in regulation of platform responsibility for moderation of content. To do so, it was first necessary to survey some of the dimensions of difference among national platform regulation structures, by comparing selected legal systems. Earlier chapters in this volume survey relevant law in Brazil, China, the European Union, India, and the US. Based on the level of difference, and the apparent level of flexibility in accommodating difference as platforms operate across borders, it is possible to analyze the needs and possibility of international cooperation. Once these needs and possibilities are understood, a second step is to examine, inductively and deductively, possible mechanisms for international cooperation in this field. The generative chapters in this volume evaluate cooperation problems and responses from other fields of international interaction – international taxation, international infectious disease control, and international financial regulation – as sources of generative thinking.

It is difficult to propose a definition of "platform," but for present purposes, it is sufficient to say that platforms are hosting services that, at the request of a recipient of the service, store and disseminate information to the public.[1] Think Facebook, Twitter, Google, YouTube, WeChat, TikTok, Sina Weibo, etc. These platforms

[*] Thanks to Dominik Hofstetter and Arpitha Desai for excellent research assistance, and to Bhaskar Chakravorti, Ravi Chaturvedi, Anamitra Deb, Ellen Jacobs, and Gus Rossi, for advice on the issues addressed in this chapter, and to the Omidyar Network for financial support for this research.

[1] This definition borrows from that contained in art. 2(i) of Regulation (EU) 2022/2065 of the European Parliament and of the Council of 19 October 2022 on a Single Market For Digital Services and amending Directive 2000/31/EC (Digital Services Act), http://data.europa.eu/eli/reg/2022/2065/oj (DSA).

perform complex integrated social functions. They themselves provide services, but they also are vehicles for communication and for commerce. Their primary distinction is in hosting user-generated content (UGC).

Platforms are a new medium or technology that greatly change the scale, pace, and pattern of communication and commerce. This medium has significant social consequences and governance consequences.[2] Physical distance makes little to no difference to platform-based interaction, and so the frequency and intensity of cross-territorial border interaction is increased dramatically. Gravity models of trade, focusing on pre-platform life, suggest that geographic distance significantly affects trade patterns.[3] The elimination of geographic distance as a source of cost will increase, redirect, and change the composition of trade in goods and services. The increase will be globalization on steroids.

This disruption involved in the move to platform-based commerce – perhaps extended in the future to metaverse activity[4] – will need to be reflected in domestic and international commercial law.[5] By "international commercial law," I mean both international trade law and private and public law applicable to international commerce, including especially the jurisdictional rules relating to applicable law, judicial jurisdiction, and jurisdiction to enforce that determine the formal effect of rules.

These jurisdictional rules are most often simply national rules relating to the scope of application of national law, but increasingly, to manage globalization, states must collectively address these rules of jurisdiction. Platforms challenge settled notions of prescriptive jurisdiction. This disruption is occasioned by the growing discontinuity between the territorial state structure of our political and legal relations, on the one hand, and the increasingly transnational structure of our commercial relations, on the other hand.

Elon Musk, in connection with his bid to purchase Twitter, said "by free speech, I simply mean that which matches the law. I am against censorship that goes far beyond the law."[6] As pointed out by Marietje Schaake,[7] he failed to recognize that

2 *See* Orly Lobel, *The Law of the Platform*, 101 Minnesota Law Review 87, 91 (2016).

3 For a recent review of the literature, *see* Luigi Capoani, *Review of the Gravity Model: Origins and Critical Analysis of Its Theoretical Development*, SSRN Electronic Journal (2021). Gravity models incorporate measures of non-physical distance, such as linguistic, cultural, and legal distance, but physical distance is a central component of these models that evaluate the effects of distance on trade relations.

4 *See* Eric Ravenscraft, *What Is the Metaverse, Exactly?*, Wired (Apr. 25, 2022), https://www.wired.com/story/what-is-the-metaverse/ (last visited Aug. 21, 2022).

5 *See* Anupam Chander, The Electronic Silk Road: How the Web Binds the World in Commerce (2013).

6 Elon Musk (@elonmusk), Twitter (Apr. 26, 2022, 3:33 PM), https://twitter.com/elonmusk/status/1519036983137509376?s=20&t=g_iIfQtvnxbde2FfJVEL6A.

7 Marietje Schaake, *If Elon Musk Does Buy Twitter, Free Speech Absolutism Will Not Be Enough*, Financial Times (May 18, 2022), https://www.ft.com/content/84ea07cc-d770-48c8-be94-56c1851a4afa (last visited Aug. 21, 2022).

different countries in which Twitter operates have different legal formulations of free speech. Multiple countries' laws can apply to the same platform, or the same platform transaction. Perhaps transactions divided in conduct or effect through platform-based dispersal can escape any regulation at all.

The trade-off between national regulatory autonomy and otherwise efficient commerce will change significantly as a result of the move to platforms.[8] As the costs of economic integration become lower, and as economies of scale and network externalities make technology more valuable as well as more indivisible, integration becomes more valuable. As integration becomes more valuable, the cost of regulatory diversity will rise, increasing the value of regulatory harmonization. This will not mean that regulatory diversity will be rejected – it will be more costly and therefore accepted less frequently.

Platform-based commerce also accentuates fragmentation. Increasingly, platform commerce replicates real commerce with its multiple and sometimes conflicting regulatory goals and mechanisms. But platform commerce is much more transnational, accentuating the need to deal with multiple and conflicting regulatory goals not just within a single polity but across multiple polities. This peculiarity will gradually necessitate the integration of multiple policies at the international level.

Legal analysts tend to think functionally about law, rather than to focus on specific subjects of law. So, we prefer to speak of human rights, election integrity, consumer protection, privacy, defamation, human trafficking, competition, tax, etc., in general, rather than how these functional subjects apply with respect to specific types of property or activities. We avoid discussion of "the law of the horse"[9] but instead discuss the general law of contract, tort, and property as it applies to horses.

Similarly, in theory, there should be little regulation that is particular to platforms – rather, platforms as a vehicle of communication might be understood to have little need for specialized substantive regulation, as opposed to regulation of the structure and procedures related to the platform. This indeed is the approach of the European Union in its Digital Services Act (DSA).[10]

But administration and enforcement of pre-platform legal rules present special challenges given the enhanced frequency and velocity of interaction that has otherwise challenged law enforcement on platforms, and special structural and procedural rules are required to meet these challenges. The US and other countries are experiencing the same set of challenges and are simultaneously considering revising their law relating to platform responsibilities for moderation of content.

8 *See* Anupam Chander & Paul Schwartz, *Privacy and/or Trade*, 90 U. CHI. L. REV. 50 (2023).

9 *See* Frank H. Easterbrook, *Cyberspace and the Law of the Horse*, 1996 U. CHI. L. FORUM 207 (1996).

10 Reda Attarca, DSA, *The New Law That Will Shake Tech Giants*, UX PLANET (Apr. 25, 2022) (quoting Ursula Von Der Leyen), https://uxplanet.org/dsa-the-new-law-that-will-shake-tech-giants-3d5cda90d5e7 (last visited Aug. 21, 2022); *see also* European Commission QANDA/20/2348, *Question and Answers: Digital Services Act* (Dec. 15, 2020).

Furthermore, and importantly, the medium is the message: within a novel medium, it may be appropriate to modify substantive regulation. For example, with faster and cheaper dissemination of user-generated content, it may be necessary to revisit free speech, privacy regulation, financial regulation, taxation, or competition regulation.

14.2 COMPARATIVE ANALYSIS OF LIABILITY/ MODERATION RESPONSIBILITIES

This comparative analysis will focus on comparative *platform* regulation, not comparative libel law, election integrity law, consumer protection law, protection of minors, privacy law, competition law, or other "substantive" law that might be applied to information disseminated through platforms or decisions to moderate. All these bodies of law are likely to be quite different from state to state. Notably, the DSA does nothing to harmonize substantive law. Nor does US Section 230 harmonize substantive law among US subnational states: by immunizing platforms from state law claims relating to UGC, Section 230 reduces the interstate (as opposed to international) choice of law problems that would arise from these differences of substantive law.

When Section 230 of the US Communications Decency Act was legislated in 1996, Facebook was seven years from introduction, and Twitter was ten years off. Social media was in its infancy, and election interference, fake news, fake science, and other modern concerns were not yet perceived as threats in this domain. The explicit purpose of Section 230 was "to promote the free development of the internet, while also 'remov[ing] disincentives' to implement 'blocking and filtering technologies' that restrict 'children's access to . . . inappropriate online material' and 'ensur[ing] vigorous enforcement of Federal criminal laws to deter and punish trafficking in obscenity, stalking, and harassment by means of computer.'"[11] The internet, and these platforms, have developed beyond 1996 legislative dreams.

Section 230 has two distinct, but mutually supportive, components:

(i) Immunization of platforms from liability as publishers of UGC (UGC liability protection), and
(ii) Immunization of platforms from liability for monitoring decisions (monitoring protection).

UGC liability protection allows user free speech in a way that exceeds the protections of the First Amendment, and monitoring protection allows platforms to avoid "speaking" or carrying UGC to which they object. Insulation from liability under Section 230 is broad, excluding only a few fields, such as federal crimes, sex trafficking and intellectual property. Thus, platforms are otherwise not required to

[11] Valerie C. Brannon & Eric N. Holmes, Cong. Rsch. Serv., R46751, Section 230: An Overview (2021) (citations omitted).

moderate in order to avoid liability. Nor does this change if platforms are apprised of information about harm or illegality: the immunity from liability applies regardless of state of mind.

India's 2021 Intermediary Guidelines, pursuant to its Information Technology Act of 2000 (IT Act),[12] provides a publisher safe harbor with apparent protection similar to Section 230's UGC liability protection. Platforms are required to remove illegal content only upon actual notice, which under the 2015 Shreya Singhal case[13] is only constituted by a court order. While this provides significant protection, Indian platforms are required to maintain terms of service that prohibit users from uploading or sharing a wide range of content, including content that is defamatory; harmful to children; obscene; infringes any trademark, patent, or copyright; threatens public order or the security of India; or violates any Indian law.[14] In addition, large platforms are required to "endeavor to deploy technology-based measures" to "proactively identify" content that (i) depicts rape or child sexual abuse material or (ii) is identical to content that either a court or government order directed be removed.[15] Finally, the Indian government has the power to block content under the IT Act for security or public order reasons. This is worth comparing to US First Amendment protections against government censorship, as well as with Brazilian and EU references to human rights.

Monitoring protection under Section 230 may be subject to incursions where monitoring may have a purpose that is otherwise illegal, such as an anti-competitive purpose.[16] Under Indian law, platforms have no liability for content moderation, although large platforms must provide due process in their moderation decisions.[17] Relevant Brazilian law, the Marco Civil, is silent on content moderation rights of platforms. However, one prosecutor has argued that Brazilian consumer protection law may require moderation to prevent dissemination of false information.[18]

UGC liability protection and monitoring protection are related. Obviously, users remain liable for their own illegal speech, but under the first component of Section 230, for most purposes, platforms have no responsibility. Yet, for public relations reasons, platform attractiveness reasons, and perhaps also reasons relating to forestalling greater regulatory intervention, platforms like Twitter and Facebook engage in monitoring and editing. In the US, monitoring protection makes monitoring less risky and costly. At the same time, this protection places monitoring decisions and

[12] Information Technology (Intermediary Guidelines and Digital Media Ethics Code) Rules, 2021, Part III.

[13] Shreya Singhal v. Union of India, (2015) 5 SCC 1 (India).

[14] The Information Technology Act, 2000, §69A(3).

[15] Information Technology Rules, *supra* note 13, Part III, Rule 4(4).

[16] *See* Jane Bambauer & Anupam Chander, *Bills Meant to Check Big Tech's Power Could Lead to More Disinformation*, Washington Post, June 6, 2022.

[17] *See* Chapter 5.

[18] *See* Chapter 6.

the discretion that comes with them squarely in the online platforms' area of responsibility.

As noted above, ordinary law and law enforcement, relating to users and their content, still applies, and it might be imagined that this is enough: what is sufficiently proscribed in the real world is sufficiently proscribed in the platform world. But in this high frequency and high velocity world of platforms, this does not seem sufficient.

As Marshall McLuhan said in 1964, "the medium is the message." "The 'message' of any medium or technology is the change of scale or pace or pattern that it introduces into human affairs." "The personal and social consequences of any medium – that is, of any extension of ourselves – result from the new scale that is introduced into our affairs by each extension of ourselves, or by any new technology."[19] The social consequences of platform technology are significant and constitute a shock to the world's commercial and legal equilibrium.

Administration and enforcement of pre-platform legal rules present special challenges given the enhanced frequency and velocity of interaction that has otherwise challenged law enforcement on platforms, and special structural and procedural rules are required to meet these challenges. The US and other countries are experiencing the same set of challenges and are simultaneously considering revising their law relating to platform responsibilities for moderation of content. Furthermore, and importantly, the medium is the message: within a novel medium, it may be appropriate to modify substantive regulation. For example, with faster and cheaper dissemination of UGC, it may be necessary to revisit free speech, privacy regulation, financial regulation, taxation, or competition regulation.

What is needed? Perhaps quicker identification of violations and quicker action to cease violation. New problems may also require new laws, such as relating to the way in which algorithms accentuate certain messages or the way in which platforms may insert false information into social activities such as elections. Of course, different politicians, and different countries, will have different perspectives on what indeed is false, and in some cases decisions will be required to avoid the consequences before the fallacy of a statement is fully adjudicated.

To some extent, China has solved the problem of managing information on platforms, because it subordinates free speech to party power and harnesses platforms to carry out the moderation, or control, desired by government and party. Government power is exercised through platforms, and China deputizes platforms to assist with surveillance. In order to assist in surveillance, under Chinese law, real user-names are required, real-time monitoring is required, platforms are required to cooperate with government user-monitoring websites, users are classified by risk presented, and foreign ownership of platforms is prohibited.[20]

19 Marshall McLuhan, Understanding Media: The Extensions of Man (1st ed. 1964).

20 *See* Chapter 4.

This type of extensive governmental control is possible in the context of an authoritarian state, by simply deputizing platforms and obliging them to follow, facilitate, and enforce the party line. Party values and power are prioritized over freedom of speech. This system seems to fit within a relatively totalitarian system, where party values, and power, are seen as paramount, and where nominally private members of society are required to cooperate in advancing them. But it would not be acceptable in a liberal society.

The EU has tried to square this circle in the DSA. First, the DSA is predicated on the concept that "what is illegal in the real world must also be illegal on platforms."[21] The DSA is focused on assigning to platforms responsibilities to assist in enforcement of existing law, given the enhanced frequency and velocity of interaction that has otherwise challenged law enforcement online.

But in addition to enforcement of existing law, the DSA enters a gray area of possible state action that may at times exceed the permissible powers of government, especially with respect to freedom of expression. It does so by assigning platforms due diligence responsibilities beyond enforcement of existing law. It also requires platforms to take due consideration of fundamental rights enshrined in the EU Charter of Fundamental Rights.[22] This is at least a start toward imposing fundamental rights–based duties on private persons. Note that Brazil seems to go further with this concept, imposing direct human rights–based duties on private persons.[23]

Article 34 of the DSA requires very large platforms to "diligently identify, analyze and assess any systemic risks in the Union stemming from the design or functioning of their service and its related systems, including algorithmic systems, or from the use made of their services." These systemic risks include (i) dissemination of illegal content, (ii) negative effects for the exercise of certain fundamental rights, and (iii) actual or foreseeable negative effects on civic discourse, and electoral processes, and then to take "reasonable, proportionate, and effective measures" to mitigate the risks. The EU Commission and perhaps other regulators are assigned to supervise this process and may thereby implicitly exercise governmental authority through these platforms.

This gray area regulation may be prompted by the difficulty of regulating platforms extraterritorially, as well as the frequency and velocity of platform interaction, combining to render traditional regulatory methods inadequate. Yet it raises interesting questions on the extent to which platform due diligence actions, when mandated by governments, amount to state action and when they violate fundamental rights by constraining speech. For example, to the extent that the DSA requires greater moderation than a US platform would otherwise carry out, DSA-based takedowns that would otherwise violate US First Amendment freedoms might result.

[21] Attarca, *supra* note 10 quoting Ursula Von der Leyen.

[22] *See* Chapter 5.

[23] *See* Chapter 2.

In addition, under the DSA, liability would be based on a knowledge standard, so platforms would be required to maintain a mechanism for notice and takedown and provide due process to complainants.

14.3 JURISDICTION AND CONFLICT

Thus, platforms increase *both* collision among national rules (jurisdictional collision) and collision at the international level among functional rules (fragmentation). Revised normative and organizational tools will be needed to manage the increased globalization and fragmentation resulting from the rise of platform commerce. These tools may include rules of harmonization and rules of recognition (acceptance of home state regulation as satisfying regulatory requirements in host state).

Throughout history, human interaction has occurred in geographic space: land, sea, and air. Geographic space, imposing natural costs for communication and transportation across distance, served as a useful proxy for the scope of political concern and power. States were concerned about the people within their territory and action within their territory.

To be sure, there were overlaps in which a person within one state's territory, or with the nationality of one state, caused adverse effects to persons within another state's territory. In international trade law, informally and to a significant extent formally, jurisdiction is divided with respect to imported goods. The exporting state ordinarily has jurisdiction over the production of the good, while the importing state ordinarily has jurisdiction over its consumption: this allocation of jurisdiction is based on territoriality.[24] For some goods and for many services, production and consumption cannot be neatly divided. However, platform markets are divorced from territory, and their production and consumption externalities are highly dispersed.

For example, a good entails both production externalities and consumption externalities. In traditional commerce, and traditional approaches to jurisdiction, the producing state is largely concerned with the production externalities, while the

[24] This jurisdictional allocation is implicit in much state behavior and in one position on the debate regarding the application of WTO anti-discrimination law to PPMs – processes and production methods. To the extent that the PPM is not reflected in the product itself, as consumed in the destination state, some argue, the products may be "like" despite the difference that triggers a distinct regulatory outcome. Thus, destination state regulation of the PPM would generally be seen as treating like products less favorably, subject to possible defenses under GATT exceptions or in the WTO Technical Barriers to Trade Agreement. *See, e.g.*, Joel P. Trachtman, Regulatory Jurisdiction and the WTO, 10 J. INT'L ECON. L. 631 (2007); Steve Charnovitz, *The Law of Environmental "PPMs" in the WTO: Debunking the Myth of Illegality*, 27 YALE J. INT'L L. 59 (2002); Robert Howse & Donald Regan, *The Product/Process Distinction – An Illusory Basis for Disciplining Unilateralism in Trade Policy*, 11 EUR. J. INT'L L. 249 (2000); and the cogent response to the Howse and Regan article in John H. Jackson, *Comments on Shrimp/Turtle and the product/process distinction*, 11 EUR. J. INT'L L. 303 (2000).

importing state focuses on regulating the consumption externalities.[25] Where production and consumption are no longer territorially cabined, and where it makes increasing sense for people around the world to consume the same product produced in the same way, platforms implicate every regulatory concern of every state. Even more importantly, the effects of regulatory action or inaction are more dispersed around the world.

Platforms tend to be relatively indivisible, although they will increasingly challenge attempts by states to impose their preferred regulatory formula at the cost of splintering the platform. This splintering approach will be unstable because, to a significant extent, platforms are valuable precisely because they are global, establishing a global common communications space and providing generous economies of scale and scope. This very global nature makes platforms vulnerable to divergent national regulation. States set rules focused on their own territory, but these rules inevitably have effects beyond their territories. On the other side, states that wish to have different rules may be unable to effectuate their policies, especially if they are not the home state of the platform.

Different states' regulation may contradict that of other states: one state's regulation may require platforms to allow certain types of speech, while another's may prohibit platforms from allowing such speech. As Daphne Keller has pointed out, some countries' "must carry" requirements – requiring platforms to carry certain types of posts – may well conflict with other countries' "take down" requirements – where those countries prohibit certain types of posts.[26] A slightly less explicit form of this type of conflict is where one state permits what another prohibits – in that case, the prohibition may conflict with a permissive policy in the first state, but it may be that the permissive policy is not too strongly held.[27]

Where these conflicts occur, one state must defer to the other, either unilaterally or in accordance with an agreed jurisdiction-allocation rule, or, alternatively, the relevant platform must use technological means to limit access to the prohibited posts in the prohibiting state, assuming that the prohibiting state (a) does not intend to act extraterritorially and (b) is satisfied that the limits will be effective.[28]

[25] One of the important themes of modern regulatory diplomacy is increasing concern in importing states regarding production externalities, such as greenhouse gas emissions or labor conditions, that present either physical externalities, in the case of greenhouse gas, or pecuniary externalities and possibly political externalities, in the case of labor conditions.

[26] Daphne Keller, *Why D.C. Pundits' Must-Carry Claims Are Relevant to Global Censorship*, The Center for Internet and Society (2018), http://cyberlaw.stanford.edu/blog/2018/09/why-dc-pundits-must-carry-claims-are-relevant-global-censorship (last visited Aug. 21, 2022).

[27] *See* Hartford Fire Ins. Co. v. California, 509 U.S. 764 (1993).

[28] These issues have arisen in the Google "right to be forgotten" cases. In Case C-507/17, Google Inc, v Commision nationale de l'informatique et des libertés (CNIL), ECLI:EU:C:2019:772 ¶¶ 72-73 (Sept. 24, 2019), the Court of Justice of the European Union determined that the full right to be forgotten does not extend outside the EU.

14.3.1 *Gaming Jurisdiction by Replicating Territorial Borders Online*

Online platforms routinely make use of certain technical capabilities to tailor the content available to audiences, that is, users, across the globe based on their territorial location, more specifically that of their IP address. The use of these capabilities is akin to replicating national, territorial borders online. A fragmentation of platform regulatory approaches may lead to platforms' increased reliance on these technical means, in order to remain compliant with globally divergent regulatory regimes, while still hosting most content, even if some of it is impermissible in certain jurisdictions.

The most common tool to territorially police the availability of content on online platforms involves geo-blocking specific content. Geo-blocking (also commonly known as, "Geo-IP-blocking," "geo-filtering," and "geo-locking," less accurately likened to "geo-fencing") is the process of blockading portions of the web to restrict access to websites by location. Geo-blocking renders portions of the web regional rather than global.[29] This involves restricting access to certain content on the internet, based on the location from which the content is being accessed. Geo-blocking blocks both outgoing and incoming connections to and from a platform.[30]

Previously, geo-blocking had been the tool of choice for platforms that deal in licensed content. For licensed content such as streamed video, this tool helps prevent content from being accessed from regions outside of those permitted by the distributor. Geo-blocking has also been used to segment markets. In doing so, geo-blocking does not lead to an outright website access restriction. Instead, the geo-block may simply affect the content that may be viewed depending on the location of the user or its IP address. This allows companies that operate globally to treat and, as a result, price geographical regions differently, rather than treating the entire internet as one single market.

The most relevant use-case to the present study of online platform regulation and content moderation allows online platforms to comply with diverging sets of laws as to permissible online content through geo-blocking. For instance, anti-gambling legislation may compel platforms to reject access and traffic to offshore online casinos, betting sites, or to restrict access to domestic sites from certain locations.[31] In doing so, platforms may, prima facie, be able to comply with differing approaches to content moderation globally without sacrificing an outright exit from a certain market. What may be prohibited content in country A, could still be hosted on

[29] Romj Amon, *What Is Geo Blocking and How Does It Work?*, TECHJURY (2022), https://techjury.net/blog/what-is-geo-blocking/ (last visited Aug. 21, 2022).

[30] *What Is Geoblocking?*, TECHOPEDIA.COM, http://www.techopedia.com/definition/32362/geoblocking (last visited Aug. 21, 2022).

[31] *See, e.g.*, Simon Planzer, *The Gambling Law Review: Switzerland*, THE LAW REVIEWS (2022), https://thelawreviews.co.uk/title/the-gambling-law-review/switzerland (last visited Aug. 21, 2022).

Platform X and disseminated to all other countries where the content is not prohibited, so long as Platform X ensures that access to such content is geo-blocked for users attempting to access the content from within country A or with an IP address assigned to country A.

Beyond mere geo-blocking, the "Great Firewall of China," officially known as the "Golden Shield Project," is likely the most prominent internet censorship operation in the world. The technical capabilities include IP blocking, which denies the IP addresses of specific domains, and packet filtering, which scans packets of data for controversial keywords, credit records, and speech and facial recognition.[32]

This "firewall" thus combines a host of different technical means to limit accessible content on platforms from within China. Though these are measures taken by the Chinese state, an example of action taken by a platform to territorially fragment its operations is of particular relevance to the study at hand: namely, Google's adaptation of its offerings in the Chinese market prior to its exit in 2010. When Google launched Google.cn, a platform that censored content that was deemed objectionable by the Chinese government, it was accused of supporting the Chinese government's censorship efforts. This episode seemingly laid bare an online platform's willingness to censor material that a government deems objectionable, in order to maintain operations in that jurisdiction.[33]

Far from erecting firewalls or creating regional iterations of their services, reliance on geo-blocking to offer different content in different jurisdictions still begs the question of whether such efforts to replicate national borders in the online space will suffice to comply with diverging platform responsibility and content moderation approaches around the globe.

Two issues arise in this regard: First, mere geo-blocking measures do not ensure a total exclusion of access to the restricted content given that users in a restrictive jurisdiction can employ easily accessible means to circumvent geo-blocks, such as VPN or proxy servers, as well as Tor networks.[34] Given the widespread use of such means to circumvent geo-blocks, which have been erected for other purposes, for example, to enforce licensing agreements for online content, it is likely that geo-blocks on the basis of content moderation rules would simply not be effective enough a measure to ensure that users are unable to access the restricted content in question.

[32] *China's Great Firewall*, Free speech vs Maintaining Social Cohesion (2011), https://cs.stanford.edu/people/eroberts/cs181/projects/2010-11/FreeExpressionVsSocialCohesion/china_policy.html (last visited Aug. 21, 2022).

[33] On the ethical implications of Google's local platform adaption, *see, e.g*, Sung Wook Kim & Aziz Douai, *Google vs. China's "Great Firewall": Ethical Implications for Free Speech and Sovereignty*, 34 Technology in Society 174 (2012).

[34] Kearns, *Why Geo-Blocking Fails and What Service Providers Can Do About It*, Cartesian (2020), https://www.cartesian.com/why-geo-blocking-fails-and-what-service-providers-can-do-about-it/ (last visited Aug. 21, 2022).

Second, it is unclear whether the mere exclusion of access to users from a certain geographical space can satisfy the legal threshold to be compliant with platform regulation on content moderation. Notably, the Delhi High Court in 2019 ordered the global removal of defamatory content by social media platforms and ruled that simply geo-blocking the content, so that it would no longer be accessible in India, was not a valid alternative.[35] Similarly, the European Court of Justice held that national courts across the EU could order the global removal of defamatory content, provided such possibility exists under their own private international laws.[36] In sum, the possibility of courts and legislatures recognizing a right or duty for "global content removal" will render geo-blocking as a means for platform regulatory compliance mute. Moreover, the extraterritorial application of removal orders would equally call into question the viability of a fragmented, regional, geo-blocked internet.

While jurisdictional fragmentation poses a significant business and existential risk to globally operating online platforms, geo-blocking may initially appear as a means for platforms to remain global while regionally or territorially restricting access to certain content. Through geo-blocking, an online platform such as Facebook could potentially continue to provide access to content in the United States, which it has been ordered to take down or moderate in the European Union, on the basis of the DSA. Technically, a platform could remain compliant, provided that access to the restricted content is denied to users from the jurisdiction in question. However, given the system's easy circumvention as well as an increased trend toward global content removal orders, the viability of technical means, such as geo-blocking, to replicate national borders online is subject to debate.

Ultimately, a globally fragmented platform, catering to different regulatory straitjackets by geo-blocking its content, runs the risk of losing the inherent characteristics that make such a platform attractive to users globally, and, perpetuating illiberal content moderation practices, in order to remain active in every market.

14.4 JURISDICTIONAL ALLOCATION IN THE ABSENCE OF BORDERS

Accentuating the fact that multiple national regulatory regimes may apply in each functional area is the fact that the relevant rules regarding applicable law – choice of law in private law and prescriptive jurisdiction in public law – vary depending on

[35] *See* Mathangi Kumaresan, *Delhi High Court Orders Global Removal of Defamatory Content on Consideration of Inappropriateness of Sole Geo-blocking*, 15 JOURNAL OF INTELLECTUAL PROPERTY LAW & PRACTICE 90 (2020). The Court differentiates between the place of origin of the content: "in cases where defamatory content has been uploaded from India, then the removal of such content shall be worldwide and not just restricted to India. However, for uploads of defamatory content from outside India, the Defendants [online platforms] would have to use adequate geo-blocking measures, so that Indian users, i.e. IP addresses from India, could no longer access the contents."

[36] Case C-18/18, *Glawischnig-Piesczek*, ECLI:EU:C:2019:821 (Oct. 3, 2019).

which regulatory regime is being applied by which state. This is a veritable kaleidoscope of law, with multiple prisms changing the configuration of relevant law as the viewer's perspective changes: allocation of jurisdiction depends on the field of law and the state purporting to apply its law. For example, privacy law, tax law, defamation law, intellectual property law, and consumer protection law, to name but a few, each has a different rule regarding applicable law. Furthermore, each state has its own rules regarding the circumstances under which its law applies. To summarize: multiple states, multiple (fragmented) bodies of law, and multiple and overlapping and underlapping rules regarding applicable law.

This kaleidoscope of law existed before platforms were developed, but its complexity, velocity, and frequency are heightened by platforms. The medium is the message. Nor is it possible to develop a single clear, formally realizable rule for allocation of jurisdiction over platforms. The obvious one would be nationality of incorporation, but this is easily manipulable and would deprive affected states of important regulatory power over activities that affect their citizens. Alternatively, location of consumer would be considered, but this results in dispersal of jurisdiction for a transnational platform, and even a particular transaction might involve multiple consumers of platform services located in multiple jurisdictions.

Uncoordinated national regulation of platforms can splinter – destroy – global commerce. To the extent that foreign producers are unable to comply, or find it too costly to comply, with importing state regulation, in areas such as cybersecurity,[37] privacy,[38] monitoring,[39] free speech, libel, taxation, or competition – commerce will be impossible or impeded. The social problem is one of multiple goals – fragmentation – in which the best solutions maximize a combination of values: the value of liberalized commerce and the value of regulation, including regulatory autonomy. There is a trade-off between these values, and different societies may set the trade-off at different points.

The international law of trade does not yet provide for integrated negotiation and management of these trade-offs. Trade law focuses on liberalization: addressing barriers to commerce. Barriers that are intended to serve as barriers, and that serve no non-trade purpose, are easier to address than barriers that have a regulatory, or "prudential," purpose: reductions can simply be negotiated on a reciprocal and aggregate welfare-increasing basis. In the context of prudential regulation, the welfare effects of reduction are ambiguous and must be evaluated by each state on a case-by-case basis: harmonization or mutual recognition, or deregulation, may reduce welfare in an amount greater than the benefits of trade. And, especially in

[37] *See* Joel P. Trachtman, *Cybersecurity versus Trade in Internet of Things Products*, 16 MANCHESTER J. INT'L ECON. L. (2020).

[38] *See* Anupam Chander & Paul Schwartz, *Privacy and/or Trade*, 90 U. CHICAGO L. REV. 50 (2023).

[39] *See* Susan Ariel Aaronson, *Can Trade Agreements Help Solve the Wicked Problem of Disinformation?*, SSRN ELECTRONIC JOURNAL (2021).

trade in goods, many of them have been addressed over the GATT/WTO period, although they have resurged in important sectors more recently. Many of the barriers to trade in services have a prudential purpose. Even data localization requirements may be intended to ensure that the host state will have the jurisdiction necessary to regulate for prudential purposes.

Yet it is apparent that diversity of regulation of platforms – for privacy, taxation, competition, political integrity, free speech, defamation, and other purposes – while not novel per se, presents novel types of prudential barriers. These prudential barriers loom especially large in a field where there are no natural barriers of distance or transport cost and no legacy non-prudential barriers. So, this diversity of regulation is the main type of barrier to trade, given the durability so far of a moratorium on customs duties applied to e-commerce, and it can be significant. The WTO Joint Statement Initiative negotiations on digital commerce, preferential trade agreement provisions on digital commerce, and the US-EU Trade and Technology Council have begun to address some of these issues but in modest and superficial ways that provide a basis for free commerce in platform services.

Fragmentation is not new, but it is especially challenging in the platform context, which seems to implicate many policies at once. There may be conflicts among prudential policies: defamation policy or political integrity policy versus free speech policy, competition policy versus industrial policy, etc.

But all of these prudential policies conflict with liberalization – with market access – insofar as they pose barriers to certain national markets. For example, a digital service tax may present obstacles that were unexpected or that are not normal for other types of business. Variations in competition, defamation, or privacy law can require inefficient variation in platform structure in different markets or keep some platforms out of certain markets altogether. These are questions of interoperability: to what extent will platforms be required to be splintered, utilizing geo-blocking or other technical means and custom-designed for specific jurisdictions? There are important economic incentives to avoid the costs of separation and customization.

Trade law has traditionally emphasized market access, while seeking to avoid unnecessary constraints on states' "right to regulate." Early multilateral trade law – GATT 1947 – merely prohibited discrimination and even allowed discrimination where it was justified by prudential or security concerns expressed in Articles XX and XXI of GATT. The WTO, which was established in 1995, added limited requirements of proportionality, and of compliance with international standards, for goods, in the Technical Barriers to Trade Agreement and in the Sanitary and Phytosanitary Measures Agreement. In connection with services, the WTO has added requirements of proportionality in very limited areas. But it has been recognized, in connection with the European Union project, and in connection with deeper non-EU integration proposals such as the Trans-Atlantic Trade and Investment Partnership, that deeper integration requires more attention to prudential regulation. The EU model of regulatory integration is one of essential harmonization as a condition for mutual recognition.

The world has muddled through these questions of allocation of regulatory authority over transnational commerce, in part because in the past the natural borders between states were more congruent with the international structure of commerce. Digital commerce has the potential to be more transnational and to integrate across borders more deeply. In some sense, platform commerce on a global scale may be comparable to the EU phenomenon within Europe: there are important incentives for deeper integration, but the deeper integration requires greater management of differences, and overlaps, in prudential regulation of the types discussed above.

14.5 GENERATIVE ANALYSIS

Cooperation between people, or between social groups, occurs in different ways in different contexts. The distribution of resources, the distribution of preferences, the strategic structure of the cooperation problem, path dependence, and other factors affect whether and how states cooperate in the international system. Of course, cooperation need not be only among states – private actors are an increasingly important part of international cooperation, especially in the information technology field.

Furthermore, we must begin with a unit of analysis, both in terms of the number of states involved, and in terms of the number of issues addressed together, or in linked negotiations or rules. To begin to imagine how cooperation in the area of platform responsibility and moderation might evolve, we might derive ideas from some areas that may display similar cooperation problems or structures. Here, we begin with informed conjecture to suggest a few areas to examine: international bank regulation, international taxation, and the international infectious disease control.

In the area of international bank regulation, there are several bases for analogy with international platform regulation, as suggested by Federico Lupo Pasini (Chapter 8): First, platforms and international banking both operate in transnational markets. Second, both lack a transnational regulatory power, although in international banking, the Basel Committee and the IMF play limited regulatory roles. Third, both involve cross-border externalities, with the possibility of contagion in the banking field. Finally, there are substantial benefits from cross-border activity, including economies of scale, network effects, increased innovation, and more efficient capital flows. In the banking area, cooperation has been possible, despite different national regulatory preferences and market structures, through rules formulated by the Basel Committee on a nonbinding basis. Basel Committee rules are then made more binding through adoption as part of IMF or World Bank conditionality and "reviews of standards and rules." Interestingly, national rules of recognition, conditioned on compliance with Basel Committee rules, link commerce to regulation and establish an informal and expanding "club" of states in which cross-border commerce is permitted. There is a trade-off between breadth of membership in this club and depth of regulatory cooperation. This type of cooperation may provide some basis for proposals regarding international platform regulation.

In international taxation, Carlo Garbarino compares a globally distributed and manipulable tax base to the problem of globally distributed information (Chapter 9). The problem of international cooperation can be understood as a "race to the bottom," as experienced in the tax context where states reduce their taxes in order to attract investment. In the platform regulation context, to the extent that states have the ability to block platform access or hold platforms to account, it is also possible that the result would be a "race to the top," in which states agree together on a higher standard and avoid a race to the bottom. The goals and methods, for example, of China as compared to the US, however, suggests that states may have strongly differing goals, leading more to a "club" structure in which states join with those holding comparable regulatory preferences and exclude others from their markets. This is a type of "minilateralism," in which breadth of membership is traded for depth and consistency with regulatory preferences.

Infectious disease, as addressed by Mark Jit and Dominik Hofstetter (Chapter 7), also contains some analogies of interest. The global internet can be understood as a space for transmission of global infection. However, information is more normatively ambivalent than disease, although there are variations in concern about various diseases. Diverging agendas may limit cooperation. Some areas of concern may be "low-hanging fruit" for which there is wide agreement among many governments. Material regarding child pornography or sex trafficking may fall into this category. Governments can work together to reduce transmission and may work together with private sector partners. For example, transmission of virulent material may be reduced by control over algorithmic amplification.

In sum, an observation of the strides accomplished in some fields, and the careful treading on display in others as it relates to solving transnational cooperation problems, offers valuable suggestions for any attempt at achieving a transnational consensus on the regulation of online platforms. The feature in both international banking regulation as well as international taxation, where the creation of groups of like-minded regulatory polities form clubs and thus enable further harmonization, has been reflected in work on content moderation relating to election interference and national security.[40]

[40] David L. Sloss, Tyrants on Twitter: Protecting Democracies from Information Warfare 6 (2022) (proposing a "new alliance of democratic states," an "Alliance for Democracy," to shield themselves from "Russian and Chinese information warfare" while ensuring robust speech and informational privacy protections).

14.6 EVALUATING THE NORMATIVE AND ORGANIZATIONAL TOOLBOX

Considering the potential for conflicts between different countries' laws in this area, and the impediment to interaction, including commerce, that these conflicts may cause, states have already begun to act to cooperate on these issues. The chosen forum and vehicle for harmonization varies from inclusion in trade agreements to less binding principles and guidelines.

14.7 PRIOR ACTIVITY: EXISTING EFFORTS AT HARMONIZATION

There has already been much preliminary international discussion and normative activity with respect to platform responsibility. We have already mentioned the EU's Digital Services Act, which is an intensive international effort to harmonize and engage in mutual recognition of platform responsibility regulation. Note, importantly, that the DSA does not harmonize substantive law of EU member states, but the EU benefits from broad informal consensus and substantial formal agreement on many important areas of law.

The US has sought to require certain trade partners to adhere to the US Section 230 approach to platform responsibility. In 2019, the US and Japan signed the US–Japan Trade Agreement and the US–Japan Digital Trade Agreement. While the former deals with tariffs on agricultural products, the latter includes provisions on data localization, cross-border data flows, and online intermediary liability.[41]

Article 18 (Interactive Computer Services) of the Digital Trade Agreement is similar to Section 230, stipulating that "neither Party shall adopt or maintain measures that treat a supplier or user of an interactive computer service as an information content provider in determining liability for harms related to information stored, processed, transmitted, distributed, or made available by the service, except to the extent the supplier or user has, in whole or in part, created or developed the information."[42] The provision also protects online platforms from liability arising from content removal by dint of language directly mimicking Section 230.[43] And, much like Section 230, the Digital Trade Agreement contains exceptions for IP law and criminal law.[44]

Several months after the Digital Trade Agreement was signed between the US and Japan, the United States-Mexico-Canada Agreement (USMCA) was ratified to replace the North American Free Trade Agreement (NAFTA). The USMCA went into effect on July 1, 2020, requiring that US trade partners adopt provisions modeled

[41] Trade Agreement US–Japan, October 7, 2019, T.I.A.S. no. 20-101.2; Digital Trade Agreement, US–Japan, October 7, 2019, T.I.A.S. no. 20-101.1 [US–Japan Digital Trade Agreement].

[42] US–Japan Digital Trade Agreement, art. 18(2).

[43] *Id.*, art. 18(3).

[44] *Id.*, art. 18(4).

on Section 230. The online liability provisions of the USMCA largely contained in Chapter 19 are aligned with Section 230.[45] The purpose of these provisions, too, is to ensure that interactive computer service providers are not held liable for third-party content published on their platforms.

The rationale for the inclusion of such provisions in trade agreements has been said to stem from the international nature of the internet.[46] The USTR Factsheet frames the Interactive Computer Services provision from a "recognition" standpoint.[47] While much literature has focused on the exporting of Section 230 to advance the commercial interests of US-based social media companies,[48] a closer examination of relevant arrangements indicates a more nuanced observation.[49] For instance, while Canada has accepted the digital trade provisions of the USMCA without qualification, Article 19.17.5 has subjected the online liability clause to Annex 19-A, which essentially exempts Mexico from compliance for the first three years after the USMCA becomes effective and later provides that Mexico shall comply "in a manner that is both effective and consistent with Mexico's Constitution."[50]

Similarly, the signing of the US–Japan Digital Trade Agreement was accompanied by a Side Letter on Interactive Computer Services in which both parties to the Agreement recognize that Japan's law on online platforms is inconsistent with Article 18 of the US–Japan Digital Trade Agreement. However, the letter reads that in spite of this, "based on a review of information on the operation of Japan's legal system and discussion between the Parties, the Parties agree that Japan need not change its existing legal system, including laws, regulations, and judicial decisions, governing the liability of interactive computer services suppliers, to comply with

[45] USMCA, Chapter 19, art. 19.17.

[46] Ashley Johnson & Daniel Castro, *How Other Countries Have Dealt with Intermediary Liability | ITIF*, ITIF (2021), https://itif.org/publications/2021/02/22/how-other-countries-have-dealt-intermediary-liability (last visited Aug. 21, 2022) (arguing that it is "beneficial for these online services and businesses, and for their users and customers, to have a similar set of rules that apply across borders").

[47] "The United States-Japan Digital Trade Agreement parallels the United States-Mexico-Canada Agreement (USMCA) as the most comprehensive and high-standard trade agreement addressing digital trade barriers ever negotiated. This agreement will help drive economic prosperity, promote fairer and more balanced trade, and help ensure that shared rules support businesses in key sectors where both countries lead the world in innovation." *See* USTR, *Fact Sheet on US–Japan Digital Trade Agreement*, https://ustr.gov/about-us/policy-offices/press-office/fact-sheets/2019/october/fact-sheet-us-japan-digital-trade-agreement (last visited Aug. 21, 2022).

[48] Vivek Krishnamurthy & Jessica Fjeld, *CDA 230 Goes North American? Examining the Impacts of the USMCA's Intermediary Liability Provisions in Canada and the United States*, SSRN Electronic Journal (2020); Joshua P Meltzer, *The United-Mexico-Canada: Developing Trade Policy for Digital Trade*, 11 Trade, L., & Dev't 239 (2019).

[49] For a detailed account of the carve-outs, *see* Han-Wei Liu, *Exporting the First Amendment through Trade: The Global "Constitutional Moment" for Online Platform Liability*, 53 Georgetown Journal of International Law (2022).

[50] USMCA, Chapter 19, Annex 19-A.1-3.

Article 18."[51] This Side Letter suggests that Japan has also managed to essentially contract out of any potential effects of Article 18.

Despite the obvious qualifications and carve-outs, which challenge the economic rationale of including Section 230 language in trade agreements, this development in US trade negotiation policy has garnered a substantial share of criticism from different circles.[52] Notably, a coalition of internet accountability groups asked the Biden administration to eschew Section 230 language in future trade deals.[53] In the US Congress, too, calls to refrain from including Section 230 language in trade agreements is accumulating bipartisan support.[54] While some voices fear that this practice helps shield "tech giants" from foreign regulators and further entrenches their ability to make content moderation decisions void of government oversight,[55] others point to a more fundamental misconception. Namely, exporting Section 230 language through trade agreements is contentious when the receiving jurisdictions lack the constitutional and public law context that gave rise to this provision in the US.[56]

On the face of it, the inclusion of Section 230 language in US trade agreements may precipitate a bargained-for harmonization of platform responsibility regulation. As trade agreements of the future may routinely include digital trade provisions, they may provide a suitable vehicle for harmonization. However, the carve-outs negotiated by Mexico and Japan suggest that, while Section 230 language may be included in the agreements, individual countries seek to maintain their regulatory autonomy over platform responsibility and content moderation. Given the public law and constitutional nuances of online platform responsibility regulation, imposing one country's regulatory standard by trade fiat may prove significantly more challenging than "simple" tariff negotiations.

[51] US–Japan Digital Trade Agreement, Side Letter on Interactive Computer Services, October 7, 2019, https://ustr.gov/countries-regions/japan-korea-apec/japan/us-japan-trade-agreement-negotiations/us-japan-digital-trade-agreement-text (last visited Aug. 21, 2022).

[52] *See e.g.*, Anna Edgerton, *Tech Liability Shield Has No Place in Trade Deals, Groups Say* (2021), https://news.bloomberglaw.com/tech-and-telecom-law/tech-liability-shield-has-no-place-in-trade-deals-groups-say (last visited Aug. 21, 2022).

[53] *See* Press Release, American Economic Liberties Project, *16 National Orgs Urge Biden to Keep Section 230 Out of Trade Agreements* (May 27, 2021), https://www.economicliberties.us/press-release/15-national-orgs-urge-biden-to-keep-section-230-out-of-trade-agreements/ (last visited Aug. 21, 2022).

[54] *See* Letter from Richard Blumenthal, Charles E. Grassley, Rob Portman & Mark R. Warner, US Senate, to Robert E. Lighthizer, USTR (Dec. 18, 2020), https://www.warner.senate.gov/public/_cache/files/8/7/873e5ca4-6959-4ec8-ac01-62b78bc909d4/06A4505EDD4B887956702C3A8091DCD3.uk-230-letter-final.pdf (last visited Aug. 21, 2022).

[55] David McCabe & Ana Swanson, *U.S. Using Trade Deals to Shield Tech Giants From Foreign Regulators*, New York Times, Oct. 7, 2019, https://www.nytimes.com/2019/10/07/business/tech-shield-trade-deals.html (last visited Sept. 4, 2022).

[56] Liu, *supra* note 49, at 56–58.

14.8 PRIOR ACTIVITY: DEVELOPMENT OF PRINCIPLES

Apart from attempts at harmonization through the inclusion of platform liability provisions in international trade agreements, most of the discussions and movements have culminated in sets of principles and guidelines published by international organizations, NGOs, and internet governance organizations.

The Communiqué attached to the 2011 OECD "Recommendation of the Council on Principles for Internet Policy Making"[57] took a pragmatic approach to platform responsibility for user behavior by noting that appropriate limitations of liability for intermediaries play a fundamental role in promoting innovation and creativity, the free flow of information, incentives for cooperation among stakeholders, and economic growth. The Communiqué, however, also stressed that intermediaries play a vital role in addressing and deterring illegal activity, fraud, and misinformation on their platforms. Moreover, the Communiqué mentions that proportionality and respect for the protection of fundamental rights are important considerations for such intermediaries in addressing such content.

The 2014 OECD "Principles for Internet Policy Making"[58] consequently builds upon the 2011 Communiqué and supports a flexible, multistakeholder approach to internet policy-making and strengthened international cooperation. In particular, Principle No. 12 "Limit Internet Intermediary Liability" reflects the notions outlined in the 2011 Communiqué.

The Manila Principles on Intermediary Liability, published in March 2015, provide best practices guidelines for limiting intermediary liability for content to promote freedom of expression and innovation. The principles are the result of deliberations between various internet governance organizations and civil society groups.[59] The Manila Principles are among the few available guideline formulations addressing intermediary liability and platform responsibility as it relates to content. A similar attempt at formulating best practices specifically centered around content moderation can be found in the Santa Clara Principles, which provide recommendations for platforms engaging in content moderation. The second iteration of these Principles, published in 2021, is divided into Foundational and Operational Principles. Foundational Principles are overarching and cross-cutting principles that should be taken into account by all companies, while Operational Principles set out

[57] OECD, *Recommendation of the Council on Principles for Internet Policy Making* (Dec. 13, 2011) https://www.oecd.org/digital/ieconomy/49258588.pdf (last visited Aug. 21, 2022).

[58] OECD, *Principles for Internet Policy Making* (2014) https://www.oecd.org/digital/ieconomy/oecd-principles-for-internet-policy-making.pdf (last visited Aug. 21, 2022).

[59] *See Manila Principles on Intermediary Liability, Best Practices Guidelines for Limiting Intermediary Liability for Content to Promote Freedom of Expression and Innovation* (Mar. 14, 2015) https://www.eff.org/files/2015/10/31/manila_principles_1.0.pdf (last visited Aug. 21, 2022).

more granular expectations for the largest companies.[60] This distinction reflects the regulatory differentiation included in the DSA. Notably, however, the Santa Clara Principles explicitly state that they are not designed to provide a template for regulation.

The 2016 "One Internet" report,[61] published by the Global Commission on Internet Governance (GCIG) on the eve of the OECD's third internet-related Ministerial Meeting in 2016, addresses several issues relating to platform responsibility. In its chapter on "Corporations as Digital Gatekeepers," the report outlines various approaches to intermediary liability and content moderation by platforms. It highlights jurisdictions with "safe harbor" rules and presents the Manila Principles on Intermediary Liability, which the GCIG "fully supports."[62] These principles include shielding intermediaries from liability for third-party content, the requirement of judicial authority for content takedowns, necessity and proportionality, clarity and due process, and transparency and accountability. The GCIG believes that intermediaries "should not be required to perform the functions of law enforcement, except as required by the appropriate judicial order."

The Global Network Initiative (GNI) was launched in 2008 to address the question of private tech companies balancing freedom of expression, privacy, and other interests in deciding whether to censor content. GNI is a unique multistakeholder platform that came out of deliberations by information and communications technology (ICT) companies, human rights and press freedom organizations, academics, and investors. Among other issues, GNI also addresses intermediary liability and content regulation.[63] In 2020, GNI published a policy brief analyzing twenty legislative initiatives around the world that claim to address various forms of digital harm.[64] The report concludes by formulating recommendations on how to legislate to adequately account for fundamental rights as well as moderation concerns.[65] GNI has also published the "GNI Principles on Freedom of Expression and Privacy,"[66] which is largely based on internationally recognized laws and standards for human rights, including the Universal Declaration of Human Rights, the International Covenants on Civil and Political Rights, and on Economic, Social and Cultural Rights, as well as the UN Guiding Principles on

60 *Santa Clara Principles on Transparency and Accountability in Content Moderation*, Santa Clara Principles, https://santaclaraprinciples.org/images/santa-clara-OG.png (last visited Aug. 21, 2022).

61 GCIG, *One Internet*, Report (2016), https://www.cigionline.org/sites/default/files/gcig_final_report_-_with_cover.pdf (last visited Aug. 21, 2022).

62 *Id.* at 45–46.

63 GNI, *Intermediary Liability & Content Regulation*, Global Network Initiative, https://globalnetworkinitiative.org/policy-issues/intermediary-liability-content-regulation/ (last visited Aug. 21, 2022).

64 GNI, Content Regulation and Human Rights. Analysis and Recommendations (2020).

65 *Id.*, Appendix A.

66 GNI, Principles on Freedom of Expression and Privacy (as updated May 2017).

Business and Human Rights, the "Protect, Respect, and Remedy" Framework, and the OECD Guidelines for Multinational Enterprises. The GNI principles stipulate rather vague aspirations as to the responsibilities of companies, largely in favor of ensuring freedom of speech and prevention of censorship.

On a more supranational level, the UN Office for the High Commissioner for Human Rights (UN OHCHR) has expressed its concerns over the introduction of various content moderation laws across the globe.[67] As a result, UN OHCHR has proposed five actions for States and platforms to consider when engaging in content moderation: First, UN OHCHR urges that the focus of regulation should be on improving content moderation processes, rather than adding content-specific restrictions. Second, restrictions imposed by States should be based on laws, should be clear, and should be necessary, proportionate, and nondiscriminatory. Third, companies need to be transparent about how they curate and moderate content and how they share information, and States need to be transparent about their requests to restrict content or access users' data. Fourth, users should have effective opportunities to appeal against decisions they consider to be unfair, and independent courts should have the final say over lawfulness of content. Finally, civil society and experts should be involved in the design and evaluation of regulations.[68] UN OHCHR also invokes the UN Guiding Principles on Business and Human Rights[69], reiterating that business should respect fundamental rights and also provide appropriate means for appeals and decision review. On November 1, 2020, UN OHCHR also published an explainer, "Regulating online content – the way forward,"[70] with seven key stipulations for businesses and government.

Discussions on platform responsibility and content moderation practices are being led in various international fora, engaging stakeholders from across the board. While the 2014 OECD Principles and 2015 Manila Principles on Intermediary Liability form the most prominent attempts at formulating common principles, their success remains isolated to the supranational discursive sphere. At the moment, there are no sufficiently concrete regulation-like documents that could form the basis for transnational negotiations and rule-making. That being said, the vast and diverse expertise and bodies engaged in the discussion on platform responsibility and content moderation may serve as fruitful grounds for transnational attempts at regulation.

67 UN OHCHR, *Moderating Online Content: Fighting Harm or Silencing Dissent?*, Latest Stories (July 23, 2021), https://www.ohchr.org/en/stories/2021/07/moderating-online-content-fighting-harm-or-silencing-dissent (last visited Aug. 21, 2022).

68 *Id.*

69 UN OHCHR, Guiding Principles on Business and Human Rights, HR/PUB/11/04 (2011).

70 Press Release, UN OHCHR , *Regulating Online Content – The Way Forward* (Nov. 1, 2020), https://www.ohchr.org/sites/default/files/Documents/Press/Regulating-online-content-the-way-forward.pdf (last visited Aug. 21, 2022).

14.9 TOWARD A ROADMAP TO NEGOTIATING INTERNATIONAL RULES FOR PLATFORM REGULATION

The problem of platform regulation will require significant diplomatic, legal, and industry attention in coming years. This attention will not be confined to procedure but will extend to substance. However, the initial issues required to be addressed will entail the general issue of responsibility of platforms for UGC and the scope of freedom platforms have to moderate UGC.

To maximize the joint benefits of liberalization and regulation in the platform context, and to distribute those joint benefits in a politically sustainable manner, norms and organizations are required. This is true in all areas of commerce and especially true in the context of platform "globalization on steroids."

Rules of national treatment or most-favored-nation treatment prohibiting discrimination are necessary, but not sufficient, as they would leave in place divergent national regulation, and so would likely fail to achieve the optimal level of commerce. Rules of proportionality might allow greater commerce but would require that national measures be structured in the least restrictive manner necessary to achieve their objectives. However, proportionality might also fall short in achieving optimal levels of commerce. In addition, it is difficult for tribunals to measure proportionality, and the results may be unpredictable.

While the trade system has begun to address explicitly in plurilateral agreements a limited set of issues relating to data, such as customs duties, data localization, source code disclosure, privacy, and access to networks, it has not addressed a number of other issues, including political interference, free expression, libel, moderation, taxation, competition, and other issues. Of course, these issues predated platforms. However, these issues did not present the relative magnitude of potential barriers to commerce that they do in the context of the technological integration presented by platforms. As the barriers of distance have declined, the barriers of legal difference have increased in relative and absolute terms.

As discussed above, the world has muddled through with limited and ambiguous understandings of the scope of national jurisdiction in several private and public law areas. To reduce the barriers of legal difference, states may begin by reducing areas of overlapping application of law, by agreeing on rules of exclusive jurisdiction. This has been difficult and is especially challenging given the dispersed effects of platform operations. It is difficult for any state to give up jurisdictional authority with respect to an issue that has effects on its citizens. In some areas, such as taxation, the need to have a principle of single taxation – one, and only one, tax applies to all income, is more obvious. In some other areas, states may be more willing to allow overlap where the worst outcome is a race to the top. However, one state's race to the top is another's race to the bottom: states determine their own optimal level of regulation, and regulation at a more stringent level is often suboptimal.

A second step that states might take to reduce the barriers of legal difference is to eliminate differences by harmonizing rules. Indeed, in areas such as those covered by the GDPR, the DSA, and the Digital Markets Act (DMA), the rationales presented for harmonization of rules within the EU in terms of subsidiarity may be lightly edited to refer to the multilateral system instead of the EU context and would be equally accurate. For example, the 2020 memorandum accompanying the then proposed DSA includes the following statement:

> Taking into account that the Internet is by its nature cross-border, the legislative efforts at national level referred to above hamper the provision and reception of services throughout the Union and are ineffective in ensuring the safety and uniform protection of the rights of Union citizens and businesses online. Harmonizing the conditions for innovative cross-border digital services to develop in the Union, while maintaining a safe online environment, can only be served at Union level.[71]

The DMA contains the following notable language in its 6th recital:

> Gatekeepers have a significant impact on the internal market, providing gateways for a large number of business users to reach end users everywhere in the Union and on different markets. The adverse impact of unfair practices on the internal market and the particularly weak contestability of core platform services, including the negative societal and economic implications of such unfair practices, have led national legislators and sectoral regulators to act. A number of regulatory solutions have already been adopted at national level or proposed to address unfair practices and the contestability of digital services or at least with regard to some of them. This has created divergent regulatory solutions which results in the fragmentation of the internal market, thus raising the risk of increased compliance costs due to different sets of national regulatory requirements.[72]

The same reasons given for harmonizing competition regulation of platforms within the EU also apply in the broader global setting. Of course, the economic and social similarity of states and regulatory perspectives within the EU makes harmonization easier in that context than in the multilateral context. Subsidiarity demands harmonization within the EU, but it may to some extent also demand harmonization globally. However, the optimal approach is not necessarily harmonization:

[71] DSA, *supra* note 1, at 6. *See also* the Regulation 2016/679 of the European Parliament and of the Council of 27 April 2016 on the protection of natural persons with regard to the processing of personal data and on the free movement of such data, and repealing Directive 95/46/EC (General Data Protection Regulation), 2016 O.J. (L. 119) [hereinafter *GDPR*] recital 170; Proposal for a Regulation of the European Parliament and of the Council on contestable and fair markets in the digital sector (Digital Markets Act) 2020/0374 (COD) final (May 11, 2022) recitals 7–10.

[72] Regulation (EU) 2022/1925 of the European Parliament and the Council of 14 September 2022 on contestable and fair markets in the digital sector and amending Directives (EU) 2019/1937 and (EU) 2020/1828 (DMA).

optimality depends on the value to states of diversity and the costs of legal integration. This will be different within the EU than in the multilateral system.

This type of harmonization could take place within one or more specialized international bodies, or within a trade agreement. If developed in specialized bodies, the resulting rules could be incorporated by reference into trade law through a reference arrangement in the WTO treaty or in preferential trade agreements, along the lines of the incorporation of intellectual property rights in the TRIPS (Trade Related Intellectual Property Rights) agreement or the incorporation of product standards in the TBT (Technical Barriers to Trade) or SPS (Sanitary and Phytosanitary Measures) Agreements within the WTO.

Because each area of law has its own rationale, and the intensity and combination of rationales will differ in each state, fragmentation means that the optimal legal and institutional response to platforms will differ depending on the area of law involved. In addition, multiple international organizations or other fora take responsibility for different fields of law, and indeed, within national governments, multiple ministries or other agencies take responsibility for different fields of law. The result of this institutional fragmentation can be to impede integrated management of different but overlapping areas of regulation. We have seen this in the relationship between the trade system, in particular the WTO, and other areas of international law, such as environmental protection, labor rights, taxation, competition, etc.

Similarly, because different states and groups of states have different preferences, capabilities, and perspectives in these different fields of law, we can expect that there may be some degree of plurilateral action in particular areas. So, for example, we might see multilateral action regarding competition on platforms but plurilateral action regarding responsibilities of platforms for moderation.

It is not clear how this organizational fragmentation should be bridged, or whether the WTO or another organization should serve as a cross-functional clearinghouse. But it has become clear that no organization can achieve its mandate effectively or legitimately while ignoring the concerns associated with functions assigned to other organizations, so bridges will be necessary.

What diplomatic or international relations techniques could be used to achieve harmonization and/or recognition? As suggested in the generative analysis above, it may be useful to begin with lowest-common denominators, or low-hanging fruit, in the form of certain types of pornographic or trafficking content, terrorist content, or intellectual property violations. Some of these areas are already exceptions from the US Section 230 limits on platform responsibility. Beginning with low-hanging fruit will allow the development of diplomatic expertise and experience, and institutional structures, to address further issues of cooperation.

Market access conditionality may be a unilateral method to promote cooperation, and it could be structured through an initial club of states with relatively homogeneous preferences and resources that may establish agreed rules and then require moderation arrangements consistent with those rules as a condition for market access.[73] For example, liberal states might be able to agree on monitoring substance and process in many areas, while authoritarian states may group together in a system of state-controlled platforms. In a sense, the US approaches in the USMCA and in the US–Japan Digital Trade Agreement may be viewed as initial attempts along these lines. This approach could splinter platforms, or require costly geo-blocking fragmentation of platform activity, but may begin to precipitate negotiation toward international cooperation in this area. Cooperation among groups of states along these lines might be based on a transnational regulatory network, like the Basel Committee in bank regulation, with nonbinding standards that then become the basis for unilateral market access conditions.

Where state preferences are not excessively divergent, but state resources are, one result might be to negotiate arrangements for wealthier countries to provide technical or financial assistance in order to ensure that resources to fund moderation are available to less wealthy states. This might follow the model of international vaccine policy, especially if moderation in developing countries can stop the spread of undesirable content to wealthier countries. Indeed, as in the vaccine space, there may be private charitable foundations concerned with the growth and coherence of platforms that would be willing to provide funding for moderation in developing countries.

It may be possible for private actors – platforms – to utilize a "highest common denominator" strategy: complying with the most stringent national regulation to which they are subject on a worldwide basis, on the assumption that this level of regulation will also include compliance with each other national regulatory regime to which they are subject. There are two problems with this approach, which is sometimes called the California Effect or Brussels Effect.[74]

First, it is not necessarily true that more stringent regulation encompasses all other regulation. Regulation has varying concerns, varying exceptions, and varying administrative features. So, the relationship between different jurisdictions' regulation may well be nonlinear. Second, the highest common denominator strategy may be excessively costly. For example, if the highest common denominator requires a high level of human moderation, this may stifle competition and utilization in the market, in a way that is inconsistent with the policies of states with less stringent regulation. The optimal level of moderation for poor countries might be different from the optimal level for wealthy countries. Private actors could act to promote this type of result or, alternatively, to preempt greater state regulation, through private codes of conduct in this area.

[73] *See* Sloss, *supra* note 40.

[74] Anu Bradford, *The Brussels Effect Comes for Big Tech*, Project Syndicate (2020), https://www.project-syndicate.org/commentary/eu-digital-services-and-markets-regulations-on-big-tech-by-anu-bradford-2020-12 (last visited Aug. 21, 2022).

There is much work to be done by diplomats and international lawyers to negotiate and articulate useful arrangements to optimize the combination of benefits from intensified platform-based commerce and regulatory action to reduce the social costs of that commerce. In the words of Marshall McLuhan, a "new scale [has been] introduced into our affairs by [this] new technology," and it is incumbent upon us to manage its social consequences.

15

Conclusion

The Future of Defeating Disinformation

Bhaskar Chakravorti and Joel P. Trachtman

Even as it presents a threat to the institutions of democracy, the industry of disinformation is highly democratic: the tools to produce it and distribute it are readily accessible, whether to a humble farmer in India who has discovered WhatsApp, a teenager anywhere in the world with time and a smartphone on hand, or a former US president hyperactive on social media.

It takes little to piece together digital falsehoods. With some strategy, luck, and timing, there are tools and platforms that could spread the messages to millions, who could, in turn, spread them even further. AI has added a fresh boost of creativity to the disinformation industry. Now anyone can become a political content creator[1] thanks to generative AI tools, such as DALL-E, Reface, DeepFaceLab, and scores of others. Even before the year 2024 – declared as the "biggest election year in history" – commenced, the tools of AI have already turbocharged disinformation campaigns in Bangladesh setting the tone for all elections to come.[2]

The democratization of the disinformation process has even the experts worried: Former Google CEO Eric Schmidt warned[3] that "you can't trust anything that you see or hear" in the elections thanks to AI.[4] Sam Altman, CEO of OpenAI – the company that gave us the generative AI tool, ChatGPT – told US lawmakers that he is nervous about the future of democracy. Besides, the state of the wider environment adds to the potential for problems. Political polarization, major conflicts,

[1] Darell M. West, *Comparing Google Bard with OpenAI's ChatGPT on political bias, facts, and morality*, BROOKINGS (Mar. 23, 2023), https://www.brookings.edu/articles/comparing-google-bard-with-openais-chatgpt-on-political-bias-facts-and-morality (last visited Feb. 16, 2024).

[2] *2024 Is the Biggest Election Year in History*, THE ECONOMIST (Nov. 13, 2023), https://www.economist.com/interactive/the-world-ahead/2023/11/13/2024-is-the-biggest-election-year-in-history (last visited Feb. 16, 2024).

[3] J. Frank, *The 2024 Presidential Race Is the AI election*, AXIOS (June 27, 2023), https://www.axios.com/2023/06/27/artificial-intelligence-ai-2024-election-biden?utm_source = dlvr.it&utm_medium = twitter (last visited Feb. 16, 2024).

[4] S. Frenkel & K. Conger, *Hate Speech's Rise on Twitter Is Unprecedented, Researchers Find*, AXIOS (June 27, 2023), https://www.axios.com/2023/06/27/artificial-intelligence-ai-2024-election-biden?utm_source = dlvr.it&utm_medium = twitter (last visited Feb. 16, 2024).

culture wars, ethnic divisions, worries about the environment, and even about technology itself have all added fuel to the disinformation machine.

One would think that social media platforms would be investing in war rooms especially in a big election year, such as 2024 – as they have done in the past[5] – and putting in place plans to catch disinformation before it spreads. Instead, companies across the tech sector caught in an industry-wide slowdown have had other pressing business to attend to, such as propping up profitability and staking out territory in the ever-widening space of emerging AI opportunities. Since the pandemic era highs, priorities have shifted to reducing staff and making cuts in parts of the company that do not directly contribute to increasing revenue, bringing in new users, or encouraging existing users to post messages that engage others.

Meta offers a case in point. CEO Mark Zuckerberg had declared 2023 as the "year of efficiency."[6] The trust and safety team that moderates content on Meta's platforms – which include Facebook, Instagram, and WhatsApp – was drastically reduced,[7] a fact-checking tool that had been in development for six months was shelved,[8] and contracts with external content moderators were canceled.[9] These developments at Meta were mirrored by the dismantling of content moderation resources elsewhere across the industry. Under Elon Musk, Twitter (now called X) decimated its content moderation teams, steadily lifted restrictions, and restored accounts that had been suspended because of their track records of spreading disinformation.[10] YouTube announced[11] its intention to lift a ban on videos making false claims over the 2020 US election. Google had cut[12] the team that monitors misinformation and toxic speech by a third by February of 2023. In fact, those who

5 Sheera Frenkel & Mike Isaac, *Inside Facebook's Election "War Room,"* New York Times (Sept. 19, 2018), https://www.nytimes.com/2018/09/19/technology/facebook-election-war-room.html/ (last visited Feb. 16, 2024).

6 J. Vanian, *Meta's "Year of Efficiency" Was Everything Wall Street Needed to Hear from Zuckerberg*, CNBC (Feb. 1, 2023), https://www.cnbc.com/2023/02/01/metas-year-of-efficiency-everything-wall-street-needed-to-hear.html/ (last visited Feb. 16, 2024).

7 *Id.*

8 H. F. Vanian Jonathan, *Tech Layoffs Ravage the Teams That Fight Online Misinformation and Hate Speech*, CNBC (May 26, 2023). https://www.bbc.com/news/technology-64225270 (last visited February 16, 2024).

9 Chris Vallace, *Meta Denies African Content-Moderator Firm Exit Poses Risk*, BBC (Jan. 10, 2023), https://www.bbc.com/news/technology-64225270 (last visited Feb. 16, 2024).

10 Sheera Frenkel & Kate Conger, *Hate Speech's Rise on Twitter Is Unprecedented, Researchers Find*, New York Times (Dec. 2, 2022), https://www.nytimes.com/2022/12/02/technology/twitter-hate-speech.html (last visited Feb. 16, 2024).

11 *An Update on Our Approach to US Election Misinformation*, YouTube Official Blog, June 2, 2023, https://blog.youtube/inside-youtube/us-election-misinformation-update-2023/ (last visited Feb. 16, 2024)

12 T. Brewster, *Google Cuts Company Protecting People from Surveillance to a "Skeleton Crew," Say Laid Off Workers*, Forbes (Feb. 3, 2023), https://www.forbes.com/sites/thomasbrewster/2023/02/02/jigsaw-google-alphabet-layoffs/?sh=5efab4c52d71 (last visited Feb. 16, 2024).

work in trust and safety have found that there aren't many job openings in their area of expertise.[13]

This raises the question of the pressing need for regulation and its effectiveness in controlling the spread of disinformation on digital platforms. The regulation of platforms – including but not limited to the assignment of responsibility to platforms – is, of course, secondary, "gatekeeper" regulation, intended not so much to regulate the behavior of the platforms themselves but to regulate user-generated content. Gatekeepers are regulated in other areas, where, from a regulatory standpoint, they have better access to information than government regulators would have, and where their incentives are distinct from those of the actors whose underlying behavior is sought to be addressed. For example, in the US, securities offerings underwriters are required to apply "due diligence" in ensuring that prospectuses for securities offerings are not fraudulent.

In the digital platform context, the sheer volume and velocity of speech is a challenge to regulators, and so in this relatively novel field, some governments have sought to assign responsibilities to platforms. It is noteworthy that in the European Union's Digital Services Act (DSA), the main obligation of platforms is one of "due diligence." Due diligence is not specifically defined, and moreover, the underlying "offensive" addressed in the DSA's due diligence obligation may not itself be a violation of law. And for good reason – the "offense" may be protected free expression. It is in making the trade-off between protected free expression and legally proscribed behavior that the challenge of international platform responsibility arises. Governments may cross a constitutional or human rights line when imposing responsibilities on platforms that cause them to restrict speech.

We hasten to add that platforms can themselves engage in objectionable behavior – for example, failing to monitor and remove objectionable content, amplifying the distribution of objectionable content, whether through algorithms or otherwise, or censoring benign content. As a rapid and essentially costless global medium, platforms provoke states to regulate behavior that they formerly might have ignored. In grappling with platform responsibilities, states may be drawn to regulate speech that in a different medium would have been subject to a laissez-faire approach.

The problem of platform regulation per se is a novel problem. States may develop the capacity to regulate user generated content directly, without regulation of platforms. Governments are developing this capacity at different rates. In the US, for example, users can be prosecuted for content that violates laws governing topics such as child pornography or buying illegal drugs online or content promoting banned terror organization, among others. In general, direct censorship of the internet is prohibited in the US. Citizens are protected by the First Amendment, which grants them rights to freedom of speech and expression. As is to be expected, the rules on what is considered illegal digital content vary depending on the country.

[13] *Supra* note 8.

Different countries have different rules governing what is or is not allowed for posting on social media. Many governments are experimenting with less intrusive approaches, such as parental control tools, age-rating systems, and other controls. In some cases, governments have gone to the opposite extreme by shutting down entire platforms or the internet altogether; in fact, according to Freedom House, internet freedoms have been declining for over a decade.[14] In fact, AI has been a powerful mechanism for accelerating that decline. In at least twenty-two countries, digital platforms are required to use automated systems to remove content deemed illegal under local laws; often the content that is censored is protected according to international human rights standards. In at least forty-seven countries, governments used generative AI to push state propaganda.[15]

While all such regulations and restraints are critical to content moderation and contribute to the volume of disinformation around the world, another fundamental problem – and source of complexity – stems from the intensification of cross-border activity on platforms, which increases collisions between different states' regulatory visions.

Not only does platform activity change the regulatory calculus in ways that challenge individual states, but it also exists in what may be or should be a global commons. Thus, the novel problem of platform governance is exacerbated by globalization. The research program that formed the basis for this volume was prompted by many changes being enacted and considered in different parts of the world, from the growing demand to amend Section 230 of the US Communications Decency Act to the EU's Digital Services Act to firewalls and unilateral steps being taken in countries such as China or India to place limits on content shared on social media platforms. When all of these regulatory moves are being enacted by governments unilaterally and in the absence of international harmonization, a basic question arises: How will changes in a single jurisdiction affect the ability of other states to achieve their regulatory goals, and vice-versa? How might platforms that operate across national borders moderate content that is borderless and is, yet, governed by different rules across different regulatory jurisdictions?

As of this writing, no amendment has been made, and the US Supreme Court has recently refrained from pronouncing on the scope of Section 230 – in particular, the extent to which platforms may be treated as "publishers" or "speakers" where they algorithmically or otherwise select which content to promote. And yet, the analyses of Brazilian, Chinese, European Union, Indian, and US approaches to platform responsibilities show wide divergence in mediating the tension between, on the one

[14] Allie Funk, Adrian Shahbaz & Kian Vesteinsson, *The Repressive Power of Artificial Intelligence, FREEDOM ON THE NET 2023*, Freedom House (Oct. 4, 2023), https://freedomhouse.org/report/freedom-net/2023/repressive-power-artificial-intelligence/ (last visited Feb. 16, 2024).

[15] Allie Funk, *Advances in AI Are Compounding Internet Freedom's Decline. But They Don't Have To*, Freedom House (Oct. 4, 2023), https://freedomhouse.org/article/advances-ai-are-compounding-internet-freedoms-decline-they-dont-have/ (last visited Feb. 16, 2024).

hand, treating platforms as transparent and thereby regulating only the users who generate the content and, on the other hand, seeking to assign to platforms responsibilities to moderate user-generated content on their platforms.

Of course, one solution to this problem is a kind of platform "splinternet," in which, for example, TikTok must follow different policies in the US from those followed by its sister company, Douyin, in China, as related by Jufang Wang (Chapter 4). This is a case of two platforms with essentially the same structure, but different memberships, and most importantly, different policies. China's regulations would conflict with US constitutional free speech principles, as well as other US public policy. The Chinese state does not permit foreign platforms to operate in China, presumably because it cannot sufficiently apply its regulation to foreign platforms. As this book is finalized, the US is considering a similar approach: debating legislation to ban TikTok if its ownership structure is not changed. The EU's DSA does not bar foreign control but applies to the extent that foreign platforms provide services to EU persons.

On the other side of the jurisdictional divide, Section 230 would probably prevent enforcement in the US of platform liabilities for failure to carry out responsibilities under non-US law that are inconsistent with Section 230. But of course, a US company that provides platform services in China or the EU may find that its assets outside the US are subject to enforcement actions, or that it would be blocked from operating in those jurisdictions unless it satisfied its regulatory responsibilities there.

These jurisdictional problems operate at two levels: first, at the level of substantive law, and second, at the level of specialized platform responsibilities, such as obligations under the DSA to engage in due diligence. Global platforms increase the collision of substantive law – including law relating to elections, privacy, consumer protection, libel, securities regulation, taxation, competition, intellectual property, or others. They make it more difficult for businesses to craft a compliance strategy insofar as either one government prohibits what another requires, or insofar as a "highest common denominator" strategy that complies with all the most restrictive policies places an international platform at a competitive disadvantage vis-à-vis purely national platforms. At the level of platform due diligence, different standards also will require the platform to follow a highest common denominator strategy. On the other hand, to the extent that governments will focus on harms that occur within their own territories, platforms will have incentives to focus monitoring resources on the most restrictive and most remunerative jurisdictions, perhaps providing insufficient monitoring resources for developing countries.

In this book, we see that China has deputized platforms to assist in maintaining a state-sanctioned information environment for "public opinion management" and has excluded foreign platforms from operating in China, presumably because they would be unable or unwilling to cooperate with state control. As Jufang Wang states: "China's requirements for platforms to proactively monitor, moderate and sometimes censor content, especially politically sensitive content, make it almost impossible for foreign social media platforms to survive without full compliance." Thus, China is distinct both in substantive law and in platform regulation, and the degree of difference makes interoperability practically impossible. This is one extreme of national behavior.

The other extreme, perhaps, is the US, in which First Amendment fundamentalism limits the substantive regulation of speech. In the converse of China's circumstances described above, the US objects to foreign platforms such as TikTok regulating speech to US persons. Section 230 goes even further, insulating platforms from responsibilities applicable to users who generate content. This keeps the government out of the business of regulating speech but, in addition, leaves open the possibility of private sector regulation of speech: under Section 230, platforms may moderate as they see fit. One path to reform in the US would be to limit the scope of autonomy that platforms have to moderate – and it might be attractive to see platforms as a type of "common carrier" that have an obligation of political neutrality, while policing certain types of speech according to neutral principles, such as illegality or demonstrable falsity.

The EU, Brazil, and India may be viewed as operating in between these polar extremes. The EU is most interesting. First, in the EU, most regulation of content is provided by national law. Second, the EU, to some extent, prioritizes privacy over free speech, causing some friction with the US. Third, at the EU level, the DSA operates by imposing systemic risk management obligations on platforms without explicit specification of what the risk management obligation must accomplish, for example, in the area of election interference. As Christoph Busch (Chapter 3) notes, "the scope of this risk assessment includes the "dissemination of illegal content," "any actual or foreseeable negative effects for the exercise of fundamental rights," and "any actual or foreseeable negative effects on civic discourse and electoral processes, and public security." The DSA will apply to all platforms, irrespective of their place of establishment, to the extent they provide services to users in the EU.

As this volume's generative and interdisciplinary chapters suggest, there may be multiple means of improving the organization of allocation of authority over platform content. As Federico Lupo-Pasini notes (Chapter 8), platforms externalize costs to society without national regulation, and states may externalize costs to citizens of other states, or simply restrict international commerce, without international rules. There is a trade-off, as he suggests, among (i) a global market, (ii) regulatory sovereignty, and (iii) internalization of regulatory externalities. Regulatory sovereignty can only be achieved by compromising the global market or accepting regulatory externalities. One response is harmonization – giving up regulatory sovereignty to some extent. Regulatory competition can be permitted to operate, but it may be driven in part by externalization of costs to other states. Regulatory networks are an intermediate solution, utilizing communication and negotiation to minimize unnecessary differences in regulatory regimes. Soft rules also may be more acceptable but less satisfactory from a regulatory standpoint. Mutual recognition may be useful where goals are sufficiently shared and merely implemented in different ways. The discussion above suggests that there may be important differences in goals among different leading jurisdictions.

In Chapter 9, Carlo Garbarino also focuses on the problem of regulatory externalities, from the perspective of international cooperation and diversity in the global tax system. To the extent that common standards may be achieved, these externalities can be reduced, and states may also cooperate with one another in the absence of agreement on standards by seeking to reduce externalization of costs by their actors. He evaluates policies that counteract aggressive tax strategies based on the mobility of capital as potential models for policies for platform content moderation with mobile computational capital. One way forward, as in financial regulation, is through multilateralism among like-minded states.

Mark Jit and Dominik Hofstetter (Chapter 7) derive lessons from state regulation and cooperation in managing infectious disease. While they suggest that some areas of regulation may present "low-hanging fruit" for cooperation, other areas where states have different regulatory goals will be distinct from the field of infectious disease where states tend to have more homogeneous interests. This would suggest that an internationally negotiated agreement on standards would help to support greater cooperation in managing disinformation.

In order to manage the issue of diversity of regulatory vision, states may, to some extent, harmonize substantive regulation. This is less likely than states determining unilaterally or multilaterally to develop manageable rules of jurisdiction, so that their regulation applies only in limited circumstances. The fullest realization of this "choice of law" solution would involve geo-blocking or other technology that divides up regulatory authority according to a specified, and a perhaps agreed-upon, principle. Geo-blocking may be costly and ultimately porous, but it would allow different communities to effectuate their different visions of the good in the platform context. To the extent that the principles of jurisdiction are agreed, and are structured to be exclusive, platforms would have the certainty of knowing the requirements under which they must operate in each market. Of course, different communities may remain territorial states, but given the a-territorial nature of the internet, it may be possible for other divisions of authority and responsibility to develop. Cultural affinity, or political perspective, may be more compelling as an organizational principle to some than territorial co-location.

Eventually, our ability to defeat disinformation worldwide hinges on a critical factor: the incentives of multiple stakeholders to cooperate on several fronts. These fronts could include common standards that define acceptable content, markers of deviation from standards and actions to be taken in the case of deviations, and fact-checking ecosystems using an open-source mechanism involving designated experts of different regions.

A natural question to ask is: How likely is it that multistakeholder interests will converge? The issue of misaligned incentives across regulators as well as across the platform companies, one that Bhaskar Chakravorti returns to repeatedly, cannot be ignored. At a symposium on the subject of this book, held in December 2022 at The Fletcher School, Josephine Wolff, who contributed to this book, noted that, "While enforcing different rules and policy measures for different national versions of a platform is certainly not the same as reaching international consensus on these measures, it is no small thing that so many countries have accepted this approach as a satisfactory implementation of their domestic laws …. This widespread acceptance of a highly imperfect system of implementation and enforcement is, itself, an impressive feat of international coordination." Joel Trachtman cautions that there are many added complexities to consider; for example, even on the matter of free speech, different countries have different legal formulations of free speech. Multiple countries' laws can apply to the same platform or the same platform transaction resulting in platform-based dispersal escaping regulation altogether. Daniel Drezner, also a contributor to this book, is even less sanguine about the stakeholders getting to a state of meaningful coordination; he argues that countries have wildly divergent preferences in terms of which internet content should be regulated and notes the possibility of the creation of "sham standards" at the global level. He worries about token agreements negotiated at the global level that lack enforcement mechanisms and likely be honored only in the breach.

There are, no doubt, many gaps to be closed. We conclude our approach to the daunting task of defeating disinformation with a five closing ideas from the contributors in this book.

15.1 MIND THE POLITICAL CONTEXT

As Eric Goldman (Chapter 2) points out, online speech freedoms are intertwined with partisan politics; in the US, Democrats want more content moderation; while Republicans want fewer restrictions as they see the restrictions as disproportionately affecting those on the right of the political spectrum. He concludes that this fracture is causing the two sides to advance two radically different visions of the internet's future. This calls for finding common ground before enacting legislation – which is bound to be a slow process of negotiation. Jufang Wang (Chapter 4) offers a portrait of risks of the opposite – a single party – environment. The Chinese version of platform regulation involves heavy obligations and administrative measures for enforcement. The requirements for platforms to proactively monitor, moderate and sometimes censor content, especially political sensitive content, de facto lock out foreign social media platforms. This creates a very different kind of problem altogether.

Considering a context, such as the EU, that sits in between the US and Chinese polar extremes, Joel Trachtman (Chapter 14) notes that subsidiarity demands harmonization within the EU and possibly elsewhere. He argues that optimality depends on the value to states of diversity, and the costs of legal integration. This might call for more specialized international bodies, or the coordination to be done within the framework of a trade agreement.

15.2 BORROW FROM OTHER REGULATORY MODELS

One problem that has been raised is that regulators are limited by their jurisdictions while digital platforms are global in their reach; so there is a mismatch between what the regulators can affect and the effects of the actions of the platforms. There are potential solutions to consider from other domains. As one such source of inspiration from other domains, Federico Lupo-Pasini (Chapter 8) offers the example of the US Dodd-Frank Act. It allows for extraterritorial jurisdiction by linking the application of domestic law to local contact points.

15.3 DEFINE STANDARDS

As Mark Jit and Dominik K. Hofstetter (Chapter 7) remind us, while there may be broad consensus on goals, there may be disagreement over how the cost of reaching them is shared or even over a prioritization of the goals. What may be "political speech" to one platform user is "hate speech" to another, and vice versa. What one state may consider interference in its electoral system, another state may consider as a normal part of the electoral process. Mutually agreed-upon definitions and standards will be critical in getting to a multistakeholder dialogue on these issues and harmonizing across countries as well as across regulators and the platforms.

15.4 INVEST IN DIGITAL LITERACY

Farah Pandith (Chapter 10) highlights the value of digital literacy and hygiene – possibly through structured education programs. She is also optimistic about the effects of generational change: "digital natives," that is, Gen Alpha, Gen Z, and Millennials, are better attuned to the workings of technology and may be more amenable to interventions that encourage digital literacy.

15.4 INNOVATE IN REGULATIONS

As Bhaskar Chakravorti (Chapter 13) has pointed out, as platforms redirect scarce content moderation resources to a few important markets, such as the US, we could end up with a situation where the rest of the world pays a high price for American democracy. This calls for regulators to think a few steps ahead and anticipate the consequences of their demands. For example, one solution is to have US lawmakers pass laws not only on the nature of the content hosted by the platforms but on the investments that platforms make on content moderation and how these resources are allocated across the world. The regulations ought to require that market-specific resources be allocated in proportion to the potential risk of disinformation in any given market.

On balance, it is clear that the goal of defeating disinformation will not happen overnight. There is no silver bullet, and it will take a systemic approach to addressing the problem. Despite the many challenges, the components of a solution are also within our grasp. It is essential that we get to a workable set of solutions. The future of democratic societies depends on it.

Index

www.ingramcontent.com/pod-product-compliance
Lightning Source LLC
Chambersburg PA
CBHW070150180225
22112CB00004B/198
* 9 7 8 1 0 0 9 4 3 8 6 2 9 *